Praise for
Learning Google AdWords and Google Analytics

"This book is a comprehensive and deep explanation of how to get the most out of your online advertising. Benjamin describes in detail how Google Analytics and AdWords work both separately and together, providing the necessary background to get into field as well as advanced tips for those in it."

DANIEL WAISBERG, ANALYTICS ADVOCATE, GOOGLE

"The user manual for marketing used to be price, product, promotion, and place. How much? What is it? How do you tell people about it? How do you get it to the masses? That third one has gotten so much trickier in the last ten years, we need a new user manual. Here it is. For all of those ten years, Benjamin has been getting to know and using AdWords and Google Analytics to help clients make the most of online marketing. That knowledge is now found in these pages. Practical, definitive and straightforward, Learning Google AdWords and Google Analytics delivers on the promise of its title and puts you in a position to take on this whole new world of marketing."

JIM STERNE, FOUNDER, EMETRICS SUMMIT AND BOARD CHAIR, DIGITAL ANALYTICS ASSOCIATION

"From novice online advertiser to expert, this book is an excellent reference resource for Google AdWords and Google Analytics. Benjamin's narrative style and practical approach makes this book very easy to understand. Pay attention to the tips throughout the book, this is based on Benjamin's expertise and experience implementing all of these tools with real live customers."

EVA WOO, DIGITAL MARKETING EXECUTIVE, GOOGLE, SUCCESSFACTORS, SAP

"The Google advertising platform is AMAZING! The combination of Google AdWords and Google Analytics lets you reach the right person, at the right time, with the right message. The power is AdWords targeting capabilities and Analytics' measurement and analysis tools. But getting started can be a bit challenging if you're new to the space. Luckily we have Benjamin and Learning Google AdWords and Google Analytics! Benjamin brings all of the information you need to get started and to grow and take advantage of these powerful tools. What I really like is how he brings all of the information about both systems – AdWords and Analytics – together in one central place. He makes it easy to understand how to measure your AdWords campaigns in Google Analytics data. This makes the information very actionable, which is exactly what you want."

JUSTIN CUTRONI, ANALYTICS EVANGELIST, GOOGLE

Learning
Google
AdWords
and
Google
Analytics

Benjamin Mangold

LOVES DATA

Learning Google AdWords and Google Analytics
Proudly Published by Loves Data

First Published in 2015
Copyright © 2015 Benjamin Mangold

Published by Loves Data Pty Limited
www.lovesdata.com
For general questions contact Loves Data at info@lovesdata.com

ISBN: 978-0-9943904-0-0
ISBN: 978-0-9943904-1-7 (eBook)
ISBN: 978-0-9943904-2-4 (eBook)

Printed in Australia by Ligare Book Printers (via Inscope Books)

Acknowledgements

Writing this book was inspired by all the people I have trained and worked with over the years. The questions and informal chats I've had around conferences and training has been invaluable in forming the basis of this book. Writing has been a remarkable experience and it's been amazing to have such incredible support throughout the entire process.

Thank you to my wonderful team at Loves Data. The team have supported every aspect of the book, from ideas, right through to technical edits and publishing. It's an honor to work with such great people. Special thanks go to Marta Sengers, Dara Vongsonephet and Arzu Cidem for their work getting the book into final shape. Thank you to Michael Fridman, Johann de Boer, Caitlin Hodgson, Namita Joseph, Harsha Mudradi, Samuel Nirmal, Andrew Wineberg, Anmol Gupta and Jason Lam.

I would like to thank the incredible people at Google who put their heart into making truly great products. Special mention goes to Justin Cutroni, Daniel Waisberg and Avinash Kaushik. Finally, I would like to thank Michael Mangold and Barb Moore. This book would not have been possible without their support and advice.

BENJAMIN MANGOLD

About the Author

Benjamin Mangold is the Co-Founder and CEO at Loves Data. His unique approach to online marketing and digital analytics helps organizations of all sizes make their data actionable. He translates complexities into simple and logical steps for people to measure, test and improve their results.

In 2010, Benjamin was the first trainer certified by Google for both Google AdWords and Google Analytics. He has worked closely with Google to present the annual Google Analytics User Conference in Australia since 2012.

Today, Benjamin and the specialists at Loves Data are amongst the world's most up to date experts, as they simultaneously work on client accounts, and provide high-quality training to users of Google's tools.

Book Updates

Google AdWords and Google Analytics are continually updated and improved by the teams at Google. You will find the latest updates to the book at http://lovesdata.co/uET4H

Contacting the Author

Have a suggestion? Noticed a new feature you would like covered in the book? Just want to connect? Visit http://lovesdata.co/hhNAL to contact the author.

Foreword

When was the last time you spent money on marketing or advertising for your company and you knew exactly who saw your effort, if they took any action, if they hated or loved your response to that action, and/or if they ended up doing business with you?

I'll give you a minute. In all seriousness, think about it.

Not a pretty answer, right?

Ok.

One more.

When was the last time your billboard at Sydney airport felt it spoke to a person for whom it was relevant? When was the last time the person at the billboard felt your sexy ad was relevant for them? Or, if it's easier, think about your TV ads or the ones in the Sun Herald?

Very hard to imagine, right?

Yet, both of these scenarios have very straight-forward answers when it comes to digital. #hurray

Measurement solutions like Google Analytics can tell you exactly who saw an ad you delivered, what their experience was when they landed on your mobile or desktop website, and if they did something that delivered economic value to your business. How crazy amazing is that?

Advertising platforms like AdWords don't care about a person's age, sexual orientation, salary, or religion. They are built to react to strong customer intent. Person X wants a pair of jeans. Company Y sells jeans. X meet Y, be happy! And, it comes with a fantastic dose of accountability as you can extremely precisely measure everything from impressions to clicks to brand equity created to profit to, get this, lifetime value of the customers!

#omg

Digital unlocks a new layer of creativity in our business strategy, it unlocks the imagination of our marketers and product engineers, and it does so at a speed and scale that is breath taking. As the above two stories illustrate.

And, it all starts with data.

The ability to capture it smartly, the ability to analyze it with passion, and the ability to deliver insights that drive both tactical and strategic decisions every day.

Hence, I could not be more excited about Benjamin's book. It's got intent marketing (holiness!) and creative measurement (uber holiness!) right there in the title.

Most books on analytics tend to just focus on the tactical or on which buttons to press in which reports. Benjamin's does not. It balances for the critical strategic elements that need to be present in any digital discussion (jump to Chapter 5), and the tactical elements that you'll find useful every day (for example, Chapter 13 or, my favorite, Chapter 21).

If you are reading this foreword on amazon.com, now's the time to look for the orange Buy Now button. If you are reading it in a bookstore, start walking to the cashier (and don't forget to smile). With this action, you would have completed the first step in your journey to becoming an Analysis Ninja!

All the very best.

AVINASH KAUSHIK
Author: *Web Analytics 2.0*, *Web Analytics: An Hour A Day*
Digital Marketing Evangelist: Google

Contents

I

Google AdWords

Google AdWords gives you the ability to reach your target audience with your advertising messages. The beauty of Google AdWords is that it is quick to get started, you can measure the results of your efforts, maintain control of your budget and tweak performance as you become more advanced. The popular advertising platform allows you to display your ads on Google search results, as well as other search-related websites, like Google Maps, plus content websites like the New York Times.

You are probably familiar with the text-based ads that are displayed on Google search results, but Google AdWords can also be used to get your message out in other forms, including image ads and even video ads on YouTube. All these options can make Google AdWords confusing at first and although it is easy to get started, it is important to understand the options available to refine how and when your ads are displayed. This allows you to focus your budget and effort on areas that are more likely to achieve results based on the objectives you define for your advertising.

We will begin by looking at the foundations required to run a successful campaign before moving into specific details for structuring, creating and optimizing campaigns. If you are just getting started with Google AdWords it's important to spend time learning about the full capability of the platform, because you will discover that particular features and options can allow you to improve your results. While you can always modify your campaigns, it is easier to set things up correctly the first time. If you're already using Google AdWords then you will want to spend time in the chapters covering optimization and advanced features.

1

Online Advertising Opportunity

Online advertising is measurable and gives you the opportunity to target your messages to particular people as they search and browse online. It is an accountable form of marketing which can be positive and negative. The upside is that we can quickly evaluate what is working and what is not working, allowing us to make changes that can dramatically improve results. The downside is that performance data can be seen quite quickly too (this could be in a few hours or the next day), making it quite tempting to jump to a conclusion before there is enough information.

If we compare online advertising to traditional advertising like ads in magazines, local papers or even radio and TV, typically more conversions would be received at a lower cost with online advertising. This is because the message can be directly targeted to the people most likely to purchase a product or enquire about a service. It is no longer necessary to pay for people who are not interested in the marketing message, instead we pay for people who have expressed interest or who engage with our ads.

Online advertising includes a number of ways to deliver your marketing message. You might promote a particular offer on your website and also use email as a way to communicate with your existing and potential clients and customers. Both of these options are low cost and should be quick to set up, unless you have a popular website or a way of growing your email newsletter database you will eventually hit a wall in generating new interest in what you have to say. This is where online advertising plays a critical role, by allowing you to grow your audience and get your message out more widely.

Major online advertising opportunities include search, display and social. In brief, search advertising is where you target people who are actively looking for a piece of information. For example, you might want to target your advertising message to people searching for a particular term on Google. Next is display advertising, which is where your ads are shown to people browsing content. For example, you might choose to show ads to people reading the travel section of the *New York Times* website. Finally, there is social media advertising, which allows ads to be placed on particular social networks. For example, a message could be promoted using an ad on Twitter.

Each type of online advertising has unique characteristics that need to be approached with different strategies and planning. Reusing an ad that is successful on search won't automatically translate to a successful ad on a social network, so you need to consider each type of online advertising as a distinct opportunity. However, the same techniques used for improving the results of campaigns can be applied across the different online advertising platforms. The key to success with online advertising is making the effort to properly set up your campaigns for the audience you are trying to target, monitoring your results and dedicating time to improving your campaigns on a regular basis.

Tip: You can't simply create a campaign and assume it will succeed, you need to dedicate the time to continually tweak and improve your targeting and messages. If you can't dedicate the time, then you will need to find someone who can review your online advertising on a regular basis. This might be someone inside or outside your organization.

Search

Search advertising allows you to target people as they search for keywords on a search engine such as Google, Bing and Yahoo. This allows you to display ads to someone who is actively looking for information that relates to your advertising message. Compare this to advertising in a newspaper: Is the reader actually interested in your message? Do they even see your ad? Traditional advertising like newspaper ads are not targeted solely at people looking for information relating to your offer and it can also be difficult to gauge success.

Compare this to someone searching on Google for 'buy gardening book', straight away it is clear that this person is looking for a particular product and that they have expressed interest in purchasing. If you sell gardening books you are far more likely to receive a sale if someone is already actively looking for the products you offer. This is in contrast to a news-paper ad where very few people are likely to be actively looking for the specific product.

You should consider search-based campaigns as the foundation of your online adver-tising. This is because search advertising typically sees higher conversion rates and better return on investment (ROI) than display or social campaigns. There are, of course, exceptions but starting with a search campaign will give you a strong basis to then extend into the other online advertising options.

Display

Display advertising is where you show your ads as people browse and engage with content online. The majority of display ads are placed on websites, but they can also appear on mobile apps and even embedded within video content. It is important to understand the difference between display advertising and search advertising. When people use a search engine, it is a very controlled experience. You have an immediate understanding of what to expect when someone performs a search, but display advertising could mean your ads are placed on hundreds or even thousands of different websites, each with their own content, design and navigation. You also need to consider that people are browsing these different websites for various reasons and critically, they are not searching in the way someone uses a search engine. This means that the messages you use in your display ads will probably be different to the messages in your search ads.

Display advertising also allows for different ways to target your desired audience. Search is focused on the keywords people are entering into the search engine, but with display advertising there are a number of options. This can include selecting individual websites, targeting content themes on display sites, right through to behavioral targeting where ads are displayed to people that have already been to your website.

Social

Social networks provide a way to engage with your target audience and almost all social networks allow you to undertake some form of paid advertising. For example, on Twitter and Facebook you can promote your brand and particular posts to extend your audience and reach new people. Advertising on social networks can be used to increase your brand aware-ness through to generating leads and sales. However, the first thing to remember about social media is that people are in a completely different frame of mind to someone who is actively searching for information or even people browsing content where you are running display ads. This means your message has to be appropriate to people's behavior as they engage on each social network. You also need to understand that social networks will not result in the same outcomes as your other advertising campaigns. For example, your search campaigns running on Google could drive the majority of your sales, while your social media campaigns result in people re-sharing your content, registering for competitions and completing other actions on your website. Social should still be included within your marketing strategy, but it will mean defining specific objectives and goals that are appropriate to your social audience.

In this book the focus is on running search and display campaigns, but some of the core concepts can be applied to your social media ads. For example, having well-structured campaigns and defined targeting are important for both search and social advertising. The one critical difference to remember when running ads on social networks is that you typically target people based on their demographics and areas of interest. This means that unlike search, your social campaigns will have a defined group of people that will see your ads, while the people searching for particular keywords will change over time. This makes regular optimization of your ad copy even more important on social networks where you will typically want to create new ads at much shorter intervals compared to your search campaigns.

Content

Content can take many forms, from a page about your services, a video on YouTube, a text ad on a social network or your latest blog post. No matter what type of online marketing you do, content is going to be central to your efforts. Content is what people engage with when they first find you, including both paid ads and free listings. After they have become aware of your brand, the content on your website is what encourages people to engage with you to become a prospect and then a customer. This is why you can be running a perfect advertising campaign, but if your landing page and content hasn't been considered you will see poor results. You need to invest time and effort in your content, so that it relates to the audience you are trying to engage.

Remember the content of your landing pages and website can take on many forms, including headlines, text, photos, graphics and video. Different content elements work together to engage with each person on your website. The better your content relates to their needs and desires, the more people will engage and the more likely they will be to complete the goals you want them to perform.

Here's an example that will help you understand the importance of content. Someone has just moved to New York and wants to join a local gym by researching nearby gyms to see what equipment and classes they offer. A search for 'gym new york' on Google shows the following ad:

NYC Gym & Fitness Center
www.gym.com
New York Gym with Latest Equipment.
7 Day Free Trial, Register Now!

Now ask yourself how well this ad relates to what the person searched for and their objective of joining a gym. You will notice that the ad includes 'NYC' and 'New York' – these are going to immediately appear more relevant to the person searching than generic ads that don't mention the location. This is where the importance of content starts as the ad is like a small piece of content about each of the gyms. The better and more relevant the content, the more likely the person will be to click the ad to get more details.

Next, the person clicks on the ad and they are taken to the following page:

What do you think of the landing page? Does it relate to the ad? Does it relate to the original keyword that the person used?

Although the landing page is about a gym, it doesn't tell the person if the gym is going to be easy to get to as there are no details about location. Instead people are asked to do all the work and navigate through the website to find more information and to see if the gym is actually in their location. This landing page does not provide the information they were looking for as the content fails to meet the needs of the audience.

The example below of another landing page might not be perfect but at least it provides content that relates to the ad and what the person was searching for in the first place.

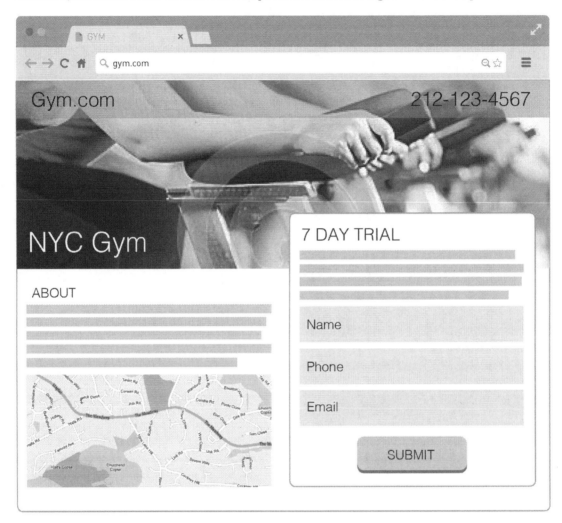

This landing page includes headings, text, photos and a map – content that is much more relevant compared to the previous example. You can quickly see how important good quality content is to provide a positive experience to your audience.

Tip: Some companies consider content as a marketing channel. This is called 'content marketing' and where you aim to get your audience to help amplify your message by sharing your content to a wider audience. For more details about content marketing visit http://lovesdata.co/SaJzu

Common Misconceptions

There are a number of misconceptions around online advertising. Typically these are around the theme of 'online advertising doesn't work'. This seems to slowly be fading away as the amount spent on online advertising increases. In some countries, the amount invested in online advertising exceeds the amount spent on traditional media like TV advertising. However, it is worth looking at a couple of key misconceptions that you might encounter as you move into online advertising.

Some people argue that they never click on the ads displayed on Google search results and question the need to run search advertising campaigns. It is difficult to believe that someone has never clicked on an ad, even inadvertently or unknowingly, but leaving that argument aside, the vast majority of Google's revenue is generated from their advertising platforms. In 2014 Google's revenue was just over $66 billion[1] and 90% of this revenue came from advertising. That's a lot of people clicking on ads. If you then take a stab at the average people pay for a click, let's say it's between $0.50 and $1.00,[2] even if you go with the higher end at $1.00 that means there were over 59 billion clicks on ads in 2014. This would mean that there are over 100 million clicks on ads every single day. Even if some people don't click on ads there is still a huge potential audience that can be reached by search advertising. The other important thing to consider is that with search advertising you pay on a cost-per-click (CPC) basis, so you are only ever charged when someone clicks on your ad. If they never click, you are not charged for someone simply viewing your ad.

Another misconception is around the performance of online advertising and the results that can be received. Some people who have tried online advertising have not seen the results that they were hoping for from their campaigns. It is common for people who are just getting started to think that their online advertising has been set up correctly and they have allocated a suitable advertising budget, when in fact their online advertising is poorly conceived and their immediate expectations have been set too high. This can happen if someone jumps into online advertising without much thought and believes that they can create a successful campaign in the time it takes to make a coffee. Although you can create campaigns quickly, you need to know what you are doing in the first place. Other people get someone else to help set up their campaigns for them, this could be a large online advertising agency, or even a relative. People placing their trust in someone else to deliver successful campaigns need to establish if that person or company actually know what they are doing.

1   http://investor.google.com/financial/tables.html
2   http://searchenginewatch.com/article/2220372/How-Google-Rakes-In-Over-100-Million-in-Search-Advertising-Daily-Infographic

2

Benefits of Google AdWords

Google AdWords enables you to create ads targeted at people based on your particular advertising objectives. For most people this means displaying ads on Google search results when people use particular keywords that relate to their products or services. Additionally, Google AdWords allows you to create display and video ads to extend the reach of your advertising.

Key benefits of Google AdWords include:

- **Show relevant ads to people** as they search and browse, allowing you to display your ad to people when they are most likely to be receptive to your marketing message.

- **Target your audience** so that your ads are displayed to the right people at the right time. Targeting covers a range of options, including the geographic location of your audience.

- **No minimum advertising spend** means you can start your advertising on a small budget and then increase your spend as you get the results you need.

- **Only pay when people engage** with your ads. You can choose to only pay when someone clicks on your ad, which means if your ad is seen and not clicked, you are not charged.

- **Make changes at any time** to make sure your ads are up-to-date and include any special seasonal offers. You can also make changes to improve the performance of your campaigns, this is covered in Chapter 12 – "Optimization Techniques."

- **Choose when your ads are shown** to only show your ads on particular days or during particular hours. You can also adjust how much you want to spend on clicks for particular times and days if you know when you are more likely to generate leads and sales.

- **Measure your results** to understand what is working and what is not working. This also allows you to make adjustment to improve the performance of your campaigns.

Overall, Google AdWords is an advertising platform that enables you to advertise to the right people at the right time and make improvements to get more out of your advertising budget. When you first jump into Google AdWords it can be a daunting experience – we will look at how to set up and manage your campaigns to achieve the best results.

Google's Advertising Network

Google AdWords enables you to display your ads in a wide variety of places, letting you choose where you want your ads to be seen based on the targeting methods you select in your campaigns. The Google Network is made up of two primary parts: the Google Search Network and the Google Display Network. The Google Search Network allows you to show your ads on Google search results and Google Shopping. You also have the option to display your ads on other search engines (known as Google Search Partners). Then there is the Google Display Network which allows you to display your ads on content websites, for example, the *New York Times*, Gmail and YouTube. You can choose where to display your ads and how you target them in the Google Display Network based on a number of factors including your advertising objectives and budget.

Here is a small selection of places your ads can be seen on Google's advertising network:

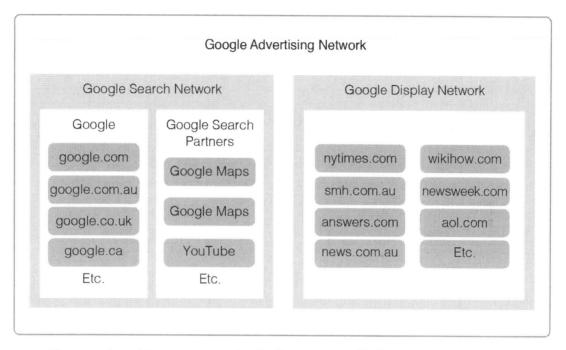

If you are launching a campaign for the first time it is likely you will want to focus your efforts on targeting the campaign to display your ads on Google search results before moving to the other advertising options. This is for two reasons: most people are familiar with Google and how search results appear and behave and the second reason is that people go to Google searching for information, meaning ads are displayed to people who are actively looking for what is being offered. If someone searches on Google for 'buy digital camera' this is a clear indication of what they want to do and if you are selling digital cameras, then targeting these types of keywords is likely to result in potential customers viewing your ad.

Did you know? Google Search Partners "include hundreds of non-Google websites like AOL, as well as Google Maps, YouTube and other Google sites"[1]. This means showing your ads on Google Search Partners will extend your reach on a range of websites that provide a search function to their users.

Once you are seeing success with your search campaign, you can then look to further extend your reach and improve your results by growing your campaigns and creating new campaigns to target people browsing on the Google Display Network.

1   https://support.google.com/adwords/answer/2616017

If you are just starting to use Google AdWords or creating a new account, then in most cases you will want to focus on targeting your ads on Google search results to give you the best results. From there you can expand your campaigns and look to use the Google Display Network to increase the visibility of your advertising messages. If you already have an established account and want maximum coverage to reach your potential customers you will want to ensure you have campaigns that display your ads on the Google Search Network and the Google Display Network.

Core Concepts for Successful Campaigns

It is important to understand different components help achieve a successful campaign. When you are running a search campaign you need to consider the keyword that you are targeting, the ad variation that you present and the landing page that you send someone to. The closer the relationship between these three elements, the better your campaign results will be.

If you bid on the keyword 'milk chocolate gift basket' and the ad specifically talks about the milk chocolate baskets you have for sale, and people are taken to a landing page on your website that shows a selection of milk chocolate baskets, then the three elements have been considered. The relationship between the elements is very close and you are much more likely to receive good results from the campaign, compared to other advertisers that are not considering the relationship between all three elements.

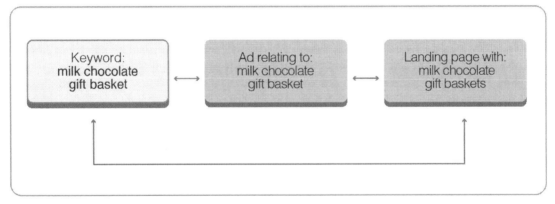

If a competitor was bidding on the same keyword of 'milk chocolate gift basket', but just had a generic ad for all their gift baskets (or even all their chocolate gift baskets) and sent people to a page on their website that contained different types of gift baskets, it is clear that each element is not as closely related. Not only are they less likely to receive the same number of sales compared to your ads, but they are likely to be paying more for their campaigns. This is because Google AdWords also looks at the quality of these three elements to determine where advertisers are placed in the paid results and quality also impacts how much people pay.

Tip: You might have some questions about quality following this example, but hold tight, we need to cover some important fundamental concepts before discussing quality in detail. If you like you can jump ahead and read about "Quality Score" in Chapter 12 – "Optimization Techniques."

When you are creating or managing campaigns always try to remember these elements and the relationship between them. The better the relationship, the better the performance.

3

Account Structure

Inside each Google AdWords account you can have one or more campaigns and in each campaign you can have one or more ad groups. This structure allows you to manage and improve the performance of your ads by grouping your keywords, ads, budget settings and more.

Here is an example of a simple account structure:

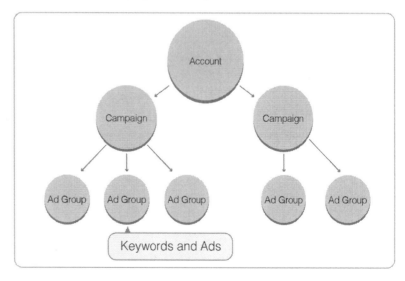

There is no one way to structure an account, so a simple account structure might suit you as you get started. You can always adjust the structure depending on your needs.

Account

Your Google AdWords account contains all of your campaigns and is designed to advertise an individual organization. There are some settings that you make at the account level, including your billing preferences for your advertising and who has access to manage your account.

Tip: You can manage multiple accounts using a My Client Centre (MCC) account for details visit http://lovesdata.co/qGXvv

Campaigns

You can think of campaigns as folders. They allow you to organize your account and create a top-level structure to keep everything neat and tidy in your account. A good structure is an important component of managing your account and can help you be more targeted and more relevant with your advertising. If you are starting out it is quite normal to just have one campaign in your account, but as you begin to grow and optimize your account, you are likely to need at least a couple of campaigns to help keep things more organized. Structuring your account into multiple campaigns can help make it easier to understand and improve performance, find things easily in your account and even allocate your budgets based on performance.

There is no set way to structure an account – this is because Google AdWords is used by so many different advertisers, from local bakeries to giant corporations. By allowing you to create your own campaign or folder structure inside your account, you can have the flexibility to set things up exactly as you need them. This can be confusing if you're new to Google AdWords, but will make more sense as you become familiar with creating campaigns.

Some common campaign structures include:

- Products.
- Services
- Keyword theme
- Brands
- Website structure
- Targeting
- Budget

You might want to use a combination of these different methods. For example, here are two campaigns that have been created to advertise different services, with different budgets applied:

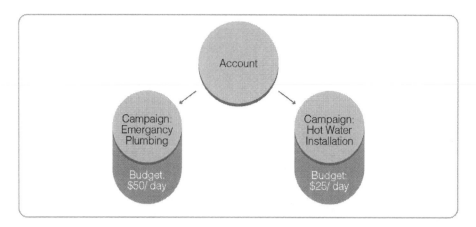

Ad Groups

You can create one or more ad groups in each campaign and you can think of them as sub-folders. They allow you to further refine the structure of your campaigns and enable you to be more granular with the targeting of your ads. For search campaigns your ad groups contain the keywords that you have selected and the ad (or ads) that you are showing to people as they search for those particular keywords.

Here is an example ad group structure:

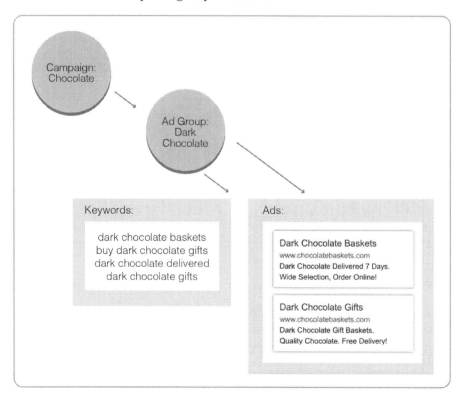

> **Tip:** For display campaigns, your ad groups still contain the ads that you are displaying to people along with the display targeting options you have selected.

Structuring Your Account

Now it is important to think about how you are going to structure your account. There is no single way to structure your account, so let's look at some common options.

Products and Services

If you offer different products or services, then these can help form the basis for your campaign structure. For example, if you sell drums and also offer drum lessons, then these would be two campaigns in your account.

If you are just focused on products, then your campaign structure can be set up to reflect the product categories you want to advertise. The same logic can be applied if you have multiple services you are looking to promote.

Keyword Theme

You can also consider structuring your campaigns around particular keyword themes. For example, if you are structuring the account for a hotel chain you might want to split your campaigns between keywords for people looking to book a room versus people researching hotels in particular cities.

Brands

If your business sells different brands of products, then you can structure your campaigns around these particular brands. For example, if you sell cameras, you might have one campaign for 'Canon' and one campaign for 'Nikon'.

Website Structure

If you are stuck, then a good starting point for structuring your campaigns is to look at the structure of your website. For example, if you have different overarching categories in your website, then these can potentially become campaigns in your account.

Geographic Targeting

If you want to create ads with a special call to action for people located in Australia and ads with a different call to action for people in New Zealand you should create two separate campaigns with different geographic targets. Geographic targeting is set at the campaign level and determines who your ads are displayed to based on their physical location and their locations of interest.

You might also combine this with another method for structuring your account, for example, if you wanted to advertise your 'Canon' and 'Nikon' cameras with different prices in Australia compared to New Zealand, then you would end up with four campaigns. Two 'Canon' campaigns, with one displayed in Australia and the other in New Zealand and then another two campaigns for 'Nikon' cameras.

Network Targeting

Google AdWords allows you to display your ads on Google search results, but you also have the ability to target your ads to display to people on other search engines, content websites, like the *New York Times* and even mobile apps. To give you the highest degree of control over your campaigns it is best to separate search from display (content websites).

Tip: Display advertising can help you reach your audience while they are browsing websites, so you are more visible to your current and potential customers. Read Chapter 6 – "Display Campaigns" – for details.

Budget

You can also structure campaigns based on the budget that you want to allocate. For example, if you know that you generate more leads for one of your services (or products) compared to another, then it makes sense to assign a greater portion of your overall advertising budget to that particular campaign. If you have a fixed campaign like this, then you might also modify budgets between campaigns based on performance and even your ability to deliver the products to your customers.

Tip: Typically you will use budget in combination with another method for structuring your campaigns, unless you have been assigned additional budget to advertise something new.

Combined Account Structures

Remember there is no one way to structure your account, so choose a structure that works for you and there is also the option of using a hybrid of these ideas.

Tip: If you are starting an account from scratch, then you have total freedom on how to set up and structure your campaigns. However, if you are taking over an existing account, then you might decide that you need to restructure the account. This might not be something that you can achieve quickly and it is likely that you will need to plan out how you are going to restructure the campaigns over several months, especially if it is a large account.

Keywords

Keywords are the particular search terms you want to target when people search on Google and other search engines. The term *keywords* can be confusing because different people can use it to refer to different things. Keywords in Google AdWords are the words and phrases that you are bidding on in your account. For example, you might want to show your ads to people searching for 'robot vacuum cleaner', so you add this phrase to your Google AdWords account, which means this is the *keyword* you are targeting.

The keyword that you bid on is not necessarily the term that someone uses to search on Google. For example, targeting the keyword 'robot vacuum cleaner' might also display your ads when somebody searches for 'buy robot vacuum cleaner' or 'robot vacuum cleaner reviews'. These phrases people use are called *search queries*, so remember that there can be a difference between the keyword you are targeting in your campaigns and the keywords that people are searching for on Google. There are ways to be more controlled about when you want your ads to display and we will look at this when we look at setting up campaigns.

Ad Variations

Ad variations are the different ads you create and they are displayed to people when they search. For example, the following ad is displayed to people when they search for 'robot vacuum cleaner':

Robot Vacuum Cleaner
www.vacuum.com/Robot-Cleaner
Clean Floors with Robot Vacuum.
From $299.00 with Free Shipping.

The ads displayed on Google search results are primarily text-based ads, but if you are selling products there is the option to create shopping campaigns that create slightly different ad variations. For example:

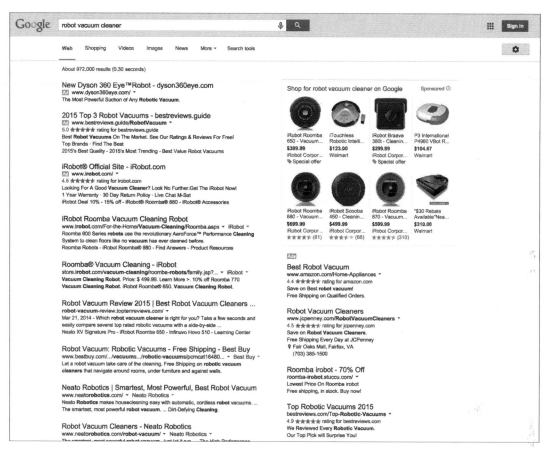

You can also choose to place ads on content sites through the Google Display Network. Display ads can be text, image, video and other ad formats. Let's start by focusing on text-based ads that are displayed on Google search results before looking at these additional options.

4

Developing a Google AdWords Campaign

There are three fundamental elements you need to develop to get your Google AdWords campaign set up. Firstly, you will need to research appropriate keywords to target, then develop a suitable campaign structure and finally develop compelling ad variations.

Tip: Having appropriate landing pages is critical to the success of your campaigns. You can have a perfect campaign inside your Google AdWords account, but if the landing page fails to engage and convert you won't receive good results. In some cases you might want to create a new landing page specifically for a set of keywords you are targeting before you launch the campaign (or ad group).

Keyword Research

Selecting keywords is a critical step in creating your Google AdWords campaign. The keywords that you select can also influence the structure you use for your campaigns and ad groups. Keyword research is something that you will come back to regularly because you will continue to add and remove keywords as part of ongoing optimization.

Brainstorm an initial list of keywords by:

- **Listing** your core products and services.

- **Looking at any recent marketing material**, including brochures, white papers or anything else you can find.

- **Reviewing your website's homepage** and any other important pages relating to your core products and services. Look for phrases that are repeated in your content and look at what is included in the headlines.

- **Asking yourself what you would search for on Google** if you were in the market for the products and services your organization offers. If you can, ask one or two of your best clients – getting an outside perspective can be really useful.

Tip: As you list your initial keywords look for logical ways to group the keywords together into related sets. This will make structuring easier as you move forward.

Now you should have a good list of initial keywords that you can then expand upon with some additional keyword research. The best way to start is by using the Keyword Planner which is under 'Tools' in your account.

The Keyword Planner gives you different options for using the tool. Start by selecting the first option: 'Search for new keywords and ad group ideas' which takes the initial keyword ideas and provides suggestions for related keywords.

Keyword Planner
Plan your next search campaign

What would you like to do?

▸ Search for new keyword and ad group ideas

▸ Get search volume for a list of keywords or group them into ad groups

▸ Get traffic forecasts for a list of keywords

▸ Multiply keyword lists to get new keyword ideas

Start by entering a few of your keywords that relate to the same product or service. For example, if you have a number of different keywords, including 'running shoes', 'training shoes', 'sports watch' and 'fitness watch', then you should start by searching based on an individual theme. So you might enter 'running shoes' and 'training shoes' to begin your additional keyword research, and then repeat the steps for the other themes of keywords from your initial brainstorming.

Once you have entered a few keywords you can skip down to the targeting section. Next you will want to select the geographic area where you will be showing your ads. In most cases you will want to select a country-level target for your keyword research. Now click on 'Get Ideas'.

Tip: The rest of the default settings should be fine, the tool should automatically pick up the language of the keywords you enter, but if you see anything strange showing up you can always make adjustments to these settings later.

The Keyword Planner will display a list of additional keyword suggestions based on the initial keywords you entered. By default the tool will show you keyword suggestions automatically grouped into different ad groups.

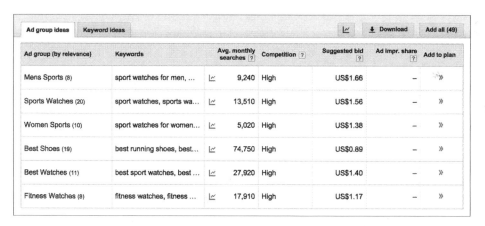

Ad group (by relevance)	Keywords		Avg. monthly searches ?	Competition ?	Suggested bid ?	Ad impr. share ?	Add to plan
Mens Sports (8)	sport watches for men, ...	⌇	9,240	High	US$1.66	–	»
Sports Watches (20)	sport watches, sports wa...	⌇	13,510	High	US$1.56	–	»
Women Sports (10)	sport watches for women...	⌇	5,020	High	US$1.38	–	»
Best Shoes (19)	best running shoes, best...	⌇	74,750	High	US$0.89	–	»
Best Watches (11)	best sport watches, best ...	⌇	27,920	High	US$1.40	–	»
Fitness Watches (8)	fitness watches, fitness ...	⌇	17,910	High	US$1.17	–	»

You can then click the name of the suggested ad group to see all the related keywords. The automated ad group suggestions can be helpful, but because it is automated you will want to take the time to review the suggestions and in most cases create your own campaign and ad group structure.

| Ad group: **Mens Sports** | | | | 1 of 49 ad group ideas | ‹ | › |
| | | | | | ⬇ Download | Add all (8) |
Keyword (by relevance)		Avg. monthly searches ?	Competition ?	Suggested bid ?	Ad impr. share ?	Add to plan
sport watches for men	〽	2,900	High	US$1.84	–	»
mens sport watches	〽	1,900	High	US$1.80	–	»
sports watches for men	〽	2,900	High	US$1.52	–	»
mens sports watches	〽	880	High	US$1.47	–	»
mens sport watch	〽	260	High	US$1.24	–	»
mens sports watch	〽	260	High	US$1.12	–	»
men sport watches	〽	110	High	US$1.42	–	»
men sports watches	〽	30	High	US$0.77	–	»

When you look at an individual ad group suggestion, you can see the average number of monthly searches for the keyword. Hovering over the graph icon will also show you the historical search volume trend for the keyword over the previous 12 months. This can be useful to understand the seasonality of the keyword and if there are particular months of the year when you can expect more people to be searching.

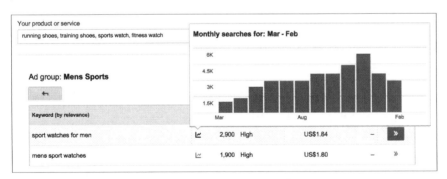

Tip: The numbers you see in the 'Average Monthly Searches' column is an overall average for the search volume over the previous 12 months.

'Competition' gives an indication of how many advertisers are competing to show their ads on a particular keyword. 'High' means that there are a higher number of advertisers competing to show their ads, compared to 'Medium' and 'Low'. This is a quick gauge as to how much effort you will need to put into your campaign optimization, keywords with higher competition typically require higher bids.

'Suggested Bid' provides an idea of how much you will need to bid for the keywords. This number is an average which means if you want to receive maximum coverage towards the top of the paid results you are likely to end up needing to use a higher bid. That being said, it is a good way to gauge your starting bids to get an idea of the budget you will need to allocate to your campaign.

'Ad Impression Share' will show 0% unless you are already bidding on the keyword or related keywords in your account. If you are bidding on the keyword 'vancouver tour' as a broad match keyword and you research additional keywords that relate to 'vancouver tour', you will be able to see how much coverage you are already receiving because of keywords you are already bidding on. This shows that there are related terms where there is an opportunity to increase your visibility by adding those keywords to your campaign.

If you don't like the automated grouping of keywords you can also see a single list of all the keywords by selecting 'Keyword Ideas'. This will provide the same suggested keywords, but without providing ad group suggestions.

Ad group ideas	**Keyword ideas**		
Search terms		**Avg. monthly searches** ?	**Competition** ?
running shoes		90,500	High
fitness watch		6,600	High
sports watch		3,600	High
training shoes		3,600	High

Either way you choose to use the Keyword Planner the most important thing is to try and think like a customer and consider each keyword that the tool suggests. Some keywords will give you an indication of someone's intent, for example if you see a keyword that includes 'buy' then it is likely that person is ready to purchase, while a keyword that is more general or includes 'reviews' is more likely to be researching before they make a final decision.

Tip: Visit http://lovesdata.co/V0p4X for more about how different keywords can show search intent.

When you find suitable keywords that you would like to target you can click the arrow in the 'Add to Plan' column. This will automatically build a list of keywords as you are using the Keyword Planner. As you add keywords you will see the daily clicks and cost estimates update and you can even adjust the bid range to understand the impacts of having higher or lower bids based on the keywords you are going to add to your campaign.

You can even add and edit ad groups as you build your plan, by clicking on the icons. This allows you to start creating your campaign structure right in the tool before you add the keywords to your campaign.

When you are ready you can click on 'Review Forecasts'. From here you can get an idea of how many clicks and impressions you will receive, along with an estimated advertising cost. You can use the slider or enter a bid amount at the top of the tool to see how changing your bid will impact the number of clicks you are likely to receive.

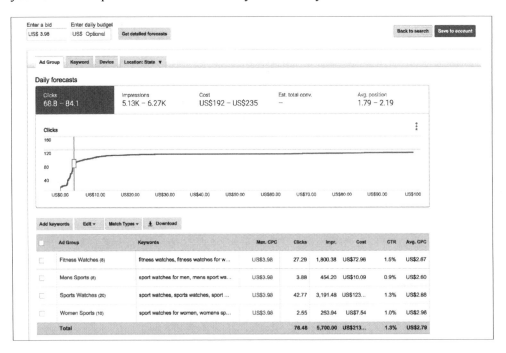

Tip: Estimating and assigning budget is covered in the "Budget" section in Chapter 7 – "Campaign Settings."

You can also use the tabs across the top of the tool to see a more granular breakdown for individual keywords, devices and geographic areas within your target. Finally, you can choose to add the keywords to a new or existing ad group, or download the keywords to save them to your computer.

Tip: There is no one way to add keywords to your campaigns. Some people like to work in Google AdWords, others prefer using spreadsheets or text files. Use whatever technique you're most comfortable with.

Keyword Matching

It's important to understand that the keywords you are bidding on are not necessarily what people are searching for when they see your ad. This is why keyword matching is important. It allows you to control the way the keywords you are bidding on are matched to the terms that people are actually using when they search.

Broad Match

Broad match is the default method in Google AdWords and will show your ads on terms people are searching for that relate to the keywords you have in your ad groups. You can think of broad match as a flexible matching option. It is the Google AdWords default to ensure that your ads are presented to people searching for terms that relate to your offering and helps increase your visibility.

For example, if you added the keyword **gardening book** to your ad group, your ad might be presented when people search for 'gardening book'. It might also presented when people search for related terms including, 'books on gardening', 'organic gardening book', 'gardening book club', 'gardening book reviews' and so on.

While some of these terms closely relate to the offering, there are terms that are not as relevant – for example, 'gardening book club' and 'gardening book reviews'. Both of these terms are unlikely to result in someone purchasing a gardening book or making an enquiry.

However, broad match does provide the greatest possible coverage for your ads and since the objective is to get your message seen by people you won't want to remove all your broad match keywords. You can refine when your ads are displayed to reduce your ads being shown for these less relevant terms (like 'club' and 'reviews' from the previous examples). This will be covered shortly, for now you should start thinking about the types of terms you do (and do not) to target for your ads.

Phrase Match

Phrase match is much more controlled than broad match because the keywords you bid on must be used within the terms people are searching for, and appear in the same order you have defined. In order to have a keyword phrase match, you need to place quote marks around your keyword. For example, using **"gardening book"**, would display ads to people searching for 'gardening book', 'gardening book sale' and 'gardening book club'. However, ads would not be displayed to people searching for 'books on gardening' or 'garden design book' because they do not contain the words in the same order as the phrase match keyword.

Phrase match is designed to be more precise than broad match (or modified broad match) since it enforces that words need to be in a particular order, but it provides greater reach than exact match.

> **Tip:** Phrase match can be used to control the amount you bid on keywords based on the particular word order people use when searching.

Exact Match

Exact match does as its name suggests: it matches exactly to what people are searching. To add an exact match keyword, you need to use square brackets around your keyword. For example, **[gardening book]** will only match people searching for 'gardening book'. Any variations of the keyword will not display your ads and there cannot be anything before or after your exact match keyword. This means that **[gardening book]** will not display your ad for 'buy gardening book' or 'gardening book sale'.

Important: Exact and phrase match keywords will also display your ads for close variants, like misspellings, plural and singular variations. Read the "Close Variants" section in this chapter for details.

Exact match is useful for your most important keywords. For example, if you have a keyword that drives the majority of your clicks and conversions, you might consider running that keyword in its own ad group as an exact match. This allows you to focus your optimization efforts on that individual keyword and ensure that you get the best results possible.

It is important to understand that what people search for changes over time. After all, Google has said that 20% of what people search for every day are terms that Google has not seen before.[1] This means you need to keep your keywords up-to-date to reflect what people are searching. This does not mean that everybody needs to change their keywords every day. For example, a plumber bidding on the keywords relating to their services, like 'New York plumber' and 'plumbing New York' won't see dramatic changes in keywords. However,

---

1   'Under the Hood' http://www.google.com/insidesearch/playground/underthehood.html 28 January 2011

if you're an online retailer and offer the latest mobile phones and tablet devices for sale, you will need to keep your keywords up-to-date on a much more regular basis, as new products are released and people begin to search for terms relating to those new products.

Broad Match Modifier

Broad match modifier is more specific than the standard broad match, but it also gives you greater reach than phrase match. Think of it as the midway point between broad match and phrase match. Broad match modifier allows you to define an individual word (or words) in your broad match keyword that you would like to match more closely.

To match a word in your keyword more closely using broad match modifier you need to add a plus sign before the word, for example 'formal shoes' would become 'formal +shoes' to match close variations of 'shoes' in what people are searching.

Broad match modifier matches close variations of words, including:

- **Misspellings:** for example **+flowers** would match 'flouers' and 'flwers'
- **Singular:** for example **+books** would match 'book'
- **Plural:** for example **+sale** would match 'sales'
- **Abbreviations:** for example **+doctor** would match 'dr'
- **Acronyms:** for example **+roi** would match 'return on investment'
- **Stemmings:** for example **+flooring** would match 'floor'

Let's look at the keyword 'formal shoes'. As a broad match keyword, ads might display for 'formal shoe', 'formal footwear' and 'evening footwear' because they all broadly relate to 'formal shoes'. By using a broad match modifier you can ensure that people searching must include a close variant of 'shoes' in their term by changing the keyword to 'formal +shoes'. This would mean ads would display for terms like 'evening shoes', 'formal shoe' and 'black dress shoes' because all of these terms include 'shoes' or a close variation of the word. If you were then to change the keyword to '+formal +shoes' this would mean that both words would need to be included or have close variations within the terms that people are searching. You would now be matching terms like 'formal evening shoes', 'shoes for formal' and even the misspelling of 'frmal shoes'.

> **Tip:** Don't forget to include spaces between your broad match modified words, for example if you miss the space between a word and the plus sign, for example 'gardening+book', you have incorrectly added the keyword. In this example, the keyword should be 'gardening +book'.

Remember that broad match modifier sits between standard broad match and phrase match, allowing you to get greater coverage on search terms, while maintaining focus on words that are important to your objectives. Broad match modifier is a great option for when you are just starting to use Google AdWords.

> **Tip:** You can broad match modify one or more words within your keyword, for example 'buy gardening +book', 'buy +gardening +book', '+buy gardening +book' and '+buy +gardening +book' are all correctly modified. If you are starting out think about the words that are important to you and that you want to ensure are contained within what people are searching, these are the words you want to broad match modify.

Negative Match

Negative match allows you to prevent your ad from displaying if a particular word is included in the term that is being searched. Negative match is indicated by placing a minus (or dash) before the particular word and works in combination with broad and phrase match. For example, if you had a broad match of 'gardening book' and you include a negative match of '-club' this will prevent your ad from displaying when people search for terms like 'gardening book club' and 'book club for gardening'. If you didn't use the negative match of '-club' these terms would ordinarily display your ad because of the broad match keywords in your ad group.

> **Tip:** In most cases you will want to use single words with the negative match type. However, you can use multiple words, for example '-free download' would prevent your ads from displaying for 'free photo download' and 'download free photos', but not 'free photos'.

Negative keywords are an important optimization technique for being more targeted with your ads. Adding lots of negative keywords prevents your ad from showing on irrelevant keywords you have identified and will therefore improve the click-through rate (CTR) of your ads because those terms will no longer generate unnecessary impressions. Apart from improving your CTR, negative keywords will also improve your website conversions because people using irrelevant terms will no longer be driven to your website.

You can add negative keywords for individual ad groups and entire campaigns. To add negative keywords, click on 'Negative Keywords' at the bottom of the 'Keywords' tab. You can also centrally manage negative keywords across multiple campaigns, read the "Negative Keyword Lists" section in this chapter for details.

> **Tip:** You can quickly add negative keywords to an ad group when you are adding other keywords by entering a minus sign (or dash) before the word. For example, entering 'gardening book' and '-free' would automatically add the broad match and negative match keywords to your ad group.

Negative Phrase and Negative Exact Match

In most cases you probably won't need to use negative phrase or negative exact match, but if you have a specific need that isn't met by regular negative keywords then it can be useful.

If you are targeting the keyword 'leather iphone case' and notice that your ads are occasionally showing when people search for 'leather briefcase' you can add the negative phrase match keyword of **-"leather briefcase"** to your campaign (note: the double quotes need to be included in the Google AdWords interface). This will prevent your ads from showing on the irrelevant term and any search queries that include the phrase, but they will continue to show for 'leather iphone case'.

Continuing the example, this time targeting the keyword 'iphone case', you might notice that your ads are appearing for people searching for 'iphone case' as well as 'iphone'. You can use the negative exact match keyword of **-[iphone]** to prevent your ads from showing when someone just searches for 'iphone', but your ads will continue to be seen if someone searches for 'iphone case'.

Close Variants

Since late 2014, phrase and exact match keywords automatically match to close variants. This means that your phrase and exact match keywords will display your ads if someone searches using a misspelling, abbreviation or other slight variations of your keywords. For example, the keyword **[gym new york]** is likely to match 'gym new york', 'gyms new york' and 'gyms new yrk'.

This means that your phrase and exact match keywords might not work exactly the way you expect them to when people are searching. The benefit of automatically including close variants is that it reduces the need to manage very specific keywords and allows you to expand the reach of your ad groups.

Google says that, "The AdWords system prefers to trigger ads using keywords that are identical to search queries",[2] which means that adding the different variations of your keywords and adjusting the bids will give your more control over how your keywords are matched.

Since your exact and phrase match keywords include close variants, it is important to monitor the search queries people are using to identify potential negative keywords. Techniques to do this will be covered after looking at keyword matching.

---

2   http://adwords.blogspot.com.au/2014/08/close-variant-matching-for-all-exact.html

Using Keyword Matching

Here is a quick summary of how the different keyword match types work:

Table: Broad Match Type

Match Type	Keyword	Examples of Search Queries Matched
Broad match	**gym new york**	gym new york new york gym gym in new york gym new york city new york fitness new york sports club boxing new york best gym new york new york athletic club new york boxing club climbing gym new york 24 hour gym new york boxing gym new york city
Broad match modifier	**+gym new york**	gym new york new york gym gym in new york gym new york city best gym new york climbing gym new york 24 hour gym new york boxing gym new york city

Table: Phrase Match Type

Match Type	Keyword	Examples of Search Queries Matched
Phrase match	**"gym new york"**	gym new york gyms new york gym new york city best gym new york climbing gym new york climbing gyms new york 24 hour gym new york boxing gym new york city

Table: Exact Match Type

Match Type	Keyword	Examples of Search Queries Matched
Exact match	**[gym new york]**	gym new york gyms new york

Table: Negative Match Type

Match Type	Keyword	Examples of Search Queries Matched
Negative match	**-boxing** and **-climbing** with broad match **gym new york**	gym new york new york gym gym in new york gym new york city new york fitness new york sports club best gym new york new york athletic club 24 hour gym new york
Negative match	**-boxing** and **-climbing** with broad match modifier **+gym new york**	gym new york new york gym gym in new york gym new york city best gym new york 24 hour gym new york
Negative match	**-boxing** and **-climbing** and **-24** and **-best** with broad match modifier **+gym new york**	gym new york new york gym gym in new york gym new york city

Identifying Potential Negative Keywords

Adding negative keywords improves your relevance by preventing your ads from displaying on irrelevant terms that you have identified. There are a number of different techniques for identifying potential negative keywords that you can add to your account.

When looking for potential negative keywords, it is important to consider the intent behind the keyword, or in other words, why somebody was searching using that particular term. For example, people searching for 'digital camera reviews' might be starting their research to look for a digital camera, whereas somebody searching for 'buy canon powershot g15' has already decided on the particular camera they want to purchase. So when you're looking for negative keywords, you will also need to consider the strategy and objectives of your Google AdWords campaign. Some people might want to add 'reviews' as a negative keyword, while others might want to include this as a keyword they want to target to drive clicks.

Using the Keyword Planner

When you are using the Keyword Planner, always keep an eye out for potential negative terms. As you research keywords you want to include in your ad groups you will also find negative keywords that don't directly relate to your objectives. When you find a negative keyword, add the most important word from that keyword, for example if you don't want your ads to display for 'digital camera reviews', then adding '-reviews' will prevent your ad from displaying for that term, but also other terms that include reviews, for example 'slr digital camera reviews', 'compact digital camera reviews' and so on. This will save you from having to add each separate keyword and ensure you prevent your ads from displaying on other variations that you might not have encountered.

Using Actual Search Terms

Using the different keyword match types means that the keyword you're bidding on is not necessarily the keyword that someone has actually entered to see (and then click on) your ad. This is especially the case with broad match keywords, where bidding on 'tennis shoe' as a broad match would mean your ad could display for keywords like 'buy tennis shoes', 'tennis shoe photos' and even 'used tennis shoes'. This means that ads can be found using lower quality keywords that you might want to exclude from your campaigns.

You can see the actual search terms people use to find your ads in Google AdWords and this is a fantastic way to optimize your keyword lists. Navigate to the 'Keywords' tab in a particular campaign or if you have a smaller account you can follow these steps after selecting 'All Online Campaigns', which will include all keywords across all of your campaigns. Click 'Details' and under 'Search Terms' click 'All'.

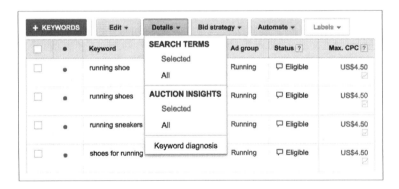

You will now have a list of all the actual keywords people are searching for that have triggered your ad and resulted in a click through to your website.

	Search term	Match Type ?	Added / Excluded ?	Campaign	Ad group	Clicks ? ↓
☐						969
☐	running shoes online	Broad match	None	Shoes	Running	260
☐	sport shoes discount	Broad match	None	Shoes	Sport	89
☐	latest running shoe	Broad match	None	Shoes	Running	53
☐	running shoe photo	Broad match	None	Shoes	Running	24
☐	buy running shoes	Broad match	None	Shoes	Running	22
☐	shoes for gym	Broad match	None	Shoes	Gym	17
☐	running shoes	Exact match	Added	Shoes	Running	10
☐	gym shoes	Exact match	Added	Shoes	Gym	10

You will see all the different keywords people use in the 'Search Term' column and you can also see how these keywords have been matched to the keywords in your campaigns and ad groups by looking at the 'Match Type' column.

The 'Added/Excluded' column is useful because it shows you if you are bidding on that particular keyword or have already excluded the keyword. If you see 'none' in this column it means that you don't currently have that particular search term in any of your ad groups. For example, if someone searched for 'brand new tennis shoes' and you were bidding on 'tennis shoes' then the column would read 'none' if you didn't have 'brand new tennis shoes' in any of your ad groups.

If you haven't run the actual search term report before, it is important to spend some time scanning through the list of keywords and deciding if any should be added into your ad groups (or if you should be adding any as negative keywords).

You can select the checkbox next to one or more keywords and then click the 'Add as Keyword' button at the top of the report. This will automatically add the keyword into an ad group, however, if you want to add the keyword to a different ad group one option is to download the keywords and manually add them to appropriate ad groups.

If you find negative keywords in the actual search terms report, you can use the checkbox to select one or more keywords and then click 'Add as Negative Keyword'. This will add the keyword as a negative exact match.

In most cases I recommend editing the search term to only include an individual word to use as a negative keyword. For example, you scan the list of actual search terms and you see 'used tennis shoes', since you only sell new tennis shoes this keyword won't result in any conversions, so you select the keyword and use the 'Add as Negative Keyword' button. You will see the keyword shown as [used tennis shoes] which means your ad will only be prevented from displaying when somebody searches for that exact term again, but your ad will continue to show for people searching for 'used tennis shoe' or 'used tennis footwear'. So instead of adding the search term as an exact negative keyword, you can edit it to 'used' and this will now mean that anybody that searches for a keyword that includes 'used' will no longer see your ads. This is much more efficient than adding every single term individually.

The other option that you have when adding negative keywords in the actual search term report is that you can choose to add the keyword at the ad group level, the campaign level, or even to an existing negative keyword list.

> **Tip:** When using the 'Add Negative Keyword' button to add a search term to a negative keyword list, you might see the option to 'Add negative keyword list to associated campaigns'. This option will display if you are adding a negative keyword to a list that is not currently assigned to the particular campaign. Selecting this will mean that you add the negative keyword to the list and the list will also be applied to the campaign.

Reviewing the actual search terms report for negative keywords should be part of your regular account optimization and will help ensure your ads are displayed to the most appropriate audience. It is also critical to use this report regularly if you have a large portion of broad match keywords to help refine when your ads are being displayed.

Using the Opportunities Tab

The opportunities tab in Google AdWords provides automated suggestions for your account, including keyword suggestions. This is another great way to identify new keywords and even potential negative keywords for your account. Since the suggestions are all automatically generated, it is worth spending a little bit of extra time and care when reviewing the recommendations.

Navigate to the 'Opportunities' tab in your account and check that you are on the 'Keywords' tab. There will be keyword suggestions for different ad groups in your account. Clicking on the keyword suggestion will open up a panel that includes the different keywords that are being recommended for your account.

> **Tip:** If you have just created your account there will not be any automated suggestions – Google looks at the performance of your account over time to generate these ideas. If you don't see any suggestions now, then check back in a couple of weeks.

Spend some time scanning through each set of keyword recommendations. You can add keywords to your ad group by checking the box next to one or more keywords and then click 'Apply Now' at the bottom of the panel. Since the keywords are automatically being recommended you should take a moment to ensure that they are appropriate for the particular ad group, if they are not suitable for the ad group you can click the 'Ad Group' column and select a more appropriate ad group for the keyword.

If you identify a good potential keyword, but you don't have a suitable ad group to add it to, then you can download those keywords by selecting the checkboxes and then clicking the

'Download as .csv' button. Once you have downloaded the file you can later create a new ad group (or multiple ad groups), upload the keywords and then create suitable ads.

When you are scanning the keyword recommendations you should also keep an eye out for negative keywords that you can add to your campaigns, ad groups and negative keyword lists. Using the same technique covered when using the actual search terms report, you can identify terms in the keyword suggestions. For example, if you are advertising a real estate agent course and you see the keyword suggestion of 'real estate coaching' you can add 'coaching' as a negative keyword if you don't offer a coaching service as part of your services.

You can't add negative keywords directly from the keyword suggestions panel, so you can copy negative terms you identify into a separate document and then later add them into your account. Alternatively you can use the checkboxes to select potential negative keywords and download your negative keywords using the download as CSV option for later review and placement into your account.

> **Tip:** Once you have reviewed a keyword and have decided not to add it to your account or you have added it as a negative keyword, you can select the keyword and click the 'Remove' button to remove if from the list of recommendations.

Using Google Analytics

Google Analytics is another great way to identify potential keywords to target and negative keywords to further refine your campaigns. Log into your Google Analytics account and navigate to the Queries report (under 'Acquisition' and 'Search Engine Optimization'). Start by scanning through the organic (free) keywords that people are using on Google to find your website. If you don't see any data within the report read "Search Engine Optimization" in Chapter 17 for details.

You are likely to have hundreds or thousands of different keywords sending people to your website, so focus on the keywords that are driving the majority of traffic, these will be at the top of the report. You can then expand the number of rows by changing the 'Show Rows' option or simply navigate through the report using the arrows in the bottom right corner.

Quickly scan through the list and copy any potential keywords into a separate document so you can then load them into suitable ad groups later. You are also likely to find terms that can be added as negative keywords. You can copy them into a separate document or into a new sheet if you are using a spreadsheet to organize your potential keywords.

Negative Keyword Lists

Now that you are actively identifying negative keywords and managing multiple campaigns, you will begin to find that there is overlap in the negative keywords you are using for different campaigns. Rather than manually adding the negative keyword to each separate campaign you can create a list of negative keywords which you can then apply to multiple campaigns. Negative keyword lists will help streamline your management of negative keywords across multiple campaigns.

To set up a negative keyword list, navigate to the 'Campaigns' tab and click on 'Shared Library'. You will find the item on the bottom left corner under the names of your campaigns. Then click 'Campaign Negative Keywords'. If there are already negative keyword lists set up in the account you will see the names of these lists, if there are no lists set up you can click the 'New Negative Keyword List' button to start creating your first list.

Start by adding all the negative keywords you want to apply to multiple accounts into your new list. Alternatively, if you already have identified a large number of negative keywords you can create multiple lists that can then be applied to particular campaigns. For example, you might create a negative keyword list called 'Free' where you include all the lower quality keywords like 'free', 'cheapest' and 'bargain'. If you notice that people are searching for career-related search terms and you are not trying to drive these visitors to your website, you can create another list called 'Careers' where you include keywords like 'jobs', 'career', 'apprenticeship' and 'intern'. This will help ensure your ads are only being displayed to your potential clients and not being displayed to people looking for employment.

Once you have saved your negative keyword list, click on the name of your list and click the 'Apply to Campaigns' button. You'll now see a list of your campaigns – click the arrow button next to each campaign that you want to apply the list to. Once you've added all the campaigns that you want to use the negative keyword list for, click the 'Save' button.

Tip: Remember that negative keyword lists apply at the campaign level, so if you only want to add negative keywords to individual ad groups, you will need to add these using the standard method of adding negative keywords.

You can also apply your negative keyword lists to your campaigns from within the 'Keywords' tab. From the shared library, click on 'All Online Campaigns' under the search box in the left hand column. Now click on the name of an individual campaign and navigate to the 'Keywords' tab. At the very bottom of the keywords you will see a link that says 'Negative Keywords', click this to open up the negative keywords panel (if it isn't already open) and then click on 'Keyword Lists' on the right hand side. Here you can see if any negative keywords lists have been applied to the campaign and you can also add additional negative keyword lists by clicking 'Add' and then selecting 'Add Keyword Lists'.

5

Model for Successful Online Advertising

The continued success of online advertising requires ongoing work to improve performance and results. Developing a framework that can be consistently applied will help ensure that key campaign elements are reviewed on a regular basis. Before you begin any campaign, it's important to outline the business objectives, goals and audience for the campaign. If you already have a campaign running you should review these key elements to ensure your campaigns still meet their original purpose.

This model guides you through the different stages of managing a successful campaign.

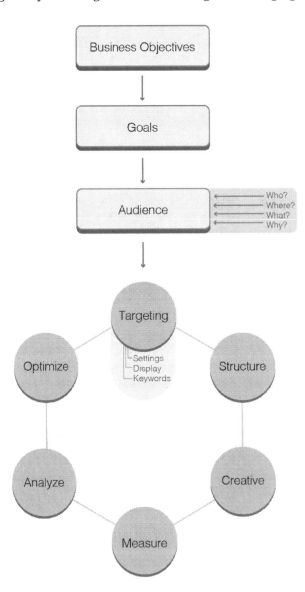

1. Objectives

Start by outlining your objectives. You need to be able to clearly and concisely answer the question 'Why do I need this campaign?'[1] And you also need to be able to tie the purpose of the campaign to tangible objectives.

---

1   http://www.kaushik.net/avinash/digital-marketing-and-measurement-model/

Your objectives for an advertising campaign for a new product launch could include 'growing awareness', 'product sales to new customers' and 'product sales to existing customers'. If you're not selling a product, but instead focused on services or content, then your objectives might be slightly different – instead of sales you might want to drive leads or engagement with your content.

If you're stuck, refer to the core marketing funnel steps to help shape your objectives. The steps include:

- **Awareness** to build an initial audience for your product or service
- **Engagement** for people to form an understanding about the offering
- **Conversion** to make sales and generate leads
- **Retention** to keep your existing clients and customers happy

You can use all of these steps or a combination of them. For example, if you are launching a new product or service into the market, you might want to begin with a focus on awareness and engagement before you begin trying to tie your campaign objectives to conversion and retention. Using a template can be helpful to map out the objectives for the marketing funnel steps.

Awareness	
Engagement	
Conversion	
Retention	

For example, if we are looking to develop a campaign for a new gym that is opening, we might outline the following objectives:

Awareness	Increase number of people who know about the gym
Engagement	Increase number of people interested in joining
Conversion	New gym memberships
Retention	Continue gym membership

Since this campaign promotes a new offering, the initial objectives should focus on awareness and engagement. This does not mean conversion and retention should be ignored (you should aim to set up goals for all four stages), but objectives should be guided by the understanding that the first stage is build an audience. This means that initial success should be judged against goals that reflect awareness and engagement objectives.

2. Goals and Measurement

Now we need to define what we want people to do – our goals. They should relate closely to each of the objectives and also be measurable and tangible. You might have more than one goal for particular business objectives you have defined.

Continuing the gym scenario, we might develop the following goals for each of the objectives:

Increase number of people who know about the gym

- Increase ad impressions
- Increase number of people viewing the website

Increase number of people interested in joining

- View the location page
- View the pricing page
- Email newsletter sign up
- Social media follow
- Opening event registration

New gym memberships

- Purchase gym membership
- Free trial registration

Continue gym memberships

- Log in to members section of the website
- Refer a friend
- Participate in online promotions
- Click through from email newsletters

> **Tip:** In most cases it is difficult to set up goals in Google Analytics to measure the awareness stage. Instead these are usually metrics, for example, impressions of your ads that you compare over time. That being said, you might be able to use engagement-based goals based on time or pageviews to help measure awareness.

Goals can be used to define your macro and micro conversion actions. A macro conversion is a high priority goal, for example a sale or a lead. A micro conversion is a secondary conversion objective, like watching a video, engaging with a number of pages on your website, commenting on your blog or even signing up for your email newsletter. Your micro conversions might not immediately contribute to your bottom line, but they do have a value in that they are indicators of potential future macro conversion actions.

Try to set up goals for all of your macro and micro conversion actions. Even if you set up too many goals, you can always refine these moving forward by disabling particular goals. By having all of your conversion actions defined you will have a much clearer understanding of what actions your campaigns are driving.

3. Audience

Defining the target audience for your online advertising is an important step as this will help you develop the campaign structure and inform the way you create the campaign. Focus on the most important aspects of your target audience and start by answering the following questions:

Who are they?

- Depending on the objectives and the type of campaign you are looking to develop, this can be a useful question to establish any key demographics and general areas of interest of your target audience.

Where are they located?

- This will inform the geographic targeting of your campaigns. If you answer this question with a very broad answer, like 'Worldwide' or 'North America', you might want to consider changing this to 'Where are my most valuable audience members located?' as this will provide a better starting point. Once you see success you can always come back and adjust your answer and modify your geographic targeting.

What are they looking for? What are they interested in?

- If you are looking to develop a search campaign you will want to have some initial ideas of the types of keywords your target audience are using to search. If you are focused on a display campaign write down the types of websites your audience are likely to be interested in and the types of content that appeals to them.

What do they do online?

- Are they actively searching for information, or are they are casually browsing content? Answering this question will allow you to determine if you should be running a search campaign or a display campaign. It can be good to spend time going beyond the initial answer of the type of campaign you are looking to run as it might provide ideas for the future direction of your online advertising. For example, even if you want to focus on people who go to Google to search for keywords relating to your product or service, taking the time to consider the other things they might be looking for or browsing can help build a more complete picture of the future opportunities for the campaign and other campaigns you might consider running.

Why would they want this?

- Thinking about the unique benefits you are offering to your potential customers and clients will help shape the messages you develop for your advertising campaign. When you answer this question you should focus on your unique selling points and what makes you different from your competitors. This will help inform the ad creative you develop for your campaign.

4. Targeting

Based on your audience insights, you'll now be able to determine the starting point for your campaign targeting. In most cases you will want your initial targeting to be focused. You can always broaden the scope of your targeting once you are achieving the objectives you have defined. Consider the primary campaign targeting options:

Type

☐ Search Network with Display Select

☐ Search Network Only

☐ Display Network Only

☐ Shopping

☐ Video

> **Tip:** In most cases you will start by running ads using the 'Search Network Only' option. This gives you more control over your campaigns and is likely to produce the best results as you are starting out.

Location

☐ All Countries

☐ Country

☐ State

☐ City

☐ Region

☐ Postal Code

Consider starting with a location target that is more specific than country, but not too targeted. This will give you enough reach without displaying your ads too widely. Remember that although your products and services might be available globally or to a large area you should start by targeting areas where you already have success.

Devices

- ☑ Computers*
- ☑ Tablets*
- ☐ Mobile

* Note: Ads always target computers and tablets

Tip: Bid adjustments let you disable mobile targeting or adjust your final bid amounts.

Ad Schedule

- ☐ All days and times
- ☐ Certain days
- ☐ Certain times

Now that you have defined your initial campaign targeting, you need to start researching the keywords or placements for your ads. You can start with an initial list before moving onto the next step or you can spend time creating a comprehensive list.

Tip: Read Chapter 4 – "Developing a Google AdWords Campaign" – for details on researching keywords and placements.

If you are checking your targeting for an existing campaign you should begin by reviewing the targets against the objectives and goals that have been defined. You can then review your historical data to understand the performance of your different targeting selections. A good option for reviewing previous performance is to use the 'Dimensions' tab in the campaign. For example, selecting 'User Location' allows you to see the performance by the places people are located when they view your ads.

5. Structure

Now you need to structure your campaign. If you are working on a search campaign the structure will be based on keywords, while a display campaign will be structured around the display placements you have selected. Start by reviewing your keywords or placements against the most common account structures:

- ☐ Products and services
- ☐ Keyword theme
- ☐ Brands
- ☐ Website structure

☐ Geographic targeting

☐ Network targeting

☐ Budget

Remember that you can use a hybrid of two or more of these common structures for your campaigns. You can also review the "Structuring your Account" section in Chapter 3 for additional details. After you have structured your campaigns you can begin to structure your ad groups in those campaigns.

6. Creative

Your ads form the creative component of your campaigns and can take different forms depending on the type of campaign you are running. For search campaigns all of your ads will be text-based, while display campaigns give you the flexibility to run text, image and other ad formats. The ads you create need to be informed by your:

☐ Objectives

☐ Audience

☐ Targeting

☐ Structure

Remember to create at least two ad variations for each ad group within your search campaigns. This allows you to test different messaging to improve your CTR, onsite engagement and even conversions. You should also test different ad variations when targeting the display network, including image and other ad formats. Using different imagery and calls to action can impact the success of your display campaigns.

7. Measure

Ensure that goals are set up for your campaign, that these goals are available in your Google AdWords account and that the data you have available inside Google Analytics is accurate. In most cases, once you have set up your goals you should only need to make adjustments if your objectives change or if changes are made to the way your website functions. Things to check include:

☐ Google AdWords and Google Analytics are linked

☐ Goals are set up inside Google Analytics

☐ Goals are imported into Google AdWords or
Google AdWords conversion tracking has been set up

☐ Goals reflect the objectives that have been defined for the campaign

☐ Conversion numbers appear to be accurate

Tip: Creating regular reports on the performance of your campaigns can help highlight any problems that might be occurring with the way you are tracking success. Regular reports can also help you quickly identify changes that are occurring in your campaigns that might need to be reviewed in more detail.

8. Analyze and Optimize

After your campaign has been running and collecting data, it is time to begin analysis and optimization. The focus of your analysis will depend on the maturity of your campaign. If you are looking after a younger campaign you will typically focus on impressions, clicks and CTR to increase visibility. This is in comparison to a mature campaign that is already meeting your objectives for conversions and return on investment (ROI), where you will focus on identifying new opportunities, historical trends and further tweaking to improve performance.

You should aim to analyze what is working and not working for each of these components of your campaign:

☐ Ad variations

☐ Keywords

☐ Placements

☐ Structure

☐ Targeting

Remember to consider your campaign objectives before you begin to make changes to your campaign. Some campaigns might have a focus on driving conversions, while others might be designed to increase brand awareness.

Tip: Consider macro and micro conversions when analyzing the performance of a campaign. You can extend this further by using the Multi-Channel Funnels report in Google Analytics to understand how your Google AdWords campaigns work in conjunction with your other marketing efforts.

Applying the Framework

Review your campaigns on a regular basis and create your own checklist that meets the needs of your campaigns. If you are setting up a new campaign, or reviewing a campaign for the first time, it is a good idea to run through each step. Once you are familiar with the steps you can begin to adjust and extend the framework based on your requirements. There might be steps you only review every six months (for example the measurement step) while other steps you might review every week.

The main thing is to review your campaigns on a regular basis and use the framework to ensure you check critical campaign elements. Managing your Google AdWords account is not a static process and something only done once – continually reviewing performance and testing will lead to better outcomes.

Display Campaigns

The Google Display Network is made up of over two million different websites,[1] allowing you to target your ads to users as they view content and browse online. As you begin to target your ads on the Google Display Network, it's important to understand that people's behavior and intent is different from when they are searching for information. Since they are not actively searching, it means that they are less likely to be actively seeking out your product and services. This means you need to consider your display campaign objectives and choose the best targeting options to meet those objectives.

Apart from websites, the Google Display Network also gives you the ability to place your ads on mobile websites, video content and even in mobile apps that have allocated space to display ads. Google AdWords allows you to choose from multiple targeting criteria to get the best results, so if you want to show on news websites, but not on travel blog or vice versa, you have the flexibility to choose and adjust your targeting.

---

1   http://adwords.blogspot.com.au/2013/09/reach-relevance-and-trust-big-three-in.html

Fundamentals

Display campaigns can be an effective way to drive brand awareness, increase engagement and even increase conversions, but you have to understand the best techniques for creating and targeting your ads before you jump into the Google Display Network.

If you are just getting started with Google AdWords, then the best thing to do is focus on your search campaigns and then come back to display after you have optimized your search campaigns and are seeing a level of success. If you immediately start by jumping into display, then you are less likely to achieve the results you may be hoping for. This is because the Google Display Network has multiple targeting options and your ads can easily start showing on websites that might not be suitable for your message and offering. Your display campaigns also need to be configured and optimized if you are specifically trying to drive conversions, which takes more time and effort compared to your search campaigns.

The best way to run display ads is in their own dedicated campaigns. This is for a number of really important reasons. Firstly, you will want to develop ads with specific messages and calls to action for the Google Display Network. It is likely that the ads which are successful on search are less successful on display (or even worse, not successful at all). By having a dedicated display campaign, you can create new ads that have specifically targeted offers and messages. This also allows you to test particular ads against one another, just like you would for search but this time for display.

Secondly, by having your display campaigns separate from your search campaigns, you can allocate your budget appropriately. Let's say that you are advertising a frozen meal delivery service and you receive 100 conversions on your website. If 20 of these conversions are from your display ads and 80 conversions are from your search ads you probably want to allocate your advertising budget based on these results. By having separate campaigns for display and search inside your Google AdWords account, you can then allocate 20% of your budget to display and 80% of your budget to search. Alternatively, if you had your display and search ads in the same campaign with 100% of your budget allocated to the single campaign, you would not have control over how your budget is spent. Your display ads might start receiving a disproportionate amount of your advertising budget, resulting in less conversions because your search ads are shown less frequently.

The other benefit of having your display and search ads separated into different campaigns is that it makes reporting and analysis easier. This is because you can see performance at a glance in your account, instead of having to segment your data or create special reports to tease apart the insights you need to make decisions.

Defining Objectives

The objectives for your display campaigns are going to be different to the goals defined for your search campaigns. This is because of people's intent and behavior when browsing or engaging with content is different to when they are searching for something. Before you begin building your display campaign, spend some time listing out the key objectives for the campaign. The objectives and goals you choose will inform the way you set up and target your display campaign.

You can also use your objectives to define how you are going to measure and evaluate success. This includes the goals you are going to define and the reports you are going to use to analyze your campaign results.

Branding and Awareness

Display campaigns can be used to improve your brand recognition or increase awareness of your products or services. This objective is the most difficult to evaluate when it comes to assigning new and ongoing budget, however, assigning a branding or awareness objective can be an important component of your digital marketing efforts. If you are trying to break into a market or build your reputation this type of campaign is a good starting point. When you begin to develop your ad variations, consider the content that you write and the imagery you use to convey your brand and offering.

> **Tip:** For branding and awareness campaigns, keep your messages short and catchy. Ensure your logo and branding elements are highlighted in your ad variations. Focus on image and video ad formats that engage with your target audience and use a call to action to encourage people to find out more.

If you are focused on branding or awareness as a campaign objective, then when you evaluate your campaigns you will want to look at data for impressions (to see how many times your ads are displayed) and reach (to understand how many people have been exposed to your ads). Reporting is covered in Chapter 11, but there are additional metrics that will help complement impressions and reach to give you a more detailed understanding of performance and success.

Engagement

You can encourage different types of engagement using display campaigns. You might want people to get more information about your product or service, or maybe build an initial connection with your organization. You might even want people to engage with your ad directly – for example, if you have created a rich media ad, you might want people to interact with the ad itself. If you have created video on YouTube you might advertise the video with the objective of getting people to engage and watch the video.

Defining objectives around engagement are similar to branding, in that they are not directly tied to a dollar value, but they step beyond someone just seeing or being aware of your ad or brand. You are focused on encouraging people to take the next step. If you are focused on engagement, you might want to consider additional objectives around branding, and potentially even conversions to build a more complete picture of success when you are reporting and analyzing your results.

Conversions

You can use display campaigns to drive particular conversion actions. You might define a conversion as a new lead, a sale of a product or even a registration. It is important to define your core conversion objectives along with your secondary objectives. For example, you might want to sell a particular product on your website, but people also have the option of signing up for your email newsletter and following you on Twitter. If you define product purchases as your sole objective, you are not going to consider all the other actions being taken by people as they find you online.

> **Tip:** Read Chapter 23 – "Goals" – on macro and micro conversions for more ideas on primary and secondary objectives for your display campaigns.

You might find that your display campaigns are not ideally suited to driving your primary conversion objective. In this case you might want to consider altering your display strategy to focus on secondary objectives. For example, display ads that specifically direct people to sign up for your email newsletter or engage with you on social media might be more effective in the medium and long term, rather than trying to explicitly get people to purchase your products or enquire about your services. Test different strategies for your objectives to see what is most successful.

Retention

Display campaigns can also be used to retain your existing clients and customers and potentially even expose them to new products and services you are offering. Defining your retention objectives might have some overlap with the other objectives, including awareness and conversions. For example, you might want to get existing customers to log into your customer section or view a landing page that highlights a new product offering. Alternatively, you might want people to renew their subscription or upgrade to a new service level or new product.

> **Tip:** Consider dedicated campaigns or ad groups for extremely different objectives. For example, if you want to target ads to existing customers write an ad copy that is different to ads targeting prospective customers. Keeping these in separate campaigns can help you segment your messages and allocate budgets more effectively.

Display Targeting

You can present your display ads to people based on a number of different targeting options, and this will depend on the objectives you have defined for your campaign. Targeting options include targeting particular keywords as they appear within pages on the display network – this is called display keyword targeting. Other options include targeting people based on how they have previously engaged on your website which is known as remarketing (or behavioral targeting). The different targeting features will be covered shortly, but here is a snapshot of the options available:

- **Display keyword targeting** (also known as contextual targeting) allows you to target your ads based on particular keywords in the content of sites on the Google Display Network.

- **Placement targeting** allows you to choose the specific sites, apps and other placements where your ads will be displayed.

- **Topic targeting** enables you to choose particular content categories. If a placement on the display network includes content about the topic your ad can display on that placement.

- **Interest categories** allow you to target your ads to people based on their particular interests. Google determines their areas of interest based on their browsing behavior and other data.

- **Remarketing** enables you to target your ads to people who have already engaged with you. For example, you can target people who have been to your website, but who have not yet converted.

- **Gender** allows you to target your ads based on gender.

- **Age** allows you to target your ads based on particular age ranges.

- **Parental status** allows you to target your ads to people with or without children.

- **Display Campaign Optimizer (DCO)** automates the process of selecting placements for your ads using your historical conversion data and Google's automation tools.

Google has presented details on the best targeting strategies for advertisers focused on conversions and getting people to take action from ads on the display network. Advertisers receive the best results when using remarketing, which might not be that surprising because these are people who have already been to your website or engaged with your brand before they are shown your ad. If your display campaign objective is for people to perform some sort of action, then you should consider starting with a campaign that uses remarketing to get the best results.

This diagram from Google[2] shows that advertisers receive the highest conversion rate and lowest cost-per-conversion (also known as cost-per-acquisition) when using remarketing to target their ads:

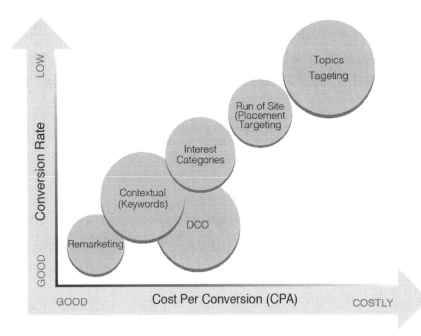

As you move up and to the right in the diagram the conversion rate reduces and the cost-per-conversion increases. It is important to understand that particular targeting techniques like remarketing can potentially mean that only a small number of people are ever exposed to these ads, so it is critical to monitor the audience size of your targets to ensure your campaigns are viable. If ads will only be seen by a handful of people, then it probably isn't an efficient method of advertising and you will want to balance defined targets with the potential audience size.

Display Keyword Targeting

Display keywords (also called contextual targeting) allow you to display your ads on placements on the Google Display Network that relate to the keywords you choose. For example, if you used the display keyword 'tropical holiday', then Google would look for pages that relate to that particular keyword. This is not the same as search campaigns, where someone is actively searching to see an ad. Instead Google looks at content that relates to your keyword and then places your ad alongside that content.

2   http://www.google.com/ads/displaynetwork/webinar.html

Tip: Google also looks at recent browsing behavior to display your ads when using display keywords. This means that if someone was looking at content relating to your keywords and then browsed to other types of content, your ad might still be displayed even if the particular page does not relate to your keywords. You can check to see if your ads are being placed based on recent browsing behavior by selecting 'Placements' in the 'Display Network' tab. Then click 'Segment' and select 'Targeting Mode'. Where you see 'Extended Keyword Match' this tells you that recent behavior was used instead of contextual targeting.

When using display keyword targeting you should use a similar approach to structuring your ad groups as you would for your search campaigns. By using tight groupings of display keywords, you can help ensure that your ads relate to what people are browsing on the Google Display Network.

Placement Targeting

Placement targeting allows you to control where your ads are displayed on the Google Display Network, including websites, apps and other placements. This gives you granular control and for some placements you can even select sub-sections of the website. For example, you could select to display your ads across the *New York Times* website, or just on the 'jobs' section. The ability to choose particular sections of a placement varies depending on the website.

You can use the Display Planner tool to check to see if a website is included within the Google Display Network to place your ads. Click on 'Tools' and then 'Display Planner'. Here, you can enter the URL of the website and click 'Get Placement Ideas'.

If the placement shows up, then you can target it. However, if it does not show up at the top of the results, then this means the website is not accepting ads through the Google Display Network. You will also notice additional suggestions for related websites as you scroll down the list of results.

If you do not have a particular website in mind to show your ads, then you can also enter general keywords into the Display Planner to see suggested placements. You will want to take your time going through the list of recommended placements and look at each website to get an idea of where your ads will potentially be displayed. Some placements in the Google Display Network will be better than others.

> **Tip:** You can use a combination of automatic and managed placements. *Automatic placements* are where Google automatically identifies suitable places to display your ads, while Managed Placements are where you have complete control using the placement targeting option.

Topic Targeting

Topic targeting is similar to display keywords, but rather than having to add multiple keywords around a particular theme, you can select the appropriate topic. This will mean that your ads are displayed with content that relates to that particular topic. This provides broader coverage for your ads. For example, using the topic target of 'home improvement' would mean your ads are placed on Google Display Network sites alongside content that relates to home improvement.

It is important to remember that topic targeting gives you broad coverage, so you will typically want to combine this with another targeting method to ensure your ads reach your desired audience. You can combine topic targeting with placement targeting to make your ads appear on relevant areas of a website on the Google Display Network. For example, if you were selling t-shirts online you could combine the 'fashion and style' topic target with the 'nytimes.com' placement target to only display your ads on fashion-related pages of the *New York Times*. This would mean that your ads are displayed to people more likely to be interested in your product.

If you are looking to run remarketing ads, then combining your remarketing list with a topic target can also mean that your ads appear alongside relevant content. For example, if you were trying to get people to register for your 'business tips' email newsletter, you could create a remarketing list for people who visited your website but did not register. By combining this list with the 'business and industrial' topic target your remarketing ads would only be displayed to people who had been to your website as they browse business related content on the Google Display Network. If you did not add the topic target, then the ads could appear on various display network sites and alongside unrelated content, like entertainment and holiday content. Although this might sound OK, do you really feel someone would be likely to sign up for your 'business tips' if they were researching their next holiday? By combining the appropriate topic target, ads immediately become more relevant to what people are browsing. How to set up combined targeting methods is covered shortly.

Interest Categories

Interest categories display your ads to people who are interested in particular types of content. Unlike the previous targeting methods, this is based on individual behavior. For example, if someone browses the travel section of the *New York Times*, then looks at travel blogs and other travel related content, Google AdWords can determine that the person is interested in *travel*. This allows you to target your ads to anybody who has shown an interest in travel.

Since interest categories are based on behavior, it also means that you can target someone based on their interest, even if they are not on a website that relates to that topic. After someone has shown an interest in a topic (like travel), you can target them while they are browsing any content, this might be travel-related or any other type of content. For example, someone with a travel interest might see your ad on a news or business website. Combining interest category targeting with another targeting method, like topic targeting makes it more precise. Combining the 'travel' interest category with the 'travel' topic target, means your ads would display to people who are interested in travel while also browsing travel related content.

Remarketing

Remarketing allows you to target your ads to people who have already engaged with your website. If you are starting your first display campaign, then this is the best option if you are looking to drive conversions from your advertising budget. This is because people who are already aware of your brand are far more likely to convert than people who are not. You can also create highly targeted remarketing lists to target your ads to people who have the highest likelihood of converting. For example, you could target people who added an item to your shopping cart, but did not complete their purchase. Or you could target people who viewed your contact page or lead form, but did not complete it.

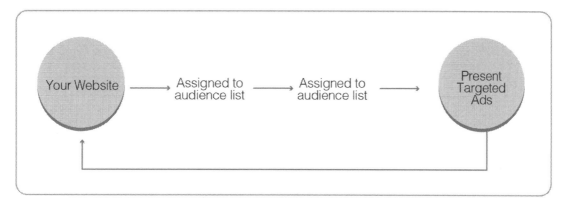

By creating targeted remarketing lists you can also create specific ads to encourage people to convert. For example, you could provide a special offer or incentive to bring people back to your website and complete their purchase. If you have not run display campaigns before, then remarketing can be a good starting point, especially if you are trying to drive conversions on your website.

Tip: Setting up remarketing campaigns is covered in the "Remarketing" section in Chapter 6.

Gender, Age and Parental Status

You can target your ads based on gender, age and parental status on the Google Display Network. These demographic targeting options are determined in a number of ways. Google can determine demographics based on the content that someone browses. For example, someone viewing gardening related sites on the Google Display Network would be placed into a different demographic than someone browsing alternate music sites. Some sites allow people to create a profile, which can be used to understand demographic information. Google can also use details from Google profiles to understand demographics. When Google cannot determine particular demographic details, for example someone's age, they will be included in the 'unknown' category.

Combining Targeting Options

Combining two or more targeting options can help improve the performance of your display campaigns by refining when your ads will be displayed. As you layer targeting options you also need to balance the refinement with the number of people who will see your ad, as being too refined could mean that your ads are rarely displayed. Start by selecting your display campaign and then an ad group in the campaign. Then, select 'Display Network' and click the 'Add Targeting' button. This will show you the current display targeting that has been set for the ad group. Here the ad group is using 'Topics' for targeting ads:

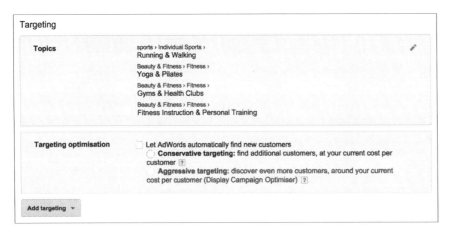

You can click 'Add Targeting' to layer another targeting method for the ad group. Since 'Topics' has already been used, the additional targeting options are 'Display Keywords', 'Placements', 'Interests and Remarketing', 'Gender', 'Age' and 'Parental Status'.

If you then select 'Interests and Remarketing' and add the interest category of 'Athletic Shoes' you can see visualization update and the estimated research is updated.

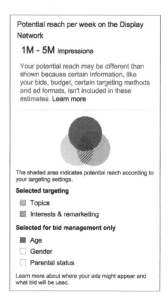

If you then layer another targeting method (this time a particular placement), the information is updated again and you can quickly see if your audience size is suitable or if it is small and will have a limited reach.

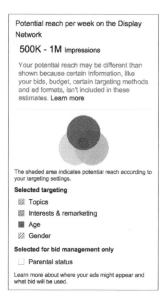

For each target that you add there is the option to select 'Target and Bid' or 'Bid Only'. The default option is 'Target and Bid' because this requires all of your targeting to match before ads are displayed.

For example, someone needs to be viewing a pet-related page on the Google Display Network *AND* be in the 'Pet Lover' interest category. Selecting 'Bid Only' is like saying someone needs to be viewing a pet related page *OR* be in the 'Pet Lover' interest category.

You can test different targeting combinations in your display campaigns to see what drives success based on your objectives.

Suggestions for targeting combinations include:

- **Placements and display keywords** to only display your ads with relevant content on management placements.

- **Placements and topic targeting** to only display your ads with types of content on management placements, without the need to manage keywords.

- **Topic targeting and interests** to only display ads to people interested in particular content while they are also browsing content related to your topic.

- **Topic targeting and remarketing** to only display your remarketing ads while people are browsing content related to your topic.

Tips for Display Campaigns

To run a successful display campaign you need to follow a similar process to the one outlined in Chapter 5 – "Model for Successful Online Advertising." But remember that your display campaign is unlikely to drive the same actions as your search campaigns. People who see your display ads are not actively searching for information about your products or services. So if your search campaigns are designed around conversion actions like leads or sales, then display is unlikely to result in the same number of conversions or the same conversion rate. However, they can be used to increase your visibility in the marketplace and even focus on conversions, but they might not result in exactly the same outcomes as your other campaigns. It is important to consider this before you begin creating your display campaign.

Consider using the following strategies for your display campaigns:

- **Start with remarketing** so that your ads are only shown to people who are already aware of your brand and more likely to convert.

- **Aim for micro conversions instead of macro conversions**, as your campaigns might be better suited to generating initial engagement with your audience and not driving high value conversions.

- **Use landing pages that align with the objectives** of your display campaign. If you are leading people towards a micro conversion, then ensure the landing page has a softer tone than the ones you use for your search campaigns.

- **Testing different display ads** can be just as effective as testing search ads. For example, a charity could test an ad that includes an image of a child against an ad that includes an image of an adult.

- **Create ads in all sizes** in order for your ads to achieve the widest reach possible. Different placements on the display network will only accept particular size ads.

- **Create high quality banner ads** that appeal to your audience, that stand out on placements without clashing and are well designed.

- **Test different targeting combinations** in different ad groups. This can help you identify the best way to target your ads.

- **Structure ad groups that use display keywords** in a similar way to structuring your search ad groups. Display keywords should be grouped to reflect the landing page and ad variations.

- **Create an ad group with automatic targeting** and use this ad group to identify potential placements for a managed ad group. This technique allows you to identify higher quality placements that can be managed with a specific bid based on results.

- **Align display with your other marketing initiatives** so that you present a clear message across marketing channels. This includes ensuring that your display ads use the same style and messages as any other offline and online advertising you are running.

- **Use the Multi-Channel Funnels reports** in Google Analytics to understand the full impact of your display campaigns.

- **Consider your website and landing pages** so the style and message of your ads reflects the experience on your website.

7

Campaign Settings

Google AdWords allows you to define specific configurations for each of your campaigns to help you target your ads to the best possible audience. Campaign settings allow you to target people in different geographic locations, the time of day your ads are displayed through to budget and whether your ads should appear on mobile devices or not.

Campaign Type

Campaign type allows you to quickly select common predefined campaign settings, for example you can select 'Search Network Only' to show your ads only to people searching, or 'Display Network Only' to show your ads to people viewing display sites (or other display placements).

> **Tip:** Never run ads on both search and display within the one campaign. This makes it difficult to understand what is working and not working. It also makes it harder when you are reporting on results and performing analysis. Simply create one campaign for your search ads and another campaign for your display ads. You can also apply different settings to each campaign and use different ad group structures.

Select either 'Search Network Only' or 'Display Network Only' and then select the 'All Features' option, this will allow you to adjust all campaign settings.

> **Tip:** Additional campaign types include 'Shopping' and 'Online Video' for promoting products in Google search results and videos on YouTube. These are covered in Chapter 10 – "Video and Shopping Campaigns".

Networks

Networks allow you to refine where your ads are displayed, including on Google's search results, other search-based websites (Google Search Partners) and content placements (Google Display Network).

For a search network campaign you have the ability to include or exclude search partners. Deselecting search partners will mean that your ads only run on the Google Search Network and will no longer appear on third party search sites.

For a display network campaign you have the option to control targeting at the ad group level, which is called 'Flexible Reach'. In order to further refine your targeting, you can drill down in the individual ad group, select 'Display Network' and then click on the 'Change Display Targeting'.

Locations

You can choose the geographic targeting of your ads within the locations setting. To target a particular location, start by searching for the name of the country, region (state, province, etc.), or city and then click 'Add' next to the appropriate result. You can repeat the process to target multiple locations.

> **Tip:** Clicking 'Advanced Search' provides additional location targeting options, including 'Radius Targeting' which allows you to select a radius around a particular location.

For example, if you wanted your ads to show to people located in the United States or Canada, you would first search for 'United States' and click 'Add' and then search for 'Canada' and click 'Add'. Now your ads will target both countries.

> **Tip:** Location targeting is set at the campaign level, so the geographic target you define will apply to all the ad groups within the campaign. It is generally a good idea to create separate campaigns for different geographic targets because this allows you to include geographically specific messaging in your ads and include the appropriate details.

Before selecting your locations take some time to consider the best audience for your campaign. If you are running ads for a large company with nationwide reach targeting an entire country might be appropriate. However, if you are a smaller business, targeting a more defined geographic location, an individual city might get you better results. Before you make a decision on the locations you want to target, let's look at how location targeting works.

> **Tip:** Clicking on 'Advanced Search' within the location settings allows you to search for locations using a map, enter a radius around a particular location you want to target, or add locations in bulk. Radius targeting is useful for local businesses wanting to target an area around their physical location and the bulk option allows you to paste in multiple locations at once.

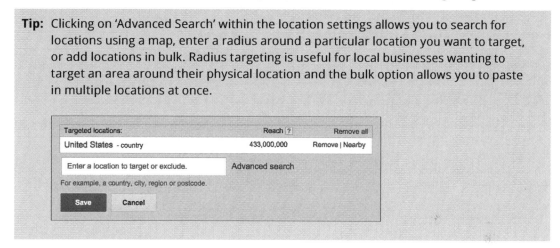

How Location Targeting Works

Google AdWords uses a number of different elements to determine when to display your ads based on your location targeting. Google AdWords will look at the particular search term that is being used, the particular Google domain and details of the physical location of somebody searching.

Location Search Terms

Google AdWords will look for geographic indicators within the search term that someone is using. For example, if your ads are targeted to Canada and somebody searches for 'hotel vancouver' then your ads can appear because Vancouver is located within the location target of Canada.

This is useful because if people are not physically located in your targeted location, your ads will still display as they research products, services and offers that they are looking for in a particular location.

Google AdWords will also look at the search area people are using on Google Maps and any custom location settings selected on Google search results for location targeting.

In the following example there is an ad targeted to a location in New York:

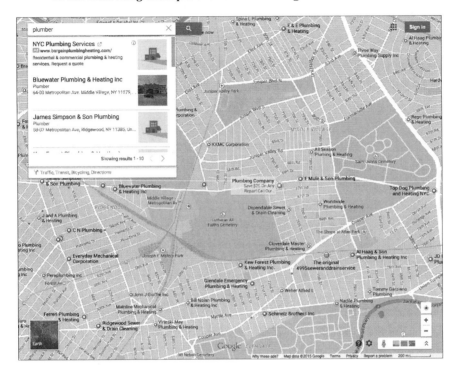

Notice that the geographic term of 'new york' was not used when searching because the map has been zoomed in to only view a particular area within Google Maps.

Google Domain

Geographic targeting looks at the particular Google domain that someone is searching in order to provide more relevant results. For example, if someone is searching on google.co.uk then they are more likely to be looking for websites and content relating to the UK, where as people searching on .com.au are looking for information and websites relating to Australia.

Physical Location

Google AdWords will also consider the physical geographic location of somebody searching in order to present ads based on your location target. In order to determine this location, Google AdWords looks at IP addresses. If you are non-technical you can think of IP address as an identification of your computer's connection to the internet. This identification can contain details of the physical location of the computer.

The accuracy of geographic targeting based on IP address depends on the particular location you are targeting with your campaign. Generally, accuracy decreases as you become more precise with your location targeting. By targeting a country you are typically 99% accurate, or in other words, you are highly likely to display your ads to someone within that country. If you target a city, the accuracy of targeting will reduce and the accuracy will depend on the country where the city is located. For example, the city level accuracy for the United States is reported to be 81%, while the city level accuracy for the UK is 72% and Australia is 58%.[1]

The level of accuracy comes down to how well IP addresses are matched to geographic locations. This is out of the control of Google AdWords and can also be impacted by the number of IP addresses assigned within each country. Accuracy at the city level in Australia is lower than some other countries and this is because Australia has less IP addresses than other countries and therefore geographic information is less precise.

Where available, Google AdWords will also use GPS, WiFi and cell tower ID to determine physical location. These are based on a user making their location available on their mobile device.

Excluding Locations

You can also exclude certain areas from within your targeted area. For example, if you wanted to target people in suburban or rural areas you could target a particular region and then exclude the city location from within that particular geographic target.

To do this start by adding the area you want to include, then perform a search for the area within that location you want to exclude and click 'Exclude' in the search results.

Matches	Reach ?	
Minnesota, United States - state	10,300,000	Add | Exclude | Nearby
Minnesota State University, Mankato, Minnesota, United States - university	2,000	Add | Exclude | Nearby
Minnesota Lake, Minnesota, United States - city ⚠ Limited reach ?	--	Add | Exclude | Nearby
Locations that enclose:Minnesota, United States		
United States - country	433,000,000	**Added** | Nearby
Related locations		
Roberts County, South Dakota, United States 💬 - county	16,000	Add | Exclude | Nearby
Burke County, North Dakota, United States 💬 - county	1,000	Add | Exclude | Nearby
Yellow Medicine County, Minnesota, United States 💬 - county	3,000	Add | Exclude | Nearby
University of Minnesota, Minnesota, United States 💬 - university	22,000	Add | Exclude | Nearby

---

1   http://www.maxmind.com/en/city_accuracy

> **Tip:** There are additional settings that give you even more control over how location targeting allows (or prevents) your ads from being displayed to people. Additional location options are covered in Chapter 8 – "Advanced Settings".

Best Practices for Location Targeting

The best way to choose what locations to target is by identifying your target market, and the geographic location of your existing and potential customers. If you're starting out, then your campaign will be more successful if you are more defined with your geographic target (rather than choosing a wider geographic target). This is because you can be more specific about your messaging and by selecting the area around your office or store location, you'll be able to connect with people searching for your product or service. It might be tempting to select a whole country when you start, but by selecting a large geographic target, your budget is going to be quickly spent and your messaging is not going to be specific to the audience in individual geographic locations.

Consider the scenario of an independent digital printing shop located in downtown Chicago starting a new Google AdWords campaign to advertise their large format poster printing service. Although they might be able to deliver large format posters all across the United States, they are far more likely to be known by locals who walk past their storefront (or even just know of their location) if they saw the store marked on a city map. They will also be able to deliver posters quicker and cheaper to people located nearby and people will feel more comfortable ordering from a company located in the area. As a result, starting a Google AdWords campaign that only targets downtown Chicago will deliver better results for their budget, than a campaign that targets the whole of the United States. Once they achieve success in their local market, they can then look to build out additional campaigns to target surrounding areas. After they see success with those campaigns they can look at campaigns that target areas further away. Although this approach is conservative, it is more likely to be successful and it is going to be easier to grow the campaigns as sales are tracked and the ROI (Return On Investment) calculated against the investment in Google AdWords.

If you are a local business, for example an electrician, an independent store or a local restaurant, and you primarily service a well-defined geographic area, it is best to select that area as your location target. If you are going to create a campaign that targets a city or other well-defined local area then it is worth taking the time to set up a second campaign that has a wider geographic target, but includes slightly different keywords. Start by thinking about how this might look inside an account and then discuss why this type of structure can achieve better results.

First, create a campaign with a specific geographic target along with appropriate keywords:

Campaign Name: **Poster Printing [Location Targeted]**
Location Target: **London, England, United Kingdom**

- Ad Group Name: **Poster Printing**
  - Keywords:
    - poster printing
    - large poster printing
    - print posters
    - etc.
  - Ads:

Poster Printing London

www.printing.co.uk/Posters

High Quality, Fast Delivery for
Poster Printing. Great Prices!

London Poster Printing

www.printing.co.uk/Posters

Poster Printing Services in
London. Great Posters, Fast!

Then create another campaign that has a larger geographic target, but uses keywords with specific geographic terms:

Campaign Name: **Poster Printing [Location Keywords]**
Location Target: **England, United Kingdom**

- Ad Group Name: **London**
  - Keywords:
    - poster printing london
    - large poster printing london
    - print posters london
    - etc.
  - Ads:

Poster Printing London

www.printing.co.uk/Posters

High Quality, Fast Delivery for
Poster Printing. Great Prices!

London Poster Printing

www.printing.co.uk/Posters

Poster Printing Services in
London. Great Posters, Fast!

- Ad Group Name: **Chelsea**
  - Keywords:
    - poster printing chelsea
    - large poster printing chelsea
    - print posters chelsea
    - etc.
  - Ads:

Poster Printing Chelsea

www.printing.co.uk/Posters

High Quality, Fast Delivery for
Poster Printing. Great Prices!

Chelsea Poster Printing

www.printing.co.uk/Posters

Poster Printing Services in
Chelsea. Great Posters, Fast!

The benefit of taking the time to create a location targeted campaign and a location-based keywords campaign is that you can create more targeted ads for the location keywords. The campaign structure also allows you to adjust the bids in each of the campaigns. For example, you can increase the bids on the location keywords based on the results you receive.

You also have the option of using bid adjustments to increase or decrease your bids based on people's location. The "Bid Adjustments" section in Chapter 17 contains further details.

Tip: If you are targeting a very specific location using radius targeting it is recommended to set a minimum radius of 10 miles or 20 kilometers to ensure you reach your desired audience.

Language

Language targeting allows you to select the language of your ads. This setting will not automatically translate your ads, so you will want to pick a single language and ensure your ads are written in that language.

You can choose a language to target particular people within your location target. For example, selecting 'Italian' as your language and 'United States' as your location will target your ads to people who speak Italian that are located within the United States. For more details on language targeting visit http://lovesdata.co/iz07k

Bidding

If you are starting out, then selecting 'I'll manually set my bids for clicks' means that you define the maximum you are willing to spend on any given click. This gives you more control and also allows you to use more advanced campaign settings.

There is also automatic bidding, where Google AdWords will automatically adjust your bids to try and get the highest number of clicks on your ads. This gives you less control, but could be an option if you want to quickly launch your campaign without defining a maximum CPC. If you do select this option, then consider changing to manual bidding once you have a feel for the amount you are spending on clicks. To use automatic bidding, select 'AdWords will set my bids to help maximize clicks within my target budget'.

With manual and automatic bidding you also have the option to select 'Enhanced CPC', which adjusts bids when Google AdWords predicts that someone is likely to convert on your website. This works based on the historical data available within your account and signals that are not available for you to bid on within your campaigns. For example, if people located in Hawaii using an Android phone are more likely to convert based on the historical data within your account then Google AdWords will automatically increase your bid.

Additional bidding options include 'Focus on Conversions' which allows you to define the maximum you are willing to spend on a conversion (as opposed to a click). For display campaigns you also have the option to select 'Focus on Impressions', which means you set the maximum you are willing to spend for a thousand impressions. There is also a 'Flexible Bid Strategy' option that allows you to create an automated bidding strategy based on the particular objectives you define.

Manual Bidding

When you select 'I'll manually set my bids for clicks', it puts you in complete control of the amount you spend for each click on your ads. This sets a maximum CPC that applies to the keywords you are targeting or placements on the Google Display Network. This default maximum CPC is defined at the ad group level which means each time you create a new ad group you will be asked to enter the default bid. This allows you to adjust your bidding strategy based on the particular groups of keywords (or placements) you are targeting. As you optimize the campaign, you have the option to increase and decrease the default bid for each ad group within the campaign.

Tip: If you're just getting started, then consider setting the same default bid for all your ad groups within a particular campaign. You can then monitor the performance of your ad groups based on conversions, CTR, average position and the overall number of clicks and adjust your bids based on the results you are seeing for each ad group.

Manual bidding also allows you to adjust bids for individual keywords. You can do this by navigating to 'Keywords' where you will see 'Maximum CPC'. If you haven't adjusted the bid for a particular keyword it will be displayed in grey. This indicates that the keyword is using the default bid that has been set at the ad group level. You can edit the bid for the individual keyword by clicking on the bid within the 'Maximum CPC' column. Your new bid can be either higher or lower than the default bid for the ad group.

> **Tip:** The same technique can be applied to the targeting methods applied within your display campaigns. For example, you can adjust bids for individual placements.

It's important to remember that when you define your bids using manual bidding that you might actually end up paying more for a click than your maximum CPC. This can occur if you are using bid adjustments, your final bid can be different from the default bid that you have set. For example, if you have set your default bid to $2.00 and you have added a bid adjustment of an additional +15% for people who click on your ads located in New York and another bid adjustment of an additional +20% for people using their mobile devices, then your final bid can vary based on those factors. This means someone located in New York using their laptop to find your offer will end up with a final maximum bid of $2.30 which is the $2.00 bid plus $0.30 for the +15% location adjustment. Furthermore, someone in New York using their mobile will end up with a final maximum bid of $2.76 which is the $2.00 bid plus an additional $0.76 for the +15% location adjustment and +20% mobile adjustment. Setting bid adjustments is covered in Chapter 8 – "Advanced Settings".

> **Tip:** Enhanced CPC is an additional bidding option you can select to enable Google AdWords to automatically adjust your bids up and down based on the likelihood of a conversion. Enhanced CPC can also modify your final maximum bid. Read the "Enhanced CPC" section in this chapter.

When you set manual bids, remember that you are setting the maximum you want to pay for a click on your ads. However, the actual amount you pay for a click will vary and typically will be below your maximum amount, once combined with any bid adjustments you have made. This is because Google AdWords uses an auction-style system where the final amount you pay for the click is dependent on additional factors such as what other advertisers are bidding on and the quality of your campaigns. This is covered in the "Quality Score" section in Chapter 11. You can compare the difference between the maximum CPC you have defined and the actual CPC that you are being charged by looking at the 'Average CPC' column within the 'Ad Groups' tab. This shows you the average amount you have actually ended up paying for the clicks you have received. Typically your actual CPC is less than your maximum CPC.

Selecting a Default Bid

The amount that you select for your default bid will depend on the historical data that you have available. If you have previously been bidding on the keywords (or placements) you can use the historical data to help you select and refine your bid amounts. But what if you are creating a new ad group or even setting up a account? In this case there are a number of strategies you can use to help you select a starting point for your bids.

Using Keywords

If you have already spent time researching and building out your keywords, then you can use the Keyword Planner to estimate your bids. Navigate to 'Keyword Planner' under 'Tools'. You will see an option called 'Get traffic forecasts for a list of keywords', which allows you to copy and paste your keywords or even upload a file that contains your keyword research.

Once you click 'Get Forecasts' you will see a graph that compares maximum CPC to the estimated number of clicks for the particular keywords you have provided. You will see that as the bid increases, so does the likelihood of additional clicks. The tool allows you to enter a maximum bid amount to then see the estimated number of clicks and impressions you would receive for that bid amount. The tool also shows you the estimated average position of your ads, based on the bid you have provided and the estimated daily cost for those clicks.

> **Tip:** Accuracy of the forecasts seen within the Keyword Planner vary by keywords, location and the other selections you make. This means that you will need to start your campaign and monitor your costs for an accurate understanding.

For example, if you are creating a new campaign to advertise camera bags that are being sold in an online store you can begin by researching keywords for your campaign. To keep things simple for this exercise focus on 10 keywords. However, you will want to extend your keyword list for the actual campaigns you are going to launch, since a more complete list will give you a better overall idea of costs.

Keyword list	
camera bags	dslr camera bags
buy camera bag	slr camera bags
camera bag	slr camera bag
dslr camera bag	digital slr camera bags
digital camera bag	padded camera bag

Since the online store only ships to customers located in the UK, you can set the location target to 'United Kingdom' in the Keywords Planner. This will mean that the estimates are more accurate. Now click on 'Get Forecasts' and you will see data for the particular keywords you have entered.

You can quickly see that your bid is likely to be below $9.00. This is because the graph flattens out and you are unlikely to receive any additional clicks if the bid goes beyond $9.00. So try entering a lower value to see how many clicks you are likely to receive – enter $0.50 as a starting point. Looking at the daily estimates you can see that only a handful of clicks is likely. If you know your website converts 5% of people who view one of your camera bags, then three or four clicks a day won't be enough sales to make the campaign a success.

Try adjusting your bid to $1.50 – you can see that you will receive approximately 5 clicks per day based on the keywords. This means that based on your 5% conversion rate you might make a sale every few days. You could start at this point, but really you want to be making a sale every day, so continue to play with the bid amount. You can see that at around $3.20 the estimate is around 20 clicks per day and based on your conversion rate you are likely to hit the daily sale target for the keywords. The Keyword Planner also shows you the estimated daily cost is between $40.00 and $49.00, so you also have a guide for the campaign's daily budget.

If you have conversion tracking set up then your conversion rate will be used to help inform the bidding strategy, however you might not have access to this data when you're starting a new campaign. In this case (like the previous example) you might want to base your decision on bid selection on a combination of clicks, average position and daily cost. There are also times when you might want to bid slightly higher as you start a campaign to ensure you are visible on search results against your competitors who are already advertising on the keywords you are looking to target.

It is also important to look at the estimated average position when you are adjusting your bids in the tool. There is nothing wrong with displaying your ads lower down on search results pages, but the majority of people searching click on results that are towards the top of the search results page. If you are focusing on clicks it is best to aim for an average ad position that is somewhere between one and three, meaning that your ad is visible towards the top of the search results. Remember that the actual amount you pay for clicks will vary. You will need to monitor the results you receive and you can adjust your bids as part of your campaign optimisation.

To get a better idea of the costs of individual keywords you can change the segment to 'keywords' and you will see estimates for the individual keywords. This is useful to understand if there are particular keywords that are going to cost you more than others, and which keywords are going to drive more traffic to your website. A good idea is to make a note of the keywords that have higher estimated average CPCs and monitor these more expensive keywords when you launch your campaign. You may also want to refine your keyword list based on this information. If there are keywords that are very expensive, then you might want to launch the campaign with the more economical keywords and then supplement them with the more expensive keywords after you see results.

From here you can create your campaign and set the default bid for the ad group at $3.50. Once you launch the campaign, it is important allow enough data to become available before making final decisions about the campaign. Not all campaigns are immediately successful, and some will require more optimisation than others. Assigning initial budgets and optimization is covered in the "Budget" section in Chapter 7.

Starting with a Calculated Bid

If you have details about the existing conversion rate and the amount you are making off your product or services, then you can use this data to calculate a maximum bid amount. You will need to start by establishing the profit that you make from a sale. If you are just starting with Google AdWords then I recommend starting at a top level, by looking at your average profit across your business, and as you progress you can begin to calculate this at a granular level.

Let's look an ecommerce example to see how this works (this technique can be applied even if you aren't selling products). Say that you sell your product for a retail price of $300 and make $150 after all your costs are subtracted. Based on historical analytics data you also know that 5% of your website traffic converts into sales. From here you can calculate the expected value that you will receive from each click to your website. To do this, take your profit (in this case $150), and multiply it by your conversion rate of 5%.

Profit × Conversion Rate = Value Per Click

This means that on average, each click to your website is worth $7.50. This also means that you can bid anywhere up to $7.50 and at worst, break even. This can then be used to help guide the amount you set as your maximum bid. If you set your bid at 50% of your value per click (or $3.75) and maintained a conversion rate of 5%, then for every 1,000 people coming to your website from Google AdWords you could expect a profit of $3,750.

Using the Suggested Bid

If you haven't created an extensive keyword list, or are just looking for a quick guide to get a campaign up and running quickly, then you can consider using the 'Suggested Bid' column in the Keyword Planner. This will not be as accurate as using an extensive keyword list to esti-mate your costs, but if you are happy to jump into Google AdWords and adjust your maximum CPC bids in the first few days, then it can be a quick way to get a campaign up and running.

Head to the Keyword Planner and search for a selection of keywords that relate to your campaign. For example, if you are advertising a local wood-fired pizza shop, you might enter 'woodfired pizza, gourmet pizza, pizza delivery' within the 'Search for new keywords and ad group ideas' option. When you click on 'Get Ideas' you will be presented with a list of suggested ad groups. This can be helpful in guiding how you group your keywords within the campaign, but in this case you really want to get an approximate idea for your default bid. Clicking on the 'Keyword Ideas' will allow you to see a long list of keywords that relate to your original keywords. You will also see the keywords that you entered highlighted at the top of the page.

Depending on how much time you have, you might want to consider building out your keyword list. If you just want a quick guide for your bids, then you can use the 'Suggested Bid' column. This gives you a guide based on the targeting you have selected within the Keyword Planner. If you look at the keywords entered, you can see that you should bid somewhere between $1.93 and $4.32 as a starting point. In this case you could choose to start at the lower end and set a default bid of $2.00 or if you are trying to get greater visibility you might start at $3.00 or $4.00. Once you have a starting point you can launch your campaigns, but you will want to monitor progress closely and be ready to adjust bids.

Another option is to scan the list of keywords, rather than just using your initial keywords to inform your starting bid. You will need to focus on keywords that are more relevant to your offering though, as the keyword suggestions will include a combination of good and bad keywords. Continuing the pizza example, you might see keywords like 'wood fired pizza oven', if you are not selling pizza ovens, you won't want to consider this keyword. If you have time you can even add keywords from the list to build up a more complete estimate. For keywords that are relevant, just click on the arrow in the 'Add to Plan' column and once you have a more complete list you can use the more detailed estimator tool.

Starting with a Set Bid

As a last resort you can always start with a set bid. For example, if you start with a default bid of $1.00 for your ad groups you can then monitor the number of clicks you are receiving along with average position to help guide your bid adjustments. Once you have set your bid you can use the 'Keywords' tab and scan down the list of keywords to quickly see if your default bid is too low for any particular keywords. Using the 'Status' column, look for any keywords that have a message that says 'Below First Page Bid', this means that your bid amount might not be high enough for your ad to appear on the first page of search results. You can then make a decision about increasing your bid for that particular keyword.

> **Tip:** When you see keywords that say 'Below First Page Bid', it can be worth quickly performing a search to see how many advertisers are competing on that particular term and if your ad is showing or not. There are cases when you will see this alert even if your ad is visible on the first page of search results. This is because Google AdWords estimates the first page bid for each keyword and since it is an estimate the accuracy can vary.

Automated Bidding

Automated bidding puts Google AdWords in control of your bids. This is only recommended if you know you are not going to be proactively managing your own bids. Google AdWords will use your daily budget and automatically adjust the bids to try and get you the highest number of clicks for your allocated budget. This might sound like a good idea, but you will quickly discover that some keywords are more valuable than others and automated bidding means that you can't control the bids for individual ad groups, keywords or placements. Automated bidding also prevents you from using advanced features, like ad scheduling, so even if you start with automated bidding you will probably want more control to further optimize your campaigns and account. The good news is that you can change your bidding strategy at anytime, even if you have already launched your campaign.

> **Tip:** If you are going to use automated bidding, then it is best to combine this with a maximum bid to give you additional control over the maximum amount you pay for any given click.

Enhanced CPC

Enhanced CPC (ECPC) is an additional bidding option that can be used in combination with manual and automated bidding. The feature uses your Google AdWords conversions to automatically adjust your bids when someone is more likely to convert. It will automatically bid up to an additional 30% when a conversion is likely and also adjust your bids down if a conversion is unlikely. It is a useful feature to help you drive additional conversions and works by looking at signals that are impossible to optimize on your own. Although the Enhanced CPC option does not require a minimum number of conversions, the more conversions you receive, the more effective the feature is at identifying potential conversion signals. This is because it looks at your historical conversions to identify if people are more likely to convert or not.

Signals for Enhanced CPC include the words within a search query, where someone is located, the browser and operating system they are using and the time of day. For example, if you have received 100 conversions and 90% of those conversions have been from people using Chrome as their browser, Google AdWords will begin to recognise this and automatically adjust your bids based on that signal.

> **Tip:** You need conversions in order for Enhanced CPC to work, so if you don't have conversions set up in your Google AdWords account, read the "Conversion Tracking" section in Chapter 11 for details.

Conversion Optimizer

Conversion Optimizer allows you to shift your bidding strategy from CPC to setting a target for how much you want to spend for each conversion on your website. This is called cost-per-acquisition (CPA) bidding and is available when you select the 'Focus on Conversions' as your 'Bid Strategy' when you have received at least 15 conversions in the last 30 days.

If you have not set up conversion tracking within Google AdWords, or you have not received the minimum number of conversions, then the option to select Conversion Optimizer will not be available. This is because the feature relies on conversion data in order for you to bid based on conversion actions occurring on your website.

When you select Conversion Optimizer you will be asked to select an initial CPA bid. The recommended bid is based on your historical data and is designed to maintain the existing performance of your campaign. It is best to start by using the recommended bid before you begin to make changes to the CPA target. This is because decreasing the CPA bid is the same as decreasing your CPC bid and is likely to result in a change to the position of your ads in search results.

> **Tip:** Conversion Optimizer allows you to switch between a target CPA and a maximum CPA. *Target CPA* is the average amount you pay for a conversion and is the absolute maximum you pay for a conversion.

Conversion Optimizer then begins to automatically manage your campaign based on your CPA target bid. This means that although you define a CPA target bid, Google AdWords continues to work based on CPC by automatically converting your CPA bid into a CPC bid. Conversion Optimizer builds an understanding of when conversions are likely to occur based on differences the system sees for people using different devices, when people convert and geographic locations. This allows the system to increase bids when conversions are likely and decrease them if someone is unlikely to convert.

> **Tip:** Conversion Optimizer works best when you receive a steady number of conversions along with a steady conversion rate. If your conversion rate continually fluctuates, then you might want to continue to manage your own bids until you see steady conversion metrics.

Once your campaign has been running using the recommended bid for a few weeks, you can begin to test CPA tweaks and monitor the impact. For example, if you have a CPA bid of $15.80 then you could adjust the CPA bid down to $14.80 and then monitor the impact this has on conversions. If your conversions remain steady then you should leave this bid for a few more weeks before making further adjustments. However, if the number of conversions decrease then you should increase the bid slightly and again monitor the change in performance. Using small tweaks, you can find the best CPA bid amount. If you are happy with the CPA and number of conversions you should consider raising the campaign's budget to further increase the number of conversions you are receiving from the campaign.

Conversion Optimizer is not compatible with some features within Google AdWords including:

- Advanced ad scheduling (for example, bid adjustments based on time or day)
- Separate bids for display
- Shopping campaigns

> **Tip:** If you find that your actual advertising cost-per-conversion is higher than your CPA bid then you should review your conversion data for changes in your conversion rate.

Flexible Bid Strategy

Selecting 'Flexible Bid Strategy' allows you to define an automatic bid strategy that is based on criteria that you define. For example, if you want to outperform a competitor within the search results you can create a bid strategy based on outranking the particular competitor's website. The feature also allows you to apply flexible bidding strategies across multiple campaigns and even define separate strategies to individual ad groups and keywords even if they are in different campaigns.

Flexible bid strategies include:

- **Target search page location**, which allows you to adjust your bids in order to target the top of the paid results.

- **Target CPA** is similar to Conversion Optimizer, but you can also define minimum and maximum bid limits.

- **Target outranking share** allows you to adjust your bids to outrank a particular competitor's website.

- **Maximize clicks** is similar to the default automatic bidding option.

- **Target return on ad spend** allows you to define a particular percentage based on conversion value that you want to achieve.

> **Tip:** You can set up and manage your flexible bid strategies from within the 'Shared Library' which is available on the bottom left corner of the Google AdWords interface.

You can set a flexible bid strategy for a campaign within 'Settings' under 'Bid Strategy'. To define a bid strategy at the ad group level, select one or more of the checkboxes within the 'Ad Groups' tab and then select 'Use Flexible Bid Strategy' under 'Bid Strategy'. This is also available within the 'Keywords' tab.

To easily understand the bid strategies used for your campaigns, ad groups and keywords, add the strategy column by clicking 'Columns', then 'Modify Columns' and then selecting 'Bid Strategy' within 'Attributes'.

Optimizing Bids

Bid optimization is the process of adjusting and testing bids to improve the performance of your campaigns. Generally the idea is to increase bids for keywords that are profitable to increase traffic and decrease bids for keywords that are unprofitable.

Before you get started you will need to ensure you are measuring conversions inside Google AdWords by using conversion tracking or data imported from Google Analytics. Now, navigate to an individual campaign within Google AdWords and select 'Ad Groups'. Next, add columns for 'Converted Clicks', 'Cost/Converted Click' and 'Click Conversion Rate' (look for 'Modify columns...' after clicking the 'Columns' button).

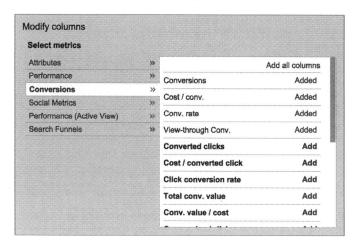

Click on the column heading for 'Impressions' to order the ad groups by overall number of impressions. You can then scan down the list and look for ad groups that have a higher number of impressions along with a lower CTR and a higher conversion rate.

You can also use the 'Cost-per-conversion' column to establish if the ad group is profitable. The best way to do is to compare this to your sales and revenue data or targets to establish profitability. From here you can review the default bid and either adjust the bid or set up an experiment to test a new bid amount.

Tip: You can also drill down into individual ad groups and look at the performance of your individual keywords. You might not have enough data at the individual keyword level to begin optimization, in this case you can begin optimizing bids at the ad group level.

To get an idea of how much you could potentially increase your bid, click on the name of the ad group to see the keywords. Now click on 'Columns', then 'Modify Columns' and add the following columns to the tab:

- **Within 'Attributes' add:**
  - **'Estimated first page bid'** to see an estimate of how much you need to bid to be on the first page of search results.
  - **'Estimated top page bid'** to see an estimate of how much you need to bid to be at the very top of the paid results on the first page.

- **Within 'Bid simulator' add:**
  - ◦ **'Estimated additional clicks/week (+50% bid)'** to see an estimate of additional clicks if you were to increase your bid by 50%.
  - ◦ **'Estimated additional clicks/week (+300% bid)'** to see an estimate of additional clicks if you were to increase your bid by 300%.
  - ◦ **'Estimated additional clicks/week (top page bid)'** to see an estimate of additional clicks if you were to increase your bid to the top page bid amount.

Tip: Remember that these are estimates, so the accuracy can vary. You can also use the Bid Simulator to inform a potential bid that you could then test using Google AdWords experiments.

Once you have determined how you want to change your bid you can either apply the change directly or use Google AdWords experiments to test the bid for a portion of your audience. Testing bids is a good way to understand the impact the change will have on your key metrics like clicks, CTR and conversions. This is covered in the "Google AdWords Experiments" section in Chapter 9.

Budget

Your budget setting allows you to control how much you are willing to spend for each of your campaigns on any given day. You need to enter a daily budget which is then applied to all the ad groups, including keywords and ad variations within the campaign. Unlike traditional advertising, there is no minimum financial commitment to launch your Google AdWords campaign. You can start with $5.00 or begin with a much higher daily budget. It's up to you to decide on an appropriate budget. Here are some options for how to determine your starting budget.

Budget Based on Traditional Advertising Costs

If you have been advertising through traditional media, like newspapers, magazines, radio or even TV, you can use your previous budget allocations to help you inform and guide your online advertising budget.

For example, if you have previously run ads in an industry publication that is distributed quarterly throughout the year, you can use that as a way to calculate a budget for your Google AdWords campaign. If it costs you $4,000 to run an ad in one edition for January, February and March, you can perform the following calculation:

($4,000 ÷ 3 months) ÷ 30.4 days = a daily budget of $43.86

Now you have a daily budget that reflects your investment in a traditional advertising channel. Since the results of your Google AdWords campaigns are much easier to track than the outcomes you receive from print-based advertising, you will find that you will be able to quickly justify this investment in your campaigns.

If you have been running traditional advertising over a long period of time, it is best to start with a controlled budget like this and continue running your offline advertising. This will enable you to see the results before you start committing larger budgets or even reallocate budgets to your Google AdWords campaigns.

> **Tip:** If you are starting out then it is best to dedicate at least three months (preferably six months) of advertising budget to your Google AdWords campaigns. It is going to take some time to understand what works and what doesn't work. You need to run your ads consistently and spend time optimizing your account over this period to really see the results of your efforts. Remember Google AdWords takes time to manage and is not an instant fix.

Budget Based on Keywords

Another option for determining your daily budget is by using the keywords you are going to target within your campaigns. After you have spent some time developing a list of keywords, you can then use the traffic forecast option to estimate a budget based on those particular keywords.

It is best to use broader keywords when forecasting as highly specific keywords generally do not have enough data for this tool to provide an accurate estimate. For example, instead of using a very specific keyword like 'accountant services new zealand', use keywords like 'accountant services' and 'accountant' to get a better picture of advertising costs.

You can find the traffic forecast option within the Keyword Planner. Then you can enter the list of keywords that you have researched and you will be presented with a chart that shows you the number of daily clicks you are likely to receive based on how you set your maximum CPC (cost-per-click) bid.

Then enter a maximum CPC bid. If in doubt just enter $1.00, as you can change this when you are using the tool. You will now see daily estimates for the number of clicks, impressions, average ad position and advertising cost for the keywords you have entered. Start adjusting the maximum CPC amount down (or up) until your average ad position is around position two or three. If you are starting a new campaign it is generally best to aim for a position that is three or above because this will mean that your ads are more likely to display at the top of the search results. Being at the top of search results will mean you are also more likely to receive clicks.

Once you have found the sweet spot where you are receiving clicks and are likely to show in a good position, you will now have a better feel for the maximum CPC you will need to bid, along with a daily budget estimate.

> **Tip:** Remember that the traffic forecast is providing an estimate, so if in doubt it is best to start with a smaller daily budget. Once you have launched your campaign you will be in a better position to tweak your bids and daily budget.

Budget Based on an Allocated Amount

One of the simplest ways to choose a daily budget amount is by allocating an amount for a month and then divide this amount by the number of days. For example, if you want to allocate $1,000 per month to your campaign, then divide this amount by 30.4 which gives you a daily budget of approximately $32.00.

Although there is no minimum advertising spend, aim for a daily budget of at least $30.00 a day. Anything less tends to make the campaign less viable by the time you invest resources managing the campaign. If you were to begin a campaign with a daily budget of $5.00 a day and the average CPC is $1.00, then you will only receive around 5 clicks per day. If your website has a 3% conversion rate, which is actually quite respectable, then you will only receive 4 or 5 conversions in a month.

Shared Budgets

Shared budgets allow you to set a daily advertising spend which can then be applied to multiple campaigns. The daily budget is then shared by the campaigns. This is a great option if you prefer defining a single budget, rather than managing multiple daily budgets individually. Defining a shared budget is useful if some of your campaigns are not spending their total allocated budget. For example, you might have two campaigns and you notice that on some days one campaign stops showing because its daily budget is reached, while the other campaign fails to spend its allocated budget. By using a shared budget both campaigns can make use of the defined budget and if one fails to spend the allocated budget, then the other can use the unspent budget.

To create a shared budget click on 'Shared Library' on the bottom left corner under 'Campaigns'. Then click on 'New Budget' and enter a name for the shared budget so you can easily identify the budget later on. Click on 'Edit' next to the 'Apply to Campaigns' option. You can click on the campaign names that you would like to add to the shared budget, and you will see the total daily budget for your selected campaigns. Then you can define your total daily budget for your shared budget and click 'Save'.

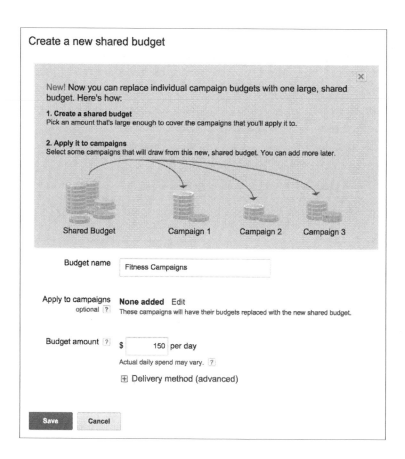

Tip: If you add existing campaigns when setting up your shared budget, their daily budgets will be replaced. If you then want to go back to managing a campaign's budget separately you will need to click on the 'Settings' tab for the campaign and select 'Individual Budget' for the campaign's 'Budget'.

Actual Daily Advertising Spend

When you set your daily budget you need to know that Google AdWords can actually spend slightly more or less than your defined amount on any given day. This is because search volume and the number of people seeing your ads changes each day (different people are searching and browsing websites on different days), so by allowing the budget to vary slightly, Google AdWords ensures that your ads remain visible even if search volume changes slightly.

Although your actual daily ad spend might vary slightly, Google AdWords will never charge you more than 30.4 times your daily budget for any given month if you leave your budget setting unchanged. For example, if your daily budget is $100, then for any given month you will never be charged more than $3,040 (which is 30.4 × $100). Google AdWords if very good at understanding these changes or fluctuations in volume, but in the unlikely event that Google AdWords spends more than that amount you will receive a credit back for the amount it overspent. Continuing the example, if Google AdWords charged $3,100 for a given month (instead of $3,040) then you would receive a credit back of $60.00.

Best Practice for Search Campaigns

Correctly setting up your search campaigns will help ensure that you receive the best possible results for your advertising budget. The next step is to use a checklist on a regular basis to review campaigns and apply best practice techniques on an ongoing basis.

1. Network Targeting

In order to get the best possible results from your search campaigns and to streamline your reporting and analysis, you will want to use dedicated campaigns that only target the search network. If you are using 'Search Network with Display Select' this will mean your campaigns are targeting both the search and display network. Splitting the campaign into two separate campaigns will give you more control over the allocation of your budget and reporting on performance will be easier.

To check if your campaigns are targeting both search and display, look at the campaign icon in the left column under 'All Online Campaigns'.

Icon	Network Targeting
🔍	Google Search and Google Search Partners
▦	Google Display Network
🔍	Google Search, Google Search Partners and Google Display Network
▷	Google Search and Google Shopping

If you're running a campaign that targets both search and display, then you can change the campaign to only target search and create an entirely new campaign to target the display network. To do this, click on the campaign and navigate to 'Settings'. You will see 'Search Network with Display Select' listed as the campaign type. Click 'Edit' and then select 'Search Network Only' from the drop-down options and click 'Save'.

Tip: If you have been running display ads, including image ads in a 'Search Network with Display Select' campaign, you should copy your display ads into your new dedicated campaign before changing the network targeting of your existing campaign.

2. Ad Group Structure

Reviewing the structure of your ad groups on a regular basis and optimizing them to include tightly grouped keywords will help improve the performance of your search campaigns. Ideally you should have a maximum of 10 keywords in each ad group as this typically indicates that the keywords are closely related. You might find that your ad groups contain more keywords, in which case you should review them to ensure they share a common theme and are grouped correctly.

If you have large numbers of keywords in each ad group you might need to plan out how you are going to restructure your campaign. It might mean that you need to create a plan over two or three months as you move keywords into more appropriate groupings and write specific ads for each ad group.

> **Tip:** Remember that you don't need to change everything in one go – it can take time to refine your ad group structure. Read Chapter 3 – "Account Structure" – for ideas on how to restructure your ad groups.

3. Ads Relate to Keywords

Check that your ads relate closely to the keywords you are targeting in each ad group. In most cases you should aim to include the overarching keyword from the ad group in the ad variations. By including the keyword in the ads, that term will be shown as bold type when people see your ads. This helps your ad stand out as people are searching.

4. Landing Pages

Ensure that the landing pages you have selected relate to the keywords you are targeting and the ad variations. If you don't have an appropriate landing page for a particular ad variation, then consider creating an appropriate page first, this is because conversions are reliant on the performance of your website.

> **Tip:** Google AdWords allows you to set the final URL (previously called destination URL) for each of your ads. The final URL can be very specific, while the display URL that is presented to people as they search can be more generic (for example, the homepage of your website). You are still likely to see reference to destination URL in Google's products (like Google Analytics). For details visit http://lovesdata.co/EQYv2 for details.

5. Conversion Tracking

In order to report on performance and to optimize your campaigns, you need to tie your campaigns to your objectives. Conversion tracking helps you to understand what is working and what is not working, allowing you to make valuable decisions about what needs to be improved in your account. Ensure that you have defined appropriate conversions for your campaigns that align with your objectives, and that these set a realistic expectation for your campaigns.

You should measure your campaigns against your most important goals and also use Google Analytics to understand how your campaigns drive micro conversions or secondary objectives. For more details, read the Google AdWords "Conversion Tracking" section in Chapter 11 and Google Analytics "Goals" Chapter 23.

6. Ad Testing

Testing at least two ad variations in each ad group means that you are optimizing your ads to improve the performance of your campaigns. In most cases you will want to stick with two ad variations as this makes it easy to understand your top performing ad. You can test three ad variations at a time if you have a higher volume of clicks, but this will increase the amount of time needed to identify the winning ad.

Start by testing dramatically different ad variations and then review the performance of the ads based on CTR, conversions and conversion rate. Once one ad is clearly outperforming the other ad variation, pause the under-performing ad and create another ad. The idea is to continue this on a regular basis with the aim of continually improving the performance of your ads. Read the "Google AdWords Experiments" section in Chpater 10 for additional testing options.

7. Ad Rotation

Changing your ad rotation so that your ad variations are displayed evenly will give you more control over the optimization process when you are testing your ads. This allows you to easily understand the best performing ads that you are testing. If you are testing two ads an even ad rotation will mean that each ad is seen approximately 50% of the time. This gives you control and can also speed up your tests since lowering the amount of times a particular ad is displayed will mean that additional time is required to achieve a definitive result.

Check your ad rotation by navigating to the 'Settings' tab in your search campaign. Under 'Advanced Settings' you will see 'Ad Delivery' – check that 'Rotate Indefinitely' is set. Read the "Ad Rotation" section in Chapter 8 for additional details.

8. Review Actual Search Terms

Regularly reviewing the search queries that are triggering and resulting in clicks on your ad is critical for ensuring the best possible traffic is being delivered to your website. Head to the 'Keywords', click on 'Details' above the keywords table and select 'All' under 'Search Terms'. This will show you all the search queries that have resulted in clicks on your ads. Use this report to identify keywords to add to your ad groups and potential negative keywords.

9. Ad Extensions

Ad extensions help your ads to stand out when people are searching. Since they also impact your ad rank, you should take the time to set up suitable ad extensions for your search campaigns. Ensure that your ad extensions are up-to-date and appropriate for your campaign, and consider creating ad extensions at the ad group level. If you have a different offering based on time or day then you should also consider scheduling different offers to display with your ads.

10. Bid Adjustments

Once you are comfortable optimizing your search campaigns, you should look at using bid adjustments to improve the results of your campaigns. Bid adjustments allow you to increase or decrease bids based on insights you have about your audience. For example, if you know that people located in a particular city are more likely to convert, you can increase your bids when people are identified as being located in that city.

You can use your historical data in the 'Dimensions' tab to identify over and under performing attributes of your audience. You should also consider using existing insights you have about your audience along with data available inside Google Analytics.

8

Advanced Settings

Google AdWords allows you to have more granular control over when your ads are displayed with advanced campaign settings. These settings can help you be more targeted, but are more complicated, so you will need some time to understand how they work and how they can impact your campaigns before changing these settings.

> **Tip:** If you do not see these advanced options in your 'Settings' tab it is usually because the campaign has been set to use the 'Standard' settings. Look for 'Type' in the 'Settings' tab and click on 'Edit'. Then select 'All Features' and click on 'Save'. You should now have access to all the advanced setting options for your campaign.

Advanced Location Options

The location targeting of your ads can be refined by using the advanced location options in the campaign settings. These options allow you to be more precise about when you want your ads to be displayed (or not displayed). You can find these options in the 'Settings' tab under 'Location Options (Advanced)'.

Target Options

By default the 'Target' option will be set to 'People in, searching for, or viewing pages about my targeted location'.

⊟ Location options (advanced)	
Target ? **People in, searching for, or who show interest in my targeted location** Edit	
Exclude ? **People in, searching for or who show interest in my excluded location** Edit	

Let's look at how the different 'Target' options work if these ads were targeting 'Singapore', along with the keyword 'hotel'. With the default setting of 'People in, searching for, or viewing pages about my targeted location' then these ads would be eligible to appear for all of the following scenarios:

Someone located in	Action	Ads display?
Singapore	Searching for 'hotel'	Yes
New York	Searching for 'singapore hotel'	Yes
Singapore	Viewing pages on the Google Display Network about 'hotels'	Yes
New York	Viewing pages on the Google Display Network about 'singapore hotels'	Yes

Now if you were to change the 'Target' to 'People in my targeted location' and kept the location targeting as 'Singapore' with the same keyword, then the ad would only be showing to people actually located in Singapore:

Someone located in	Action	Ads display?
Singapore	Searching for 'hotel'	Yes
New York	Searching for 'singapore hotel'	No
Singapore	Viewing pages on the Display Network about 'hotels'	Yes
New York	Viewing pages on the Display Network about 'singapore hotels'	No

If you change the option to 'People searching for or viewing pages about my targeted location', the following would occur:

Someone located in	Action	Ads display?
Singapore	Searching for 'hotel'	No
Singapore	Searching for 'singapore hotel'	Yes
New York	Searching for 'singapore hotel'	Yes
Singapore	Viewing pages on the Google Display Network about 'hotels'	No
Singapore	Viewing pages on the Google Display Network about 'singapore hotels'	Yes
New York	Viewing pages on the Google Display Network about 'singapore hotels'	Yes

You can see that changing the 'Target' option provides more control over where these ads are displayed. In most cases you will probably want to use the default option, but if you are specifically trying to target people who are not currently near your business, for example, a hotel, then you can use the 'People in my targeted location' option.

Exclude Options

The 'Exclude' options can be used in combination with the targeting options to further refine when your ads are displayed. By default, your campaign will be set to exclude 'People in, searching for, or viewing pages about my excluded location'.

If you're targeting ads to 'Canada' for the keyword 'hotel', with the location target to exclude the location of 'British Columbia' and you use the default 'Exclude' option, then the following would occur:

Someone located in	Action	Ads display?
Vancouver	Searching for 'hotel'	No
Toronto	Searching for 'hotel in british columbia'	No
Vancouver	Viewing pages on the Google Display Network about 'hotels'	No
Toronto	Viewing pages on the Google Display Network about 'vancouver hotels'	No

If you change the 'Target' option to 'People in my excluded location', then you would see the following:

Someone located in	Action	Ads display?
Vancouver	Searching for 'hotel'	No
Toronto	Searching for 'hotel in british columbia'	Yes
Vancouver	Viewing pages on the Google Display Network about 'hotels'	No
Toronto	Viewing pages on the Google Display Network about 'hotels'	Yes

One thing to consider when adjusting the exclusion option is the accuracy of targeting. This can vary widely by country, for example, in the United States location targeting is highly accurate, while in Australia the accuracy is lower. This is because there are less IP addresses in Australia and this is what is used to identify the location of people as they are searching and browsing online. Another consideration is the audience that you are targeting. It is possible that if you are advertising a B2B (Business to Business) product or service that you may not receive the results you're looking for as some larger organizations control their internet usage. These larger organizations can choose to run all of their internet usage though a specific geographic location (using dedicated IP addresses), even if they have offices in different cities.

It is generally recommended that if you are trying to target people in very specific locations (for example, in particular cities), then you should consider this when setting up your account. You can use location bid adjustments to set lower bids for the fallback locations or you can use separate campaigns. For example, you could have one campaign with your specific location target, and another campaign with a larger location target as a fallback, in case people are not correctly pinpointed based on their physical location.

Here is an example of how you might configure this type of account structure:

Located Targeted Campaign:	Location Keywords Campaign:
Location target: Vancouver Default bid:$2.50 Daily budget: $150.00	Location target: Canada Default bid:$1.00 Daily budget: $50.00
Keywords: accounting services certified accountant tax accountant corporate tax specialist etc.	Keywords: accounting services vancouver certified accountant vancouver tax accountant vancouver corporate tax specialist vancouver etc.

This strategy of having a highly targeted location with slightly more general keywords, along with a second campaign with location keywords and a broader location target, can be highly effective. It also helps ensure that your ads are displayed to more people in your target audience.

Scheduling

Scheduling allows you to set a start date and end date for your campaigns, and also select the hours of day and days of week you want your ads to run.

Click on 'Schedule: Start date, end date, ad scheduling' to view and make changes to your Scheduling settings.

> **Tip:** Scheduling is based on the country and time zone settings that were selected when your account was created. If you want to use scheduling for multiple time zones, you will need to convert the time or consider setting up separate Google AdWords accounts for each time zone you are targeting.

Start Date and End Date

For newly created campaigns, you also have the option for setting a start date for when you want your ads to automatically start displaying. If the campaign has already been launched, then the start date cannot be edited.

You can also set an end date for your campaign to automatically stop your ads from displaying. This is useful for seasonal and time-limited promotions where you might forget to log into Google AdWords to pause your campaign. You can set the end date for a campaign even after it has been launched and you have the option to change the end date at any time.

Ad Scheduling

Ad Scheduling lets you choose when you want your ads to display. Including the hours of the day when you want your ads to run and the particular days of the week.

By default, ad scheduling will be set to show ads continuously 24 hours a day, seven days a week. Selecting 'Ad Schedule' in the 'Settings' tab for a campaign opens up the ad scheduling panel, where you'll see the hours of the day that your ads are currently being displayed.

If you only want your ads to display from 9:00 am to 6:00 pm on Mondays, click 'Ad Schedule'. You'll now be able to select when you want your ads to display. Select '09 AM' as the starting hour and '06 PM' as the ending hour and click on 'Save'.

> **Tip:** You can also set multiple start and end times within each day by clicking 'Add'.

This means that your ads are only running during the particular set hours and at all other times they are not going to be displayed. Think of this as switching your ads on and off during the course of a day. This is most useful for companies that are trying to drive calls or online enquires that they can only respond to during particular hours of the day. This might be standard office hours, or maybe even an after hours service, like an emergency plumber or dentist.

You can also use ad scheduling to adjust your bids during the course of a day. To do this, click on the 'Bid Adjustment' column for the particular time period you want to adjust.

This allows you to adjust your bids by a percentage at particular hours of the day (or days) of the week. If you haven't made any bid adjustments yet, this column will say '+0%'. This means that if your default bid is $1.00, then for the particular times of the day your ads are displaying your bid will be +0% of $1.00, which means it is still $1.00 for those particular hours.

Continuing this example of only displaying ads between 9:00 am and 6:00 pm, if your website conversions are better between 1:00 pm and 4:00 pm, you can adjust your bids up slightly to try and receive even more conversions. Start by adding the time period and then click in the 'Bid Adjustment' column for that time period.

Let's say you want to the bid to be $1.20 from 1:00 pm to 4:00 pm. If the default bid is $1.00, then you'll need to set the percentage adjustment to +20% (since +20% of $1.00 is $1.20). Based on this, change the percentage to '20' for the '1:00 pm – 4:00 pm' time period and click 'Save'.

You'll notice that there is information now on your settings page to indicate the percentage of hours that your ads are being displayed and if you are making any bid adjustments.

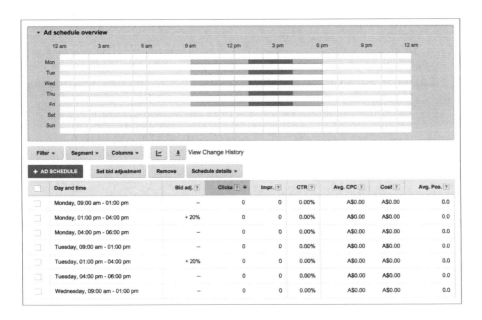

If there are particular times of the day, or days of the week, where you receive less conversions you can also adjust your bids down accordingly.

Bid Adjustments

Bid adjustments allow you to modify your final bid amounts based on particular audience traits. For example, if you find mobile users are more likely to convert you can increase your bids for those users. If you also find that users in a particular location are less likely to convert you can decrease bids for those users. This allows you to increase or decrease bids based on the insights you have about your desired audience.

Bid adjustments can be used to adjust bids based on:

- Location
- Ad schedule
- Mobile devices
- Display network targeting
- Remarketing lists

Bid adjustments are combined to create the final bid amount. If you have a default bid of $2.00 and a bid adjustment of +10% for mobile users and +25% for a particular location then your final bid for a mobile user within the targeted location would be $2.75.

The order of bid adjustments doesn't matter. For example, $2.00 with the +10% bid adjustment equals $2.20 and then by adding +25% it becomes $2.75. Looking at the reverse order – $2.00 with a +25% bid adjustment equals $2.50 and then by adding +10% it becomes $2.75.

> **Tip:** Setting a mobile bid adjustment of -100% means that your ads will not display on mobile devices. There is no way to apply a bid adjustment to desktops or tablets, so this means your ads will always show on these devices.

The "Ad Scheduling" section in this chapter (above) and the "Manual Bidding" section in Chapter 7 include examples of bid adjustments.

Ad Delivery

The ad delivery options allow you to adjust how Google AdWords displays your ads.

Ad Rotation

By default, your ad rotation will be set to 'Optimize for Clicks'. This means that if you are running more than one ad in an ad group, Google AdWords will automatically display the ad that receives more clicks more often. This is fine in theory, but the problem is that Google AdWords can make this decision quite quickly, and in the medium-term and longer-term it might not actually be the best ad. So you might end up showing a poorer quality ad more often.

If you launch a new ad group with two ad variations, Google AdWords will begin by evenly displaying each ad to people searching. So someone searching on one of the keywords you were bidding on has a 50% chance of seeing the first ad and a 50% chance of seeing the second ad. This is because Google AdWords will never display both of your ads at the same time.

Then, Google AdWords monitors which ad is receiving more clicks. If your first ad receives 10 clicks and your second ad receives 2 clicks, it begins to show the first ad more often. So now, rather than displaying the first ad 50% of the time, it will begin to increase this – it might go up and be displayed 70% of the time. This also means that your second ad is only displayed 30% of the time.

Google AdWords can make this decision about how to display your ads quickly – it can even be within the first day of launching your new ad group. The problem with this is that it might not make the decision based on enough data. There might be something happening on that particular day which results in a few more people clicking the first ad, or a trend on that day might be occurring for your keywords. In short, those first few days might make the first ad appear to be more relevant and get more clicks, but over the course of a week or two it might actually be the second ad that is better at engaging your audience. However, Google AdWords will continue to display the first ad more often and the percent of people seeing the second ad might have decreased further, making it even less likely that the second ad will ever be able to outperform the first ad. This happens regularly in accounts.

Here is an example based on data from a real Google AdWords account:

- The campaign is launched and the first ad receives 1,486 impressions and 7 clicks with a CTR of 0.47%. The second ad receives 871 impressions and two clicks with a CTR of 0.23%. Google AdWords immediately sees this and accordingly displays the first ad just over 63% of the time.

- On day two, the first ad is being displayed over 76% of the time, receiving 2,807 impressions and 14 clicks with a CTR of 0.50%. The second ad receives 876 impressions and one click with a CTR of 0.11%.

- Jump forward a week and the first ad is now being displayed over 99% of the time. It received 1,705 impressions and 13 clicks with a CTR of 0.76%. On the other hand, the second ad only received 12 impressions and 1 click with a CTR of 8.33%.

- The second ad has a much higher CTR than the first ad, however, this is based on very low numbers because ad rotation has already made its decision about which ad to display more often. Extending the date range confirms that the results are accurate (statistically significant) by providing enough data to ensure the second ad has a higher CTR.

- As a starting point, you should base your analysis on at least 100 clicks, so looking at the data in this account, you'll need to extend the date range to almost 12 months. You can then see that the first ad received 87,778 impressions and received 3,558 clicks with a CTR of 4.05% and the second ad received 2,892 impressions and received 179 clicks with a CTR of 6.19%.

Tip: Using a test calculator is the best way to ensure you have enough data to decide on your winning ad variation. Go to http://lovesdata.co/C68VJ for a split test calculator

The better performing ad could be determined in less time by changing the way Google AdWords displays your ads. You can tell Google AdWords to continually rotate the ads evenly, or in other words display each ad approximately 50% of the time. This way you can compare the performance of the ads in Google AdWords and make your own decision about which is the best performing ad.

Changing Ad Rotation

In order to get Google AdWords to evenly display your ads from your ad groups, you'll need to change your 'Ad Rotation' setting in each of your campaigns. Click on 'Ad delivery: ad rotation, frequency capping' under 'Advanced Settings' in your campaign settings tab.

If your setting has not been changed from the default you will see 'Optimize for clicks: show ads expected to provide more clicks', click on 'Edit' to change this. To ensure your ads are always rotated evenly select the 'Rotate indefinitely' option and click 'Save'.

I would always recommend you select the 'Rotate Indefinitely' option if you are going to be actively managing your Google AdWords account. It really is the only way to be 100% in control of how your ads are displayed. It also allows you to begin testing your ads and decide which ads are working and which ads are not working. Read the "Best Practices for Search Campaigns" section in Chapter 7 for details.

Ad rotation options include:

- **Optimize for clicks** is the default setting explored earlier. It will automatically decide which ad is more likely to receive clicks, but as shown in the example, it might not make the right decision.

- **Optimize for conversions** is like optimize for clicks, but requires you to set up conversion tracking on your website. It will then try and display the ad that is more likely to result in a conversion more often. This might sound like a good option, but the issues outlined around optimize for clicks also applies to this setting. Instead, use the 'Rotate Indefinitely' setting and monitor your conversions and conversion rate to decide which ad drives more conversions.

- **Rotate evenly** will evenly display your ads for 90 days and then automatically change back to 'Optimize for Clicks'. This could potentially be a good option if you're not planning on actively managing your account or creating new ad variations, however, this might not be the best choice if you want to receive long-lasting results from your investment in Google AdWords.

- **Rotate indefinitely** is the best option if you want to be in control of your ads, and if you're going to be actively managing your account and testing the ad variations.

Frequency Capping

Frequency capping is a setting that only applies to campaigns targeting the Google Display Network. By setting a frequency cap, you are defining the maximum number of times your ads will display to an individual as they browse the Google Display Network.

You can set frequency capping per day, week or month, and the setting can be applied at the campaign level, the ad group level, or even for individual ads.

If you set your frequency capping to 10 impressions per day at the campaign level, this would mean that someone browsing the Google Display Network would see your ads a maximum of 10 times on any given day. This would apply to all ads contained in the particular campaign.

Or if you set frequency capping to 4 impressions per month at the individual ad level, and the campaign contains 10 different ad variations, then each ad could show a maximum of 4 times to somebody browsing the Google Display Network. This means that over the course of a month, someone could see your ads 40 times.

Frequency capping is useful for ensuring that people don't get sick of seeing your ads and can help improve your CTR, by reducing the number of impressions you receive. When deciding on your frequency cap it's important to remember that an impression on the Google Display Network does not necessarily mean that someone actually saw your ad. They may have been focused on other content on the page, or your ad might even be out of view and lower down on the page, requiring someone to scroll to see your ad.

Defining a Frequency Cap

Google AdWords provides average frequency data that can be used to help understand the performance of your campaigns. Your existing data can be found in the 'Campaigns' tab by selecting 'Columns' and 'Modify Columns', then look for 'Reach Metrics'. You will find 'Unique Cookies' (or reach) and 'Average impression frequency per cookie' (or frequency). You can then segment your data further by applying a time-based segment. This will now give you average frequency data for your campaigns, if you want more detail, then consider using Google Analytics.

To use Google Analytics to help determine your frequency cap, you will need to ensure that Google AdWords is linked to Google Analytics and that you have goals (or ecommerce transactions) setup. You will then need to check the following configurations have been made in Google Analytics:

1. Navigate to 'Property Settings' in 'Admin' and ensure that 'Enable Advertising Features' is set to 'On'. (Enabling this feature might require a change to your website's privacy policy.)

2. Then navigate to 'AdWords Linking' (also in 'Admin') and for each Google AdWords link configuration click 'Edit' and ensure that 'Enable Google Display Network impression reporting' is enabled.

Once everything is configured and data is coming into your reports you can navigate to 'Top Conversion Paths' under 'Multi-Channel Funnels' in the 'Conversions' reports. At the top of the report you will now be able to select 'Impressions' as the 'Interaction Type' to only view impression data for your campaigns. This will now show you the number of impressions along with the number of conversions you have received.

Tip: Visit http://lovesdata.co/uM8F3 for a short video explaining the steps to find impressions data in the Multi-Channel Funnels reports.

Campaign Setup Options

Ad Extensions

Ad extensions are additional pieces of information that can be displayed with your ads when people search on Google, and on some sites on the Google Display Network. Common ad extensions include sitelinks which allow you to display additional details along with your ad text when they are displayed in the top positions on search results.

Plumbing Services – plumbing.com
www.plumbing.com
Free Quote, Reliable Service. Experienced & Certified Plumbers.
$99 Drain Unblocking - 24/7 Emergency Service - Client Testimonials

Ad extensions include:

- **Location extensions** for displaying your address details with your ad
- **Call extensions** for displaying your phone number
- **Sitelinks extensions** for adding additional links to your ad

- **Call-out extensions** for highlighting additional information
- **Review extensions** for showing credible third party reviews
- **App extensions** for adding a link to your Android or iOS App to your ad

You can find your ad extensions by selecting 'Ad Extensions' under 'Campaigns' and then selecting the ad extension you want to set up or edit the 'View'.

Tip: If you don't see the tab, then the tab might be hidden. Make the tab visible by clicking on the grey arrow icon to the right of the visible tabs and select 'Ad Extensions'.

Extensions can be set up at the account, campaign or ad group level, depending on the extension type. You can also set up multiple extensions and Google AdWords will use the most granular extension available. For example, if you have a location extension for the campaign and another for the ad group, then the ad group extension will be displayed.

Location Extensions

Location extensions allow you to provide your address details, which can then be displayed along with your ads. If you have multiple locations you can provide multiple addresses and Google AdWords will automatically determine the most appropriate locations details to display with your ad. Ad extensions are displayed to people searching based on your geographic targeting settings for the campaign. It also considers where the person is located and what search terms they are using.

Before using location extensions you will need to claim your listing in Google My Business, which is a tool that allows you to claim and edit your business information on Google Maps, Google search results and Google+. Visit http://lovesdata.co/qmcke to claim your listing (and view your verified listing).

Navigate to 'Ad Extensions' and select 'View: Location Extensions'. If Google My Business is already linked to Google AdWords you will see details of the locations that are available to display with your ads. If the accounts are not linked you will need to navigate to 'All Online Campaigns', select 'View: Location Extensions' and click 'Add Extension'. You will then be prompted to link the accounts.

If your Google My Business account is not set up under the email address you use to access Google AdWords, then click 'Use a Different Account' and enter in your Google My Business login details.

Tip: If you have a lot of different locations in your Google My Business account, use the filter option to refine the locations for the campaign.

Once you have linked Google My Business to Google AdWords you can manage the locations that are displayed at the account, campaign and ad group-level. You can choose to display all or some locations at each of these levels with the more granular selections being displayed with your ads. For example, an ad group location extension would take preference over a campaign or account location extension.

Call Extensions

Call extensions allow you to display a phone number along with your ad. On mobile devices your phone number will be displayed as a button, allowing people to click to call your number directly.

> **Tip:** You can only set one phone number per campaign, so if you need to direct people to different numbers you will need to structure your campaigns accordingly.

To enter your phone number as a call extension, select 'Call Extensions' as the 'View'. Click 'New Extension', then 'Select Extension' and 'Create New Extension' to add your phone number.

When you create a call extension, you have the option of displaying your own phone number or using a Google forwarding number. When you use Google forwarding it means that people will see a phone number provided by Google, and when they call that number, they will be connected to your phone number. The advantage of using the forwarding feature is that it automatically provides you with data about the calls received from your ads. This includes the number of phone number impressions, number of calls, phone-through-rate or PTR (which is CTR for calls) and details on call costs.

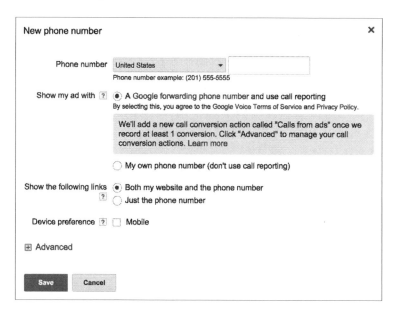

When you select call forwarding, there aren't any additional fees, but each time someone calls the number you are charged the same amount that you would pay for a click on your ad.

Tip: For additional details about how call tracking works visit http://lovesdata.co/dvqOG

For people viewing your ad on a mobile device you can choose whether you display your website and your phone number, or just your phone number. If you select 'Just the Phone Number' then clicking on your ad will connect people to your phone number and not direct them to your website.

Example of an ad displayed on a mobile device with 'Just the Phone Number':

Example of an ad displayed on a mobile device with 'Both my website and the phone number':

Tip: You can create mobile and non-mobile preference call extensions to display different numbers to people on desktops and tablets, compared to people using their mobile. Plus you can also choose when to display your call extensions.

You can set up different conversions for people who use the forwarding number. For example, you could set up a conversion after someone has made a call that lasts for at least a minute. To do this, make sure you select 'Count calls as phone call conversions'. You can then edit the settings for your call conversions under 'Tools' and then 'Conversions'. Click 'Calls from Ads' to see when a phone call using the call forwarding feature is being counted as a conversion.

Tip: Call forwarding numbers only available for select countries. See http://lovesdata.co/iEy2D for details.

Tip: You can also use the call forwarding number to replace the number you display on your website. This allows you to measure calls from your website as conversion and is called 'Website Call Conversions'. For details, read the "Call Conversions" section in Chapter 11.

Sitelinks Extensions

Sitelinks are additional links that can be shown along with your ad when your ad is displayed on the top or bottom of Google search results. Use sitelinks to add additional calls-to-action, present people with related offerings that you could not fit in your ad variation, and direct people to important sections of your website. Google AdWords can display two, four or six sitelinks along with ads on Google search results.

> **Tip:** Sitelinks can also be displayed with the descriptions from other ads in your account. These are called 'Enhanced Sitelinks' and are automatically created by Google AdWords to improve your ads.

You can create up to 10 sitelinks for each of your campaigns and Google AdWords will automatically select the most relevant links to display. If you're not seeing sitelinks displayed with your ads, it's likely because your ad is not displayed at the top of Google search results. Other common reasons for sitelinks not being displayed are ads with a low Quality Score, or other ad extensions being displayed along with your ad instead of sitelinks.

To set up sitelinks, select 'Sitelinks Extension' as the 'View' and click on 'New Extension'. You can then enter in the text to describe the link and the destination URL for each sitelink. Continue to 'Add Another' until you have all 10 sitelinks available.

Ensure each of your sitelinks direct people to a unique page (destination URL) on your website and remember they should closely relate to your keywords and ad variations. Try to include call to action phrases and secondary offers that might appeal to your audience.

> **Tip:** For account optimization, it is best practice to always add 10 sitelinks to each of your campaigns, even if the sitelinks do not display with your ads.

Did you know? Google can also automatically add sitelinks to your ads. These are called 'Dynamic Sitelinks' and you are not charged if someone clicks on them to view your website. For details visit http://lovesdata.co/UhAuo

---

Call-out Extensions

Call-out extensions allow you to highlight additional information about your products and services with your ads. This allows you to highlight your unique selling points without necessarily having to include them in your ad's heading or description lines. For example, if you offer free shipping and free returns then these could be highlighted using call-out extensions.

Here is an example of an ad with **call-out extensions**:

Tax Accountant Services - accountant.com

www.accountant.com/Services

Experienced Accountant for Personal & Corporate Tax
Certified Accountants • Open 7 Days • Over 500 Clients

And the same ad **without the extensions**:

Tax Accountant Services - accountant.com

www.accountant.com/Services
Experienced Accountant for Personal & Corporate Tax

Call-outs are limited to a maximum of 25 characters each and can be created at the ad group, campaign or account level, depending on your account structure and which call-outs are appropriate for particular ads. When you create them it is best to create four call-outs, although the minimum is two. By creating four, they will be more likely to display with your ads as Google automatically determines which call-outs to display based on the performance of each call-out you have created.

> **Tip:** Google recommends keeping your call-outs shorter than the maximum allowed number of characters – they suggest 12 to 15 characters. This means more call-outs are likely to display with your ads. Google also recommends using sentence case for call-outs, for example, 'Free shipping' instead of 'Free Shipping'. They also suggest trying to be more specific when including particular features, for example, '35 hour battery' instead of 'long life battery'.[1]

To create a call-out extension, navigate to the ad group, campaign or account level and select 'Call-out Extensions' under 'View' and click 'New Extension'. Now you can either select an existing call-out to use or click 'New Call-out'. You can then enter your call-out and click 'Save'.

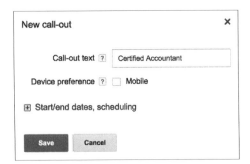

You can create call-outs that display on desktops and tablets and others for mobiles by selecting 'Mobile' for the 'Device Preference'. You will need to have both mobile and non-mo-

---

1   https://support.google.com/adwords/answer/6079510

bile preference call-outs for this to work correctly. You can also schedule each call-out to show on particular days or even particular hours by using the scheduling option when you create the call-out.

Review Extensions

Review extensions allow you to add third-party reviews that can be displayed along with your ads. Reviews need to be from a credible publication or organization and you can use a direct quote or paraphrase the review.

An example of an ad with a review:

Music Lessons

www.musicteacher.com

Professional Music Teacher for Individual or Group Lessons
"A true maestro with amazing skills and passion." - **musicnews.com**

Select 'Review Extension' under 'View' and click 'New Extension'. Then you can either select an existing review or click 'New Review'.

The source needs to be matched to the source URL, for example 'NY Times' would match to 'nytimes.com'.

Tip: To ensure your review extensions are approved, you cannot use personal reviews from individuals. You also need to ensure the review is not over 12 months old, that the review is taken from the source you provide, and that you are not altering the review.

App Extensions

App extensions allow you to add a link to your Android or iOS App in Google Play or the Apple App Store.

To create a link to your app, select 'App Extensions' under 'View' and click 'New Extension', then 'Select Extension' and 'Create New Extension' (or select an existing app extension). Select the type of app and then click 'Look up App'. This will automatically fill out the fields. You can then edit the fields, including 'Link Text' if required.

> **Tip:** You can modify the destination URL in the app extension, so that people who click your ad will automatically download your app. For details visit http://lovesdata.co/YKKuv

Display Network Exclusions

When you are running a campaign that targets the Google Display Network, there are additional options available to refine when your ads are displayed. Display exclusions include negative keywords, just like those for a search campaign, but there are also other options to prevent your ad from appearing based on additional criteria. By adding exclusions you can further target ads by reducing the number of impressions they will receive.

To set up exclusions, navigate to the 'Display Network' tab in a campaign that is targeting the Google Display Network. Then scroll to the bottom of the page and click 'Exclusions'. You can modify existing exclusions or add new exclusions to the ad group or campaign.

Display Keywords

You can reduce the likelihood of your ads displaying on pages that contains a particular term by adding display keyword exclusions at the ad group or campaign level. Review the display keywords you are targeting and only exclude terms that are clearly not performing, or strongly conflict with your brand.

Placements

Adding excluded placements will prevent your ad from showing on particular Google Display Network sites (or sections of a site). If you have found that an individual placement has not performed well inside your campaign, you can add it as an exclusion and your ads will no longer be displayed on that placement. If a placement has received a significant number of impressions and has not received a single click or view-through conversion, then it is worth evaluating the placement and deciding if you want to continue displaying your ads on that particular website. You will need to factor in the value of awareness and branding, as people who simply view your ad but don't click might still have a value depending on your objectives.

> **Tip:** Placement exclusions are best used when you are using automatic placement targeting. As you review your automatic placements you might see individual placements that are not aligned with your campaign objectives, these individual placements can then be excluded.

Categories

Category exclusions reduce the likelihood of your ads from showing on particular categories of websites. For example, if you don't want your ads to be placed on error pages or on pages containing adult language (think swearing), you can choose to stop your ads running on these pages.

To view the available category exclusion options, click 'Exclusions', then 'Add Campaign Exclusions' and then select 'Site Category Options'. A panel will load with all the available categories.

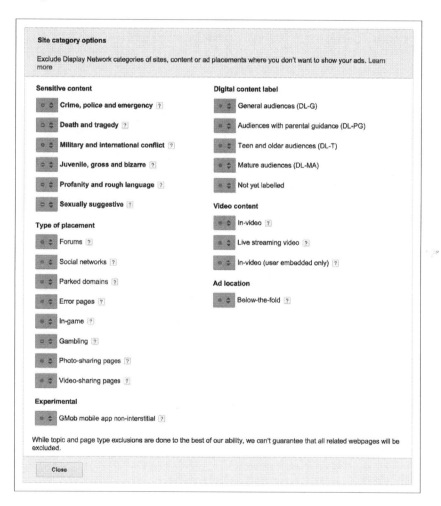

Tip: Selecting to exclude 'Below the Fold' will mean your ads are visible in a person's browser window when they are on a Google Display Network site. Check the available data before excluding this category as it might significantly reduce the impressions and clicks you receive from your Google Display Network campaign.

Additional Exclusion Options

You can also prevent your ads from appearing by defining exclusions based on topics, interests, remarketing lists, gender and age. Be careful when excluding based on very broad criteria like interests, as you are likely to exclude a portion of your target audience and they will no longer see your ads. It is best to run your Google Display Network campaigns for at least a few months so you have enough data available to make informed decisions about your targeting refinements.

Remarketing

Remarketing allows you to present highly targeted ads on the Google Display Network to people who have already been to your website. Since you are targeting people that are already aware of your brand, offering remarketing campaigns typically have a much higher conversion rate than standard display campaigns.

Here is an example of how remarketing works: somebody comes to your travel deals website, views a summer holiday package, and clicks on your 'enquire' button, but doesn't fill in their details, instead leaving your website. Using remarketing, you have the ability to reconnect with this person by showing them ads after they have left your website to remind them about your summer holiday package (and your brand) as they browse different sites on the Google Display Network.

Maybe a week has passed and they are again thinking about relaxing on a beach, so they head to a travel blog or the travel section of a news website. Using remarketing, you can target those content websites and even display an ad that includes your summer holiday package to bring them back to your website. You might even include a special incentive, such as a special saving or 'free extra night' to draw them back to your enquiry form.

Setting Up Remarketing

Remarketing works by assigning people who visit your website into particular categories that you define based on how they interact with your website. The simplest way to place people into a particular category or audience list is by defining which page or which content area on your website they visit. For example, if you wanted to create an audience list that included anybody who viewed your 'contact us' page, you could create a list for anybody who went to '/contact-us.html' on your website.

There are two options for setting up remarketing: you can use a special tag in your

Google AdWords account or you can use Google Analytics. There is no right or wrong in selecting how to set up remarketing, but in most cases you will want to use the Google Analytics option, because it provides more flexibility than the dedicated Google AdWords remarketing tag and is quicker to set up. We can start by looking at how to set up the dedicated Google AdWords remarketing tag, followed by the Google Analytics remarketing option, and you can decide which one suits your needs.

> **Tip:** Remarketing for search ads allows you to target ads to people on Google search results (instead of on the Google Display Network).

Before you set up remarketing you will need to check that you are eligible to create remarketing campaigns. There are some types of businesses that are not allowed to use remarketing, for example if you advertise alcohol. You can review the restricted categories by visiting http://lovesdata.co/3PThw

You also need to ensure that your privacy policy tells people that you are using remarketing, some details about remarketing, and how people can opt-out of remarketing campaigns. You can find details on these requirements at http://lovesdata.co/2f1AP

> **Tip:** Once you have met these requirements it is a good idea to check the local laws in your country around privacy and targeting ads to people online.

Once you have set up remarketing you will need a minimum of 100 people and 1,000 for search ads (based on unique remarketing cookies) in a list before your ads will begin to display.

Google AdWords Remarketing Setup

To set up remarketing using Google AdWords remarketing, navigate to 'Campaigns' and click on 'Shared Library' towards the bottom of the right-hand column. Now click on 'Audiences'. If remarketing has not been configured in your account, you will be prompted to set up the feature.

If you are using the Google AdWords remarketing tag, then it needs to be placed on all the pages of your website, just like your Google Analytics tracking code. When you open the 'Audiences' page there is an alert on the top right corner that tells you if you have any remarketing tags installed on your website.

> **Tip:** You can find your Google AdWords remarketing tag by clicking 'View Tag Details' in the top right corner of the 'Audiences' page. Then click 'Setup' and select 'View AdWords remarketing tag and instructions'.

Once you have installed the Google AdWords remarketing tag on all the pages of your website, you can begin to create audience lists for targeting your ads. To create a list, click on

'New Remarketing List'. When you create a remarketing list for your website, you have the following options:

- **Visitors of a page** allows you to target people who have viewed a specific page, for example, you could define the thank you page for your email newsletter subscribers. You could then use the list to display ads to promote your paid products or services.

- **Visitors of a page who did not visit another page** can be used to create a list that targets people who viewed a particular landing page, but failed to convert or engage deeper into your website.

- **Visitors of a page who also visited another page** allows you to target people who have engaged beyond a single page on your website.

- **Visitors of a page during specific dates** can be used to create lists for seasonal campaigns, for example, people who converted on your website two weeks before Valentine's Day.

- **Visitors of a page with a specific tag** gives you the ability to create different remarketing tags that can be used to meet specific needs. For example, you could have a separate remarketing tag that you use in the members section of your website to classify people who have logged in. (In most cases using Google Analytics remarketing will be easier than adding extra tags to specific pages or sections of your website).

- **Custom combination** is the most powerful option and allows you to create a list from lists you have already created. For example, if you can create a custom combination that includes people who have been to the product pages on your website, but exclude people who have already converted.

To create your remarketing list you can enter the particular page URLs that you would like to match. For example, if you wanted to target people who viewed one of your landing pages but did not convert then you would create a remarketing list where people visited '/landing-page.html' but did not visit '/thank-you.html'.

Google Analytics Remarketing Setup

Remarketing with Google Analytics gives you greater flexibility for targeting particular audience segments. Start by logging into Google Analytics and navigating to 'Admin'. Now click on 'Property Settings' and turn 'Enable Advertiser Features' to 'On'. If you have already linked your Google AdWords and Google Analytics accounts you will now be able to create remarketing lists in Google Analytics.

Did you know? Previously you needed to modify your Google Analytics tracking code to use remarketing. If you are using the Universal Analytics tracking code you might see an extra line of code that was used to enable the feature: **ga('require', 'displayfeatures');** . This extra code is no longer required.

If you are using Google Tag Manager to implement your Google Analytics tracking code on your website, then it is as simple as checking a box. Here is the option to enable remarketing inside Google Tag Manager:

☑ Enable Display Advertising Features   Includes Demographics and Interest Reports, Remarketing with Google Analytics, and DCM Integration. Learn about Display Advertising features and their impact on your privacy policy.

Now that remarketing is enabled you can begin to create lists inside Google Analytics and each list you create will automatically become available in your Google AdWords account. Examples of remarketing lists you should consider setting up are covered later in the book, but below are some steps to set up a simple remarketing list.

In Google Analytics navigate to 'Admin' and click on 'Remarketing' in the center column. Now click on 'Audiences' – if you already have lists set up they will be displayed. Start by clicking 'New Audience' and select the view that you want to use (the session and user data from this view will be used to create your remarketing list). Under 'Advertising Account' you will need to select the Google AdWords account where you want to use the list. Now click 'Next Step'.

You can now define how people are included (or excluded) from your remarketing list. There are a number of default options which include:

- **Smart List** is a list that is automatically managed by Google. This type of list uses machine learning to identify people who are likely to convert on your website using a number of different signals. Smart Lists are best suited to larger scale ecommerce websites that are generating a significant number of transactions. For details visit http://lovesdata.co/HheGe

- **All Users** allows you to target ads to anybody who has been to your website. This can be useful when creating lists based on 'Custom Combinations' inside your Google AdWords accounts. For example, you can subtract people who have converted from 'All Users' to target ads to prospective clients.

- **New Users** for targeting people who have not been to your website before. Remember this is based on users not having the Google Analytics cookie in their browser.

- **Returning Users** for targeting people who have already been to your website.

- **Users who visited a specific section of my website** allows you to only include people who have viewed a particular page or pages on your website.

- **Users who completed a goal conversion** if you have already configured your goals, then you can target people who have already converted. You can use this to cross-sell and up-sell, or use it in combination with another list like 'All Users', to target people who have not converted.

- **Users who completed a transaction** similar to 'Users who completed a goal conversion' but for websites using ecommerce tracking.

You can create a custom list by clicking 'Create New' and you also have the option to use an existing segment for your remarketing list. Clicking 'Import Segment' allows you to select and import a segment.

Create a basic list that includes everybody accessing your website. To do this, click 'All Users', you can then set how long people are included in the list. Change the default of '30' to '90' days and then name the list 'All Users' and click 'Save'.

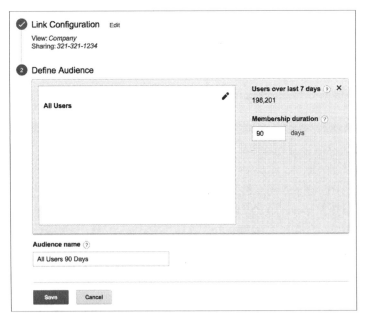

The list has now been created and you will select this list when you create a custom list inside Google AdWords.

> **Tip:** You can delete lists in Google Analytics by clicking on the name of a list and then clicking 'Close Audience' on the right hand side. Be careful if you are deleting lists because there is currently no undo option.

How Remarketing Works

Remarketing uses a browser cookie with a unique ID to display ads back to that person as they browse other websites on the Google Display Network. Let's look at a simplified scenario to understand how this works in more detail. Someone browses your website and the Google Analytics tracking code creates (or updates) a first party cookie (one that is stored under your domain name). This cookie is used along with the JavaScript tracking code to send information about the session to Google's servers which then gets processed into your reports. Since you have also set up remarketing with Google Analytics, the tracking code creates (or updates) a third party cookie which is stored under a Google domain name for remarketing. This cookie contains a unique ID.

Once you have set up a remarketing list inside Google Analytics for all of your website users, you can then display your ads to this person. This is because Google knows that the ID in the remarketing cookie is for the person who previously viewed your website. Since it is a third party cookie it means that Google can find the details of the unique ID even if they are on a different website.

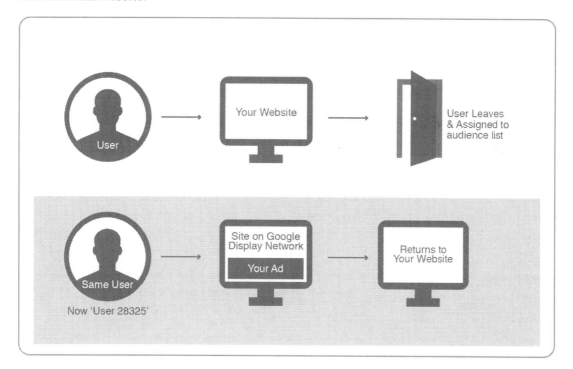

Did you know? Some people set up their browsers to only allow first party cookies which means that cookies are only stored on the current domain the person is browsing. This means that the person will not have a third party remarketing cookie and therefore will not be included in your remarketing lists.

The remarketing cookie is also used for other types of behavioral campaigns inside Google AdWords. For example, campaigns that target people based on a particular interest. People can choose to opt-out of seeing remarketing ads by visiting Google Ad Preferences at http://lovesdata.co/huEKL

Defining Membership Duration

You can choose how long someone should remain in each of your remarketing lists. The duration you choose will depend on how long it typically takes people to convert. For example, if you are selling products at a competitive price on your website you might set a membership duration of 15 to 30 days, since the majority of people quickly make a decision about buying from your website. On the other hand, a high cost item or service will typically have a much longer buying cycle and it can take longer for people to make a decision about contacting you for details. In this case you might set a membership duration of 120 days.

> **Tip:** The maximum duration for a display remarketing list is 540 days and 180 days for a search remarketing list.

One consideration when setting your membership duration is to understand that a long membership duration will mean that people are exposed to your ads for a longer period of time. Overexposure to your ads could lead to negative feelings towards your brand, so you need to balance your objectives against your audience's experience of seeing your ads for the duration you have defined. You can use Google Analytics along with your own experience of your customer's buying cycle to determine your membership duration.

If you have ecommerce tracking already set up then you can use the 'Time to Purchase' report in the 'Ecommerce' section. This report shows you the number of days between someone finding your website with the most recent source and medium combination, and when they made a purchase. This allows you to identify the time it takes for the majority of your transactions to occur. In the following example almost 95% of transactions occur between 0 and 27 days:

Days to Transaction	Transactions	Percentage of total
0	340	88.77%
1	4	1.04%
2	4	1.04%
3	3	0.78%
4	1	0.26%
5	1	0.26%
6	1	0.26%
7-13	4	1.04%
14-20	1	0.26%
21-27	4	1.04%
28+	20	5.22%

If you do not have ecommerce tracking, but you have set up goals, then you can use custom segments to see how many days occur between sessions before a conversion occurs. To do this multiple segments are used – each segment includes a particular number of days between sessions.

In the following example, multiple segments have been applied to the Goal URLs report. It shows that over 95% of users convert between zero and 30 days.

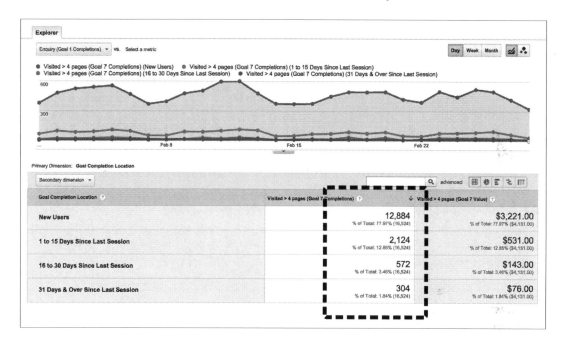

The following segments have been applied to the report:

- New users

- 1 to 15 days since last session

- 16 to 30 days since last session

- 31 days and over since last session

Applying the default 'New Users' segment allows you to see people who immediately convert along with the custom day ranges. Visit http://lovesdata.co/GfPhn to add the custom segments to your reports. Since there is a maximum number of segments you can apply at a time, you can edit the custom segments if you want to analyze different day ranges.

Tip: Try adjusting and extending your date range to balance any large spikes in conversions. This can help provide more accurate data to inform your membership duration.

Audience Lists You Should Set up

The best starting point for your remarketing lists is to target people with the highest potential value to your organization. You can create lists for people who are more likely to convert, people who have expressed an interest in your products or services, and people who have shown higher levels of engagement. Below are remarketing lists you can set up inside Google Analytics.

All Users

Defining a remarketing list for all your website users allows you to create a branded campaign that will only targeted to people who have already been to your website. Using this remarketing list for your branded ads on the Google Display Network might not drive a high number of conversions, but it will achieve a much better result than a similar display campaign that does not use remarketing. This is because without the remarketing list, many more people will see your ad, but they are far less likely to be aware of your products and services and not very likely to convert.

Creating a remarketing list that includes all your website users is important because it will also be used when you create custom combinations in Google AdWords. A custom combination is simply where you target your ads based on two or more remarketing lists. For example, if you want to target someone who has not yet purchased on your website you will need to have set up two remarketing lists: one for all users and another for everybody who has already purchased. By subtracting people who have purchased from all your users you end up with the desired target audience.

Users Who Converted

It might sound strange to create a remarketing list that targets people who have already converted on your website, but this will actually allow you to create two types of remarketing lists. Firstly, it allows you to up-sell and cross-sell to people who have already converted (this is covered later). Secondly, it allows you to create a remarketing list for people who didn't convert. Defining a conversion will also allow you to create a list for people who didn't convert. This will be covered in detail shortly.

To create a remarketing list for a Google Analytics goal, click 'New Audience', select your 'Advertising Account', click 'Next Step' and select 'Users who completed a goal conversion' and name the list.

You can adjust the membership duration based on the type of goal. If the goal is for a low-value lead, like a new email newsletter subscriber, then it is generally best to define a membership duration of between 90 and 180 days since they have engaged, but have not committed to becoming a client or customer. Finally, click 'Save'.

Users Who Didn't Convert

Once you have set up remarketing lists for users who have converted on your website, you can create a custom combination list in Google AdWords that allows you to define multiple criteria for matching and excluding particular users. For example, you could create a list that will target all your website users, but exclude anybody who converted for your contact form goal. This means that your ads will only display to people who have been to your website, but who have not yet converted.

> **Tip:** You can also create a remarketing list for people who haven't converted by creating a custom list inside Google Analytics where the condition is to exclude users who have already converted.

This is an important remarketing list to set up because it allows you to target ads to people who are far more likely to come back to your website and convert. These people are already aware of your brand and have already engaged to some degree with your website.

Create ads that will help push these undecided people over the line to generate conversions. This could include a special offer or promotion or highlighting unique benefits. If the conversion you are trying to achieve is a hard-sell or has a high price point, then consider creating ads that promote an alternate goal conversion.

For example, if you are trying to sell a premium product or service, then you could run ads that allow people to receive a free whitepaper download or an ad that encourages people to sign up for your free email newsletter. This might not result in an immediate high-value sale or conversion, but does allow you to build a relationship and connect with them which is far better than not getting their contact details and never hearing from them again.

To create a custom combination list, log into Google AdWords, click on the 'Campaigns' tab, click on 'Shared Library' in the bottom right corner and then 'Audiences'. Click the 'New Remarketing List' button and select 'Custom Combination' (as the 'Who to add to your list' option).

Let's continue the example and create a custom combination list that targets all users, who have not yet converted on the website. To do this, name the custom combination 'Users Who Haven't Converted'. Now select 'Any of these audiences (OR)' as the criteria, and click 'Select Audiences'.

Then find the 'All Website Users' list previously created in Google Analytics and click the arrow button to add it to the selection. Now click 'OK'.

Now click 'Add Another' and select 'None of these Audiences' as the criteria.

Click on the 'Select Audiences' button and add the Google Analytics remarketing list for the goal conversion you want to exclude and click 'OK'.

Once you click 'Save', you'll now have a remarketing list that will display to anybody who has been to the website, but who has not yet converted.

Abandoned Shopping Cart

Creating a remarketing list for people who abandon your shopping cart is similar to the remarketing list for users who did not convert. Start by creating a remarketing list that includes people who view your shopping cart page and another remarketing list that includes people who navigate to your checkout page. Once these users have been defined, you can then create a custom combination list inside Google AdWords that will only show ads to people who have viewed the cart, but not navigated through to checkout.

Shopping Cart Remarketing List

Start by identifying the URL of your shopping cart page on your website. You can do this by adding an item to the cart and then noting down the URL. For example, you might see http://www.company.com/cart/ which means that /cart/ is the page for your shopping cart.

> **Tip:** The URL of your shopping cart might change for each person on your website, so if you see something like http://www.company.com/cart.aspx?userid=1234 then you should just use /cart.aspx when you define your remarketing list.

Head back to 'Remarketing' in the Google Analytics 'Admin' area and click on 'New Audience'. Select your 'Advertiser Account', click 'Next Step' and then select 'Create New'.

Select 'Conditions' and click 'Ad Content' and change it to 'Page', since the remarketing list is based on people viewing the shopping cart and then the checkout page. Leave 'Contains' as the matching criteria and then paste in the page URL for your shopping cart. In this scenario, enter **/cart/** as the page.

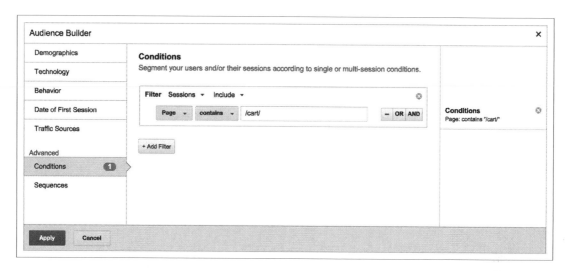

Now click 'Apply'.

Name the remarketing list 'Viewed Cart'.

For this remarketing list, set the membership duration between 15 and 45 days. You can adjust this based on the type of products you are selling online and their cost. Higher cost products will take longer for people to make a decision about, while lower cost products will generally be purchased quicker with less time spent considering alternate options.

Finally, click on 'Save'.

Checkout Remarketing List

Now you need to identify the URL of your checkout page. Navigate to the page and again note down the URL. If you see http://www.company.com/cart/checkout/, then your checkout page is /cart/checkout/ and you can now use this to set up the remarketing list inside Google Analytics.

Tip: If your checkout page is on a third party website, like PayPal, then you will need to set up Event Tracking to track the people who navigate away from your website to complete the checkout process.

Click on 'New Audience', select your 'Advertising Account', click 'Next Step' and then 'Create New'.

Select 'Conditions', click 'Ad Content' and change it to 'Page' and then enter the page URL of your checkout page. Continuing the scenario, enter **/cart/checkout/** as the page.

> **Tip:** If you have multiple next step options from your shopping cart page then you can change the matching criteria from 'Containing' to 'Matching RegExp'. This allows you to use regular expressions to define multiple next steps. For example, if you give people the option to register or to login with an existing account you might have two paths people can take during checkout. This might allow people to go to /cart/checkout/ but also to /login/ if they are already members. In this case select 'Matching RegExp' and enter **(/cart/checkout/|/login/)** as the value. This will now match people going to either page. Read the "Regular Expressions" section in Chapter 27 for more details.

Click 'Apply' and set the membership duration between 15 and 45 days (depending on the type of products and their cost).

Name the remarketing list 'Checkout Users' and click 'Save'.

> **Tip:** You could just create one remarketing list in Google Analytics that only includes people who viewed the shopping cart, but did not continue on to the checkout. However, this will reduce the flexibility you have in the future. For example, you might want to target people who reached the checkout page, but did not end up purchasing. By creating multiple lists you will have more options for creating custom combinations in Google AdWords.

Next, log into Google AdWords to create the remarketing campaign. Click on 'Shared Library' in the bottom right hand corner under 'Campaigns'. Now click 'Audiences', then 'New Remarketing List' and select 'Custom Combination' (as the 'Who to add to your list' option).

Name the custom combination 'Viewed Cart Didn't Checkout' and select 'Any of these audiences (OR)' as the criteria. Click 'Select Audiences', find the 'Checkout Users' list and click the arrow button and click 'OK'.

Click the 'Add Another' link and select 'None of these Audiences'.

Again, click 'Select Audiences' and add the remarketing list called 'Checkout Users' as the selection (using the arrows) and click 'OK'.

Click the 'Save' button.

This new custom combination list will now only display ads to people who have viewed the shopping cart, but not travelled through to the checkout page.

> **Tip:** Consider creating Google Analytics remarketing lists that include people who viewed your high value products (or even particular categories of products). This will allow you to target very specific product ads to people who have shown a level of intent to purchase.

Specific Content or Content Areas

Remarketing lists can be set up based on important content and even important content areas from your website. These lists enable you to display ads to people who have shown a level of interest in your products or services based on how they have engaged with your website content.

For example, if someone navigates to your ecommerce website that sells electronics and then navigates to the product category for TVs you could define that product category as a remarketing list. This would allow you to create a special ad that would be displayed to people who had shown an interest in purchasing a TV. You could then create additional remarketing lists for your other product category pages.

Content based remarketing lists are also suited to non-ecommerce websites. For example, if you are an accountant with an information page about your personal tax services, you could create a remarketing list that includes anybody who saw that particular page. Again, this would allow you to create a specific ad to appeal to anybody who viewed that particular page.

You could also extend your remarketing list to apply to multiple pages. Continuing the previous example, the personal tax services page might have additional sub-pages that people can navigate to, including a benefits page, a testimonials page and page with additional service options that all relate to personal tax. You could define all of these pages as a 'personal tax' content area for your remarketing list.

Tip: Dynamic remarketing allows you to automatically create ads that include content and products that people have engaged with on your website. For more information visit http://lovesdata.co/MI6pH

Cross-Selling

Remarketing lists can be used to create additional sales opportunities by cross-selling additional products to customers who have already purchased. To do this you will need to ensure that you are defining product names and categories in the Google Analytics ecommerce tracking code, which hopefully you are already doing. The next step is to think about the products that will lead to cross-selling opportunities.

For example, if you are selling TVs online, then you could create remarketing lists that promote popular accessories and additional options to people who have already purchased. This could include things like promoting surround sound systems, media players and maybe even installation services or extended warranties.

If you have a lot of products, then it is best to start with ones that you already know lead to additional purchases. If you begin by using remarketing to enhance what you know works, then you are far more likely to achieve a good return on your time in setting up the campaign.

In Google Analytics navigate to 'Remarketing' (under 'Admin'), click on 'New Audience' select your 'Advertising Account' and click 'Next Step'.

Click 'Create New' and select 'Conditions'. Click 'Ad Content' to change the condition and then search for either 'Product' or 'Product Category'. This will depend on if you want to create your remarketing list based on someone purchasing a particular individual product or if someone purchased a product from a particular product category. Remember you will need to ensure ecommerce tracking is collecting the correct details. For this example, select 'Product Category' since every TV that is sold through the website is reported as 'TV Screens' for the product category.

Now select 'Exactly Matches' as the match type, so that other product categories are not unknowingly included. You can use one of the other match types if it is more appropriate for your needs.

Then enter 'TV Screens' as the value for the filter and click 'Apply'. This will mean that anybody purchasing online where the product category is set to 'TV Screens' in the ecommerce tracking code will now be included in this remarketing list.

Set the membership duration to 365 days. This will mean that people are included in this remarketing list for a maximum of one year. If you sell products that people need to buy on a regular basis, like ink cartridges for printers or any other consumable goods, then you will want to reduce the membership duration to a period that make sense for your products.

Name the list and click 'Save'.

From here specific offers can be developed for people who have purchased a particular products, allowing you to cross-sell and create new revenue opportunities.

Upselling

The same concept covered under cross-selling can be applied for upselling people who have converted on your website. This is not just limited to ecommerce websites either. For example, if someone subscribes to your email newsletter on your website, you could upsell with ads to get them to download a whitepaper or you could even upsell to encourage people to complete your contact form. The idea here is to increase the level of engagement and commitment people have with your brand.

If you know that people who buy one product are likely to want to upgrade in a couple of weeks you can build remarketing lists to appeal to them at exactly the right time in your upselling purchase cycle.

Tip: Upselling based on a long purchase cycle might not achieve great results using remarketing because when people clear their browser cookies they will no longer be included in the remarketing list.

Click 'New Audience', select your 'Advertising Account', click 'Next Step' and then click 'All Users'.

Enter '14' as the 'Membership Duration'. This will be used as an exclusion when you create the custom combination inside Google AdWords. Name the list '14 Day Buffer' and click 'Save'.

Now create another remarketing list using the steps covered in the "Cross-selling" section above in this chapter. This should be for the product (or conversion action) that relates to the item you are cross-selling.

When you create this remarketing list, ensure that you set the duration to be longer than the previous list. For example, if you set 14 days for the first list, you would then set a duration between 30 and 60 days for this new list.

Then head to Google AdWords and create a custom combination list that includes people from the last list you created and exclude people from the 14 day buffer list. You will now be able to advertise to people who purchased (or converted), but ads will not begin to display until 15 days after the conversion.

Members and Loyal Customers

If you have members or a customer loyalty program you can create a remarketing list to promote your new offers or members specials. You can track your members and customers by defining a remarketing list based on people who view the members area on your website. For example, if members login and are then taken to https://www.company.com/members-area/ then you could create a page-based remarketing list for anybody who navigates to /members-area/ after they complete their login details.

A better option would be to track your members and customers using a custom dimension and then creating a remarketing list based on the information collected. Although this method does require implementation on your website, you can track things like your different membership levels and create ads targeted to those different levels. This would allow you to present different offers to your gold and silver members.

Once implemented, you can create a remarketing list based on the values you are collecting into the custom dimension.

Highly Engaged Users

If you are looking after a content or branding website that is designed to increase awareness, then you can create a remarketing list that will display ads to your highly engaged users. Remarketing lists can be created based on how long people are spending on your website, including how many pages they have viewed and how many times they have been to your website.

To create a remarketing list based on engagement, follow the steps previously outlined (in the "Specific Content or Content Areas" section above in this chapter), but after selecting 'Create New' select 'Session Duration' for 'Conditions'. Session duration is based on seconds, so if you want to target people who have spent longer than 5 minutes on your website, select 'Greater Than' and enter 300 as the value.

You can create engagement-based lists using other criteria too, for example, based on people viewing a certain number of pages (using 'Pageviews'). A remarketing list can also be created based on the total number of times someone has been to your website. You can do this by selecting 'Count of Sessions' and then defining how many times they need to have been to your website before they are included in the remarketing list.

Bid Simulator

The Bid Simulator allows you to see how making adjustments to your bids impacts on the number of clicks you are likely to receive. You can use the Bid Simulator at the campaign, ad group and keyword level, depending on the level of detail you would like to see. Under the 'Campaigns' tab you will find the bid simulator under 'Budget' – it is a small icon that looks like a graph. When you click on the icon, the tool will open.

This shows you the current performance of your campaign and the estimated impact of changing all your bids in the campaign.

Tip: The Bid Simulator is not available all the time, you will notice that it is greyed out and unavailable for particular campaigns, ad groups and keywords. There are a number of reasons why the Bid Simulator can be unavailable including:

• If you have just added a new campaign, ad group or keyword. The Bid Simulator uses data from the last 7 days to provide estimates. If there is not enough data it won't be available.

• If your daily budget has been reached at least once in the last 7 days.

• If you are using automatic bidding or CPA (cost-per-acquisition) bidding.

• You can find a full list of reasons under the "Troubleshooting" section at **http://lovesdata.co/hBPQP**

You can also use the Bid Simulator for particular ad groups. You'll find the icon under 'Default Maximum CPC' in the 'Ad Groups' tab. This shows the default bid for your ad group and the impact of changing the bid on the number of clicks and impressions you are likely to see.

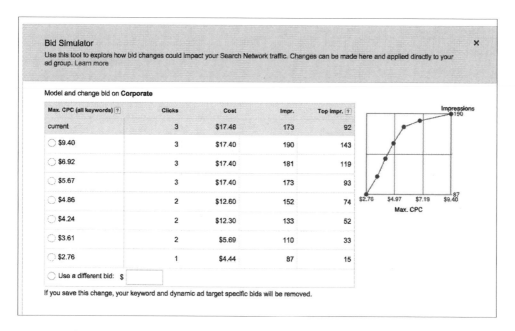

In the example above the default bid for the ad group is $1.10, which means dramatically increasing the bid will have a minimal impact on impressions and is unlikely to result in additional clicks. In this case you might want to look at the Bid Simulator for the other ad groups, to see if there are areas that are more likely to see improvement if bids are changed.

If you decide that you would like to adjust your bids based on the Bid Simulator, then running a Google AdWords Experiment to test the change can be a good way to ensure that making the change will have a positive impact.

Dynamic Keyword Insertion

Dynamic Keyword Insertion (DKI) allows you to automatically change your ads depending on the particular keyword that triggers the ad. This allows you to create ads that are more relevant to what people are searching without having to create lot of different ad groups with different ads.

For example, if you look at the following examples you will see that the only thing that changes is the headline of the ads:

Plumber Seattle
www.plumber.com
Fast, Reliable Plumbing Services.
Available 24/7. Call Now!

Plumber Tacoma

www.plumber.com

Fast, Reliable Plumbing Services.
Available 24/7. Call Now!

Inside Google AdWords, these ads are both created using the following single ad variation:

{KeyWord:Plumbing Services}

www.plumber.com

Fast, Reliable Plumbing Services.
Available 24/7. Call Now!

You will notice that the ad looks different. The curly brackets (and everything inside them) is replaced by the keywords you are targeting in your ad group. This means if we have 'plumber seattle', 'seattle plumber', 'plumber tacoma' and 'tacoma plumber' in the ad group, then the headline of the ad will automatically change based on the keyword that triggers the ad.

You can change the capitalization of 'keyword' in order to change the final ad that people see. For example, using {keyword:Plumbing Services} along with the keyword of 'plumber seattle' means the ad would read 'plumber seattle'. Using {KeyWord:Plumbing Services} would display 'Plumber Seattle'. This gives you additional control over how your ad is capitalized.

Usage	Keyword	Result
{keyword:Plumbing Services}	emergency plumbing seattle	emergency plumbing Seattle
{Keyword:Plumbing Services}	emergency plumbing seattle	Emergency plumbing seattle
{KeyWord:Plumbing Services}	emergency plumbing seattle	Emergency Plumbing Seattle

Now you have probably also noticed that 'Plumbing Services' is included in the Dynamic Keyword Insertion. This is the fallback that will be used if the keyword is too long to fit in the ad. For example, the headline of an ad can contain a maximum of 25 characters. If we use {KeyWord:Plumbing Services} and the keyword 'quick emergency plumbing service seattle' triggers our ad, then this clearly won't fit within the character limit. In this case the fallback is used and the headline of the ad will read 'Plumbing Services'.

> **Tip:** You can also use Dynamic Keyword Insertion in the description lines and display URL for your ads. If you do, it's important to ensure that the ad remains readable and continues to make sense for each of the keywords you are targeting.

When you use Dynamic Keyword Insertion it doesn't automatically improve Quality Score, so you will need to ensure your keywords and ads are still grouped appropriately. You should also consider the fallback, as this is what will contribute to the relevance of your ad with the keywords you are targeting.

Important: When using Dynamic Keyword Insertion, it is the keyword you are bidding on (from within your ad group) that is displayed in your ad. It will not use the actual search query that someone enters. For example, if you are bidding on the keyword 'plumber seattle' and this keyword broadly matches the search query of 'certified plumbing seattle', then the ad will still read 'plumber seattle' (and not 'certified plumbing seattle').

Google AdWords Experiments

Experiments is a feature of Google AdWords that allows you to test different changes in your account. For example, if you have an ad group with a default bid of $2.50 and you want to understand what will happen if you change the bid to $4.00, you can run an experiment where 50% of the time the bid will be $4.00 and for the other 50% of the time the bid will be your original amount. After enough data is collected, you can see what impact the change has made and you can decide to alter the bid or not. This means you can test different changes and you can even choose what percentage is allocated to the original and to the experiment. Instead of a 50/50 test you might want perform an 80/20 test, so that you are only experimenting 20% of the time.

Things you can test with experiments include:

- Bid changes for ad groups
- Bid changes for individual keywords
- Changes to your maximum CPA bid
- Completely new ad groups
- Additional keywords
- Different keyword match types
- Additional display placements
- Additional display keywords
- Different ad variations

Experiments are set up in individual campaigns, so to create an experiment, select a particular campaign and click on the 'Settings' tab. Towards the bottom of the settings page you will see 'Experiment' under 'Advanced Settings'. Click 'Add Experiment Settings'.

> **Tip:** If you don't see 'Advanced Settings' then your campaign is using the 'Standard' features option. To use experiments you will need to click on 'Edit' next to the campaign 'Type' at the top of 'Settings'. Now select 'All Features' and click 'Save'.

Next you will need to name your experiment. I suggest using something descriptive that describes what you are going to test along with the date, for example, 'Ad Group Bids 06/10/14'. Now you'll need to select the split between the control (original) and your experiment. The smaller the amount you include in the experiment the longer the test will take to find a winner, so unless you are running campaigns with a reasonable number of impressions and clicks you will probably want to stick to allocating at least 50% to your experiment. Finally, you can select a start and an end date for your experiment. I recommend starting your first experiment manually and using the default end date of 30 days after you launch the experiment.

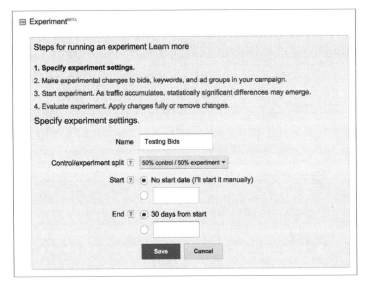

Now that the experiment has been set up, you need to create the changes in the campaign. Test the default bids for each ad group, to do this, navigate to the 'Ad Groups' tab. You will notice the status icon for your ad groups has changed from a green circle to a testing icon. To make the changes between the control (original bids) and the experiment, click on 'Segment' and select 'Experiment'. This will allow you to see the difference between your control and experiment, since changes haven't been made yet, you will see that the bids are the same.

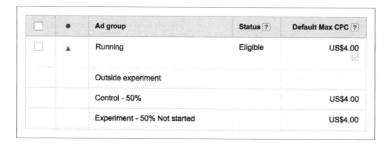

Now click on the default bid for the experiment and enter the amount that you want to adjust the bid for your test. The default bid is $4.00 and adjusting the bid by +50% means you will now be experimenting with a $6.00 bid.

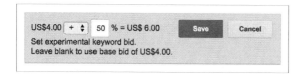

Once you're happy with your experiment, head back to the 'Settings' tab and click 'Start Running Experiment' to launch the test. You can use the segment previously applied to check on the progress of your experiment. Once you have enough data you can then decide if you want to keep the changes or remove them.

You can see that the experiment has enough data and that increasing the bid has improved the number of clicks and impressions. So for this experiment, you will want to make the experiment bid the default for the ad groups. To do this you can head back to the 'Settings' tab and click 'Apply: Launch Changes Fully'. This will mean that your experiment bids become your default bids.

Tip: When you apply the experiment segment you will see arrows that indicate the statistical significance of the data. This basically tells you the certainty of your experiment in having an impact. Three arrows indicate 99.9% certainty, two arrows 99% and one arrow 95%. Look for arrows that point up, this means they've increased performance, while a downward arrow indicates a decrease. If you see two grey arrows pointing up and down this tells you that the change isn't statistically significant.

10

Video and Shopping Campaigns

Google AdWords for Video

Google AdWords for video is a video-specific campaign type. It allows you to promote your YouTube content using cost-per-view (CPV) bidding on YouTube and across the Google Display Network. There are two types of TrueView ad formats available: *TrueView In-stream*, where your YouTube content is played before another video, and *TrueView In-display*, where your YouTube content is displayed as an ad (with an image and text).

The TrueView In-stream format is a bit like a TV commercial, as it plays before the video content someone has selected to watch. However, you are only charged when someone watches your video for at least 30 seconds (or until the end of your video if it is shorter than 30 seconds).

When someone sees your ad they have the option of skipping it after watching the first 5 seconds. This means you are not charged if they click 'Skip Ad' before watching 30 seconds of your video (unless your video is shorter).

This means that you need to ensure the content you are promoting with your video campaigns is highly engaging in the first 5 to 15 seconds to encourage people to watch your entire video.

Tip: TrueView In-stream ads allow you to add a display and destination URL that direct people through to your website. This can then be displayed to people watching your video ad and allows you to add a clear call to action to encourage people to visit your landing page.

The TrueView In-display format is more like a display ad in that a thumbnail image of your video content is displayed along with a headline and description lines. Your ads can appear on YouTube search results pages or alongside other videos.

For your TrueView In-display ads you need to ensure you are writing engaging content, just like you would for your other text-based ads. If the headline and description lines are not interesting, then people will not click to watch your video.

You are only charged when people click to watch your ad and you have the choice of sending people to watch the video on its own page or watching the video on your YouTube channel page.

Tip: If you want people to watch your promoted video content on your YouTube channel page then you need to ensure that 'Browse' is enabled for your channel. To do this navigate to your channel page to where you see the menu that says 'Home, Videos, etc'. Hover over this section and you will see an edit icon displayed in the top right corner. Click on this icon and select 'Edit Channel Navigation' and ensure that 'Browse' is enabled. For details visit http://lovesdata.co/M7ehD

Video Campaign Setup

To set up your first video campaign click on 'New Campaign' under the 'Campaigns' tab and select 'Online Video'. From here you can name your campaign and allocate your daily budget. You can also choose where your ads will display, choose your location and language targeting and select your video.

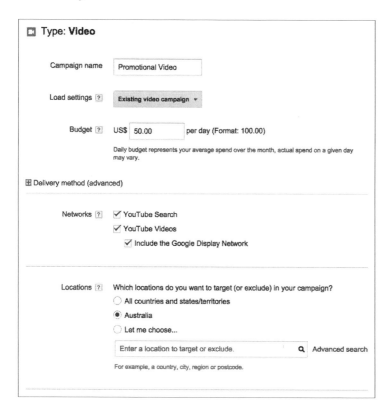

When you select a video you can choose to include In-stream or In-display formats and preview how your ad will appear. You can then name your ad to review its performance in your reports, choose additional campaign settings and save your campaign.

Tip: You can add up to 10 videos to each of your campaigns. When you first create your campaign you can add one video, but after the campaign has been set up and you have selected your targeting you can add additional videos.

After you have created your campaign you will then need to define your targeting and maximum bid for the campaign. The targeting you use for your video campaigns is just like what you use for Display Campaigns. You can target based on:

- Gender
- Age
- Interests
- Topics
- Remarketing
- Keywords
- Placements
- Parental Status

In most cases, you will want to begin with broad targeting where you target all ages and genders along with some general interests. If you want to run some video ads to advertise your cooking classes for the first time, you should start by targeting all ages and genders along with the following interests:

- 'Cooking Enthusiasts' and 'Foodies' from in the 'Affinity Audiences'
- 'Home & Garden' and 'Food & Drink' from within 'In-market Audiences'
- 'Food & Drink' from within 'Other Audiences'

This will provide you with broad coverage as you begin to promote your videos and then you can begin to refine and test different targeting methods once you have some data available to understand the performance of your video campaigns.

Tip: For details about the difference between Affinity Audiences, In-market Audiences and Other Audiences read the "Interests" section in Chapter 16.

Once your video ads have been running you will be able to see the number of impressions and views your videos have received. Remember that a view will only occur if someone has watched your In-stream ad without skipping it, or they have clicked your In-display ad. You can also see how much of your videos people are watching under 'Video Played To' which shows you the percentage of people watching 25%, 50%, 75% and 100% of your videos. You can also segment the report using the tabs above the graph:

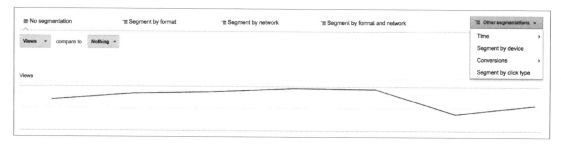

Segmenting your data can help you identify which ad formats, networks and targeting methods are working. For example, selecting 'Segment by Network' in the 'Ads' tab shows how your ads are working on the different networks.

In the example above you can see that the majority of views are coming from YouTube videos with a small number of views on YouTube search and no views on the Google Display Network. This means you can look at adding keywords to your targeting to help improve the number of times your ads are eligible to display within YouTube search results. Plus you could consider adding the Google Display Network to your targeting to increase your audience size..

You should check your targeting on a regular basis under the 'Targets' tab. When you first come into the tab you will see all of your different targeting methods. You can then click on a particular targeting group to see a more detailed view of performance. Use the links above the table to review the performance of the individual targeting methods you are using.

For example, after clicking 'Interests' you can now see performance for each of the individual interests you are targeting. You can also click on the links under 'Where your ads were shown' for additional details about placements, keywords, ages and genders. In this example, 'Placements' have been selected and you can see where your ads have been displayed on YouTube and on the Google Display Network:

Placement [?]	Type
Gordon Ramsay's Scrambled Eggs	YouTube video
Egg Roulette Challenge	YouTube video
Slow Cooked Beef Short Ribs - Gordon Ramsay	YouTube video

You can use these reports like you would for display campaigns. To modify bids for particular placements or to exclude your ads from being shown on particular placements.

Tip: Read the "Display Targeting" section in Chapter 17 for additional ideas on managing the targeting of your video ads.

Link YouTube Channel

Linking your YouTube channel to Google AdWords provides you with additional options for your video campaigns and also gives you additional data in your reports. You can either link from within your Google AdWords account or from within your YouTube account. In Google AdWords click 'Linked YouTube Accounts' and then click 'Link YouTube Channel' and follow the steps.

Tip: If you are not the owner of the YouTube account, then they can either add your Google AdWords customer ID in YouTube or you can send them a link after following the steps in your Google AdWords account. Visit http://lovesdata.co/9AHfQ for additional information.

Once you have linked the accounts you will be able to see your channel listed in the 'Linked YouTube Accounts' page.

After linking accounts you will have access to additional features and reporting data:

- **YouTube remarketing** lets you show ads to people who viewed your channel, watched your videos and many other options around how they engaged with you on YouTube. You can use these remarketing lists for your video campaigns as well as other remarketing campaigns in your Google AdWords account.

- **Call to action overlays** allow you to share additional information with people watching your video, including to promote other videos, your YouTube channel or even your website.

- **Additional data** including ad completion rates and earned actions from your videos and video ads.

Video Remarketing

Video remarketing is just like the traditional form of remarketing where you only display your ads to people who have previously engaged with you, but with video remarketing you are doing this based on people engaging with you on YouTube and not your website. For example, you could create a video campaign that only displays particular video ads to people who have already watched at least one of your other videos on your YouTube channel.

Video remarketing options include:

- Viewed any video from a channel

- Visited a channel page

- Viewed any video (as an ad) from a channel

- Liked any video from a channel

- Disliked any video from a channel

- Commented on any video from a channel

- Shared any video from a channel

- Subscribed to a channel

- Unsubscribed from a channel

- Viewed certain video(s)

- Viewed certain video(s) as ad(s)

- Liked certain video(s)

- Disliked certain video(s)

- Commended on certain video(s)

- Shared certain video(s)

Tip: For more on how to use remarketing and choosing membership duration read the "Remarketing" section in Chapter 6.

To create your remarketing list click 'Video Remarketing Lists' and then click 'New Remarketing List'.

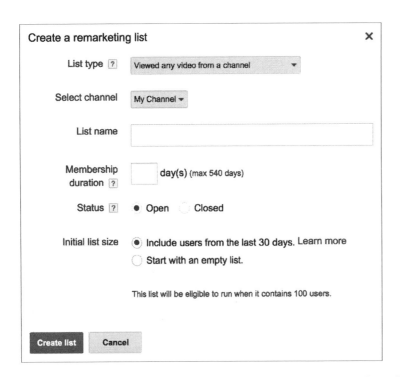

Once you have created your video remarketing list and used it as a targeting method your ads will begin to run, although your list must first contain at least 100 people. You can also make use of your video remarketing lists in your other remarketing campaigns. For example, you could show an image ad encouraging people to purchase one of your products on the Google Display Network to people who watched one of your product tutorial videos on YouTube.

Shopping Campaigns

Shopping campaigns allow you to display the products you sell on Google search results and on Google Shopping results as people are searching to buy products. Shopping ads include a picture of the product, title, price, promotional message and store name. They allow people to click through to your product page from the product listing on Google.

Here is an example of shopping ads in Google search results:

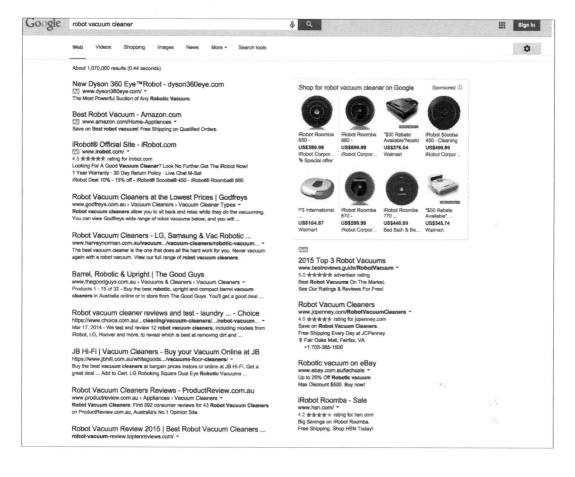

And an example of ads on Google Shopping:

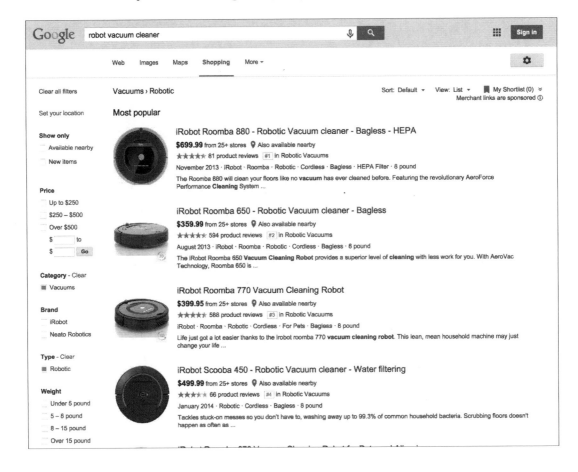

Did you know? Just like regular search ads, you are only charged when people click on your ad to view the product page on your website.

Before you create your shopping campaign you will need to create a Google Merchant Centre account. This account is where all of your product information will be collected and then you can link your Google Merchant Centre and Google AdWords account. In order to get your product information into the Google Merchant Centre, you will need to create a product feed that contains all of your products along with particular details for each product. You will need to work with your web developer or technical support resource to get your product feed set up. For details on what you need to include your feed visit http://lovesdata.co/RDaGU and for a summary visit http://lovesdata.co/78OZO

To set up your Google Merchant Centre account visit http://lovesdata.co/PR8ql

Tip: If you are using a good quality hosted ecommerce solution, like Shopify, then they will have an add-on that allows you to automatically create the feed. Search your ecommerce solution's help section for 'Google shopping'. Alternatively, if you are using a self-hosted solution, then you should contact the developer and see if there is a plugin you can download for your website.

Next you will need to link your Google Merchant Centre account to Google AdWords. To do this you will need to copy your Google AdWords customer ID which is in the top right corner once you have logged into your Google AdWords account.

Then you will need to log into your Google Merchant Centre account, click on 'Settings' and then 'AdWords'. If you have created the Google Merchant Centre account using the same login you use for Google AdWords, then you can simply click 'Link Account'.

You can now head back to your Google AdWords account and click on 'New Campaign' in 'Campaigns'. Now select 'Shopping' to create the campaign.

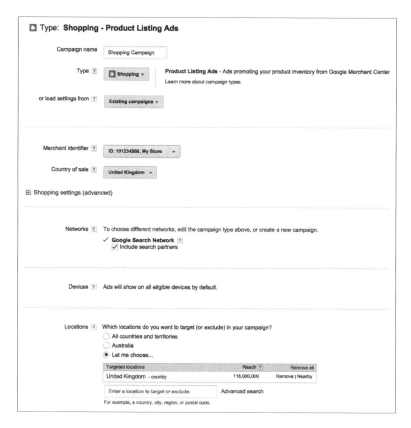

Select your network and location targeting, along with your bid strategy, default bid and daily budget.

Shopping campaigns do not use keywords, instead the details in the product feed are automatically used to display your products when people search. You can use product groups to create groups of particular products, based on product category or attributes you provide in the product feed. This allows you to group particular types of products together and then create promotions that relate to those particular product groups.

Did you know? Most advertisers use shopping campaigns to direct people to an online store, but you can also promote in-store items with local inventory ads. For more details visit http://lovesdata.co/h0EWR

You can create promotions under the 'Ads' tab in your shopping campaign. The promotions you create can be used to differentiate your store from others stores selling the same product. For example, if you have a special coupon or other offer you can highlight this by creating a promotion.

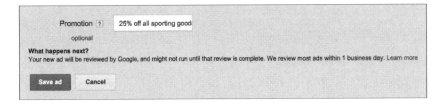

Tip: For best practice recommendations on setting up and running shopping campaigns visit http://lovesdata.co/Zqbli

11

Google AdWords Reporting

Linking Google AdWords and Google Analytics

By linking your Google AdWords account with Google Analytics you can analyze the performance of your campaigns in more detail. This is because Google Analytics allows you to see what people do after they click on your ad, including where they navigate to, where they leave and if they convert on your website.

Before you can link your accounts you need to ensure that the email address you use to log in has administrator-level access to both the Google AdWords and Google Analytics account (this is called *edit* access in Google Analytics).

Tip: If you only have administrator access to one of the accounts (only Google AdWords or only Google Analytics), then you will need to request administrator access for the other account. If this becomes problematic it can sometimes be easier to add a new login to both accounts (for example, a new Gmail address). Then once you have linked accounts, you can safely remove the new login from both accounts. This is because removing the login used to link accounts does not undo the linking process.

Linking Steps

1. Log into Google Analytics (or in Google AdWords, navigate to 'Google Analytics' under the 'Tools' tab).

2. Click on 'Admin' in Google Analytics.

3. Select the name of the Google Analytics account you want to link to your Google AdWords.

4. Click 'AdWords Linking' in the center column (under 'Property').

   a. You will see a list of Google AdWords accounts you have access to listed by 'Customer ID' (this looks something like 123-123-1234).

   b. If a Google AdWords account has already been linked, you'll see it listed on the page. Click on the name of the link (under 'Link Group Name') to see the Google AdWords customer ID. If your account is already linked, then you do not need to re-link your accounts.

5. Select the Google AdWords account (or accounts) you would like to link using the check boxes and click 'Continue'.

6. Name the link (for example, 'My AdWords Account') and select the reporting view (or views) where you would like to see your Google AdWords campaign data. In most cases you will want to use the 'Select All' link so that you have data available in all of your reporting views. You will see there is a link for 'Advanced Settings'. This allows you to disable auto-tagging. Unless you have a specific reason, you should not disable auto-tagging as this automatically sends all of your Google AdWords data into Google Analytics.

7. Click on 'Link Accounts'.

Once you have followed the steps to link your accounts, Google AdWords data will begin to appear in Google Analytics. This can take up to 24 hours from when you have linked your accounts and will only include data from the time you linked accounts moving forward. Google AdWords has its own dedicated set of reports in Google Analytics. These can be found in Google Analytics under the 'Reporting' tab, by selecting 'Acquisition' and then 'AdWords'.

Troubleshooting Google AdWords Data in Google Analytics

After the accounts have been linked for a couple of days, it is worth checking to ensure that the data you are seeing is accurate. Start by selecting a date range that includes the days when the accounts were correctly linked. Next, navigate to the 'Campaigns' report (under 'Reporting', 'Acquisition' and then 'AdWords') and select 'Clicks' above the graph (it will be in the 'Explorer' tab and to the right of the goal and ecommerce links).

The Clicks report shows you a combination of Google Analytics data and data directly imported from Google AdWords. The number of sessions will show you the total number of people interacting with your website based on the Google Analytics tracking code installed on your website. The number of clicks will show you the total number of people who have engaged with your ad. This is simply the number of clicks you have received from Google AdWords.

It is important to highlight that sessions and clicks are not the same. Think of a click as the physical action of someone clicking on your ads. The number of sessions and click should be as similar as possible, but they are not going to be identical. As a general guide, the difference between sessions and clicks should be no greater than plus or minus 10% of each other. For example, if you found 6,679 sessions and 6,115 clicks, the difference is 564 clicks and this means that there are 8.44% fewer clicks compared to sessions. Since this percentage is within the plus or minus 10% range, the variance is acceptable.

Looking at another example, you might see 3,254 sessions and 6,925 clicks, which is a much larger variance between sessions and clicks. This indicates that something has not been configured correctly. Below are some scenarios that might result in these differences in Google Analytics.

Reasons for data discrepancies:

- **Unlinked accounts**
  - If you see sessions being reported, but zero clicks this indicates that your Google AdWords account has not been linked (or that it has been linked incorrectly, or you are using a reporting view that has not been selected to include the Google AdWords cost data). You will need to either link Google AdWords, or edit the link to include cost data to be reported into the particular view.

- **Incorrect Google Analytics account linked**
  - If you see zero sessions, but clicks are being reported, then this tells you that the Google AdWords account is being used to advertise a different website.

- **Bookmarks**
  - People bookmarking the landing page after clicking your ad can lead to additional sessions being reported. This occurs if the person returns directly (without using a different method to find the website).

- **No active campaigns**
  - If you see zero sessions and zero clicks then this can mean that your accounts are linked but there are no Google AdWords campaigns running.

- **Invalid clicks**
  - If you have received invalid clicks from your Google AdWords campaigns, for example, if malicious software was used to repeatedly click on your ads, then these clicks will be automatically filtered from your Google AdWords campaign data. However, you can still see sessions reported inside your reports if the tracking code fires and sends data to Google Analytics.

- **Redirects**
  - Redirects that have been set up for your website can cause inaccurate data in your reports. When people click on your ad there is a special query parameter added to the end of your destination URL, if this parameter is stripped off by the redirect then Google Analytics is unable to match the session to the initial click on your ad. For technical details on checking redirects visit http://lovesdata.co/q8mfP

You should also keep an eye out for the following scenarios which can cause different data to be displayed inside Google Analytics:

- **Updated campaign names**
  - If you launch a campaign and then change its name while the campaign is running then your reports will automatically update to display the new name.

- **Ended campaigns**
  - Once a campaign has ended you might still see some traffic coming from the campaign inside your reports. This occurs when people return to your website without using another method to find your website. For example, if someone clicks on your ad, then bookmarks your website and returns using the bookmark in seven days, then this returning session will be credited to the Google AdWords campaign.

Google Analytics Data in Google AdWords

Once you have linked your accounts you can even configure Google AdWords to display top-level Google Analytics data from within Google AdWords. This allows you to see the bounce rate, average session duration and average pages per visit for your campaigns and ad groups, right down to individual keywords and ad variations. These top-level engagement metrics allow you to quickly establish the overall health of your Google AdWords campaigns.

For example, if you are driving people to a landing page with a contact form, then seeing a high bounce rate indicates that a large portion of people are leaving the website and not navigating to another page or completing the form to view the thank you page. From here you can check the content of the landing page against the keywords you are targeting in Google AdWords to see if there is a disconnect between what people are searching for and what is on the landing page.

Steps:

1. In Google AdWords, navigate to 'Linked Accounts' under the 'My Account' tab.

2. Select 'Google Analytics' under 'Linked Accounts' (or click 'View Details' under Google Analytics).

   a. You will now see the Google Analytics account that has previously been linked to the Google AdWords account.

3. Click on the name of the Google Analytics account you would like to link.

4. Now click on the name of the appropriate Google Analytics property.

   a. Generally a Google Analytics property is used to track an individual website. If you see multiple properties it means that different websites are being tracked in the Google Analytics account.

5. Click 'Add' for the appropriate profile you would like to link.

   a. If there are multiple profiles available, it is best to link the primary profile (the one you use on a regular basis for reporting and analysis) to Google AdWords.

Google Search Console (Webmaster Tools) Data within Google AdWords

Did you know? Google Search Console was previously called Google Webmaster Tools. Google is still updating the name within their products (including Google AdWords and Google Analytics), so you are likely to see reference to Google Webmaster Tools.

Google Search Console gives you access to data for your website's performance in the organic (free) search results. Once you have set up Google Search Console, you can link your account with Google AdWords to compare the performance of your paid ads against your organic listings in Google search results. You use this to see the effectiveness when only your ads show, when you are only in organic results and when you are in both.

In this example, when paid ads are displayed at the same time as organic listings for the keyword 'running shoes' there is an overall improvement in the 'Clicks/Queries' ratio. In other words, people are more likely to click through to the website when there is a combination of paid and organic listings.

Query	Ad stats					Organic stats					Combined ad and organic stats		
	Clicks	Impr.	CTR	Avg. CPC	Avg. Pos	Clicks	Queries	Clicks/query	Listings/query	Avg. Pos	Clicks	Queries	Clicks/query
running shoes	328	1,977	16.59%	$1.84	1.0	52,425	105,834	0.5	8.6	1.9	52,753	105,843	0.5
Ad shown only	0	9	0.00%	$0.00	1.1	0	0	0.0	0.0	0.0	0	9	0.0
Organic shown only	0	0	0.00%	$0.00	0.0	51,587	103,866	0.5	8.6	1.9	51,587	103,866	0.5
Both shown	328	1,968	16.67%	$1.84	1.0	838	1,968	0.4	8.9	1.0	1,166	1,968	0.6
gym shoes	126	3,947	3.19%	$3.00	1.0	49,593	234,468	0.2	3.6	1.5	49,719	234,486	0.2
Ad shown only	0	18	0.00%	$0.00	1.0	0	0	0.0	0.0	0.0	0	18	0.0
Organic shown only	0	0	0.00%	$0.00	0.0	48,716	230,539	0.2	3.6	1.5	48,716	230,539	0.2
Both shown	126	3,929	3.21%	$3.00	1.0	877	3,929	0.2	4.2	1.0	1,003	3,929	0.3
sport shoes	26	203	12.81%	$2.55	1.0	6,280	13,836	0.5	7.8	1.8	6,306	13,844	0.5
Ad shown only	1	8	12.50%	$3.16	1.0	0	0	0.0	0.0	0.0	1	8	0.1
Organic shown only	0	0	0.00%	$0.00	0.0	6,194	13,641	0.5	7.8	1.8	6,194	13,641	0.5
Both shown	25	195	12.82%	$2.52	1.0	86	195	0.4	7.6	1.6	111	195	0.6

Clicks/Queries is a bit like CTR, but the closer the number is to one, the better the performance in getting people to click through to the website. A clicks to queries ratio of 0.1 means that approximately 10% of people click through to your website, while a ratio of 0.9 means that approximately 90% of people are clicking through.

Tip: Visit http://lovesdata.co/Vudwt for more details on Google Search Console and how to set up your account. You can also read about the Google Search Console reports that are available within Google Analytics in the "Search Engine Optimization" section in Chapter 17.

After you have created your Google Search Console account, open up your Google AdWords account, click the configuration icon and select 'Account Settings'. Now click on 'Linked Accounts' in the left column and select 'Webmaster Tools'. If the email address you use to log into Google AdWords has access to Google Search Console, then you can search for the URL of the website and click 'Continue'. If you have access, then the accounts will be linked. If you don't have access then you will be prompted to claim the website within Google Search Console.

Once your accounts are linked you will be able to find your organic and paid search results data by navigating to 'Campaigns' and selecting the 'Dimensions' tab. Then click on 'View' and select 'Paid and Organic'. You will see search queries listed down on the left hand column and then a breakdown for when you have only had ads displayed, only organic listings and a combination of both.

Tip: Use the columns on the right under 'Combined ad and organic stats' to view all of the data together. Alternatively, click on 'Columns' and ' Modify Columns' to limit down the amount of data you see in the report.

You can compare the performance of your paid and organic traffic to identify areas that could be improved. Start by looking for keywords where you are getting organic traffic, but where you are not currently targeting with ads. To save yourself from having to scan through all the rows, you can select 'Filter' and then click 'Create Filter'. Now select 'Ad Clicks' under the 'Performance' option, choose '=', enter zero '0' in the field and click 'Apply'. You will now have a list of keywords where you are displaying in the organic results but are not running ads.

Look for keywords that align with your advertising goals and that also have a higher average position. These are keywords that could potentially provide increased traffic and improved results if you include them in your campaigns.

You can then repeat this process, but this time for keywords where you are not receiving any clicks on organic results. To do this change your filter so that 'Organic Clicks' (which is also available under 'Performance') equals zero '0'. Use this to identify keywords to include in your organic optimization strategy. You can use this as a starting point for creating new website content and new blog posts to help improve your organic ranking for the keyword. You might see some general keywords in this report, so start by focusing on more specific keywords where you are more likely to see improvement, since generic keywords can be difficult to optimize for in organic search results.

The report can show you if you have an organic result with a higher average ad position than your ads. You can use this as a starting point to test different bids, to see if you can maintain traffic while lowering your maximum bid amounts.

Finally, you can see the combined effectiveness when you are visible in the organic results and when your ads are displayed. You can use the clicks to query ratio to see if performance is improved when you have both ads and organic results displayed to people searching. The closer the ratio is to one, the better the performance. When your ads are displayed along with an organic listing, you have a higher likelihood of people clicking through to your website:

Query	Ad stats					Organic stats					Combined ad and organic stats		
	Clicks	Impr.	CTR	Avg. CPC	Avg. Pos	Clicks	Queries	Clicks/query	Listings/query	Avg. Pos	Clicks	Queries	Clicks/query
chcolate gift basket delivery	22	499	4.41%	$13.75	2.4	221	841	0.3	1.0	1.1	243	939	0.3
Ad shown only	7	98	7.14%	$15.91	2.0	0	0	0.0	0.0	0.0	7	98	0.1
Organic shown only	0	0	0.00%	$0.00	0.0	80	440	0.2	1.0	1.2	80	440	0.2
Both shown	15	401	3.74%	$12.74	2.5	141	401	0.4	1.0	1.0	156	401	0.4

If you notice that the overall ratio is lower when ads are combined with your organic listing then this can indicate a disconnect between the keyword, the text in your listing and your landing page. If you notice that the clicks to query ratio is being lowered by your ads, then this means you should review your ad copy and landing page for the particular keyword and see if improvements can be made.

Tip: To focus on keywords where you are visible in both the paid and organic results create a filter where 'Organic Clicks' are '>=' (greater than or equal) to '0' and 'Ad Clicks' are '>=' to '0'.

Conversion Tracking

You can measure different actions as conversions into Google AdWords, in the majority of cases a conversion is someone viewing the thank you page on your website, but you can also measure apps downloads, calls and even offline conversions. We'll now look at how to measure website conversions and at the additional conversions options available.

Website Conversions

When it comes to measuring conversions occurring on your website, there are two options. You can set up Google AdWords conversion tracking or you can import a goal that has already been set up inside your Google Analytics account. If you already have Google Analytics on your website, then this is typically the easiest way to get conversion data into Google AdWords. The steps for using Google Analytics goals are:

1. Ensure you have the Google Analytics tracking code installed on all the pages of your website and link your Google AdWords account to Google Analytics.

2. Set up your goal inside Google Analytics and check that it is reporting the correct number of conversions.

3. Inside Google AdWords, navigate to 'Conversions' under 'Tools' in the main navigation.

4. Click 'Import from Google Analytics' and select the goal (or goals) you would like to use.

5. Rename them if you like and click 'Import'.

After you have imported a goal into Google AdWords, you will begin to see data. This will only include goal conversions that were the result of a click on one of your ads. If no one has converted from your campaigns, then no conversions will show inside Google AdWords.

Alternatively, you can use Google AdWords conversion tracking – this requires you to add a piece of additional tracking code to your 'thank you' page. The main differences when using this option are:

- Requires additional tracking code that is placed on each thank you page (and no other pages of your website).

- If you want to pass a conversion value it needs to be passed in the tracking code. You can also pass a dynamic (changing) value if you work with your web developer.

- Includes JavaScript and non-JavaScript tracking, so this can potentially be slightly more accurate (since Google Analytics only uses JavaScript, if somebody has JavaScript disabled the conversion will not be reported).

- Count every conversion or just count a conversion once (Google Analytics will only count a conversion for a particular goal once, even if they convert multiple times in a single session on your website).

- Choose a 'Conversion Window' to choose how long you will count a conversion. For example, if you select 30 days, then all conversions that occur within 30 days of someone clicking your ad will be counted.

To set up Google AdWords conversion tracking, navigate to 'Conversions' under 'Tools' and click 'Add Conversion'. Click 'Select' under 'Website'. You can now name your conversion and there are options for assigning a value to each conversion, if you want to count all conversions, the conversion window, assigning a category for the conversion and if you want the conversion to be used for bid optimization.

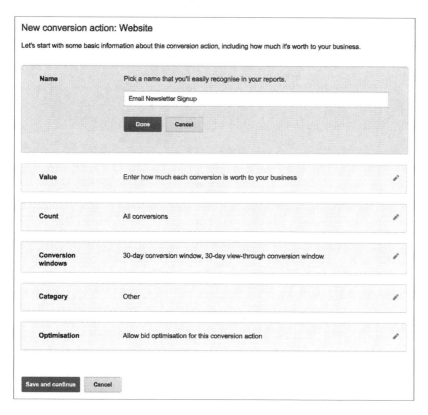

Now you can either email the tracking code to your web developer, or view the code yourself to add to the thank you page on your website.

> **Tip:** After you have either imported goals from Google Analytics or set up Google AdWords conversion tracking, you will begin to see data in the 'Conversions' section of Google AdWords. You can add this into your reports under 'Campaigns' by clicking on 'Columns' and then ' Modify Columns'. You will find the available conversion metrics in the 'Conversions' section.

When using conversion data inside Google AdWords, remember that credit for the conversion is always given to Google AdWords. This means if other methods were used to find your website along with your campaigns, the campaigns will be seen as getting the credit. If you want to see the other methods people are using to find your website, then you can use the Multi-Channel Funnels reports in Google Analytics.

App Conversions

If you are using Google AdWords to promote your app you can set up conversion tracking to measure the number of installs of your Android and iOS apps.

After selecting the app conversion. You will need to select the type of action you want to track (either people downloading your app or interacting with your app) and select 'Android' or 'iOS' as the platform.

> **Tip:** Visit http://lovesdata.co/fV9HI for technical details on tracking app installations as conversions.

Call Conversions

There are three ways you can measure calls as conversions inside Google AdWords. The first option is to measure calls from people who view your ad if you have a call extension set up that uses Google's call forwarding feature. You can set up a call extension under the 'Ad Extensions' tab after you have selected a particular campaign. The easiest way to do this is to select 'Google Forwarding Phone Number' when creating your call extension.

By default, this will create a new conversion for calls you receive and if you like you can edit the settings in the 'Conversions' area.

> **Tip:** For details on setting up call extensions read the "Ad Extensions" section in Chapter 9.

The second option you have is similar to call extension tracking, but where you also place special code on your website to display Google's call forwarding phone numbers if someone clicks through to your website from one of your ads. This is called *website call conversions.*

To measure calls from your website that have come from your Google AdWords campaigns, you will need to add additional tracking code to all the pages of your website and also modify how your phone numbers are placed on your website. Select 'Calls to a Google forwarding number on your website' when you create the conversion to set up this option. You can then configure the conversion and you will be given special code to add into the head tags of your website.

> **Tip:** Visit http://lovesdata.co/HVwap for technical details on setting up website call conversions.

The final option for measuring calls is if you have a mobile version of your website. In this case, you can use the 'Clicks on a number on your mobile website'. This allows you to wrap some extra code around the phone number you display on your mobile website, so that when people click the number on their phone it will be measured as a conversion.

Offline Conversions

You can measure conversions that happen offline by importing your offline conversion data into Google AdWords. For this to work, you need a method for collecting the 'GCLID' which is a parameter that is available when you use Google AdWords auto-tagging (which you should be using, as it is also the best way to get data into Google Analytics). If you have an ad with a destination URL of 'http://www.company.com/landing.html', when someone clicks through to your website they are taken to that page, but Google AdWords adds the GCLID as a query parameter. This means they are actually taken to 'http://www.company.com/landing.html?GCLID=87654321' and you can modify your website to capture the value of the GCLID and reuse it.

In the scenario of a car dealership with the objective of getting people to test drive cars, ads are used to direct people to the website where there is a form they can fill out to book a test drive. The website can be modified to capture the GCLID when they first land on the website and then when they complete the test drive booking form and the value of the GCLID parameter is sent as a hidden field in the form.

Then when someone comes to the showroom and completes the test drive, a note is added saying they have driven the car and converted. Then, the test drive booking form is reviewed to find the GCLID and the conversion details are uploaded back into Google AdWords. They will now be able to see offline conversions and see conversions against individual campaigns, ad groups, ads and keywords.

> **Tip:** Visit http://lovesdata.co/bafxq for technical details on setting up offline conversions and using the import option.

> **Tip:** Some of these additional types of conversion can be configured inside Google Analytics. These include app conversions and offline conversions. This gives you the flexibility to set up these conversions inside Google Analytics and then import them into Google AdWords.

12

Optimization Techniques

Optimization is the process of making changes to improve performance of your campaigns. This can include a range of techniques, depending on the campaign objectives. In most cases you will want to balance the optimization techniques you use. For example, if you are trying to drive conversions, then you will need to balance increasing conversions with maintaining or increasing visibility with your target audience.

The amount of time you need to optimize your campaigns will depend on the size of your account and how well organized your ad groups are currently. If you are taking over the management of a large account that isn't very well structured, then optimization is going to take some time. Each improvement you make will have an impact, but you might need to schedule what you are going to do over the course of several weeks or even months.

A range of options have been covered that can improve the performance of campaigns, including structuring ad groups, refining keywords and writing targeted ads. Here is a summary of techniques that have been covered:

- **Use a well-defined account structure** and ensure that keywords are tightly themed into appropriate ad groups.

- **Select the right keywords** and if you are starting out, remember to avoid very general or broad keywords.

- **Add negative keywords** to improve the relevancy of your campaigns and ensure your budget is being spent on the best possible keywords.

- **Use the search query report** to identify additional keywords to target as well as potential negative keywords.

- **Use appropriate keyword match types** depending on your objectives. Use exact or phrase to be more precise, and broad match and broad match modifier to increase the reach of your ads.

- **Choose network targeting** so that each of your campaigns targets either the search or the display network and not both. This will help you allocate budget and have a more defined structure in your account.

- **Review display network targeting options** and the performance of your different targeting methods. For example, review automatic placements to identify good quality placements for manual bids, and lower quality placements for reduced bids or exclusions.

- **Review geographic targeting** to ensure it is appropriate for your target audience. A more defined target will typically produce better results.

- **Check device bid adjustments** and review performance to tweak bid adjustment amounts. For example, if mobile users are performing better than non-mobile users, then consider increasing your bid adjustment.

- **Use ad scheduling** to display your ads at the best times during the day and week. Consider modifying your bid at particular times and on particular days if performance is better (or worse) than expected.

- **Create ad extensions** to differentiate your ads from the competition and to highlight unique aspects of your offering. Adding appropriate ad extensions can also help improve your Ad Rank.

Optimization of your campaigns is an ongoing process. The cycle you use for optimization will depend on how much time you can allocate and the size of your account. Typically you will want to be performing some of these optimization techniques on a monthly basis. If you are just getting started, then you should at least consider optimizing every two months.

You don't need to perform all of these techniques every month, but you should regularly review your account structure, keywords and ads to improve performance. You can then add additional tasks on a less regular basis. For example, you probably don't need to review your ad scheduling or geographic targeting every month. These are things you could check every three or four months. Below are additional optimization techniques to further improve campaign performance.

Quality Score

Quality Score reflects how relevant your ad variations, keywords and landing pages are to someone who sees your ad. Quality Score determines where your ad will show (position), affects how much you pay for clicks, and if your ad will even show at all.

Google AdWords uses a number of factors to determine your Quality Score.[1] They include:

- Expected CTR for your ad
- Past CTR of your display URL
- Landing page quality
- Relevance of your keywords to your ad variations
- Relevance of your keywords to what people actually search
- Geographic performance
- Performance on particular sites on the Google Display Network

Don't worry too much if you currently have a low Quality Score, by properly managing your campaigns you can quickly improve Quality Score.

Tip: Deleting your account and starting from scratch will not improve your Quality Score because Quality Score is actually tied to your website's domain name.

Improving Quality Score

Quality Score impacts what you pay for clicks on your keywords. By improving your Quality Score, your ads are going to be more likely to display at the top of search results and it is possible to achieve higher rankings in the paid results, without necessarily having to increase your bids.

---

1   http://support.google.com/adwords/bin/answer.py?hl=en&answer=2454010

> **Tip:** You can view the Quality Score for your keywords in search campaigns by selecting the 'Keywords' tab and hovering over the speech bubble icon in the 'Status' column. You can also click on 'Columns' and ' Modify Columns' and then add 'Quality Score' from within 'Attributes'. This will allow you to see the Quality Score for all of your keywords in a dedicated column.

You can start to improve your Quality Score by optimizing the relationship between keywords, ad variations and landing pages in your account. The best way to optimize the relationship between the keyword and the ad variation is by structuring your campaigns and ad groups. Ideally, you only have 5 to 10 closely related keywords in each ad group.

For example, you might have one campaign and one ad group with the following keywords:

>chocolate gift baskets
>chocolate hampers
>chocolate boxes

These keywords could be structured into three separate ad groups:

- **Gift Baskets**
  - chocolate gift baskets
- **Hampers**
  - chocolate hampers
- **Boxes**
  - chocolate boxes

By structuring your ad groups and by only having closely related keywords in each ad group you create ad variations that are highly targeted for each ad group. This will mean that your ad variations can be more relevant to your keywords.

You can further optimize your ads by running at least two ad variations in each ad group. This is covered in the "Best Practices for Search Campaigns" section in Chapter 7.

Your landing page (destination URL) should also relate to your ad variations and keywords. This means that your landing page should contain content that specifically relates to your keywords and ad variations. This will not only improve your Quality Score, but it will also mean that you will receive better results from your campaigns because people land directly on a page that relates to what they were originally searching for on Google.

Google outlines the following items it considers on your landing page when determining Quality Score: relevant and original content, transparency, and ease of navigation[2]. This might sound scary, but really Google just wants to ensure that advertisers send people to a real website and are not trying to mislead people.

---

2   http://support.google.com/adwords/bin/answer.py?hl=en&answer=2404197

- Ensure your content is unique, or in other words you have developed the content of your website yourself and haven't copied it from another website.

- Make sure your contact details or a way to contact you is clearly visible on the landing page. This also helps people to build trust with your brand.

- You can also include a link to your privacy policy to further enhance the transparency of your landing pages.

Tip: If you are targeting mobile users then you should develop either mobile optimized landing pages or a mobile optimized website. This will improve your Quality Score and also improve the results of your mobile campaign. Remember that people using mobile devices generally spend less time on individual websites, so write concise, targeted content and also consider simplifying the conversion process for mobile users.

Here is a checklist to help improve your Quality Score:

- **Review your keywords** to ensure you are including the best possible keywords and look for very general keywords that might not be appropriate for your ad groups.

- **Check the structure of your ad groups** on a regular basis and continually work towards small and highly targeted groups of keywords in each ad group.

- **Add negative keywords** to help improve the relevancy of your ads and your CTR by reducing the number of times your ads are displayed for irrelevant terms.

- **Write compelling ads** for each ad group that closely relate to the keywords you are targeting. Ideally, the ads should contain the keyword that is included in the ad group.

- **Continually test your ads** in each ad group. You should always have at least two ads that you are A/B testing to improve your CTR. Try testing an ad with dynamic keyword insertion – in some cases it might help improve your CTR.

- **Review your landing pages** and ensure they relate to your ads and the keywords in the ad group. If they don't closely relate, then you should consider creating appropriate landing pages. You can even test different versions of your landing page to improve your conversion rate.

- **Check your landing pages are mobile friendly**, if your ads are being displayed to people using mobile devices (you will be by default). Quality score is calculated separately for mobile users, but if your landing pages are not mobile friendly it will have an impact.

- **Review your display campaigns** in the same way you review your search campaigns. Quality Score is calculated separately for display, but use the same tactics to improve it.

Tip: Google has published a guide on understanding Quality Score. You can download the PDF at http://lovesdata.co/CgOqU

A/B testing

Google AdWords allows you to test different elements of your ad variations to see if particular changes lead to better results, including clicks and conversions.

Ensure you have at least two ad variations in each of your ad groups, this is known as A/B testing. When you are starting out, begin by creating two completely different ad variations with different calls to action. By testing dramatically different ad variations you will see more noticeable results.

For example, if your original ad variation is:

Chocolate Gift Baskets
www.baskets.com
Buy High Quality Chocolate Gift
Baskets. Order Now!

Test a completely different ad variation, like:

Need Chocolate Gift?
www.baskets.com/Chocolate
Fast Delivery For Chocolate
Gift Baskets. Huge Selection.

Tip: Remember to include the keyword in both ad variations. Your ads still need to relate to the keywords you are targeting.

Once you have two ad variations running in each of your ad groups, you can monitor which ad is performing better than the other in Google AdWords. You will need to wait until both ads have enough clicks for reliable data. Then look at the CTR of each ad – the ad with the higher CTR is likely to be the more engaging ad in relation to the keywords in the ad group.

For example, if your first ad has a CTR of 1.50% and your second ad has a CTR of 3%, then the second ad is the better ad based on CTR. Once you have determined the ad with the higher CTR you can pause the under performing ad and develop a new ad to try and further improve the CTR.

Following the first test where major changes were tested, you can use follow up tests to make smaller changes to refine your ad further. Try testing individual elements of your ad variation to establish which elements and particular calls to action are impacting your CTR.

For example, if your winning ad variation from the first test is:

Need Chocolate Gift?
www.baskets.com/Chocolate
Fast Delivery For Chocolate
Gift Baskets. Huge Selection.

You might develop the following ad variation that only tests the headline:

Great Chocolate Gifts
www.baskets.com/Chocolate
Fast Delivery For Chocolate
Gift Baskets. Huge Selection.

Wait until each ad variation has at least 100 clicks and then repeat the process of developing new ad variations to continue the process. You are now A/B testing your ads.

Ideas for A/B testing include:

- Different call to action
- Capitalization (including title case and sentence case)
- Including geographic terms
- Dynamic Keyword Insertion (DKI)
- Changing punctuation
- Asking questions
- Different display URL
- Including prices
- Including special offers

Tip: If you want to be more accurate with your A/B testing you can use a split test calculator to check the statistical significance (accuracy) of your test. You can find a calculator at http://lovesdata.co/C68VJ where you can enter the number of impressions and clicks for each ad variation to compare their performance.

You can also improve your ads based on conversion rate if you have conversions set up inside Google AdWords. You should still consider CTR because it does impact your Quality Score, but optimizing your ads based on conversions is another great way to improve the results of your campaigns.

Geographic Performance

Reviewing the geographic performance of your campaigns can inform your strategy for applying location bid adjustments. Start by checking if you already have any bid adjustments applied by choosing a campaign and selecting 'Settings' and then 'Locations'. Here, you can see that no bid adjustments have been applied to the campaign:

In this case, select the 'Dimensions' tab and then click on 'View' and select 'User Locations'. This will show you the geographic performance of your campaigns based on the location of people viewing your ads. By default, the report will include very specific geographic information. To make the report easier to read click on 'Columns' and then ' Modify columns' and only include 'Region' and 'Town/City/Suburb' (removing 'Metro Area' and 'Most Specific Location').

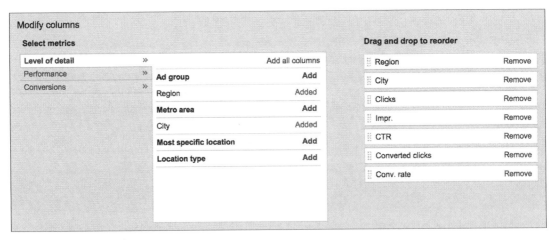

Now the report should be easier to read and you can see the performance of your campaign based on the location of your audience. From here you can identify which audience segments are more likely to click and convert. You can then use this to inform your bid adjustment. For example, if Melbourne users are twice as likely to convert, then you could consider increasing your bid for people located in that geographic area.

To modify your location bid adjustment head back to 'Locations' under the 'Settings' tab.

Tip: You can use Google Analytics to identify new markets for your products and services by using the geographic reports and including your conversion data to identify areas that have strong conversions where you are not currently displaying your ads.

Ad Position

Google says that "conversion rates don't vary much with ad position"[3], which makes sense since the likelihood of somebody converting after they click your ad is much more likely to be impacted by the content of your landing page and its relation to the your ad and their search query. However, the position of your ad will impact the number of clicks you are likely to receive. This is because people are more likely to click the top results, than the lower search results or the ads in the right hand column.

Since the position of your ad in the paid search results is determined by your Ad Rank you can use one or more of the following techniques to increase your position:

- Increase your maximum bid amount
- Improve your Quality Score
- Create appropriate ad extensions

Tip: You can use the Keyword Positions report in Google Analytics to understand performance based on the position of your ads. Read about Google AdWords reporting in Chapter 17.

If you want to increase the visibility of your ads by increasing your bid, then you can use experiments in Google AdWords. This will allow you to understand the impact of your new bid amounts on your ad position before applying the bid for your entire audience. Read the "Google AdWords Experiments" section in Chapter 9 for details.

Customer Lifetime Value

Using customer lifetime value (CLV) provides you with a better understanding of the true value of your conversions. The idea is to focus on the longer-term value of a customer, instead of just looking at the short term. If you sell products online, then customer lifetime value would take into account the likelihood of somebody coming back and becoming a repeat buyer. If you are offering services, it might be the length of time that somebody is a customer and the value you receive from the customer over the course of their subscription or fees they pay you.

---

3   http://adwords.blogspot.com.au/2009/08/conversion-rates-dont-vary-much-with-ad.html

Looking beyond the initial conversion can help you understand the true value of a lead or sale and inform your advertising and bidding strategies. For example, if an initial lead is worth $50.00 on average, but you have a high portion of repeat customers, your initial lead could be worth much more to your organization over the longer term. By moving to customer lifetime value you will have a better understanding of the true value of your campaigns for your business. This allows you to adjust your budgeting and bidding strategies to take this value into account. Typically this will mean focusing on you cost-per-acquisition (CPA) when bidding.

In order to calculate your CLV you will need the following details:

- Average cost-per-click (CPC)
- Conversion rate
- Average time that someone remains a customer
- Value of their purchases

- Profit margin

Once you have these details there is a handy tool which allows you to calculate your CLV, along with how much you are spending on each new client (CPA) and the profit you are generating from each customer. You can find the tool at http://lovesdata.co/5bQZm

Review Opportunities

Google provides automated suggestions based on the recent performance of your campaigns. You can find all of these suggestions under 'Opportunities' in the main navigation. You will find suggestions that relate to changing bids, budgets and adding additional keywords to your account.

You should review each suggestion before adding them to your campaigns. As they are automated suggestions, some are going to be good recommendations and some are going to be less than perfect, so take your time.

By default you will see recommendations for all of your campaigns, but you can use the drop-down option to select individual campaigns.

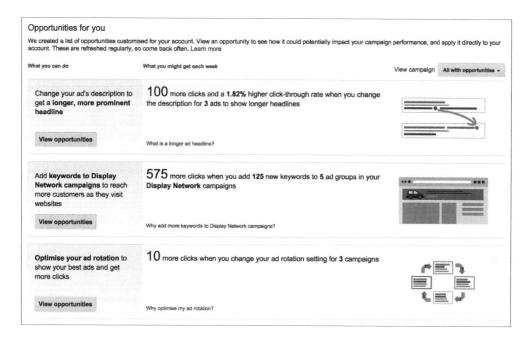

When reviewing keywords, use the same techniques you would use when researching keywords to establish the suitability and value of the suggestions. When reviewing budget and bid suggestions it can be helpful to note down the change and head back to the 'Campaigns' tab to review the performance of the campaign in more detail, including the conversion rate.

You might see the following suggestion:

Raise budget for **Free Delivery** campaign from $16.00 to **$48.00**	**250** more clicks and **110,000** more impressions at a lower cost-per-click.

Clicking on 'View' will show you that changing the daily budget to $48.00 will potentially provide an additional 250 clicks for an additional cost of $220 per week. Now head to 'Campaigns' in the main navigation and find the campaign. By looking at the historical conversion rate (by adding the 'Click Conversion Rate' column) you can estimate the number of additional conversions you might receive from the additional clicks.

For example, if you see the conversion rate is 4.5%, then from the additional 250 clicks per week you could potentially receive 11 additional conversions. This can be used by taking into account your campaign objectives to determine if you should increase the budget by the amount suggested.

Allocating Budget

Using your campaign structure along with your daily budget allocations can be a powerful way to optimize your campaigns based on conversions and ROI. For example, if you have a single campaign with a daily budget of $100 with the following ad groups and keywords:

Campaign: Delivery	
Daily Budget: $100	
Ad Group: Fruit and Vegetables	**Ad Group:** Meals
fruit delivery fruit and vegetable delivery vegetable delivery service vegetable delivery	meals delivered frozen meals delivered meals delivered to home premade meal delivery

You'll notice that the 'Fruit and Vegetables' ad group has a higher conversion rate than the 'Meals' ad group after the ads have been running for two weeks.

Ad Group: Fruit and Vegetables	**Ad Group:** Meals
Cost: $700	**Cost:** $700
Conversion Rate: 10%	**Conversion Rate:** 5%
Total Conversions: 89	**Total Conversions:** 36

Since your budget is evenly split between the two campaigns it means that the overall conversion rate for the campaign is 7.5% with a total number of conversion at 125.

Now let's look at what would happen if you were to split the campaign into two separate campaigns and allocate 80% of the budget to the 'Fruit and Vegetable' keywords:

Campaign: Fruit and Vegetables	Campaign: Meals
Daily Budget: $80.00	Daily Budget: $20.00
Ad Group: Fruit and Vegetables	Ad Group: Meals
fruit delivery fruit and vegetable delivery vegetable delivery service vegetable delivery	meals delivered frozen meals delivered meals delivered to home premade meal delivery
Cost: $1,120	Cost: $280
Conversion Rate: 10%	Conversion Rate: 5%
Total Conversions: 142	Total Conversions: 14

Assuming that the conversion rate and bids are maintained, then by reallocating your budget you could potentially receive a total of 156 conversions, which is almost a 25% increase compared to the original campaign structure. By allocating budget based on performance you are able to drive more conversions without having to increase your overall budget.

Google Analytics

Google Analytics allows you to understand how people interact with websites and mobile apps in order to improve performance. The way you use Google Analytics will depend on your particular objectives. If you are in marketing, you will be likely to focus on reports that help you understand the performance of your campaigns and to make decisions on how your resources are best applied. If you are focused on content and usability you will want to know what content is popular, how people navigate through your website and how you can improve the experience.

If you are focused on the technical performance of your website or mobile app, you can use Google Analytics to understand which devices people use and also monitor the technical performance of websites and mobile apps. If you are focused on interface and design, you will come at Google Analytics from a different angle and look at how people interact and engage with your website.

The key is to use and shape Google Analytics to meet your particular needs. It is easy to get caught up trying to understand what every single report or every single piece of data tells you, but to be productive with Google Analytics you need to instead focus on a handful of reports that help you drive improvement in your role.

Google Analytics includes over 90 standard reports allowing you to view top-level and granular detail about who is visiting your website, how they are getting there, what they are doing and whether they are converting. We will look at the reports that are available and how they can be used to make positive changes, how to customize Google Analytics, including how to create custom reports, segment your audience and tweak your implementation so you can measure exactly what you need for your organization.

13

How Google Analytics Works

Google Analytics allows you to measure how people interact with your website, mobile app and other platforms. The Google Analytics tracking code is used to understand people's behavior as they engage with your website. Mobile apps can be measured using the mobile SDKs (Software Development Kits) for iOS and Android devices. The Measurement Protocol allows you to measure interactions on other platforms.

Did you know? The Measurement Protocol allows you to feed data directly into Google Analytics without the need to use the tracking code or mobile SDKs. It opens up the opportunity to measure just about anything. For example, it can be use to measure in-store purchases, apps on gaming consoles and offline interactions. Visit http://lovesdata.co/lu2CE to watch a short video showing some of the possibilities.

Since Google Analytics is mostly used to measure websites, we will focus on the Google Analytics tracking code and how this works to report on website behavior. However, the core concepts we look at in this book apply to any interaction you are measuring – on mobile devices, a gaming console, a website or any other platform.

When somebody navigates to your website, the Google Analytics tracking code loads. This tracking code does not make any visible changes to your website, it is a small piece of JavaScript that is placed in the code of all the pages of your website.

The tracking code checks to see if there is any existing information (from previously accessing the website). This existing information is stored in cookies. Cookies are a way to store information and these cookies are kept in people's web browsers. If there is existing information stored in a cookie, then the cookie is updated. If there is no cookie, then a new cookie is created in the web browser.

The tracking code then sends information to the Google Analytics servers. This information includes details about how the person found your website, what page they are looking at and if they have previously been to your website.

Google's servers then process all the information sent by the Google Analytics tracking code into a database (taking into account any configurations that have been made). When you log into Google Analytics and view a report you are simply querying the database, this is then generating the report in the Google Analytics interface.

It's important to understand that the data that you see in your reports is the data that has been collected and processed into the database. This means if something went wrong, for example, if you forgot to install the tracking code on your website, then this will mean the data is not in the database and therefore not available in your reports. It's important to note that once data is in (or not in) the database, there is no going back. You can't change historical data or have historical data reprocessed if something went wrong. This is why having Google Analytics correctly set up and collecting data is critical.

There are also ways to get additional data into Google Analytics for deeper insights about how people interact with your website. In most cases this means getting extra data into your reports. There is no rush to collect custom data into Google Analytics, the main thing is to understand the possibilities so when the need arises you know what to do. The best way to think about this is that Google Analytics automatically gives you rich insights, but you can then build on this when needed.

Terminology

Session

A session is recorded when someone interacts with your website. In most cases this is when people view the content pages on your website. For example, if someone comes to your homepage views your 'about' page and then your 'contact' page, one session will be reported by Google Analytics because they are interacting with the pages on your website.

In Google Analytics you will see a total number of sessions. This is the total number of times people have interacted with your website within the particular date range you are viewing.

Sessions and Time

Time plays a role in how sessions are calculated, so if somebody stops navigating your website for over 30 minutes and then navigates to view another page on your website, then a new session will be reported by Google Analytics.

For example, if somebody views three pages on your website, then goes for a 45-minute lunch break and then navigates another two pages on your website, you will see two sessions in Google Analytics. This is because the period of inactivity (for lunch) is greater than 30 minutes.

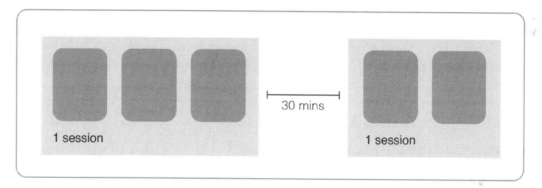

Let's look at another scenario: someone views two pages on your website, then goes for a five minute coffee break and then navigates to view a further three pages on your website. In this example there will only be one session reported in Google Analytics because the period of inactivity was less than 30 minutes (the coffee break was only five minutes).

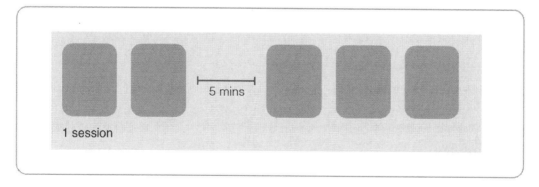

Users

The number of users you see in your reports give you a more accurate reflection of the number of individuals accessing your website. If someone comes to your website on Monday, Tuesday and Wednesday you will see three sessions performed by one user in your reports.

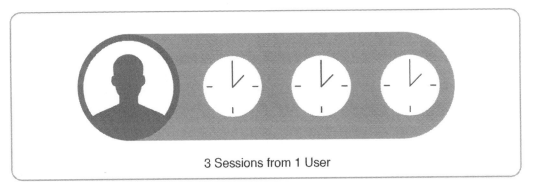

3 Sessions from 1 User

However, users are based on cookies, so remember that people might use multiple devices to access your website. In the case that somebody used their laptop and then their phone to access your website, you will see two users in your reports because each device has its own set of cookies.

Impacts on Users and Sessions

There are some impacts on the data that is collected by Google Analytics that will affect your user and session data. These are not things that you can change, but it is important to be aware of how Google Analytics works when you are reading your reports. Try not to get too hung up about the number of users and sessions that are not reported, instead focus on the improvement you are making as this is something you can measure regardless of whether a portion of people are not being tracked. For example, if you have improved your conversions by 100% compared to the same time period last year, this shows you are improving the performance of your website even if some people are not included in your reports.

Blocked Cookies and Disabled JavaScript

If someone has chosen to block cookies or disable JavaScript on their browser they will not be tracked by Google Analytics. This is likely to be a small percentage of your overall traffic. If people are choosing to block cookies or disable JavaScript, then this can mean that they don't want to be tracked. It can be tempting to focus on ways to improve the accuracy of your data, however if you focus on measuring improvement, then you don't have to worry about being 100% accurate.

Deleted Cookies

If someone deleted the cookies from their browser and then visits your website they will be seen as a new user in your reports. This will be the case even if they have previously been to your website. For example, if someone came to your website on Monday, then deleted their cookies before coming back to your website on Tuesday, you would see two users and two sessions in your reports.

Multiple Devices and Browsers

Each device people use has a different set of cookies, this will mean that you see different users in your reports even if it is actually the same person. For example, if someone views your website on their desktop and then on their tablet, this would result in two users and two sessions appearing in your reports.

> **Tip:** You can implement a cross-device tracking feature called User ID so that when someone logs into your website on their desktop and then on their tablet, just one user with two sessions is reported (with one session on the desktop and one session on the tablet). User ID can also be used to measure people interacting on your mobile app and other platforms, including offline interactions, like people purchasing in a physical store. For more information on User ID visit http://lovesdata.co/8d1Hf

Do Not Track

People can install plugins to opt out of being tracked by Google Analytics and other products. These people will not be counted in your reports.

Did you know? Google provides its own opt-out browser plugin for people who do not want to be tracked. You can learn more about the plugin at http://lovesdata.co/JBr4M

New Users

A person is counted as a new user when they access your website for the first time within the given date range. Let's look at two examples to understand how this works. First, if you select January as the date range and someone who has never been to your website interacts with your website once in the month of January. In this case you will have one session from one user and that session will be from a new user. Second, if someone else comes to your website in January, but this person previously viewed your website in December, you will have one session from one user and it will be a returning user.

Tip: If you have a large portion of new users it means you are good at acquiring new traffic to the website and you should focus on ways to bring people back to the website. This might include having an email newsletter sign-up form on your website and highlighting your social media presence.

Someone is considered a new user when there is no existing Google Analytics cookies in their browser. It is important to understand that the impacts on session and user numbers previously outlined also apply to new users. Actions that impact on new user numbers include people deleting cookies, using multiple devices, using multiple browsers and setting their browser preferences so they are not tracked.

Tip: New sessions are similar to new users. A new session is reported when somebody accesses your website for the first time. For example, if you have selected November the '% New Sessions' will include people who have never previously been to your website (based on the Google Analytics cookie).

Users and Multiple Devices or Browsers

If someone uses multiple devices or multiple browsers to access your website, each method they use to access your website will create a new set of Google Analytics cookies. For example, if someone always views your website on their laptop and then comes to your website on their mobile device for the first time, a new user will be reported for the mobile device, even though they have previously been to your website on their laptop.

New Visitor and Returning Visitor

In a small number of reports, including the Audience Overview and New vs Returning report you will see 'New Visitor' and 'Returning Visitor'. A new visitor is someone who hasn't previously been to your website. While a 'Returning Visitor' is somebody who has already been to your website and is performing a second or subsequent session.

Tip: If you have a large portion of returning visitors it means you are good at bringing people back to the website and you should focus on ways to drive new visitors to the website. This generally means new advertising campaigns to reach people not aware of your brand or even new audiences. It is also a good idea to ensure that you are clearly highlighting your website URL in your existing advertising, marketing and even printed material like business cards and brochures.

Pageview

A pageview is counted each time a page is loaded on your website. For example, if someone goes to your 'homepage', your 'about' page and then your 'contact' page, each page will be reported as receiving one pageview in your Google Analytics reports and the total number of pageviews will be three.

Bounce Rate

Bounce rate is the percentage of sessions where someone only viewed a single page on your website and then left.

For example, if you had four sessions and two of those sessions only contained one pageview, and the other two sessions contained two pageviews, the bounce rate would be 50% because half of the sessions only viewed a single page.

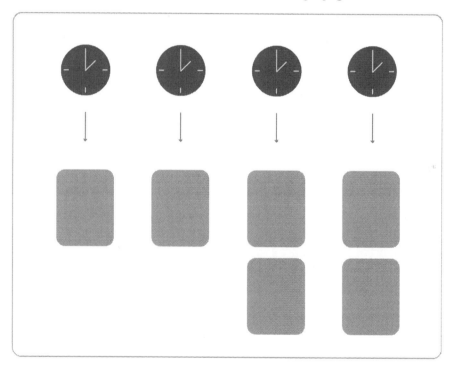

The bounce rate has also been referred to as the percent of people who 'puke'[1] because of the scenario where you go to a website, don't like what you see and puke by leaving the website. This does make sense, for example, if someone performs a search on Google, clicks on a result and the page doesn't contain what they were looking for, they hit the back button – *puke* – and then continue searching.

---

1   http://www.kaushik.net/avinash/standard-metrics-revisited-3-bounce-rate/

However someone puking or bouncing is not necessarily a bad thing. Why? Well, what if they get everything they need on the page they land on. If they found the content they were looking for and then left they still only viewed a single page and they are still considered to have bounced.

Two examples of where people get what they looking for on a single page include:

- **Your contact page** where people were looking for your address or phone number. If they used a search engine, they might have come directly to your contact page, found the appropriate information and then left your website.

- **Your blog** can also have a high bounce rate because people find your blog, read the content and leave. They have found the content they were looking for and you have had someone come to your blog and engage with your content. You might also have long articles on your blog that people take the time to read, but in the end it is still one page, so they are likely to bounce after reading your content.

If you find certain pages that have high bounce rates in your reports, the best thing to do is start by thinking about those pages and if you expect people to find everything they were looking for on those individual pages. If they are finding everything they need on a page, then you don't need to worry too much about the bounce rate. On the other hand, if the page is designed as a navigation page or to get people to another page, then seeing a high bounce rate indicates that you need to re-evaluate the effectiveness of that page and look at the content and navigation options that it contains.

For pages with a high bounce rate you might consider looking at the amount of time people are spending on the page, however there is no time recorded for people who bounce. For more on how time is tracked see 'Average Session Duration' below.

Improving Bounce Rate Accuracy

There are a number of options for improving your reports to better understand if people are actually bouncing without interacting with your website, or if they are engaging in the individual page they are viewing. The best place to start is by tracking interactions that occur in the page. Using Event Tracking you can track people watching video content, downloading files and navigating off your website using outbound links just to name a few options. By default, Event Tracking will also cancel out the bounce if someone engages with one of these elements in a page. This means that your bounce rate now only shows people who land on the page and do not interact further.

Another option is to track engagement based on how long someone has spent on an individual page. For example, you can use Event Tracking to automatically track if someone has spent five minutes on an individual page on your website. This will allow you to understand if people are spending a defined amount of time on a page even if they bounce.

When you set up Event Tracking based on time you have the option to remove the bounce based on the time you have defined, or to continue counting the bounce even after they have spent the defined amount of time on an individual page. If in doubt you might want to go with the latter option to still count the bounce. Otherwise, if you have multiple people using Google Analytics it can cause confusion because by removing the bounce you are changing the definition of the bounce rate and bounces in reports.

Tip: Even if people are viewing another tab, browser window or stepped away from their computer to make a coffee – the event will still be tracked. Just because you see time-based events in Google Analytics it doesn't mean they were actually reading your website content.

Finally, you can set up Google Analytics to track if people scroll on a landing page. If people scroll this indicates that they have engaged with the page and this can be tracked using Event Tracking. This option is the least reliable because there will be cases where people quickly scroll up and down the page that they land on, don't like what they have found and then leave. Depending on how you track scrolling as an interaction you will be removing the bounce even though they didn't really engage with you content.

If you decide to track scrolling then I would suggest you configure Event Tracking so that it doesn't remove the bounce. This will mean that if someone views a single page and scrolls on that page they will be still considered a bounce, but you will be able to then use Event Tracking to compare bounces with and without scroll interaction.

These options give you greater clarity into what is actually happening on your website and if people are engaging with individual pages on your website. For details on setting up measuring scroll depth visit http://lovesdata.co/yrDi1

Average Session Duration

Average session duration allows you to understand how long people spend on your website. The time is reported for each session and shown as an average in reports. For example, if you have just launched a website and it has only been seen by two people, the first person spent one minute on the website and the second person spend two minutes, then the average session duration would be reported as 1.5 minutes.

Average Time on Page

Average time on page is a bit like average session duration, but it only shows you how long people are spending on individual pages. This allows you to compare how engaged people are on the different pages on your website. If Google Analytics sees that two people viewed your homepage and the first person spent 30 seconds on the page and the second viewed the page for one minute, then the average time on page for the homepage would be 45 seconds.

How Time and Duration is Calculated

It is important to know how Google Analytics calculates and reports on time and duration in order to interpret the data you find in your reports. The first thing to understand is that if you are using standard Google Analytics implementation the last page people view during a session doesn't receive any time or duration. This can be confusing at first, so we'll walk through how Google Analytics works.

Someone performs a search on Google and clicks through to the homepage of your website, imagine that a little stopwatch starts as soon as that person loads your page. You have a quick look at the clock as they load your website and it is says zero seconds. The person then navigates to the 'about' page on your website and as soon as the page loads you take a quick look at the current time on the stopwatch. If this person spent 30 seconds on the page – the stopwatch says 30 seconds. Now in order for Google Analytics to understand how long someone spent on the first page they saw, in this case, the homepage, it simply subtracts the first time from the second time (30 seconds – 0 seconds = 30 seconds).

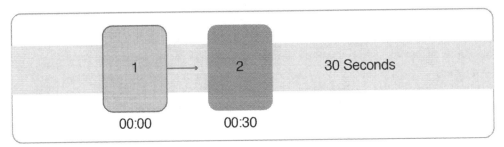

This means that Google Analytics is unable to calculate time for a page if there is no subsequent pageview. For example, if someone only views a single page before leaving your website, then this page will have one pageview reported, but zero seconds for the time spent on the page. The same occurs for the last page somebody views before leaving your website – exit pages will have zero seconds associated with them by default. You can measure interactions within individual pages to understand time spent on exit pages, read "Event Tracking" section in Chapter 28 for details.

Tip: This is a simplified example – Google Analytics actually works by looking at the timestamp associated with each pageview and subtracts the difference in the timestamps to calculate time.

Metrics and Dimensions

When looking at Google Analytics reports you are really looking at pieces of data and information. This data and information can be presented in different ways, typically it will be presented in a table, graph or another type of visualization. For example, you might want to look at the geographic report to understand the location of your website's audience. This shows you where people are located (by country) and how many people view your website from that particular location. These elements form the building blocks of reports. You are seeing metrics and dimensions.

Dimensions are the rows you see inside your reports and are typically pieces of information. In the geographic report the dimensions are the names of the different countries:

Country	Acquisition		
	Sessions ↓	% New Sessions	New Users
	112,198 % of Total: 100.00% (112,198)	82.03% Avg for View: 82.03% (0.00%)	92,035 % of Total: 100.00% (92,035)
1. United States	60,810 (54.20%)	75.68%	46,023 (50.01%)
2. Canada	4,562 (4.07%)	85.69%	3,909 (4.25%)
3. India	3,248 (2.89%)	93.44%	3,035 (3.30%)
4. United Kingdom	3,007 (2.68%)	84.47%	2,540 (2.76%)
5. Germany	2,639 (2.35%)	84.05%	2,218 (2.41%)

Metrics are the columns that are shown along with the dimensions and typically present a number or a calculation, such as a percentage. In the geographic report the first metric shown is the number of sessions and this metric is displayed for each geographic location:

Country	Acquisition		
	Sessions ↓	% New Sessions	New Users
	112,198 % of Total: 100.00% (112,198)	82.03% Avg for View: 82.03% (0.00%)	92,035 % of Total: 100.00% (92,035)
1. United States	60,810 (54.20%)	75.68%	46,023 (50.01%)
2. Canada	4,562 (4.07%)	85.69%	3,909 (4.25%)
3. India	3,248 (2.89%)	93.44%	3,035 (3.30%)
4. United Kingdom	3,007 (2.68%)	84.47%	2,540 (2.76%)
5. Germany	2,639 (2.35%)	84.05%	2,218 (2.41%)

Understanding the difference between a metric and a dimension becomes important as you become a more advanced user of Google Analytics. When you want to start building custom reports and custom dashboards, you need to know which building block goes where when you configure these custom options so that they display the information and data you want. Just remember that dimensions are the rows of information and metrics are the columns of data.

14

Interface Features

The Google Analytics interface allows you to access your data for reporting and analysis. Although the interface can be daunting the first time you log in to see your reports, it quickly becomes familiar. The great thing about Google Analytics is that you can open up your data to everybody in your organization.

Accounts

Google Analytics caters to large-scale and small websites alike, and the account structure reflects this flexibility by allowing you to create multiple accounts when needed. There are three levels in Google Analytics, and at the very top-level you will have a Google Analytics account. In the majority of cases you will only ever need a single Google Analytics account as it is designed to store data for all of the websites and apps managed by your organization. For example, an accounting firm that has two websites, one for personal accounting and another for corporate accounting, can be set up in a single Google Analytics account.

If you were to then begin looking after an unrelated website, let's say you're starting a personal blog, then this should be set up in a new dedicated Google Analytics account.

So anything that does not directly relate to what is already being measured into a Google Analytics account should use a new separate account. This helps keep things neat and tidy and prevents the wrong people from seeing the unrelated reports when they log into Google Analytics.

Properties

In each Google Analytics account you can have one or more properties. Each separate property you create will have it's own dedicated tracking code (and property ID) which is used to collect data. Coming back to the accounting firm example, where they have two websites, you would be likely to see two properties, one for each website. However, in most cases you are likely to see a single property within your Google Analytics (this is expected when you are only measuring a single website).

> **Tip:** There are more advanced cases where you might want to measure multiple websites using a single tracking code. Visit http://lovesdata.co/6speV for details on setting up cross domain tracking.

Views

Finally, for each property inside Google Analytics you will find one or more reporting views. A view is where you will find the reports for the data that has been collected and processed. In most cases you will have an account structure with a single account, a single property and a single view.

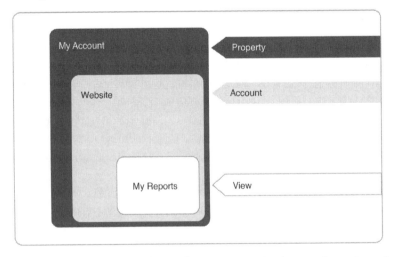

Views can be configured to meet particular needs and can be set up to include or even exclude particular data from appearing. This is covered later, but let's quickly look at one example before getting to the more technical topics. The most common reason to have an additional reporting view is to exclude your own visits from showing up inside Google Analytics. In the example below there are three different reporting views:

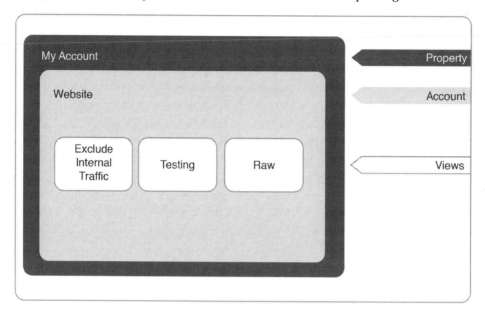

One view has been configured to exclude internal traffic to the website, this is because staff regularly check the website to review content and this internal traffic would skew the data. Think about it: you probably regularly go to your website which will mean that you appear as a highly engaged user, but are you ever going to convert? No, you are just checking different parts of your website, so you probably do not want your own interactions showing up in your reports.

There is also a view for testing purposes, and finally a 'raw' view which means that all data is included in the reports without any modifications being made.

User Permissions

It's strongly recommended that you encourage other people to use the data and reports and not hold your data hostage. The more people you can get engaging with the data that is available, the more likely people will begin to start suggesting ways to improve your website and marketing.

There are four types of user permissions that you can give people to access Google Analytics. The most common permission used is 'Read and Analyze' which allows people to log into Google Analytics and use the reports without being able to make any changes that will impact on your data. If someone else manages Google Analytics for your organization it is likely that this will apply to you.

Giving people 'Read and Analyze' level permission along with 'Collaborate' allows people to access the reports and also share custom assets with everybody else who can log into the account. This means people with 'Collaborate' permissions can create custom dashboards and share them so that anybody logging in can see the custom dashboards.

Next is 'Edit' permission. You should keep people with 'Edit' level permissions to an absolute minimum as they can make configuration changes to the account which permanently modify data. This means they can configure and delete accounts, properties and views.

Finally there is 'Manage Users' level permission which allows for the management of people who can access your reports and data. Again, the number of people with this level of permission should be kept to a minimum whenever possible.

> **Tip:** To check what level of user permissions you have, click on 'Admin' and then 'View Settings'. If all the configuration details are greyed out and cannot be selected then you do not have 'Edit' level permission. Now click back and click on 'User Management'. If there is a message that says 'You do not have permission to modify users on this account' then you do not have 'Manage Users' level permission. Finally to see if you have 'Collaborate' level permissions navigate to the 'Reporting' tab and then 'Dashboards'. Once you have created your own custom dashboard click on 'Share', if you don't see 'Share Object' (and you only see 'Share Template Link') then you only have 'Read and Analyze' level permissions.

Report Navigation

Account List

The account list allows you to quickly jump between different reporting views and accounts if you are managing Google Analytics on multiple websites.

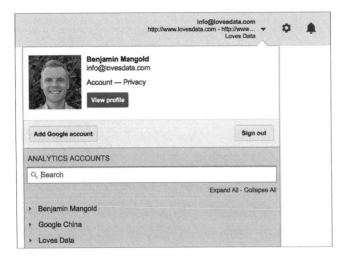

Tip: The search box is useful for quickly finding a particular view.

Home Tab

The 'Home' tab provides a list of all the accounts, properties and views that you can access. You will also see a summary showing you the number of sessions, average session duration, bounce rate and conversion rate for each view.

Tip: You can quickly compare date ranges to see top-level changes in your reporting views by using the date range selector in the top right corner.

Reporting Tab

The Reporting tab contains all the core reports that you will be using on a regular basis. The menu under Reporting is structured to help answer your questions about your website and people accessing your website.

You will find Dashboards that you can customize for top-level and topic specific reporting, Shortcuts for quickly navigating to reports you have previously saved and Intelligence Events for automated insights into changing visitor trends. Real-Time reports show you what is currently happening on your website.

Audience contains reports on who is accessing your website. This is where you can find information about where people are geographically located when they access your website. If you want to know if people are accessing your website on a mobile device, like an iPhone or Android phone, this is also available under the Audience reports.

The Acquisition reports show you how people are finding your website. You will find reports on which websites are linking to your website, social networks that are driving traffic, organic search traffic and your own custom marketing campaigns.

There is also a collection of reports for your Google AdWords campaigns that can be found in Acquisition. The AdWords reports details about the keywords people are using to trigger your ads, the keywords you are bidding on in your campaigns, the time of day people are engaging with your ads and more.

The Behavior reports allow you to understand what people are doing on your website, this includes what pages people are viewing and engaging with. You can also set up Event Tracking to report on any interactive content contained on pages of your website, for example videos, downloads and links to other websites.

Conversions contains reports on your key website objectives (goals) you are trying to get your visitors to perform. Goals need to be configured to meet your needs, but common examples include: completing a contact form, signing up for an email newsletter, downloading a particular file or purchasing a product online. If you have an ecommerce website, you can also find ecommerce reports under Conversions.

Customization Tab

The Customization tab is where you can create your own custom reports to meet your individual requirements. Custom reports can be used on any historical data, so these can be set up at any time.

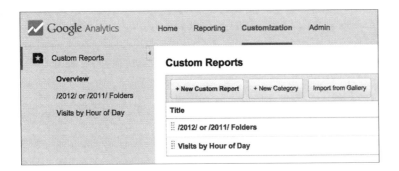

Date Range

When you open your Google Analytics reports you will be looking at data from the last 31 days. Clicking the date range will allow you to change the set of data you see in your reports.

You can click the name of a month to load that month or select a custom start date and end date.

Checking the 'Compare to Previous Period' option will automatically load the same number of days before the date range you are currently looking at. For example, if you have 1 April to 14 April selected and check 'Compare to Previous Period' it will automatically compare this range to 18 March to 31 March.

> **Tip:** When using the 'Compare to Previous Period' option you might not be comparing the same days to one another in your reports. For example, you might be comparing Mondays to Sundays or some other day of the week. You can manually change the comparison date range to correctly align the days of week for example, to ensure you align Monday with Monday.

Graph Options

Depending on the date range you have selected, you can graph by day, week or month. This allows you to change what each point represents on the graph, for example, with a six month date range selecting 'Month' will show each month as a point on the graph.

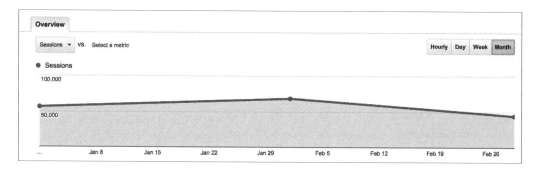

> **Tip:** The Overview Reports available under Audience, Behavior and Conversions (for both Goals and Ecommerce) allow you to graph your data by hour on the timeline.

You can change which data is graphed. The available options will depend on which report you are currently viewing.

You can also graph two sets of data in the graph by clicking 'Select Metric' and selecting the additional set of data to graph.

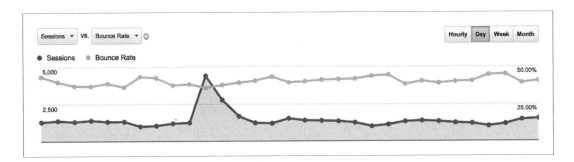

Report View

You can change how data is presented in reports by selecting a 'Report View'.

Looking at the Source/Medium report (under All Traffic) shows the different ways people are finding your website (for example, 'google/organic' are free searches on Google, 'site.com/referral' are traffic from links on other websites). The data view allows you to compare sessions by traffic source and also engagement, including the average number of pages per session and the average amount of time spent on the website.

The Percentage view and Performance view allow you to quickly compare the effectiveness of the different traffic sources in driving traffic to your website.

Percentage view:

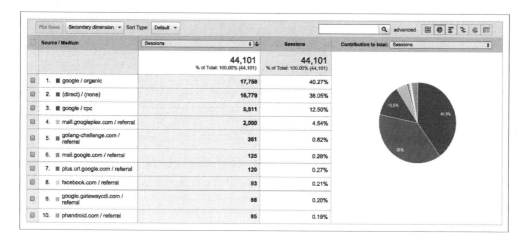

Performance view:

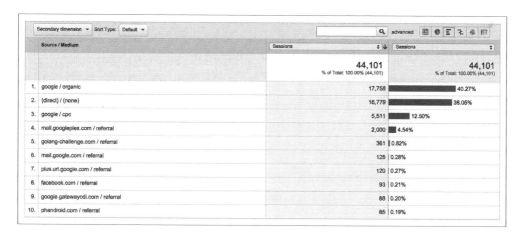

The Comparison view allows you to compare individual performance against the overall average for your whole website. Selecting 'Average Session Duration' you can quickly identify traffic sources that are performing better in comparison to the overall website average and also those that are underperforming.

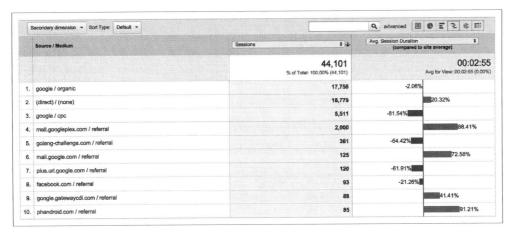

The Term Cloud is a visual representation of importance. The traffic sources resulting in the most sessions is presented the largest.

The Pivot view allows you to analyze the rows of information with additional columns. For example, selecting 'Country' allows you to see the different methods people use to find the website, ordered by importance, along with the physical location of your users.

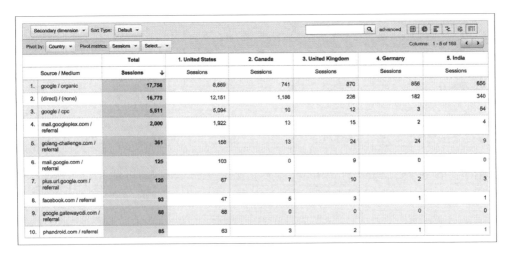

Annotations

You can add notes to particular dates in your reports by creating annotations in the interface. This is useful for documenting any activity that has resulted in a spike or dip in traffic. Noting down major marketing initiatives, including when you send out email newsletters and launch new Google AdWords campaigns, make great annotations inside Google Analytics. They become particularly useful when you are looking back at historical data. For example, if you are looking at a report that is for a couple of months ago, you may not remember exactly what drove a large spike in traffic, but by entering annotations you can quickly determine what caused the change in traffic.

To create an annotation click on the small grey tab below the timeline:

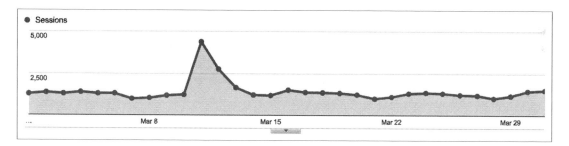

Now click the 'Create New Annotation' link, select a date and enter your comment.

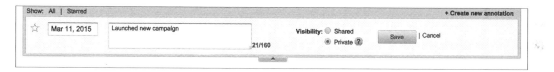

If you create a 'Shared' annotation it will be visible to everybody who has access to the particular Google Analytics view. If you select 'Private' it will only be visible when you log in – other users and administrators will not be able to see your annotation.

Tip: Annotations are only readable in the interface. If you export a report as a PDF from Google Analytics, you will see the small annotation icon in the timeline, but you will not be able to read your note for that particular date.

15

Reports

Dashboards

Dashboards allow you to quickly view key information in a single report. You can customize dashboards for particular reporting requirements and to meet the needs of particular team members in your organization.

Depending on your level of access, you will see 'Shared' and 'Private' dashboards. Private dashboards are only visible using your login details. If you have 'Collaborate' level access you can share an existing private dashboard to other people who have access to your Google Analytics account (if there are no shared dashboards in the view you will only see 'Private').

To create a dashboard, navigate to 'Dashboards' and select 'New Dashboard'. You will now be prompted to select either 'Blank Canvas' or 'Starter Dashboard'. In most cases you will want to select 'Blank Canvas' as this will allow you to build your dashboard from scratch. Then, name your dashboard and click 'Create Dashboard'.

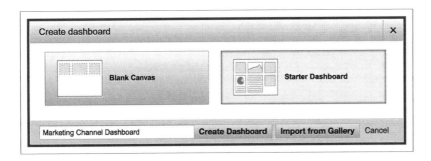

You will now be prompted to add a widget to your dashboard. A widget is simply an element that will be included in your dashboard. You can choose from the following types of widgets:

- **Standard widgets:**
  - **Metric** allows you to display a straight metric (number). For example, you can use this to display your overall bounce rate.
  - **Timeline** is used to display a trendline in your dashboard.
  - **Geomap** places a map report in your dashboard.
  - **Table** allows you to display a table of information. For example, you can include a table of your top 10 landing pages.
  - **Pie** adds a pie chart.
  - **Bar** adds a bar chart.
- **Real-time widgets:**
  - **Counter** shows the active users currently on your website.
  - **Timeline** shows pageviews from the last 30 seconds or one minute.
  - **Map** shows active users by geographic location.
  - **Table** displays information about active users. For example, you can use this to display the devices people are using to view your website.

Add a 'Metric' to the dashboard. Ensure that the 'Metric' option is selected and then click 'Add a Metric'. Search for and select 'Bounce Rate'.

A title will automatically be assigned to the widget, but this can be changed. You also have the option to link the widget to a relevant report, so you can click through to perform more detailed analysis. To do this, start typing the name of the report and select the report from the list.

Now, create the following widget to display the top performing campaigns.

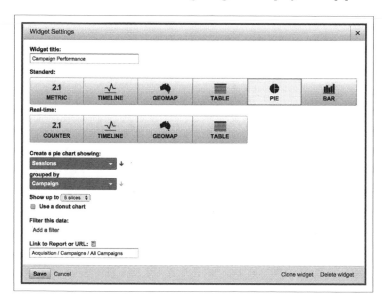

After saving the widget you will notice a large portion of 'not set' in the chart. This represents all of the sessions that are not associated with a particular marketing campaign.

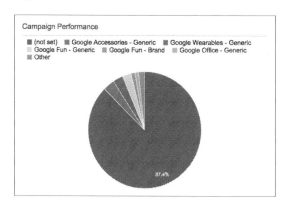

This means the widget needs to be edited to only include campaign data (by excluding the non-campaign sessions). To do this hover over the widget and click on the edit icon (in the top right corner of the widget). Now click on 'Add a Filter' and add the following filter to exclude the non-campaign sessions:

Now, when the widget is saved, the non-campaign data will be ignored and the chart will include only campaign data.

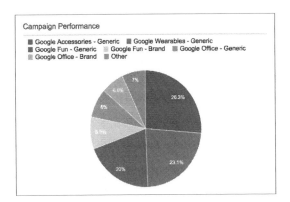

This shows how widget filters can be used to further customize what is included in your dashboards by including or excluding particular data.

Now that you are familiar with the basics of creating custom dashboards, it's time to start thinking about creating dashboards that focus on particular areas of your website and your organization.

Here are some ideas for dashboards:

- **Marketing dashboard** to present a comprehensive overview of your marketing channels.
- **Marketing dashboards** focused on particular marketing channels. For example, to view the performance of your paid search campaigns or to show the success of your email marketing.
- **Dashboards to monitor your goal** conversions and ecommerce transactions.
- **Dashboards that include technical details** about your audience, including the browsers and devices they are using.
- **Dashboards to present demographic information** about your audience.
- **Content dashboards** to understand the most popular content on your website.
- **Engagement dashboards** to see how engaging your content and website experience is.

There are two quick ways to get started using dashboards. Firstly, you can add widgets to your dashboards when you are on a standard report. For example, on the Overview report in the Behavior section, you can click 'Add to Dashboard' at the top of the report.

This allows you to select a dashboard and then add a particular component from the report you are viewing to that dashboard.

The second way to get started is to visit http://lovesdata.co/hdXcb where you can add pre-created dashboards to Google Analytics. You can then customize these existing dashboards to meet your needs.

If you have Collaborate level permissions you can share the dashboard with other people who have access to the reporting view. Click 'Share' and select 'Share Object'. This will copy the dashboard into the 'Shared' section and allow other people to use your dashboard.

> **Tip:** You can also share the template of the dashboard you have created by using the 'Share Template Link' option under 'Share'.

Shortcuts

Shortcuts allows you to save reports and report customizations so you can quickly return to them without having to repeat the steps every time you want to use the report. The following example shows the landing page report after drilling down into a page and adding a secondary dimension.

		Acquisition		
Landing Page	Source / Medium	Sessions ↓	% New Sessions	New Users
		20,523 % of Total: 37.93% (54,109)	84.32% Avg for View: 76.92% (9.62%)	17,305 % of Total: 41.58% (41,822)
1. /default.aspx	google / organic	10,596 (51.64%)	80.39%	8,520 (49.23%)
2. /default.aspx	youtube.com / referral	5,600 (27.29%)	97.16%	5,441 (31.44%)
3. /default.aspx	(direct) / (none)	2,720 (13.25%)	82.61%	2,247 (12.98%)
4. /default.aspx	linkedin.com / referral	669 (3.26%)	64.42%	431 (2.49%)
5. /default.aspx	bing / organic	163 (0.79%)	95.71%	156 (0.90%)

> **Tip:** The report above was originally created by navigating to the 'Landing Pages' report under 'Site Content' in the 'Behavior' section. Next, a landing page was clicked and 'Source/Medium' was selected as the 'Secondary Dimension'.

If you want to return to this report at another time you could repeat the steps originally used to create the report, or you can create a shortcut that will automatically bring you back. To create a shortcut, navigate to the report and apply any customizations you would like, then click 'Shortcut' at the top of the report and give your shortcut a name.

Intelligence Events

The Intelligence Events reports allows you to see significant changes that have occurred in your data. For example, if you received more sessions than expected, your conversion rate is decreasing, or your bounce rate is increasing.

The alerts you see in the reports are custom to your website. Google Analytics builds up an understanding of what should be occurring on your website based on your historical data, the alerts flag any deviation from what was expected to have occurred. This makes the Intelligence Events reports a great starting point to find new insights.

Alerts are triggered based on day, week or month as it compares each of these time periods to what was expected. A daily alert means that for an individual day there was a significant change, while a monthly alert means that the whole month experienced the change.

The Overview report provides a summary based on the date range you have selected and shows you daily, weekly and monthly alerts. By default, the most significant alerts are listed at the top of the report. The significance of each alert is indicated by the size of the colored bar under 'Importance' – the larger the bar the more important the alert.

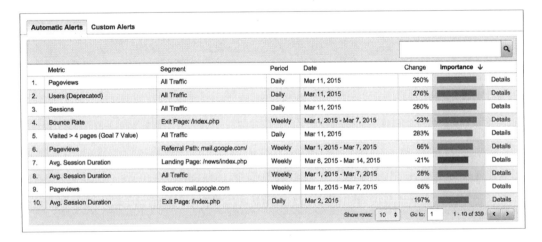

Tip: The importance (or significance) of each alert is based on the change that was experienced (compared to what was actually expected), and the number of sessions that contributed to the change.

Clicking on 'Details' will show you additional details about the alert. You can see that the expected number of pageviews was between 8,663 and 11,232 but the actual number of pageviews experienced was 34,625:

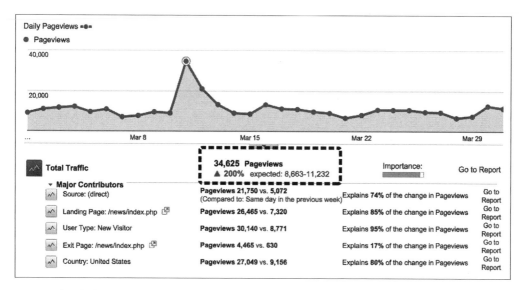

The daily, weekly and monthly event reports show you alerts based on those time periods. At the top of the reports you will see colored bars indicating on which days (or weeks or months) one or more alerts were triggered. Clicking on the bars will update the report to show you details of the alerts. By default you will see 'Custom Alerts', 'Automatic Web Alerts' and 'Automatic AdWords Alerts' that you can review in the report.

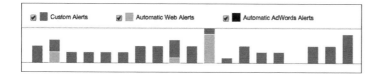

Custom Alerts

You will receive automatic alerts for people engaging on your website, along with alerts for your Google AdWords traffic. However you can also set up custom alerts based on your own defined criteria. For example, you can create a custom alert to trigger if your overall bounce rate increases by more than 10%, or if you reach a certain number of goal conversions.

You can set up custom alerts in any of the Intelligence Events reports. In the Overview report select the 'Custom Alerts' tab, or in any other report click the 'Create a Custom Alert' link. You will then be able to configure your own custom alert.

Custom alerts can be applied to one or more of your reporting views and can be triggered based on day, week or month. You can also set up your alert to send an email or a text message if they are triggered.

Important: Custom alerts are not checked in real time and daily alerts are only checked once per day to see if your conditions have been met. This means that you should not use alerts to monitor for business-critical changes, such as your website going offline.

A daily alert that triggers if the homepage bounce rate increases beyond 50% on any given day:

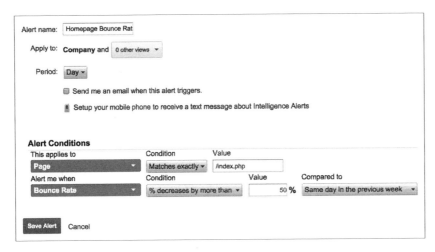

A monthly alert that triggers if the goal conversion rate increases by more than 20% in a month:

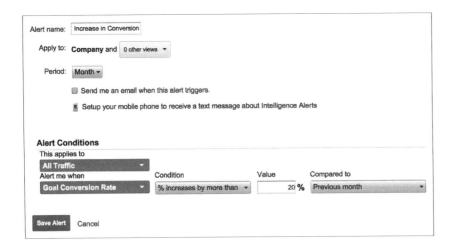

Tip: You can also create custom alerts based on custom segments you have configured in your account.

Real-Time

The Real-Time reports allow you see what is happening on your website right now. Data is processed into the Real-Time reports within seconds of someone visiting your website. As a page is loaded on your website a blue bar will appear on the right hand side of the pageviews panel and as the seconds tick by the bar will move to the left. Once they hit the 60 second mark (in the middle of the panel) they are bumped into the 30 minute section on the left hand side, where you will see pageviews grouped by minute instead of by second.

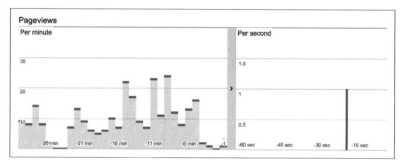

As the seconds load in the current minute you will see the bar increase just to the left of the center line.

You can drill down into the dimensions displayed to see additional detail. For example, if you click on a particular page, you will then see a breakdown of all the different mediums and sources people are using to find that individual page.

Tip: When you drill down, that particular dimension will continue to be applied. A blue label for the dimension will become visible at the top of the Real-Time reports. To remove the drill down just click on the cross for the dimension you want to remove.

For more detail you can navigate to the individual reports. For example, navigating to 'Content' will give you a full view of the different pages people are viewing and you can also view the pages people have seen over the last 30 minutes, instead of just seeing the pages that people are actively viewing right now. The individual reports allow you to drill down to see more detail about people's location, how they are finding the site, how they are engaging with the website and if they are converting.

How to Use Real-Time Reports

The Real-Time reports are a really useful way to test that your Google Analytics implementation is working as expected. If you are not sure if a particular page is being tracked, you can load the page in a browser and then use the Real-Time content report to see if it appears. If it does, the tracking code is loading correctly on the page. If it doesn't you will know within a few seconds if you need to troubleshoot the issue further. You can use a similar technique to check that goals you have configured are working and that events you have set up recently are tracking.

To speed up troubleshooting in the Real-Time reports you can add your own campaign tags to the URL of the page you are testing. For example, if you load up '/test.html?utm_medium=me&utm_source=me' then you will be able to see the custom medium and source displayed in the Real-Time traffic sources reports. If you click the custom medium and navigate to another Real-Time report you will notice that the medium filter (of 'me') is still applied so you are continuing to look only at your own interactions. This can be reset to include everybody by clicking the cross at the top of the report to remove the filter.

Tip: If you are customizing the tracking code create a test page and upload it to a testing area, then use the Real-Time reports to quickly see if your customization is working or not. This allows you to quickly check things without having to wait until the standard reports are fully processed, which can mean waiting hours instead of seconds.

Larger websites can use Real-Time reports to adjust content and monitor campaigns. For example, a news website can use the reports to understand the most popular news articles people are reading and use this to modify the placement of stories on their homepage. By adjusting the placement of stories, so that popular stories are highlighted or moved towards the top of the page, they can get more people reading those articles.

If you are launching a new marketing campaign or sending out your email newsletter, you can use the reports to ensure people are engaging with your campaign and that they are being directed to the appropriate landing pages. If you notice a problem with the landing page you have the opportunity to work with your technical team to set up redirects and ensure that people get to the correct page. You can also use the reports to see the impact of traditional media, for example, if your product is being mentioned on TV, you can monitor this in the reports.

Tip: Remember that to optimize your website in real-time you will need to have enough traffic to make your efforts worthwhile. If you are just looking at the data for a website that doesn't receive thousands of sessions every day, it is unlikely that moving content around is going to have any measurable impact.

Another use for the Real-Time reports is to display live data. Maybe you are launching a campaign and want your marketing team to see how many people are engaging with the campaign, or maybe you want to display how many people are currently on your website so your team starts to get excited about Google Analytics!

16

Audience

The Audience reports allow you to see information about who is accessing your website. For example, if you want to know the physical location of your website users, or what devices they are using to view your website, the Audience reports will give you the answers.

Overview

The Overview report gives you a quick snapshot of your website's audience. You can see how many people have been to your website with the users and sessions metrics, as well as engagement metrics including bounce rate and average session duration. At the bottom of the overview page, you can get quick top 10 grabs of user information, but it is likely you will want to jump straight into the main reports.

Demographics

The Demographic reports allow you to understand behavior by age and gender, giving you insights into how particular segments of people interact with your content. The reports reflect demographics that are available to target through Google AdWords on the Google Display Network, so you can also identify potential advertising opportunities in these reports.

Demographic data is not available for every user that interacts on your website, so you will notice that the total number of sessions in the reports does not match other reports (like the number of sessions in the Audience Overview report). This is because the demographic reports rely on users allowing third-party cookies to be stored as they navigate through your website, and also on other third-party sites on the Google Display Network. Some people choose to block this third-party cookie, which means they will not show up in the demographics or interests reports, but they will continue to be measured in the other reports as these use a first-party cookie instead.

> **Tip:** A first-party cookie is one that is created, updated and stored on the same domain that you are visiting. For example, if you browse 'www.company.com' a first-party cookie would be stored just for the 'company.com' domain. A third-party cookie is created, updated and stored on a domain other than the one you are visiting, for example if you browse 'www.company.com' and a cookie is created on doubleclick.net then this would be a third-party cookie.

You can identify potential opportunities by looking at the conversion metrics in the report. Start by selecting goal or ecommerce conversions and then look for demographics that have a high conversion rate above your overall average conversion rate.

You can then look at targeting the demographics that perform higher than average in your Google AdWords campaigns. Alternatively, you can use the report to identify demographics that are not performing as well as you had expected and use this as a starting point for further analysis. For example, if you see that the 25–34 year old age bracket is not performing well you can create a custom segment and then use the acquisition reports to identify how they are finding you in comparison to your overall traffic – perhaps they are not seeing particular marketing efforts. If you don't see any major differences in the acquisition reports, then you can move to the Behavior reports to see if they are engaging differently with your content compared to your overall traffic or even other demographic segments. You might need to consider navigation and usability for that particular demographic.

Interests

The Interests reports rely on the same third-party cookie that is used to create the demographics reports, but instead of reporting age and gender they report on people's particular areas of interest, based on their behavior while browsing sites on the Google Display Network. These reports give you three different ways to view your audience and are all based on available interest targets in Google AdWords.

- **Affinity Categories** group people based on their areas of interest. Running Google AdWords campaigns based on these categories enables you to build brand awareness. For example, if you are marketing an ebook you can focus on 'News Junkies & Avid Readers' along with any other categories that relate to the ebook.

- **In-Market Segments** group your audience into categories based on products or services that they are actively researching or looking to purchase. For example, if you sell mobile phones you can focus on segments that reflect your offering, including 'Consumer Electronics/Mobile Phones' and 'Telecom/Mobile Phone Service Providers'.

- **Other Categories** is similar to in-market segments, but is more granular, containing more categories. This option is available as in-market segments that are not available for all advertisers globally.

Although the audience groupings directly reflect those available in Google AdWords, you can also use the reports to help understand how your key audience segments (or target markets) are engaging with your website. For example, if your website provides information about the products or services you offer you can use the reports to compare engagement and conversions for your key audience segment. If the groupings show lower than expected levels of engagement, like a high bounce rate, then you can further analyze engagement by landing page using a custom segment, and maybe also review your overarching content strategy.

Setting up Demographics and Interests Reports

The demographics and interests reports require configuration in order to collect data into the reports. In order to collect data you need to complete two steps: first you need to review your privacy policy as Google requires that you let people know you are using the feature. Your policy also needs to tell people how they can opt-out. You can find Google's privacy policy requirements at http://lovesdata.co/uRSiV

> **Tip:** You can also use Google Analytics to create remarketing lists for your campaigns in Google AdWords. If you want to use the remarketing feature, then your privacy policy also needs to include some additional details about remarketing.

Once your privacy policy meets the requirements, the second step is to enable the feature in Google Analytics. Navigate to 'Admin' and select 'Property Settings', then you can set 'Enable Advertising Features' to 'On'. Alternatively, if you are using Google Tag Manager then you can enable the reports directly in the Google Analytics tag. Just look for the option to 'Enable Display Advertising Features'.

> **Tip:** If you are using an older version of the Google Analytics tracking code or are looking to set up remarketing in your mobile app you will need to modify the code before you can build remarketing lists.

Geographic

The Geographic (Geo) reports include the language report which shows you the language preferences of people accessing your website. To create this report Google Analytics looks at the language preference from the browser settings. This report is useful if you are looking to translate your website or have already translated your website.

> **Tip:** The language report is not the easiest report to read as it shows language codes. If you are unfamiliar with a particular code, like 'en-au' simply perform a search on Google for 'en-au language' and you will be able to see the details. In this case, 'en-au' is actually Australian English.

You will also find the Location report in the Geo section. The Location report shows you the geographic location of people visiting your website. At the top of the report you will see a world map – the darker green areas show you the locations where more people are located. You can hover over the map to see the number of sessions for each country. Below the map, you will see the same session information presented in a table, along with engagement metrics for each country.

> **Tip:** If you are at the global level of the location report and see '(not set)' in the table this means that there were a number of sessions where Google Analytics was unable to determine their location. This is because Google Analytics relies on information being provided by third parties, like internet service providers to find the location of your visitors based on their IP address. If there are no location details for an IP address the location will be reported as '(not set)'.

You can click on the map, or click on the name of a country in the table to drill down further into the location report. You can also use the options located below the timeline to drill down and modify what you see in the location report.

Behavior

The Behavior reports provide details on how often people access your website. You can see if people are visiting your website for the first time, or if they are returning after a previous session.

The New vs Returning report allows you to compare your new and returning users. If you have a high percentage of new visitors you should consider ways to draw people back into your website. You could add an email newsletter subscription form to your website, make it easy for people to connect with you on social networks, or develop a strategy for regularly publishing new content. These tactics will help direct people back to your website.

On the other hand, if you have a high percentage of returning visitors then you are already succeeding at getting people back. Instead you may need to think of ways to get new people coming to your website. This could include ensuring your URL is on all your print collateral, including business cards, brochures and offline advertising. It could also mean running new advertising campaigns that specifically target a new audience, or even making sure you are posting links to your website on social networks.

> **Tip:** You can drill down into either 'New Visitor' or 'Returning Visitor' and then layer another question for more detailed analysis. For example, click on 'New Visitor' and then click on 'Secondary Dimension' (below the timeline and above the graph), then search for and select 'Medium'. You will now see the ways new visitors have found your website.

The Frequency and Recency report shows you how often individuals are coming back to your website and the length of time between their sessions. This report can be confusing at first because it actually looks beyond the selected date range to show you how people behave.

When you open the Frequency and Recency report you will be looking at the 'Count of Sessions' which shows you the total number of sessions performed by people accessing your website. Let's say your current date range inside Google Analytics is March, and during the month you only had two people come to your website (you probably had more, but we'll keep it simple to understand how the report works). The first person had previously been to your website in January and February before coming back in March. This means that the first user has performed a total of three sessions on your website. The second person coming to your website has never been before, so the second user will have a total of one session on your website. In this case the report would look like:

Count of Sessions	Sessions
1	1
3	1

At the top of the report you can select 'Days Since Last Session' which allows you to see the number of days that have elapsed since they last accessed your website. For example, if someone came to your website on Monday, and then returned on Friday, it means there was three days since their last session.

This report can also be confusing because it can look past the historical date range you have selected. This is why you will see some sessions where there were a large number of days since their last session, even if you have a short date range selected. If someone last accessed your website nine months ago, and then came back within your date range then they will be counted as one session in the '121–364' bracket.

You will also see that there are a number of sessions where there were zero days since their last session. This is for all the people who have ever been to your website before, since it is their first time on your website no days have passed.

Technology

The Technology reports provide technical details about people accessing your website. When you open the 'Browser & OS' report you will see a list of all the different browsers people have used to access your website. This report includes browsers used on desktops and laptops such as Chrome, Safari and Firefox, but also includes browsers used on mobile devices such as Android Browser and Opera Mini. You might even see browsers on other internet connected devices, for example Playstations, Amazon Kindles and any other device that has a web browser.

You can access additional details about the computers people are using to access your website by selecting a different dimension (look above the table and below the timeline for available options).

To see if particular operating systems provide higher levels of engagement or higher conversion rates, select 'Operating System'. Higher performing operating systems might give you insights about your customers, including their demographics and preferences. You could even use Operating System as a way to target your remarketing ads on Google AdWords.

Tip: Regularly checking the Operating System and Browser reports is an important way to understand how people are experiencing your website. For example, if a large portion of people use Internet Explorer 7 to access your website, you should check that your website functions correctly on that particular browser. Or if you find that there are people suddenly using a device that you didn't expect, like Amazon Kindles, you might consider tailoring the experience of your website or content for that particular device.

Screen Resolution gives you details about the screen size of the device accessing your website. This includes computers, laptops, mobiles and other devices. If you want to understand screen size for just mobiles or another type of device, you can apply a segment to narrow the focus of the report. For example, if you apply the default 'Mobile Traffic' segment, you will only see the screen sizes for mobile devices being used to access your website. You could use this insight to inform graphic elements you present to mobile users – if an image is too wide it might break your layout on these particular devices.

Tip: It is difficult to use the Screen Resolution report for informing the desktop and laptop design of your website. This is because the report shows you screen size and not browser size. So although someone might have a large screen, they might be using a small browser window. To understand the browser sizes people are using you can use the In-Page Analytics report which is available in the Behavior section.

The Screen Colors report shows you the color details of the screen people are using and Flash Version shows you which versions of Adobe Flash people have installed. Under Other you will find Java Support which tells you if people have Java installed. This is not referring to JavaScript, but rather the Java plug-in that is used for web-based applications. Most people never use these three reports, but if you ever need to see the data it is available.

The Network report shows you the different internet service providers people use to access the internet and then browse your website. In most cases you will see familiar providers for your audience. For example, in the United States you would see Verizon and Comcast used by people accessing the internet from their home or mobile device. In the UK you might see BT and Tesco and in Australia you might see Telstra and Optus.

You will also see some other service providers listed in the report. This is because larger organizations (like corporations and universities) will have their own dedicated connection to access the internet. This allows you to understand who is accessing your website, if you are a larger organization yourself you can see if the competition is checking you out online. You can even create a custom segment based on a particular service provider to understand the content that they are engaging with on your website.

The Network report allows you to select 'Hostname' (above the table and below the timeline). This report shows you where your Google Analytics tracking code has loaded. You should see your primary domain name as the first row in the report. This is because the vast majority of people will load your tracking code on your website, but you might see some unexpected domain names showing up in the report. This tells you that your tracking code is loading in other domains.

It's fine if you see your domain with and without 'www.', however if you are performing SEO, then you really only want the primary website to be loading from one of these domains. If you see this you need to set up your website's server to only present your website on one primary domain and set up appropriate redirects for the second domain that you are removing. For more details visit http://lovesdata.co/pIn8A

Your tracking code can also load on 'webcache.googleusercontent.com' (a result of people using Google's cache to access your website) and 'translate.google.com' (a result of your website loading with Google Translate). This means both of these domains will appear in the Hostnames report.

It's also possible that your tracking code has been placed on other websites. If there are any sites in the Hostname report that you don't want to include in your Google Analytics data you can create a filter to exclude that portion of traffic. Read the "Filters" section in Chapter 24 for further details.

Mobile

The Mobile reports allow you to quickly understand your mobile and tablet users. The Overview report gives you a top-level break down so you can compare users on computers (including desktops and laptops), tablets and mobiles. To quickly see trends in this report, you can add these devices to the timeline. To do this select one or more of the device categories (clicking the checkbox to the right of the device in the table) then click the 'Plot Rows' button above the table.

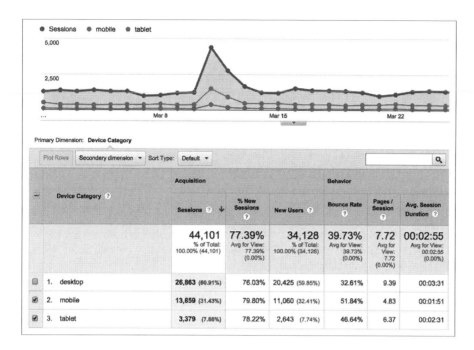

Navigating to the 'Devices' report gives you the details of all the different mobile and tablet devices people are using. You can use this to understand performance by individual devices. This report can contain a lot of rows and make it difficult to quickly compare performance by device. Selecting the 'Mobile Device Branding' tab above the table will provide a streamlined view that combines all devices under the manufacturer's brand. For example, instead of seeing 'Apple iPhone and Apple iPad' you will simply see 'Apple' in this report. You can always click on a particular brand to see all the individual devices for that particular brand.

> **Tip:** In the Mobile Devices reports you are likely to see a row for '(not set)'. This is where Google Analytics knows that someone is using a mobile device, but there is not enough information available to report on the exact device. Applying a secondary dimension (like 'Mobile Device Branding' or 'Operating System') can help provide insights for these users.

Additional options in the report allow you to see the internet service providers that people are using with their mobile devices, the way people interact with the mobile device, the operating system and screen resolution.

Custom

These reports are for historical (or legacy) features that allowed you to measure custom data into Google Analytics – they were previously called 'Custom Variables' and 'User Defined Values'. For example, measuring logged in users, categorizing content or reporting on custom data collected in website forms, like zip or postal code.

You can check these reports to see if any historical data was collected using these features, if they are still being used you should look at migrating to the latest version of the Google Analytics tracking code and replacing them with custom dimensions.

Custom dimensions and custom metrics provide even more flexibility in measuring custom information and data into Google Analytics. Read the "Custom Dimensions and Custom Metrics" section in Chapter 28 for details.

Benchmarking

The Benchmarking reports allow you to compare the performance of your website against other websites, providing greater context for your data. You can use these reports to understand how you compare based on a range of different metrics. For example, you can see how your mix of inbound marketing compares, to understand if there are particular marketing channels where you are underperforming in comparison to other websites. You might find that your website is above average, based on sessions coming from social networks, but below average for email campaign traffic. This can help inform your strategy while also providing context for your reporting and analysis.

> **Tip:** Always aim to use the Benchmarking reports to add context to your data. If you were to solely use the Benchmarking reports, it can be difficult to make them actionable. For example, if you find that you are not performing well in comparison to other websites overall, what do you do? Where do you start? However, if you see that a particular marketing channel is not performing based on your objectives, you can then use the Benchmarking reports to help support the need for more resources to be allocated to that particular channel.

To use Benchmarking reports, you need to be anonymously sharing your data with Google to contribute to the reports. To do this, click on 'Admin' and select 'Account Settings'. You will see a number of options under 'Data Sharing Settings' – ensure that the 'Anonymously with Google and Others' is checked and click 'Save'. This means that your website data will be made anonymous and combined with other data to create the Benchmarking reports.

The reports will now be available under 'Benchmarking' in the 'Audience' section. There are three sets of reports in benchmarking which allow you to view performance based on your marketing channels, geographic location of your audience and the devices people are using to access your website. Before you start looking at the data in the reports there are some elements that can be adjusted at the top of the report.

Industry Vertical (?)	Country / Region (?)	Size by daily sessions (?)	There are 16,739 web properties
Shopping ▾	**All** ▾	**1000-4999** ▾	contributing to this benchmark (?)

You can select your 'Industry Vertical' to compare against particular types of websites. Your organization might fit into multiple verticals, so you can switch between different verticals as you use the reports. You can also choose to focus on a particular country or region for the reports.

If you select very specific industry verticals and more defined geographic areas for the report, that the number of websites contributing to the reporting data will decrease on the right hand side. If there are fewer than 100 websites contributing to the report no data will be available. This is designed to ensure that the data is anonymous and that people cannot drill-down to view benchmarks against specific competitors.

You can choose the average number of daily sessions for the websites included in the benchmarking comparison. You will typically want to use the 'Default' option as this will mean that you are comparing your websites with others that have a similar volume of traffic. If you are running a small website comparison with very large websites is not a fair comparison. The same goes for large websites being compared with small websites.

Compare your data to the benchmarks and see your relative performance. You can quickly see that the website is receiving a higher than expected number of sessions from social networks and people coming directly to the website, but that the other marketing channels could be reviewed.

Default Channel Grouping	Acquisition			Behavior		
	Sessions (?) ↓	% New Sessions (?)	New Users (?)	Pages / Session (?)	Avg. Session Duration (?)	Bounce Rate (?)
	37.23% ▾ 44,101 vs 70,263	**29.04%** ▲ 77.39% vs 59.97%	**19.01%** ▾ 34,128 vs 42,138	**51.41%** ▲ 7.72 vs 5.10	**9.68%** ▾ 00:02:55 vs 00:03:14	**12.00%** ▲ 39.73% vs 45.15%
1. Direct	**5.38%** ▲ 16,779 vs 15,922	**23.64%** ▲ 77.33% vs 62.55%	**30.29%** ▲ 12,976 vs 9,959	**95.90%** ▲ 9.23 vs 4.71	**2.78%** ▲ 00:03:31 vs 00:03:25	**-31.70%** ▾ 33.43% vs 48.96%
2. Organic Search	**-42.90%** ▾ 17,862 vs 31,281	**23.84%** ▲ 77.53% vs 62.61%	**-29.28%** ▾ 13,849 vs 19,584	**37.29%** ▲ 7.38 vs 5.38	**-13.84%** ▾ 00:02:51 vs 00:03:19	**-12.65%** ▾ 37.22% vs 42.61%
3. Referral	**-59.27%** ▾ 3,423 vs 8,405	**5.10%** ▲ 57.23% vs 54.46%	**-57.20%** ▾ 1,959 vs 4,577	**142.84%** ▲ 11.82 vs 4.87	**33.68%** ▲ 00:04:17 vs 00:03:12	**-42.22%** ▾ 26.70% vs 46.21%
4. Social	**-90.51%** ▾ 457 vs 4,815	**8.85%** ▲ 67.61% vs 62.12%	**-89.67%** ▾ 309 vs 2,991	**-0.01%** ▾ 4.39 vs 4.39	**-25.95%** ▾ 00:01:53 vs 00:02:33	**10.98%** ▲ 55.36% vs 49.89%
5. Email	**-99.24%** ▾ 48 vs 6,275	**180.03%** ▲ 79.17% vs 28.27%	**-97.86%** ▾ 38 vs 1,774	**-1.68%** ▾ 5.92 vs 6.02	**-39.05%** ▾ 00:02:12 vs 00:03:37	**43.60%** ▲ 54.17% vs 37.72%

The bounce rate for the paid search campaigns is also much higher than the benchmark average which could mean that the landing pages are underperforming in comparison to other websites. This can be used to review the landing pages and identify opportunities to optimize campaigns. Other reports can also be used to investigate this further, including the Landing Page and AdWords reports.

The Location benchmarking report can be used to see if you are engaging with your target audience based on geographic location. The Devices report shows you relative performance based on the devices people are using to view your website.

> **Tip:** The Benchmarking reports are useful for checking seasonal trends for your particular industry. For example, if you notice that you have a decrease in people coming from your paid search campaigns you can check this against the Benchmarking reports to see if the drop in performance is occurring across the entire industry, or if it is a problem specific to your own campaigns.

Users Flow

The Users Flow report allows you to understand how people are navigating through your website's content. The report can be a little intimidating at first, but it does start to make sense as you begin to look at the different elements of the report.

The report is read from left to right and you can choose how you want to segment people as they find your website. The default segmentation will split people based on their geographic location. In this example it's clear that most users are located in the United States, followed by Canada and India.

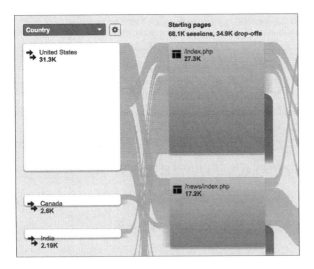

Looking to the right of these countries, you can see the top landing pages for the website, or in other words the first page someone sees as they load the website. Now you can choose how to use the report. If you are primarily interested in how people from a particular country navigate your content click on the name of a particular country and select 'Highlight Traffic Through Here'. This will immediately highlight the paths users (from that particular country) take through your website.

You can even narrow your analysis to a single segment. If you are only interested in how your Australian audience members are engaging with your content try clicking on Australia and selecting 'View Only This Segment'. The report will update you so that you are now entirely focused on that traffic segment.

Tip: If you select 'View Only This Segment' you can use the breadcrumbs to get back to the standard report, just click the 'Users Flow' link.

If you are more interested in particular landing pages (as opposed to user location) click on a landing page node and again select 'Highlight Traffic Through Here'. Now you can see how people who land on a particular group of pages then navigate through the website and you will also see their geographic locations as this is highlighted on the left.

You can also change the way the report is segmented. The default selection has been covered so far (which is 'Country'), but you can also change this selection to understand navigation paths based on different user characteristics. For example, you might be interested in how people navigate through the website based on different marketing channels. By selecting 'Default Channel Grouping' will allow you to understand how marketing channels are driving people to particular landing pages.

Tip: There are various ways to segment the report, so think about how you want to see traffic grouped and find an option that relates to your desired grouping. If the default options don't give you what you are looking for, then you can apply a custom segment to the Users Flow report for more detailed analysis.

The boxes in the report are called *nodes* and the links between the nodes are called *connections*. Although this isn't really important for using the report, it is worth highlighting that the nodes and connections are presented using relative proportions in the report. In other words, the larger the node or connection, then the more people have viewed that particular page or travelled between the pages.

As you slide the report to the right you can see how people continue to navigate through your website, viewing more and more pages. You will also see where people leave your website from particular pages, the exits are shown in red.

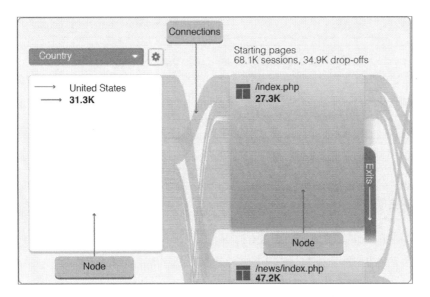

The Users Flow report automatically groups similar content into a single node. If you hover over a node and it says '20 pages' in the information panel that pops up, then you know it is more than one page that has been automatically grouped together. If you want to know which pages have been grouped together, then click on the node and select 'Group details' to see a list of URLs that make up the automatic grouping.

Using the Users Flow Report

Start by focusing on your 'Starting Pages' with the largest number of sessions. If your homepage is the most popular page, then click on this node and select 'Highlight Traffic Through Here' which allows you to see where people are traveling to from the homepage. You can then look at the pages that people are actually navigating to and compare this to the pages that are critical for your macro and micro conversion objectives. This allows you to identify suitable pages to cross-promote your content and review the on-page navigation to ensure people can easily navigate through to your most important content.

You can also use the report to quickly identify which pages have a high portion of people exiting your website. Simply look for 'Starting Pages' with the red bar on the right. You can hover over the bar to see the number of drop-offs.

Comparing two date ranges in the Users Flow report allows you to see the changing trends in the pages people are engaging with on your website. This example shows an increase in traffic to the news page, but a decrease in traffic to the homepage:

Tip: Applying different segments to the Users Flow report allows you to compare the behavior of your different audience members. For example, apply the 'Converts' default segment to see how people navigate through your website before they convert, then compare this to the 'All Sessions' segment and look for differences in people's navigation paths.

17

Acquisition

The Acquisition reports show you how people are finding your website. This enables you to understand the marketing channels that are performing well and identify opportunities to improve your campaigns. Google Analytics will automatically track some of your most important channels, including people finding your website by using search engines and by following links on other websites to find you, such as blogs, forums and social networks.

The reports allow you to understand which channels are driving the most number of people to your website, which channels are most engaging, and whether they are resulting in conversions. You also have the option to view your inbound marketing from a top level as well as drill down into the reports for really granular insights, like individual keywords people are using to find your organization.

> **Tip:** To build a complete picture of your initiatives you will also want to extend these reports by measuring your own custom marketing initiatives, like email newsletters and paid advertising. This can be achieved using campaign tags, which are covered in "Campaign Tracking" – Chapter 18.

Terminology

Before looking at the acquisition reports here are some definitions of the different terms used to explain how people are finding your website.

Referral

Referrals are links on other websites that are sending traffic to your website. This will include blogs, forums and maybe even other companies you work with that have decided to link to your website.

Organic

Organic traffic are people who are finding your website by clicking on the free, or organic results in a search engine. This will include your free search traffic from Google, Bing, Yahoo and other search engines.

CPC

CPC stands for *cost per click*. If you are running ads with Google AdWords then you will see this traffic showing up as 'CPC' or 'Paid Traffic' inside the Acquisition reports.

Direct

Direct traffic includes people who type your website URL directly into their browser or click on a link in an email client. For example, if someone sees your business card or brochure they might open a new browser window and type in your URL to learn more about what you offer. You might also have a link to your website in your email signature, if someone is reading your email in Windows Mail or Apple Mail and they click the link to your website a new browser window opens up and they are taken directly to your website.

> **Tip:** Direct traffic is actually any inbound traffic where Google Analytics cannot identify its originating source and medium. Campaign tags can be used to define a source and medium, so this allows you to distinguish your email campaigns and other custom initiatives and prevent the traffic being defined as 'Direct' in your reports.

> **Tip:** A technical problem with your website or tracking can lead to traffic being reported as 'Direct'. This can occur in some cases where there are JavaScript redirects or if the cookies are removed by the website in the middle of a visitors session. Luckily this isn't very common, but if you notice a large portion of direct traffic it is worth investigating. Visit http://lovesdata.co/JFrra for more on understanding direct traffic in detail.

Campaigns

Google Analytics allows you to measure your custom marketing initiatives as campaigns, this gives you greater clarity in your reports to understand how people are finding your website and how they behave. Apart from Google AdWords, you need to choose how you are going to label your marketing initiatives as campaigns. Until you start measuring campaigns you might be missing out on valuable insights. For example, if you send out an email newsletter to your subscribers and you haven't used campaign tags your email traffic will show up as a mix of referrals and direct. This is because people using hosted email solutions (like Gmail and Yahoo Mail) will be seen as referrals and those using email clients (like Outlook and Apple Mail) will be seen as direct. This is not ideal because what you probably want to know is if your email marketing is working or not, unless you have this reported as its own campaign you will never be sure. Using campaigns to measure marketing initiatives is covered in Chapter 18.

Direct Traffic and Bookmarks

Sessions to your website from direct traffic sources are not automatically reported as direct traffic inside Google Analytics, instead someone visiting your website from a direct source (for example, using a bookmark) is reported based on the most recent method they used to find your website.

For example, someone found you using Google and then bookmarked your website. A couple of days pass and they come back to your website using the bookmark. Both sessions will be shown as coming from Google.

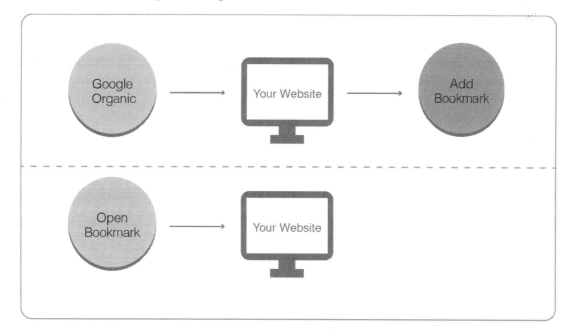

If another person found your website using Google and then bookmarked your site. Then the next day they click a link in a Tweet to return to your website and the following week they used their bookmark to open your website, in this case the session from the bookmark would be seen as coming from Twitter.

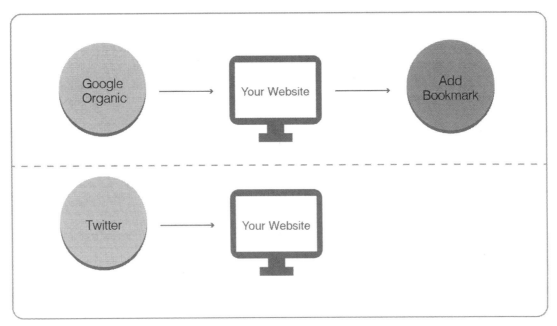

By default, Google Analytics will remember the most recent source and medium and uses the source/medium combination in place of 'Direct' for six months (this can be modified in the property settings). However, Google Analytics does attribute conversions to the 'Direct' channel in the Multi-Channel Funnels reports. Read Chapter 21 – "Multi-Channel Funnels" – for details.

Overview and Channels

The Overview report (and Channels report under 'All Traffic') allow you to analyze your inbound marketing at a top level, enabling you to understand performance at a glance.

Here you can see that organic search is driving the highest number of sessions, but that referrals are more likely to result in conversions. This information can be used to prioritize your initiatives. In this example, you could look at developing additional inbound links and even enhancing referrals with display advertising. You can also see that paid search has a good conversion rate, but that the higher bounce rate means that a large portion of people are immediately exiting from the landing page. This insight can be used to analyze the paid landing pages and to begin landing page tests to see if the bounce rate can be reduced further.

The Acquisition reports include default channels that are predefined in Google Analytics. The default channels include:

- Direct
- Organic Search
- Social
- Email
- Referral
- Paid Search
- Other Advertising
- Display

You can configure the channel groupings to separate your branded paid search and your generic paid search. This allows you to see a top level grouping of your branded keyword performance for your company, and product names that you are bidding on compared to your descriptive (or generic) keywords. Read Chapter 21 – "Multi-Channel Funnels"– for configuring the branded and generic paid search channels.

The channel groupings can be further customized if you would prefer to group your traffic into different categories. For example, if you are using campaign tagged URLs, you might see a channel called 'Other'. This occurs when Google Analytics doesn't recognize your particular naming convention. In this case, you might want to define an additional channel (or channels) to identify these campaigns appropriately in your reports.

Before you jump into creating custom channels, you will need to know which campaigns are contributing to the 'Other' channel. To do this click on 'Other' and you will see the source that is being used for the campaign.

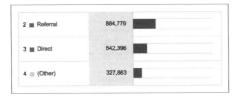

Source	Acquisition		
	Sessions	% New Sessions	New Users
	327,863 % of Total: 10.71% (3,060,970)	33.84% Avg for View: 43.23% (-21.72%)	110,960 % of Total: 8.38% (1,323,379)
1. brochure	73,834 (22.52%)	24.62%	18,177 (16.38%)
2. email-promotion	59,811 (18.24%)	40.91%	24,468 (22.05%)

This example shows a number of sessions attributed to 'brochure' and 'email-promotion'. In this case a custom channel can be created for the offline brochure and the email channel modified to include the custom source that has been defined for the promotional emails. To do this, click on 'Edit Channel Grouping' at the top of the Acquisition Overview report.

Tip: Changing the default groups permanently modifies future data coming into your view, and you need Edit level permissions to make changes. If you don't want to modify the default groups you can also create a new channel grouping by navigating to 'Admin', select 'Channel Settings' under the particular view and click 'New Channel Grouping'. This allows you to add different groupings to meet different reporting needs.

Now click 'Define a New Channel' and name the channel 'Offline'. Since 'brochure' is used as the source of the offline campaign select 'Source' and enter 'brochure' as the value.

Channel groupings are applied in a cascading order, so channels defined at the top of the report will be applied first. To be safe, drag the new 'Offline' channel to the bottom of the list. This will mean that if there is a default channel that already matches and the report won't be messed up.

Now it's time to modify the default 'Email' channel to add the 'email-promotion' source. To do this, click to edit the 'Email' channel and then click 'Or'. Now select 'Source' and enter 'email-newsletter' as the value, click 'Done' and then click 'Save'.

You can also create additional channel groupings and switch between them in the reports, depending on the way you want to present the data. For example, if you just wanted to focus on your paid channels you could create channels for 'Paid Search', 'Paid Social', 'Display' and 'Paid Email'. This would mean you can just focus on those channels, while other traffic would be grouped as 'Other'. Once you have defined additional channel groupings you can switch between them using the drop-down at the top of the report. Click on 'Default Channel Grouping' and then select one of your custom groupings instead.

Channels

The Channels report is similar to the Overview report, but presents the data in a table. Both reports allow you to click on the name of a particular channel to then drill-down into that channel for a more detailed view.

For example, clicking on the 'Referral' channel will then give you a report showing all the top level domains that have sent traffic to your website. Clicking on the 'Social' channel will give you a list of social networks. Remember that the Channels report is all about providing you with a top level overview, so if you want to perform more detailed analysis for a particular channel, you can use other reports available in the Acquisition reports.

Treemaps

The Treemaps report provides a visualization of the different channels that people are using to find your website. When you first load the report channels with the most traffic will be larger and color is used to highlight the channels that generate higher engagement (based on people viewing more pages in a session).

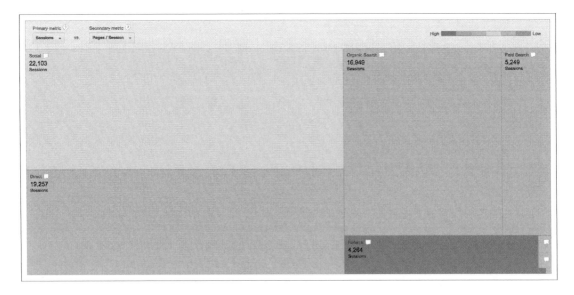

You can use the report in the same way as the Channels report, but you also have the option of clicking on the visualization to then see more granular details for a particular channel.

Source/Medium

Compared to the Channels report, the Source/Medium report gives you a more granular view of all the different ways people find your website by showing you all the different source and medium combinations that are driving traffic. For example, the Source/Medium report would show the following:

Source / Medium	Sessions
google / organic	100
company.com / referral	80
gmail.com / referral	50
yahoo / organic	10

While the Channels report would show the same data aggregated together:

Channel	Sessions
Organic Search	110
Referrals	130

The Source/Medium report will contain many more rows than the Channels report, so there is more information to digest. Use the report to establish your most important source and medium combinations and combinations that have higher levels of engagement driving more conversions or transactions.

Tip: Remember when using the Source/Medium report that 'Source' shows you where the message is seen and 'Medium' tells you how the message was communicated. So 'google/organic' means the website was seen on Google in the free search results before someone clicked through to the website.

You can also identify source and medium combinations where you have a high amount of traffic, but lower conversion rates. To do this look for source/medium combinations that have a high number of sessions, but a lower than expected conversion rate.

Source / Medium	Acquisition			Behavior				Conversions All Goals ▼		
	Sessions ↓	% New Sessions	New Users	Bounce Rate	Pages / Session	Avg. Session Duration	Goal Conversion Rate	Goal Completions	Goal Value
	68,097 % of Total: 100.00% (68,097)	85.04% Avg for View: 85.04% (0.00%)	57,907 % of Total: 100.00% (57,907)	43.45% Avg for View: 43.45% (0.00%)	5.52 Avg for View: 5.52 (0.00%)	00:02:15 Avg for View: 00:02:15 (0.00%)	25.09% Avg for View: 25.09% (0.00%)	17,086 % of Total: 100.00% (17,086)	$4,131.00 % of Total: 100.00% ($4,131.00)
1. youtube.com / referral	21,223 (31.17%)	97.24%	20,637 (35.64%)	44.95%	2.52	00:01:25	6.82%	1,447 (8.47%)	$361.50 (8.75%)
2. (direct) / (none)	19,257 (28.28%)	80.56%	15,513 (26.79%)	39.11%	7.41	00:02:50	34.23%	6,591 (38.58%)	$1,597.25 (38.66%)
3. google / organic	16,712 (24.54%)	78.95%	13,194 (22.78%)	40.59%	6.63	00:02:38	35.29%	5,898 (34.52%)	$1,429.75 (34.61%)
4. company / email	5,379 (7.90%)	91.36%	4,914 (8.49%)	72.30%	2.03	00:00:30	8.29%	446 (2.61%)	$111.25 (2.69%)
5. google / cpc	1,233 (1.81%)	47.93%	591 (1.02%)	10.82%	16.72	00:05:50	76.97%	949 (5.55%)	$214.75 (5.20%)

This example shows that 'company/email' is driving a good amount of traffic to the website, but has a lower conversion rate. The next step is to perform some more detailed analysis. Start by clicking the name of the source medium combination. Now you will be on a more detailed report that just focuses on that method people used to access your website. You can now ask additional questions about the email newsletter to determine what might be causing the lower conversion rate.

To ask an additional question, click on 'Other' which allows you to change what is seen in the report. Let's start by asking the question "What pages do people land on from our email newsletter?" After clicking 'Other', search for 'Landing Page' and click it (to apply it to the report). You will now have a list of the first pages people see as they click through from the email.

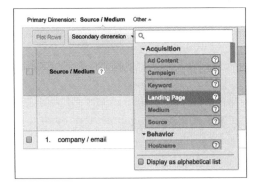

This allows you to understand the pages that are better at driving conversions by looking at the conversion rate associated with each landing page. You can then use these insights to tweak future email newsletters to ensure people are sent to the pages that are more likely to result in conversions.

Now you can ask a different question, like "Are people in particular countries more likely to convert?". To do this click on 'Landing Page', search for 'Country' and click it to apply it to the report. The report will now show you the geographic location of people clicking through to your website from your email newsletter. This can provide you with insights to inform the way you segment your email subscribers and help determine offers you make to people in particular locations.

Tip: You can layer even more questions to perform analysis. Instead of selecting 'Landing Page' or 'Country' in this example, try selecting different options that are available.

Referrals

Although you can see referrals in other Acquisition reports, like the Source/Medium report, the Referrals report gives you a consolidated view of all the sites that link to your website. So remember that this report shows you the same data that you saw in the Source/Medium report, but all combined in one place.

The report also allows you to drill-down into individual referring websites to see the particular page or pages on that website that have linked through to your website. This is useful to understand how the website is linking to you and also to understand what is being said about your brand. Look for referrals from forums and blogs and then click on the particular referring website to then see all the individual pages linking to your website. You can quickly view the page that links to your website by clicking on the little outbound link icon that appears next to the URL of each page in the report.

Tip: If the link to your website is in a forum or a blog's category page, then remember that the link might have been pushed onto another page on the referring website. Try navigating to the earlier pages and looking for the link to your website.

If you find a good quality blog or forum that is driving high quality traffic to your website you might want to consider engaging regularly on that website. If the website accepts advertising, you might also want to consider running paid ads on that website to drive even more people to your website.

Tip: You can check if a website accepts ads (for your Google AdWords campaigns) by using the Display Planner Tool in Google AdWords. If you search for the website and it is listed in the tool you can target that website in your display campaigns.

You will see hosted email solutions in the report, for example, sessions originating from 'mail.google.com' are coming from people clicking links in emails on Gmail. Some hosted email solutions can appear as multiple referring websites, you might see traffic coming from 'us-mg5.mail.yahoo', 'us-mg6.mail.yahoo.com' and other similar domains. These are all from Yahoo Mail.

Source	Acquisition		
	Sessions ↓	% New Sessions	New Users
	610 % of Total: 0.15% (411,187)	**50.33%** Avg for View: 83.37% (-39.64%)	**307** % of Total: 0.09% (342,824)
1. mail.google.com	**430** (70.49%)	46.28%	199 (64.82%)
2. us-mg5.mail.yahoo.com	**21** (3.44%)	66.67%	14 (4.56%)
3. us-mg6.mail.yahoo.com	**17** (2.79%)	76.47%	13 (4.23%)
4. mail.aol.com	**12** (1.97%)	66.67%	8 (2.61%)
5. bay177.mail.live.com	**8** (1.31%)	12.50%	1 (0.33%)

You will also see social networks in the Referrals report, as Twitter, Facebook and LinkedIn are all websites. Some social networks will be easier to spot than others, **t.co** for example is traffic coming from Twitter. If you want to report on social networks, then you probably want to jump to the dedicated set of social reports in the Acquisition section, it will give you the same data in a more readable format.

Google AdWords Reports

The Google AdWords reports are a dedicated set of reports for all your Google AdWords campaigns, allowing you to analyze your campaign performance in detail. The reports allow you to understand how people engage with your website after they have clicked your ads. This helps you identify what is working and what could be improved with your campaigns, through to your landing pages and website experience.

Campaigns

The Campaigns report reflects the campaign structure created in your Google AdWords account. You can click on the name of a particular campaign to see a list of the ad groups contained in the campaign. Clicking on an ad group will give you the list of keywords you are targeting or details of the particular targeting method you are using in the ad group. For example, if you drill down into an ad group targeting topics on the Google Display Network, you'll see a list of the topics. However, if you drill down into an ad group displaying search ads you will see the keywords that are included in that ad group.

Start by looking for campaigns that have a higher than average bounce rate. This can be a great way to identify opportunities to either change the destination URLs in your ads, or to improve the landing pages on your website. A quick way to identify campaigns with higher than average bounce rates is to click on the comparison icon above the table on the right hand side.

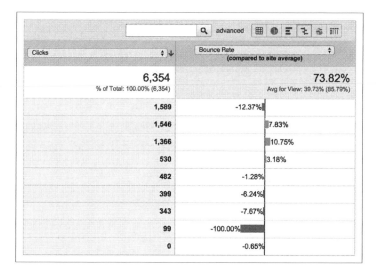

Now on the drop-down select 'Bounce Rate'. You will immediately be able to see which campaigns have better bounce rates compared to your overall website average. Now click on a campaign with a higher than average bounce rate (these will be the ones with the red bar). Next, click on 'Secondary Dimension' and select 'Destination URL' – this will allow you to quickly identify the landing page (or pages) you are sending people to from your ads. If you're using more than one destination URL you might find there are landing pages with a better bounce rate.

Tip: You can repeat this analysis for your goal and ecommerce conversion rates by selecting a conversion related metric instead of 'Bounce Rate'.

Treemaps

The Treemaps report is similar to the Campaigns report, but provides you with a graphic visualization of your campaign data. When you first load the report you will see your campaigns presented in a heatmap style. The larger the square, the more sessions are driven by that particular campaign. The color will show you which campaigns have better and worse bounce rates as people land on your website.

At the top of the treemap you can change the 'Primary' and 'Secondary' metrics to alter what is displayed in the visualization. For example, you can click on 'Sessions' and change it to 'Impressions' to understand which campaigns are driving the greatest visibility of your ads. You can also change the 'Bounce Rate' to other metrics, like 'Goal Conversion Rate' to see which campaigns have higher and lower conversion rates once people are on your website.

Just like the Campaigns report you can click on the campaign names in the table to drill down through your campaign structure. Clicking on an ad group will then mean the visualization shows you a treemap of the keywords you are targeting.

Bid Adjustments

The Bid Adjustments report allows you to see any changes you have made to bids based on targeting and scheduling. If you have made bid adjustments in Google AdWords for devices, locations or ad schedules, you will see these modifications to your default bid in the report. When you first load the report you will see a list of your campaigns and clicking on the small arrow next to a campaign will toggle open the bid adjustments.

Device	Location	Ad Schedule	Plot Rows	Secondary dimension ▼		
				Acquisition		
	Campaign	Device	Bid Adj.	Clicks ? ↓	Cost ?	
		ALL	--	11,427 % of Total: 100.00% (11,427)	$21,382.86 % of Total: 100.00% ($21,382.86)	
☐	1. ▼ General [Search]	ALL	--	2,822	$5,585.99	
		Computers	--	2,461	$4,904.40	
		Mobile devices with full browsers	+10%	200	$367.62	
		Tablets with full browsers	--	161	$313.98	

By default, you will see the device bid adjustments for your campaigns. Switch between the different types of bid adjustments by using the buttons above the table.

The bid adjustment percentages in the report reflect the current adjustments from your Google AdWords account. The bid adjustments that you set in your account can be informed by your own insights into your target audience, as well as your Google Analytics reports. After you have set your bid adjustments in your campaigns you can then use the report to evaluate the success of these strategies.

The way you evaluate success will depend on the objectives of your campaign. If your primary objective is to drive conversions you will want to focus on the conversion rate of your campaign. If you're driving sales look at ecommerce conversion rate, or if you are building awareness look at either clicks or sessions.

Tip: To view sessions in the Bid Adjustments report, click on 'Site Usage' above the timeline. This will give the 'Sessions' column along with website engagement data for your campaigns.

This example focuses on conversions, but remember you can use the same method to analyze performance for other campaign objectives. Let's start by looking at the 'ALL' row for a particular campaign. You can see that the overall conversion rate is 4.37%.

| Campaign | Location | Bid Adj. | Acquisition | Conversions All Goals ▾ |
			Clicks ? ↓	Goal Conversion Rate ?
ALL		--	**26,146** % of Total: 100.00% (26,146)	**4.37%** Avg for View: 6.57% (-33.52%)
▾ Remarketing [Display]	ALL	--	31,231	0.76%
	Sydney, AU	+35%	11,657	8.90%
	Melbourne, AU	+47%	10,239	8.45%
	Victoria, AU	+22%	7,691	3.93%
	New South Wales, AU	+27%	904	4.42%
	Western Australia, AU	+44%	740	5.70%
	View more...			

This example shows a number of bid adjustments based on audience location. Next, you should compare the conversion rates for each of these locations against the overall conversion rate.

In this example, you can quickly see that the conversion rate for Sydney is well above the overall conversion rate of 4.37%, so in this case you might consider increasing the bid adjustment further to achieve greater visibility.

Tip: There are a number of factors that will contribute to the success of increasing your bid adjustment for successful audience segments. After increasing a bid adjustment you should continue to review the performance of the segment to ensure it continues to meet your objectives.

You can also see in this example that Victoria has a bid adjustment of +22%, however the 3.93% conversion rate is lower than the overall conversion rate. In this case you might want to consider lowering the bid adjustment to reflect the reduced performance against your objectives. However, before you reduce the bid adjustment you should review the campaign and landing pages in more detail to rule out other reasons for the reduced performance. In this example looking at location bid adjustments, ask the following questions before making a final decision:

- Are there particular keywords impacting the results?

- Are there other bid adjustments that are having an impact?

- Has the default bid been modified at a more granular level? For example, keyword level or for particular display placements.

- Is there enough data to make a decision? If there are only a few conversions then this won't help you to make an informed decision.

- Are the landing pages appropriate? If the landing page doesn't appeal to the audience segment, then this can impact conversion rates.

- Did anything happen to the landing pages? For example, did the website go offline.

- Are there any seasonal or other local explanations? For example, holidays and special events.

You can use a similar approach if you are evaluating the performance of other bid adjustments for your campaigns. Also remember to consider micro conversions and your secondary objectives before making a final decision about modifying your bid adjustments.

> **Tip:** If you are selling online, or have defined the values of your goals, you can compare the ROI (based on advertising cost) of your bid adjustments. To do this select the 'Clicks' option at the top of the report.

Keywords

The Keywords report is a dedicated report for the keywords you are bidding on in your campaigns. The report also includes details about the targeting methods you are using for any display campaigns that you are running. In the following example, you can see keywords being bid on, along with content targeting, remarketing and topics being targeted on the Google Display Network.

It's important to remember that this report shows you the keywords you are bidding in your campaigns, and not the actual keywords people are searching for on Google. They are not always the same because of the different keyword match types you can use in Google AdWords. Read the "Keyword Matching" section in Chapter 4 for details.

Keyword	Acquisition			
	Clicks ↓	Cost	CPC	Sessions
	6,354 % of Total: 100.00% (6,354)	$4,007.34 % of Total: 100.00% ($4,007.34)	$0.63 Avg for View: $0.63 (0.00%)	5,511 % of Total: 12.50% (44,101)
1. (content targeting)	3,725 (58.62%)	$1,829.97 (45.67%)	$0.49	3,180 (57.70%)
2. running shoes	585 (9.21%)	$282.51 (7.05%)	$0.48	550 (9.98%)
3. gym shoes	483 (7.60%)	$270.65 (6.76%)	$0.56	465 (8.44%)
4. (remarketing/content targeting)	395 (6.22%)	$108.51 (2.71%)	$0.27	198 (3.59%)
5. latest sport shoes	200 (3.15%)	$113.90 (2.84%)	$0.57	190 (3.45%)

To understand where your ads are being displayed, click 'Secondary Dimension', then search for and select 'Ad Distribution Network'. This will allow you to see your search and display campaigns in the report.

If you would like to focus on your search campaigns you can apply a table filter to your report. Start by making sure you have the Secondary Dimension applied and then click 'Advanced' to the right of the search bar. Select 'Include', search for and select 'Ad Distribution Network' and then click 'Containing' and change it to 'Exactly Matching'. Enter 'Google Search' as the value and click 'Apply'. The report will now update and you will only see the keywords you are bidding on for your search campaigns. From here you can add the report to your shortcuts by clicking 'Shortcut' at the very top of the report.

Tip: If you prefer to use a custom report to view your keywords you can add the Google AdWords segment and custom report to your account, see http://lovesdata.co/iL3nw

Use the report to identify keywords that have higher than expected conversion rates. These keywords can potentially be placed into dedicated ad groups, allowing you to perform more detailed ad testing. You can also add them into a dedicated campaign and ad group to allocate a greater portion of your advertising budget. Analysing the ad variations that are displayed with your highly performing keywords can reveal ad variations that are working well and that can potentially provide ideas for new ads in other ad groups.

To quickly compare the conversion rate performance of your keywords, click on the 'Comparison' icon above the table on the right-hand side.

Then above the bar graph click 'Sessions' and change this to 'Goal Conversion Rate' or 'Ecommerce Conversion Rate' (you can also select to see the conversion rate of an individual goal if you choose). The report will now give you a quick visual guide showing the performance of your keywords against the overall average conversion rate for your whole website. Look for the green bars indicating a higher than average conversion rate.

You can use the report to identify keywords that have a lower than expected conversion rate. To do this, continue to use the comparison report, or you can switch back to the standard report view by clicking on the 'Data' icon above the table on the right-hand side.

Now you can use the report to look for keywords that have a lower than expected conversion. When you are reviewing the report, also look for keywords that have a high bounce rate as this can also indicate that there is a disconnect between the keyword and the expectation of users as they land on your website. Once you have identified a lower performing keyword, click on it to view the details page. Then click 'Secondary Dimension' and search for and select 'Destination URL'. You will now see where people are landing on your website.

If you are directing people to multiple pages you'll see them listed separately and you might be able to identify a page that provides better results. If this is the case, you can test new ads to see if sending more traffic to that page improves the performance of the keyword.

If you're sending people to a single page you should copy and paste the landing page URL into a new browser window to understand what people experience when they click on your ad. The landing page needs to relate closely to what people are searching. If they don't relate, this can lead to a higher bounce rate and a lower conversion rate. In most cases the landing page should contain the keyword or a close variation of the keyword in the content of the page, including the headings.

If you have reviewed the landing page and feel it closely relates to the keyword, then the next step is to compare the keyword you are bidding on to the actual search queries people are entering into Google to find your ad.

> **Tip:** You can change the report to show keywords used on desktop, mobile and tablet devices by using the options at the very top of the report.

Search Queries

The Search Queries report shows you the actual search terms people are entering on Google to find and click on your ads. By reviewing the actual search queries you can identify new keywords to add to your campaigns as well as potential negative keywords.

If you are running ads on the Google Display Network you will see '(not set)' in the report. This is because people engaging with your display ads don't have a search query associated with their clicks. You can filter these out of the report by applying a table filter or by applying a segment to the report. To apply the table filter, click on 'Advanced' to the right of the search option. Then click 'Include' and change it to 'Exclude'. Click 'Keyword' and change it to 'Matched Search Query', then click 'Containing' and select 'Exactly Matching', enter '(not set)' as the value and click 'Apply'.

You can customize the report to see search queries along with the corresponding keyword you are bidding on within your campaigns. To do this, click on 'Secondary Dimension' and search for and select 'Keyword'. You will now quickly be able to compare search queries to the keywords you are bidding on. Spend time scanning through the report and create a list of search queries that are different to the keywords you are bidding on. From here you can decide if you want to add them to your campaigns or prevent your ads from displaying by adding them as negative keywords.

> **Tip:** Another way to perform this analysis is by using a custom report. To use the preconfigured custom report visit http://lovesdata.co/2fTi9

Hour of Day

The Hour of Day report shows you the performance of your Google AdWords campaigns broken down by hour of day. This allows you to see peak times in terms of traffic volume, but also when your campaigns have the highest conversion rates and engagement. By default, the report will be ordered by hour, starting at midnight ('0' – zero) and moving through the course of the day as you scroll down the report. You can also see this on the timeline at the top of the report.

If you're focused on conversions use the report to identify the times of the day with the highest conversion rate. The quickest way to see these times it to click twice on the column heading of 'Goal Conversion Rate' (or 'Ecommerce Conversion Rate') so that the table is reordered to show the highest conversion rate first.

Since your highest conversion rate might have only occurred from a handful of sessions, you can also use the report to see the most important times based on a combination of conversion rate and the number of sessions. To do this, click on 'Default' to the right of 'Sort Types' and select 'Weighted'. This will reorder the report so that the hour of day that has the highest conversion rate, along with a significant number of sessions comes first.

> **Tip:** Weighted sort takes sessions into consideration along with the metric you are ordering by. This means the most important information is placed at the top of your report. For more details on weighted sort visit http://lovesdata.co/VcsBk

Now that you have identified your most important times for conversions, you can use this to inform your Google AdWords strategy. For example, making bid adjustments to increase visibility at particular times of the day.

You can then repeat the analysis for your micro conversions to see if there are times of day where people are more likely to complete your secondary objectives. If you find times where this occurs, you can then look at scheduling your calls to action and landing pages based on the conversions that are likely to occur at particular times of the day.

For more detailed analysis, you can use a custom report that breaks down the hour of day reporting by each campaign you are running. Visit http://lovesdata.co/ht4Ar to add the custom report to your account. Then you can click on the name of a particular campaign to see the performance of that campaign by hour of day. This will show the hour of day with the highest number of sessions at the top of the report, so don't forget to reorder the report based on 'Conversion Rate' or your metric of choice.

Destination URLs

The Destination URLs report shows you all the landing pages used in your ad variations. Start by looking for landing pages that have a high bounce rate. These are pages that might have usability issues or might not relate well to your ads and keywords. Clicking on a page will take you to the detail view and by default this will show you the types of ads that you are running. You will see 'Content' for your display ads and 'Google Search' if you are running search ads. If you're running display and search campaigns you might find your landing page has different levels of engagement based on the type of ads you are running.

Ad Distribution Network ?	Acquisition				Behavior
	Clicks ? ↓	Cost ?	CPC ?	Sessions ?	Bounce Rate ?
	1,589 % of Total: 25.01% (6,354)	$5,961.15 % of Total: 14.88% ($40,007.34)	$0.38 Avg for View: $0.63 (-40.51%)	1,459 % of Total: 3.31% (44,101)	64.63% Avg for View: 39.73% (62.88%)
1. Content	981 (61.74%)	$3,010.68 (50.60%)	$0.31	884 (60.59%)	77.99%
2. Google Search	351 (22.09%)	$1,931.01 (29.36%)	$0.50	329 (22.55%)	42.92%
3. Search partners	257 (16.17%)	$1,019.46 (20.04%)	$0.46	246 (16.86%)	54.88%

In this example, you can see that the search ads have a much lower bounce rate than the display ads. You can now review the display ads and their messaging along with the landing page. There might be insights from search ads that can also be applied to the display ads to improve performance. For example, the search ads might have a different call to action or message which could be tested in the display ads.

You might also find that particular ads perform better than other ads for the landing page. To see how your ads perform, click on 'Secondary Dimension' and search for and select 'Ad Content'. This will show you the headline or title of your ads and allow you to see if particular ads result in higher engagement levels.

If you're running search ads you will also want to check to see the performance of the landing page for your keywords. Click 'Keyword' above the table and below the timeline to see the keywords you are bidding on that send people to the landing page. Look for keywords that have a higher than expected bounce rate and determine if these are appropriate for the particular landing page. Potentially the keyword might be better suited to a different ad group or campaign, or maybe you need to create a new landing page with more targeted content to improve performance.

The Destination URLs report can also be used to identify your top performing landing pages. Head back to the main report by using the menu on the left or the breadcrumbs at the top of the report. Now click on 'Goal Conversion Rate' or 'Ecommerce Conversion Rate' to order your landing pages with the highest conversion rate at the top of the report. Then click 'Default' to the right of 'Sort Type' and select 'Weighted'. You will now have your most important landing pages based on conversion rate and sessions listed in the report.

Start from the top of the report and scan through the table for pages you didn't expect to have a high conversion rate. Then copy and paste the URL into a new browser window and look for elements in the page that are contributing to conversions. This might include content, images, buttons and other website elements. Try to compare what is on your most successful landing pages to the elements that are on your least successful landing pages. You can then rework or test new elements on your least successful landing pages to try and improve their performance.

Display Targeting

The Display Targeting report is a dedicated report for your display campaigns and allows you to analyze the performance of your campaigns, based on the different display targeting methods you are using. When you open the report you'll see the display keywords used to present your ads. The keywords are displayed along with their campaign and ad group, allowing you to see if keywords are appropriately structured in your account. Ideally, display keywords are structured in a similar way to search keywords, in that they should be grouped to reflect the ad variations and landing page.

You can click on the name of an ad group in the report to see the display keywords that are contained in that particular ad group. You can then identify keywords that should be moved to more appropriate ad groups or even identify the need to restructure the ad groups in your campaign.

When you review your display keywords in the report it's important to remember that your ad groups might be using multiple targeting methods to display your ads. For example, display keywords along with a particular website placement. So it can be useful to have your Google AdWords account open in another window to quickly check your targeting. To do this, navigate to the same ad group in your Google AdWords account, click on the 'Display Network' tab and then click 'Add Targeting'. This will show you the targets that you have set for the ad group.

The Display Targeting report allows you to see performance for all the different targeting methods. The buttons at the top of the report allow you to switch between the targeting options.

Clicking on the 'Placements' option will show you a breakdown of your automatic and management placements. From here you can drill down to view the particular placements. If you're using automatic placement targeting, this is especially important as you should review where your ads are being displayed on a regular basis. You can use this to identify automatic placements that are performing well and add these to your management placements, so you can control your bids. You can also use the report to identify poorly performing or irrelevant placements that you want to exclude in your display campaigns.

Automatic Placements
1.   youtube.com
2.   pressroomvip.com
3.   youtube.com
4.   quizzyn.com
5.   answers.com
6.   anonymous.google
7.   oasisactive.com
8.   tagged.com
9.   youtube.com
10. blogspot.com

The report provides insights about the performance of your ads within a particular website on the Google Display Network. Use this to understand if the placement is appropriate for your objectives and how well the placement relates to your offer and messaging in your ads.

You might identify pages that you want to specifically target in your display campaign or pages that you want to exclude. Spend time reviewing where your ads have been displayed – it can be useful to visit the sites if you haven't seen them before, and then determine if they are appropriate for your campaigns.

You can also use the Placements reports for your managed placements to review the performance of your ads. Head back to the main report by using the menu on the left or the breadcrumbs and click on 'Managed Placements'.

Tip: For details on managing display ads, including the different display targeting options read the Google AdWords "Display Targeting" section in Chapter 6.

You can also view the other targeting options within the report, including 'Topics', 'Interests and Remarketing', 'Age' and 'Gender'. You can apply the same technique used to analyze the performance of display keywords to evaluate the success of your other targeting methods. Look for segments within each targeting method that perform well and use those insights to inform your bidding and targeting strategy moving forward. If a segment has performed poorly for an extended period of time with a significant number of clicks, you should consider reducing your bids and even excluding that segment from your targets.

Video Campaigns

The Video Campaigns report gives you details about the performance of your YouTube video ads. Overall, the report provides the same data you will find in your Google AdWords account, but if people click through from your video ads to your website you will be able to see how they engage with you once they are on your website.

Most video ads are for branding and awareness campaigns, so the number of sessions is likely to be very low in comparison to the views of your video.

> **Tip:** You can also use the Multi-Channel Funnels report to understand the impact of people viewing your video ads even if they don't click through to your website. Read "Impression Reporting" section in Chapter 21 for details.

Shopping Campaigns

The Shopping Campaigns report allows you to understand the performance of your shopping ads. The report is similar to the Video Campaigns report and gives you data for the acquisition, behavior and conversion metrics.

You have the option to view the Shopping Categories, Product Types and Brands that you have included in your Google Merchant Center feed. The reports can help you pinpoint what is working and not working within your Shopping Campaigns.

Search Engine Optimization

The Search Engine Optimization (SEO) reports are an integration with Google Search Console (Webmaster Tools), which allows you to access additional data about the performance of your website in Google search results. If you don't already have a Google Search Console account, it is worth taking the time to set one up because it will give you valuable insights into the performance of your website. The main benefit is that you can see the number of impressions received in organic results, along with clicks, average position and Click-through Rate (CTR), just as you see inside your Google AdWords account for your paid keywords.

Under the 'Traffic Sources' menu item, select 'Search Engine Optimization' and then click 'Queries'. If you see a list of keywords and data it means the reports have already been set up. However, if you see a message saying 'this report requires Webmaster Tools to be enabled', then you will need to set up the report.

> **Tip:** You will need to be an administrator in Google Analytics to set up the Search Engine Optimization reports. If you are not an administrator, you will need to work with your administrator to set them up or request administrator access for the account.

To set up the report, click the 'Set up Webmaster Tools data sharing' button. You will now be taken to the property settings page. At the bottom of the page, you will see 'Webmaster Tools Settings' – click on 'Edit' below this heading.

You will now be taken to Google Search Console where you will need to either select the website from the list of available sites already verified in your account, or you will need to add the website. If you don't see the website in the list click the 'add a site to Webmaster Tools' button at the bottom of the page.

Click on the 'Add a Site' button and follow the steps to add and verify your website.

> **Tip:** You need to prove that you own the website in order to access Google Search Console data, which is why there is a verification process. There are a number of ways to verify your site:
> - Use Google Analytics tracking code (if you are using the asynchronous tracking code)
> - Add a special meta tag into your website's code
> - Add a DNS record to your domain name registration
> - Upload a special file to your server

Once your website is verified, you can click on the 'Manage Site' button in Google Search Console. Click 'Google Analytics Property' and select the appropriate Google Analytics property that you would like to link to. This will be the property that includes the profile (or profiles) where you want to access data from Google Search Console.

Now you will be directed back to Google Analytics where you can navigate back to the 'Search Engine Optimization' reports under 'Acquisition'. The Queries report provides you with a list of the different keywords that people search for on Google that have displayed your website somewhere in the search results. This includes the times when people search and don't click through to your website.

- **Impressions shows you the number** of times your website is displayed in search results (with or without a click).

- **Clicks are the number of** times people clicked through to your website from the search results.

- **Average Position tells you where** your website appears on average in the search results. An average position of 1 to 10 will mean that you are typically on the first page of search results.

- **CTR is your organic Click-through Rate**, which is clicks divided by impressions presented as a percentage. The higher your CTR, the better, as this indicates a higher level of engagement with your listings inside the search results.

Unfortunately, the data presented in the report is currently rounded which means you don't have access to a full, accurate set of data. You can access your full set of data directly in Google Search Console by visiting http://lovesdata.co/WZvRd, selecting your website and navigating to the 'Search Queries' report under 'Search Traffic'.

Use the reports in Google Analytics as a top-level gauge to see major changes and then jump into Google Search Console to confirm these changes and for detailed reporting. In Google Analytics you can use the 'Compare To' option within the date range selector to quickly see the major changes occurring for your website. Focus on the downward trending keywords, as these are areas where you will want to focus your optimization efforts.

Query	Impressions	↓ Clicks	Average Position	CTR
	0.34% ▲ 48,062 vs 48,226	0.73% ▲ 2,493 vs 2,475	2.28% ▲ 9.0 vs 9.2	1.07% ▲ 5.19% vs 5.13%
1. gym equipment				
Mar 1, 2015 - Mar 31, 2015	4,500 (9.36%)	50 (2.01%)	2.4	1.11%
Jan 29, 2015 - Feb 28, 2015	4,500 (9.33%)	60 (2.42%)	2.5	1.33%
% Change	0.00%	-16.67%	-3.75%	-16.67%
2. shoes for sport				
Mar 1, 2015 - Mar 31, 2015	3,000 (6.24%)	600 (24.07%)	1.3	20.00%
Jan 29, 2015 - Feb 28, 2015	3,000 (6.22%)	600 (24.24%)	1.2	20.00%
% Change	0.00%	0.00%	3.49%	0.00%

In this example, you can see that the number of clicks, average position and CTR have decreased for a particular keyword. As the performance is decreasing, you should review how your website appears in the organic search results. The best way to do this is to open a new private browsing window (for example incognito in Chrome), and then search for the keyword. This allows you to see if your headline and description are appropriate and what competitors are doing to stand out in the search results.

From here you can look to optimize the content of the page that is being displayed in search results. This can include changing the headline and content, through to writing a new title and description tag to be more relevant to the keyword. To download Google's SEO guide PDF visit http://lovesdata.co/BiRFg

> **Tip:** You can apply a secondary dimension of 'Country' to the report to see if changes are specific to your target audience.

The Landing Page report shows you data for the pages listed in search results. Use the report to identify poorly performing pages that can be optimized, and to also identify top performing pages.

Let's start by looking at the poorly performing pages. Start by clicking on the 'Clicks' column to order landing pages by overall popularity. This allows you to focus on pages that are driving the most amount of traffic to the website. Then look for pages that have a low CTR – in most cases you will want to look for pages that have a CTR less than 3%. These are pages that you will want to focus on when optimizing your content.

Tip: You can use this same process directly in Google Search Console. Just look for the 'Top Pages' tab in the 'Search Queries' report. The advantage of using Google Search Consoles is that you can click on a page to see the top keywords people are using to find the page. This can help you understand the keyword or keywords that you need to focus on when optimizing your content.

To identify your top performing pages you can repeat the process, except this time look for pages that have a high CTR. In most cases this should be above 5%. Once you have identified your top performing pages you can review them to understand what is leading to their success. Focus on the headline on the page, the content and the page title and description meta tags. Then compare these top performing pages to other pages on your website. Ideally you should do a side-by-side comparison to help quickly identify the differences between particular pages.

The Geographical Summary report shows you impressions, clicks and CTR by country. Use the report to check your overall performance and identify potential geographic areas for improvement. The report can also be used to ensure that you're maintaining performance for your primary geographic markets. A good way to do this is to use the 'Compare' option within the date range selector and look for major changes. If your impressions, clicks and CTR are improving, that is great, but if you start to notice a decline you'll want to monitor this to ensure there are no major problems impacting your organic rankings on Google. When you do this you will also need to take seasonality and other changes in search volume into account.

Tip: A quick way to search for overall seasonality is to use Google Trends. Load the Google Trends website by visiting http://lovesdata.co/MqNp4, select your primary geographic audience by clicking on 'Worldwide' and select a country. Then click on 'All Categories' and browse through the list of categories and subcategories until you have found one that appropriately reflects your business. Once you select a category you will be able to see the overall trend for keywords that are included in the category. Now you can see if there is a dip in search volume that reflects the trend you are seeing in your Google Analytics or Google Search Console reports.

Above the table in the Geographical Summary report you can select 'Google Property' to understand how people are finding your website on Google. This allows you to see if people are using the web-based version of Google, the mobile version of Google or Google Image Search.

Social

The Social reports are a dedicated place for you to find details about your social networks. Before you start, it's important to highlight that you will have seen social networks show up in some of the other Acquisition reports. For example, you will find 'Social' in the Channels report and in the All Referrals report. So think of the social reports as a place to come to focus on your social media efforts, but remember that you will find social popping up in some of the other reports you use as well.

The Overview report can be a little confusing at first, as it includes data for all of your website traffic along with data just for your social networks. I promise this will start to make sense! Basically, any numbers at the top of the report that say 'Social' are just for your social traffic, while the other numbers are for all of your traffic.

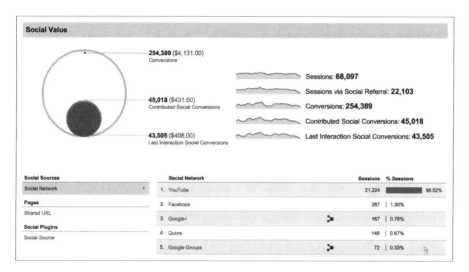

Looking at the report above you can see that overall there was a total of 254,389 conversions. Note that this is for all acquisition sources combined (not just for social). Then you'll see that there were 45,018 conversions assisted by social networks ('Contributed Social Conversions') and another 43,505 conversions resulting directly from social networks ('Last Interaction Social Conversions').

The 'Contributed' and 'Last Interaction' numbers show you the different attribution of social media for your conversions. A "Contributed' conversion is one where a social network has assisted in the conversion occurring. For example, if someone clicked through to your website from Facebook, and then later performed a search on Google before converting. In this case, Facebook assisted the conversion, but did not close the deal. A 'Last Interaction' conversion is counted when a social network was the last method somebody used before they completed the goal or transaction. For example, if someone clicked through to your website from Twitter and immediately converted, this would be a 'Last Interaction' conversion.

Attribution is covered in more detail in Chapter 21 – "Multi-Channel Funnels" – but what you can see is that the report allows you to get a full understanding of how social networks are assisting and driving conversions on your website.

The Overview report is designed to give you wider context to show you the relative performance of your social media initiatives, so you can quickly see how social is performing against your overall conversions. At the top of the report you can use the conversion selector to switch between your different ecommerce and goal objectives to see value and conversions for those particular actions. To select particular conversions click 'All' below 'Conversion' to include or exclude particular actions.

The Overview report also gives you a quick top 10 snapshot of the social networks driving the most sessions, the top shared URLs and any social interactions occurring on your website. Measuring these onsite interactions is covered later in the book.

Network Referrals

The Network Referrals report shows you the social networks that are referring traffic to your website. This is similar to the All Referrals report looked at earlier, but is just focused on the social networks that are sending you traffic. The report is also much cleaner than the All Referrals report because it provides the name of the social network and automatically combines multiple URLs that are for the same social network. For example, it will combine people coming from 'http://twitter.com' and 'http://t.co' (which is Twitter's official URL shortener) into 'Twitter'. This makes it much easier to see and report on the performance of each social network.

Clicking on the name of a social network allows you to see the links to your website that have been shared on the particular network. It also allows you to see which content is popular and the engagement with each shared URL.

Data Hub Activity

The Data Hub Activity report allows you to see what people are saying about your organization even if people don't click through to your website. This allows you to understand who is sharing and discussing your content. Before you get too excited, it's important to point out that the Data Hub Activity report requires social networks to send details about the activity to Google Analytics in order to generate the report – and not every social network chooses to send this information. You'll notice that Facebook, Twitter and LinkedIn are not included in the report. Social networks available in the report currently include Google+, Reddit, Meetup, Disqus and a handful of other networks.

> **Tip:** When you use the Network Referrals report looked at previously, you'll see a little crop circle icon next to some of the social networks. This icon tells you that they are included in the Data Hub Activity report.

Although the social networks that participate in the Data Hub are limited, you can still use the report to see what people are saying about your brand and content. For each mention in the report you can click on 'More' to perform additional actions.

- 'Filter on this Page' narrows the focus of the report to just show mentions that have included a link to that particular page on your website. For example, if you used this option on a mention that included a link to your homepage, then the report will update just to include mentions of your homepage.

- 'View Page' loads the page from your website that has been shared.

- 'View Activity' loads the post or activity on the social network. For example, selecting 'View Activity' for a Google+ mention will load the post on Google+.

- 'View Ripple' is only available for Google+ mentions and loads Google+ Ripples which allows you to see how your link has been shared. For more details on Google+ Ripples visit http://lovesdata.co/Tc6PZ

You can also see activities that don't include posts on social networks by selecting 'Events' towards the top of the report (above the table, but below the timeline). This will show activities where people are saving your content, for example saving a page to Pocket (a bookmarking application) to read later or clicking the +1 button to like the content on Google+.

Landing Pages

The Landing Pages report shows the most popular content that has been shared based on the number of people traveling through to your website from social networks. Use this report to identify the most popular content that is being shared on social networks and use this to inform the types of content you create moving forward.

Clicking on a particular landing page will then show you the social networks that have sent people to that particular page. Use this report to understand which content works on particular social networks. Depending on the social network, you could also consider amplifying the post by promoting it on that particular network. You also have the option of viewing the Data Hub activity for each landing page by selecting 'Social Network and Action' above the table.

> **Tip:** You can include the special Social report dimensions and metrics in Custom Reports in order to meet your particular reporting and analysis needs. For example, if you're looking to start advertising on social networks you could use a custom report that shows your current landing page conversion rates from social networks. To add this custom report visit http://lovesdata.co/c3liA

Trackbacks

The Trackbacks report shows you websites that have linked to your website even if people don't click through on the link. On the left of the report you'll see the website that includes the link and on the right you'll see the page that they are linking to on your website. To view the page that is linking to your website click on 'More' and then select 'View Trackback'.

> **Tip:** The Trackbacks report only contains a small selection of linking websites. To better understand inbound links, use the report along with the All Referrals report and other tools. You can use the Open Site Explorer tool from Moz to view links to a particular page. Visit http://lovesdata.co/xQJkK to use the tool.

Conversions

The Conversions report shows you the social networks that have directly led to conversions on your website. By default, the report shows you last click conversions – so somebody needs to have clicked through to your website from the social network, and then converted immediately (in the same session). To see both assisted and last click conversions, click on 'Assisted vs. Last Interaction Analysis' at the top of the report.

Now you can see which social networks are helping to assist conversions, and those that are closing conversions, along with the value of those conversions. The column on the right of the report shows you the assisted to last click conversion ratio. The lower the number and the closer it is to zero, the better the social network is at closing conversions. For these networks you can consider using calls to action in your content and ads that direct people to the conversion action. Networks that have a ratio close to one are balanced between closing and assisting conversions. For these networks, you'll also want to balance your content so you are not always trying to direct people to your macro conversions. Finally, the higher the ratio value is above one, the better the network is at assisting conversions. For these networks you should try to avoid strong calls to action and instead aim to get people engaging with your brand and your content.

When applying these insights remember that the assisted to last click conversion ratio can change over time. You can check the changes that are occurring by using the date range tool to compare your current date range with a previous date range. For example, comparing this month to the previous month or this quarter to last quarter.

> **Tip:** Just like the Social Overview report, you can select one or more conversions by clicking 'All' below 'Conversions' at the top of the report.

Plugins

The Plugins report allows you to view social interactions that have occurred on your website. For example, if you embedded a Facebook 'Like' button, a Twitter 'Follow' button or a Google '+1' button you can measure the number of people interacting with these social options.

It is quite normal to see a blank report if you don't have any social options embedded in your website. If you have added social buttons you will need to configure them to send data into your reports, this requires adding special code to the buttons. The exception to this is the Google +1 button, which automatically sends data to Google Analytics without the need for any customization.

The quickest and easiest way to add social buttons to your website is by using a third party tool like AddThis which allows you to place and manage social sharing buttons. AddThis also allows you to send data into the Plugins report by making a simple modification to their code. If you have limited web development resources this is a great way to let people engage with your content and also measure interactions into Google Analytics.

You can sign up for AddThis at http://lovesdata.co/SPj6q and learn how to integrate with Google Analytics at http://lovesdata.co/RxeVY

If you don't want to use a third-party tool, then you can also customize each social button you use to send data to Google Analytics. This requires using the social network's button API along with the Google Analytics social interaction tracking functionality. Visit http://lovesdata.co/VczvN for details. You can also find example code for the top social networks at http://lovesdata.co/us4mp

Once you are sending social plugin data to Google Analytics, the report will show you the number of social button interactions that occur on pages of your website. You will also see the total number of interactions that have occurred on each page.

Clicking 'Social Source' at the top of the Plugins report will show you the total number of button interactions grouped by their social network and 'Social Source and Action' will show you the social network along with the type of button interaction.

You can drill down into the Plugins report to see further details. If you head back to 'Social Entity', you can click on a particular page to see which social networks people have used. For example, if you see 'Facebook' and 105 'Social Actions' this tells you people have clicked the Facebook button 105 times on that page. From here you can click on 'Social Source and Action' to see both the social network and the particular type of button interaction that have occurred.

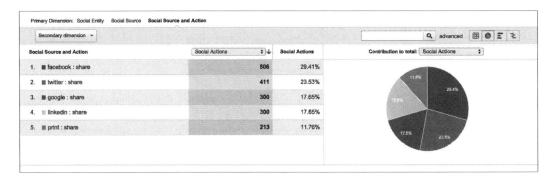

This can also be looked at in reverse where you drill down into a particular social network to see the pages that people interact with for that network. To do this, head back to the primary Plugins report (use the breadcrumbs at the top or primary menu on the left) and select 'Social Source'. Now click on the social network you are interested in analyzing, click 'Secondary Dimension' and select 'Social Entity'. This will now show all the pages people interact with for that particular social network.

Users Flow

The Users Flow report is identical to the User Flow report looked at in the Audience reports, but it only includes how people came to your website from a social network. This allows you to focus on how your social traffic navigates your website. For details on using the report head back to the "Audience Reports" section in this chapter.

18

Campaign Tracking

Google Analytics can be used to track your inbound marketing campaigns so you can understand how people are finding your website, and also compare the performance of your different marketing initiatives. There is a lot of detail that is automatically tracked by Google Analytics around how people are finding your website, including organic search and referrals directing people to your website. Don't forget to link Google AdWords with Google Analytics for detailed campaign reports in Google Analytics.

Going beyond the standard reports, you probably have your own custom marketing campaigns that you also want to track into Google Analytics. You are probably sending out email newsletters, running paid ads on social media and maybe even running offline marketing campaigns. In order to understand how these other marketing initiatives are performing you need to spend some time to get these details into Google Analytics.

Campaign Tracking

Tracking your custom marketing campaigns is achieved by defining campaign tags which become available in your Traffic Sources reports as people come through on the tagged URLs to your website.

The campaign tags you need to define are the *campaign name*, *source* and *medium*. The *campaign name* is the overarching name of your marketing initiative. You also need to define the *source*, which is where your message is seen and the *medium*, which is how your message is communicated. These are all required elements when you set up your campaign tags. There are also two optional tags which are designed for tracking non-AdWords CPC campaigns (for example tracking paid ads on Bing or Yahoo). These are: *content* (to understand the particular ad or call to action that people engaged with) and *term* (to track the particular keyword someone searched to find your ad).

Remember that source and medium has already been seen in the Traffic Sources reports. Campaign tracking is similar, but you define your own source and medium names for your own custom marketing initiatives. Also remember that source and medium are automatically tracked for referrals, organic searches and people coming directly to your website. Here is an example from the Traffic Sources report:

Source	Medium	Campaign
none	direct	none
linkedin.com	referral	none
google	organic	none

The first row, 'none', indicates people who are accessing the website directly, for example by entering the URL into their browser window. You can also see people finding the website via a link on LinkedIn, which is a referral. Finally, you can see people finding the website on Google and clicking on a free search result.

You will also notice that the campaign name for these methods of accessing the website are all 'none'. This is because all of these methods are automatically tracked. However, campaign names can be defined when you define campaign tags, along with your own defined source and medium:

Source	Medium	Campaign
your own	*your own*	*your own*

You can see this is just like the automatically tracked source and mediums, but you can also define an overarching campaign name. When defining your own source and medium, remember that these will be seen alongside the automatically tracked sources and mediums, so being clear, consistent and logical is important.

Google Analytics URL Builder

Let's start by looking at a simple example, before looking at more detailed scenarios, along with best practice recommendations. For example, you are going to track people finding your website after clicking on a link in your email newsletter. In this case the source will be 'customers' because you are only sending this email newsletter to people who have previously purchased. The medium will be 'email' because that is how the message is being communicated; and the overarching campaign name will be 'newsletter' because that describes your marketing initiative.

Now that you have decided on how to name the elements for your campaign tagged URL, you will need to tag the inbound links to your website. This can be done using the Google Analytics URL Builder. This allows you to take your campaign tag elements and get the final campaign tagged URL to use in your campaign. Continuing the email newsletter example, you would go to the URL builder and enter the source, medium and campaign name.

Step 1: Enter the URL of your website.

Website URL *

(e.g. http://www.urchin.com/download.html)

Step 2: Fill in the fields below. **Campaign Source, Campaign Medium and Campaign Name** should always be used.

Campaign Source *

(referrer: google, citysearch, newsletter4)

Campaign Medium *

(marketing medium: cpc, banner, email)

Campaign Term

(identify the paid keywords)

Campaign Content

(use to differentiate ads)

Campaign Name *

(product, promo code, or slogan)

SUBMIT   * Required field

Click 'Submit' and you are given the campaign tagged link that can be used in the email newsletter.

For this example, the final tagged URL is:

```
http://www.company.com?utm_source=customers&utm_
medium=email&utm_campaign=newsletter
```

Looking at the URL, you can identify the elements that were entered into the URL builder. Once you place this link in the email newsletter and somebody clicks the link to visit your website, they will be taken to 'http://www.company.com' and Google Analytics will automatically see the tags (utm_source, utm_medium and utm_campaign) and report the values for these tags into your reports ('customers', 'email' and 'newsletter').

You can access the URL builder at http://lovesdata.co/5D6si

> **Tip:** Once you are comfortable with campaign tagged URLs you don't actually need the URL builder to create them. Just make sure you always use utm_source, utm_medium and utm_campaign as they are the required campaign tags, and make use of the optional utm_term and utm_content tags if needed.

Campaign Tagging Non-AdWords CPC

If you are running Non-AdWords CPC campaigns (for example you are running ads on Bing or Yahoo) you need to set up campaign tagged URLs in order to correctly track these campaigns into Google Analytics.

If you are running ads on Bing you will want to go with something like the following:

Source	Medium	Campaign	Term	Content
bing	cpc	Bing CPC	{QueryString}	Ad {AdId}

The source should be defined as 'bing' because the ads are going to be seen on Bing and the medium as 'cpc' since they are cost-per-click ads. You probably want to change the overarching campaign name, from 'Bing CPC' to something more specific to the campaign you are running on Bing. The term is defined as '{QueryString}' because this will automatically take the search query and replace it in the campaign tagged URL. For example, if you were bidding on 'gardening book' and then someone searched and clicked on your ad, the term will automatically become 'gardening book' in the tagged URL. Then when you go into the reports you will be able to see all the different keywords people are using. The content is defined as 'ad {AdID}' which will automatically place the ID of the individual ad into the tagged URL. This is not perfect, but it does allow you to go back into the Bing advertising account to find the particular ad (or ads) that people clicked to visit your website.

Once you have created your campaign tag, you need to add this to all the URLs in your Bing advertising account. They need to be added to the end of your existing URLs in the destination URL for each and every ad variation in your account.

In the image above the destination URL used for the ad variation is:

http://www.gifts.com/baskets/chocolate?utm_source=bing&utm_medium=cpc&utm_campaign=Bing%20CPC&utm_term={QueryString}&utm_content=Ad%20{AdId}

If you were bidding on the keyword 'chocolate gifts online' and someone clicked on your ad the person would end up visiting:

http://www.gifts.com/baskets/chocolate?utm_source=bing&utm_medium=cpc&utm_campaign=Bing%20CPC&utm_term=chocolate%20gifts%20online&utm_content=Ad%20123456

If you are running ads on Yahoo, your campaign tagged URL will be similar to the Bing example previously covered (with just a few minor changes). A Yahoo tagged URL should be along the following lines:

Source	Medium	Campaign	Term	Content
yahoo	cpc	Yahoo CPC	{YSMKEY}	ad {YSMADID}

Just like the campaign tags for Bing Ads, you will probably want to change the campaign name to reflect the campaign you have set up in your Yahoo Search Marketing account. The term and content tags work in the same way as the ones used in the tagged URL for bing, but they insert the keyword and ad ID from your Yahoo campaign.

Tip: Instead of '{YSMKEY}' you could use '{YSMRAW}' which will insert the actual search query into your campaign tagged URL. Another option is to use '{YSMMTC:std:adv:cnt}' which will insert the match type for your keyword. This automatically inserts 'standard', 'advanced' or 'content' into your campaign tag.[1]

Tip: Visit http://lovesdata.co/Pd7CD for more details on Bing parameters. For Yahoo visit http://lovesdata.co/z9B6U

Campaign Tagging Email Campaigns

Email marketing is an effective way to engage with potential and existing customers. Campaign tagging the links to your website in your emails allows you to understand effectiveness. Your email newsletter system will include its own dedicated set of reports to understand how many people open your emails and click particular links. However, it is also important to be able to understand your campaign performance in Google Analytics. This allows you to compare email campaigns to other initiatives that you are undertaking.

If you are not currently campaign tagging the links in your email campaigns, then these will show up as both direct traffic and referrals. This is because people clicking untagged links in email software on their computer will show up as direct, while people using hosted email, like Gmail or Yahoo Mail will be seen as referrals as these are in fact websites. This means a portion of your direct traffic will be coming from your emails, but it is impossible to understand its quantity and digging through the referrals report to find those hosted email websites can be time consuming. Campaign tags solve these problems and allow you to get important details such as which email newsletter campaign is actually getting your audience to engage with your website.

Most email newsletter systems have an option to automatically add campaign tags to the links in your emails. Before looking at how these systems work, let's look at the most common ways to manually add campaign tags as it is important to understand these options, even if you decide to use automatic campaign tagging.

The first thing to understand about tagging your email campaigns is that there is no one way to execute them – it is entirely up to you to decide how you want to create them. Take some time looking at the options and choose a method that fits the needs of your organization. It's important that the campaign tags allow you to easily report on performance and provide the details you need to perform analysis.

---

1   http://help.yahoo.com/l/au/yahoo/ysm/sps/screenref/16897.html

> **Tip:** If multiple people need to be able to understand the performance of your email campaigns it is generally best to use readable campaign tags. For example, if you define the campaign name using a code such as 'E0045' it might make it difficult for other people to understand which campaign it refers to or if it is an email campaign at all. So consider something more readable like 'Email Edition 45' to make it easier for people to understand.

Editions

Source	Medium	Campaign	Term	Content
july 2012	email	Email Newsletter		Article Link
july 2012	email	Email Newsletter		Button
july 2012	email	Email Newsletter		Image

Email Segments

Source	Medium	Campaign	Term	Content
members	email	Email Newsletter		Article Link
previous buyer	email	Email Newsletter		Button
general	email	Email Newsletter		Image

Hybrids

Source	Medium	Campaign	Term	Content
july 2012	email	Members Newsletter		Article Link
july 2012	email	Previous Buyer Newsletter		Button
july 2012	email	General Newsletter		Image

Source:	Medium	Campaign	Term	Content
members	email	Email July 2012		Article Link
previous buyer	email	Email July 2012		Button
general	email	Email July 2012		Image

Popular email marketing solutions like MailChimp and Campaign Monitor include the ability to automatically add campaign tags to the links that you include in your emails. This can provide a good option if you don't want to manually tag links in your emails, but you should understand the information that they will give you in your reports before you start using their automatic tagging options.

MailChimp

MailChimp uses the name of your email list as the source, the medium is email, the campaign name is an ID along with your selected tagging name, and the term is an ID (which is the same for all links). This provides you with some top level information in Google Analytics, but it is tricky to easily read the campaign name, and the term is not useful when performing analysis. Here is an example of what you would see inside your reports:

Source	Medium	Campaign	Term	Content
Subscriber List	email	630c43e7c9-Campaign_Name	0_b8t2871tbd-840c42a7b9-427063841	

If you are sending out lots of emails and have a lot of links in each email that you are sending, you might want to use manually tagged links to make analysis easier in Google Analytics and to give additional detail about the individual links people are using.

Campaign Monitor

Campaign Monitor provides cleaner and more detailed automatic campaign tagging when you send out an email. The source is your selected name (this is 'Campaign Monitor' by default), the medium is email, the content is the campaign name with an ID, the campaign is the campaign name and the term is the link text or alt attribute of the image.

Source	Medium	Campaign:	Term	Content
Campaign Monitor	email	Campaign_Name	Learn More	Campaign_Name+CID_4cbggf4589bc2df34fa09ac7fhde5346

Campaign Tagging Paid Social Media Campaigns

If you're running paid ads on social media you should definitely tag all the links that direct people from your ads to your website. This will allow you to compare the performance of your paid ads against your other social media posts and to your other advertising channels.

When campaign tagging your ads define the source as the domain name of the social network. For example, 'linkedin.com' would be used for LinkedIn ads. Then 'social' is used as the medium and you should then create a custom campaign name to describe the marketing initiative and a custom content name for each particular ad you are running. By creating a custom content name you can understand the performance of your different calls to action and ad variations after someone has landed on your website.

Source	Medium	Campaign	Term	Content
linkedin.com	social	LinkedIn Ads		Ad Description
facebook.com	social	Facebook Ads		Ad Description

The reason medium is defined as 'social' is because this allows you to compare the performance of paid social traffic against your organic (free) social traffic. When you use the Social reports inside Google Analytics, this will combine your organic and paid social media traffic for a complete view of your social media efforts:

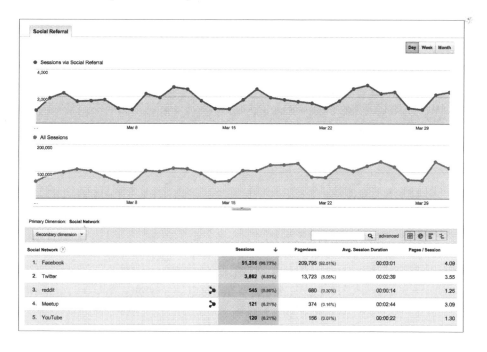

To compare your organic and paid social traffic, navigate to the 'Network Referrals' report and apply 'Medium' as the 'Secondary Dimension'. Organic social traffic will show 'Referral' as the medium, while paid social traffic will have a medium of 'Social'. Alternatively, you can use the 'Campaigns' report to only focus on your paid social media campaigns and the 'Referrals' report (in 'All Traffic') for your organic traffic.

Using this technique of campaign tagging URLs also allows you to create custom reports and segments to compare the performance of your paid and organic social media efforts. Visit http://lovesdata.co/8WEvs for custom report and segment templates you can apply to your reports.

Campaign Tagging Organic Social Media Campaigns

In most cases you will not want to campaign tag your organic social media posts. The only time you should campaign tag your organic posts is if you want to be able to see how people behave and convert after engaging with a specific post. For example, if you are looking after a travel website and you wanted to know if conversions are being driven by your posts about 'travel specials' or your posts about 'travel tips', you could campaign tag the organic posts that direct people through to your website.

In this case you should use a similar approach to tagging paid social campaigns, but this time you would define the medium as 'referral'.

Don't forget: Traffic from social networks that direct people through to your website are automatically tracked by Google Analytics and you can find them in the Social, Referrals and All Traffic reports.

Campaign Tagging for Offline Campaigns

You can measure offline campaigns by using a redirect or even a dedicated domain name for the campaign. For example, a printed flyer used to promote a landing page on your website that has a URL of 'http://www.company.com/summer-promo-offer' can use campaign tags along the following lines:

Source	Medium	Campaign	Term	Content
print flyer	offline	summer brochure		

Since this would end up being a very long URL with the campaign tags, you can print a shorter URL on the flyer like 'www.company.com/summer' and your web developer can set up a redirect that sends people to the campaign tagged link when they enter the shorter URL. If you are using a .htaccess file the redirect would look something like this:

```
Redirect 301 /summer
http://www.company.com/summer-promo?utm_source=print%20flyer&utm_
medium=offline&utm_campaign=summer%20brochure
```

Tip: It is important to give people a reason to make the extra effort to type in your special URL. This could be a promotional offer or special content that provides additional information for people interested in your products or services.

You can create URLs that redirect for other offline campaigns, like billboards and ads running on traditional media like TV and radio. Here is an example of a campaign tag for a billboard that is promoting a free trial:

Source	Medium	Campaign	Term	Content
billboard	offline	free trial		

A redirect can then be set up using the same technique for the printed flyer. If the campaign is important, you could also consider setting up a dedicated domain name that redirects to a particular landing page on your website. For example, you could register 'www.springfreetrial.com' and have this redirect to the campaign tagged URL on your main website.

Tip: You can define the optional 'Content' parameter, but this typically won't provide you with any additional insights as the source, medium and campaign name give you all the details about your offline campaign.

All Campaigns

The All Campaigns report allows you to measure and compare your different marketing initiatives in Google Analytics. This allows you to see the performance of your campaigns, including how effective your campaigns are at getting people to your website, engaging with your audience and generating conversion.

The reports can include two types of campaign data. First, if you are running Google AdWords you can link your accounts to see all of your Google AdWords campaigns. Secondly, you can measure other marketing initiatives into Google Analytics using campaign tagged URLs for your inbound marketing. This allows you to compare a whole range of your marketing campaigns and perform in-depth analysis to improve performance. Creating custom campaign tagged URLs is covered earlier in this Chapter in the "Campaign Tracking" section.

Here you can see Google AdWords campaigns along with custom campaigns:

Campaign	Sessions ↓
	13,775 % of Total: 32.06% (42,972)
1. Email Newsletter	3,256 (23.64%)
2. Holiday Promotion	2,414 (17.52%)
3. Branded [Search]	1,595 (11.58%)
4. General [Display]	1,384 (10.05%)

Tip: Can't see your Google AdWords campaign names in the report? This means your Google AdWords account is not correctly linked to Google Analytics. You will need to link them to have accurate data in Google Analytics.

If you find it difficult to distinguish the names of your Google AdWords campaigns from your custom campaigns, then you can apply a secondary dimension to make it easier to read the report. To do this, click on 'Secondary Dimension' above the table and then search for and select 'Source'. This will now make it easy to see which campaigns are from Google AdWords as the source column will say 'Google'.

Your different marketing campaigns are likely to have different objectives, so taking this into account when comparing performance is important. For example, your paid search campaigns are likely to have the objective of increasing the number of new users and sessions to your website, while your email newsletter will have a higher conversion rate because people have already subscribed to receive your updates. This means you will need to apply context to the data you see from your experience and understanding of the campaigns. It is also likely that you will find particular campaigns are better at generating different types of conversions than other campaigns, this can help focus the objectives of individual campaigns on the best possible outcomes for your organization.

Tip: Ensuring that you have both macro and micro conversions set up will give you a better understanding of how particular campaigns perform. You can switch between ecommerce transactions and individual goals for the 'Conversions' columns in the campaigns reports by selecting your desired conversion action from the drop-down list:

Campaigns and Bounce Rate

A good starting place for your campaign analysis is to identify campaigns that have a high bounce rate. This can indicate that the landing pages people are being sent to are not engaging them deeper into your website. When you have identified a campaign with a higher than expected bounce rate, click on the name of the campaign. Now click on 'Other' and search for and select 'Landing Page'.

This will show you the first page (or pages) that people are landing on when they come from a particular marketing initiative. You might find that the majority of sessions originate on a single landing page – in which case you should review that page and consider changes that will make the page more engaging. You might also want to consider testing an alternate landing page for that particular campaign.

You should also review your marketing messages to see how closely they relate to the content on the landing page. If there is a disconnect between these elements it can lead to a large portion of people quickly leaving your website.

Tip: You can repeat this process for campaigns that have a lower than expected bounce rate to get ideas of how to improve your other campaigns.

Campaigns and Conversions

The Conversions columns in the campaigns reports provides you with insights about whether your campaigns are resulting in conversions. Start by selecting a particular conversion – this could be an individual goal or your ecommerce transactions. Now click on the 'Goal Conversion Rate' (or 'Ecommerce Conversion Rate') column heading to order your campaigns starting with the highest conversion rate first.

Look for campaigns with a small number of sessions, but a high conversion rate – these are campaigns that provide the opportunity to significantly increase your conversions. Depending on the type of campaign, you can establish what would be required to increase the number of people finding your website from that initiative. This might include allocating additional budget or emphasising the calls to action in your marketing messages.

You are likely to find that different campaigns are better at driving particular conversions. For example, your email newsletter might have a strong conversion rate for online sales, while your paid search campaigns are better at generating leads, and your remarketing campaigns are stronger at getting people to sign up to your email newsletter. If your primary objective is online sales, this does not mean that your other campaigns are failing, it just means that they are better at getting people to perform different conversion actions. Having these insights can help direct your efforts to ensure that each marketing channel is used to its own advantage. It can be difficult to see which channel is generating particular conversions using the standard campaigns reports, so you might want to create a custom report that allows you to see your different conversions in an easier format.

Here you can see a custom report that includes five different conversions, quickly showing the relative performance of the campaigns by conversion rate:

Campaign	Sessions	Lead (Goal 1 Conversion Rate)	Newsletter (Goal 2 Conversion Rate)	Support (Goal 3 Conversion Rate)	Subscription (Goal 4 Conversion Rate)	Social Interaction (Goal 5 Conversion Rate)
	13,775 % of Total: 32.06% (42,972)	2.54% Avg for View: 2.39% (6.42%)	2.37% Avg for View: 1.88% (20.68%)	0.84% Avg for View: 0.75% (10.71%)	0.21% Avg for View: 0.25% (-16.23%)	0.09% Avg for View: 0.24% (-64.01%)
1. Email Newsletter	3,256 (23.64%)	0.03%	0.00%	1.09%	0.00%	0.00%
2. Holiday Promotion	2,414 (17.52%)	4.64%	1.51%	0.00%	0.21%	0.00%
3. Branded [Search]	1,595 (11.58%)	7.59%	3.82%	0.00%	0.63%	0.31%
4. General [Display]	1,384 (10.05%)	0.00%	0.80%	0.00%	0.00%	0.00%

This can be used to support your strategy for each campaign and to ensure that your marketing messages direct people to the conversion action that is most appropriate for the particular channel. Visit http://lovesdata.co/yu7mx to add the custom report to your reporting view. You will probably need to customize the report further to include the appropriate goals into the report and remove any goals that you are not currently using.

Paid Keywords

The Paid Keywords report allows you to see the paid keywords that are sending traffic to your website. If you have linked Google AdWords the paid keywords report will show you all the keywords that are resulting in clicks from your Google AdWords account. Remember that by default these keywords are the keywords that you are bidding on in the account, the actual terms people search for can vary because of keyword match types.

The paid keywords will also include any non-Google AdWords campaign that you have manually campaign tagged and that have a keyword defined in the tags. For example, if you are running ads on Bing, you might have a destination URL like:

http://www.example.com/page.html?utm_source=bing&utm_medium=cpc&utm_campaign=bing%20ads&utm_content=buy%20coffee%20mug&utm_term={keyword}

Using '{keyword}' will automatically include the particular keyword you are bidding on and pass that keyword straight through to the Google Analytics tracking code. Using 'cpc' as the medium will mean that the details of the Bing paid traffic appear in the paid keywords report. This is because Google Analytics will see 'cpc' and associate the campaign tagged URL with paid search.

Tip: You can use the same technique for other third party paid search campaigns.

Along with the paid keywords you are bidding on, you might see some additional elements in the paid keywords report. If you see '(content targeting)' in your keyword list, this is for display advertising that you are running through Google AdWords. This is because Google Display Network ads that are clicked do not have a search term associated with them, instead people are browsing content when they see your ad and then click through to your website.

If you see '(remarketing/content targeting)', this is for remarketing ads running on the Google Display Network. If you are running display ads and you are targeting particular types of content using topic targeting, your paid keywords report will also include topic areas.

If you are running these types of display campaigns you will want to use the dedicated display reports in the Google AdWords section. If you are running a mixture of search and display campaigns in Google AdWords good best practice is to name your campaigns (inside Google AdWords) so that they indicate the type of campaign you are running. For example, using 'General [Search]' and 'General [Display]' makes it easy to understand where these campaigns are being displayed. You can select 'Campaign' as the secondary dimension in the paid keywords report to quickly understand the types of ads people are engaging with to find your website.

Keyword	Campaign	Acquisition		
		Sessions ↓	% New Sessions	New Users
		5,511 % of Total: 12.50% (44,101)	90.67% Avg for View: 77.39% (17.17%)	4,997 % of Total: 14.64% (34,128)
1. (content targeting)	General [Display]	922 (16.73%)	94.79%	874 (17.49%)
2. (content targeting)	Remarketing [Display]	886 (16.08%)	92.33%	818 (16.37%)
3. +bag	General [Search]	550 (9.98%)	89.27%	491 (9.83%)
4. +speakers	General [Search]	465 (8.44%)	91.40%	425 (8.51%)

If you see '(not set)' showing up in your paid keywords report, this can indicate that there is potentially a problem with the way that Google AdWords is linked to your Google Analytics account. It can even indicate that Google AdWords has not been linked at all. Start by clicking on '(not set)' – this will load up the detail page for that particular keyword. Now click on 'Other' and select 'Source'. If you see a familiar source name this can indicate that you are using campaign tagged URLs where you have defined medium as 'cpc'.

Remember the campaign tags used for ads on Bing? Well this is similar, but since someone didn't define a value for 'term', Google Analytics won't have any keyword to report and instead it simply says it is 'not set'.

If you did not see something familiar when you selected 'Source', try going back and repeating the process but this time select 'Campaign'. If you are unable to determine where the traffic is coming from, it is likely to do with your Google AdWords account linking. Visit http://lovesdata.co/hVqAL for details on linking your accounts.

Organic Keywords

The Organic Keywords report shows you all the free, organic keywords that people are using in their searches to find your website. This first thing you are likely to notice is the large portion of '(not provided)' keyword traffic. This occurs when people securely search on Google and Yahoo. For example, if you perform a search on Google you will notice that your browser show 'https://www' at the start of the URL. The 'https' indicates that the search is secure. These search engines do not share the particular keywords people search for when they use secure search and they do this to help ensure that people's search terms are kept private.

In 2011 Google made the decision to make all searches secure, meaning that all organic keywords originating from searches on Google will be reported as '(not provided)' in Google Analytics. This is not something you can control and it is also important to highlight that it's not specifically a Google Analytics issue. Any analytics tool you use will show this traffic as 'not provided'. Alternate methods for getting some insights into the types of keywords that people are using will be covered in a moment, but first let's come back to keywords that are available in the report.

Ignoring the 'not provided' traffic for a moment, you will still see a number of keywords displayed in the organic keywords report. This will be all your keyword traffic from other search engines. The majority of this traffic will be from Bing, as they are still currently passing search queries through to analytics tools. You can check this by clicking 'Secondary Dimension' and selecting 'Source'. Now you will see the keywords along with the particular search engines people are using.

Since there are a large portion of keywords that are not provided, you might want to focus the report on the keywords that are available. You can do this by clicking on 'Advanced' to the right of the search bar, then click 'Include' and change it to 'Exclude' and click 'Containing' and change it to 'Exactly Matching'. Now enter '(not provided)' as the value and click 'Apply'.

The report will now focus on the keywords that are available. This can be a useful report to come back to. To make it easy to use again click on 'Shortcut' just below the main menu at the top of the page and name it 'Available Organic Keywords' (or something similar). This will mean you can quickly go back to the same report that you filtered from the Shortcuts menu.

Identifying Landing Pages

Now let's check which keywords are sending traffic to appropriate pages on your website. Click on a keyword that you would like to check, then click 'Other' and select 'Landing Page'. You will see the pages that people are finding when they search and you can look for unexpected pages being found for particular keywords.

In most cases you will see more than one page being found for a particular keyword. Look for cases where pages that you would expect to receive the majority of traffic are only receiving a small number of sessions. This can indicate that those pages are not well optimized for the particular keyword.

For example, for the keyword 'financial planner' you will notice that people are finding your homepage and your financial services page. You were expecting that the financial services page would receive the majority of the traffic for the keyword, instead it is only accounting for a handful of sessions. This tells you that the page could be improved in order to be more relevant for the keyword. Start by looking at the page to see if it contains the keyword in the content, you can also perform the search on Google to see why your homepage is attracting more traffic.

> **Tip:** When analyzing search results pages it's best to use your web browser's private mode. This helps remove any customization that might occur in the search results. If you are using Chrome select 'New Incognito Window' before performing the search.

Paid Keyword Research

If you are running paid search campaigns you can use the Organic Keyword report to identify new potential keywords to target in your campaigns. Start by reordering the keyword report based on conversion rate. To do this click on the column header name (either 'Goal Conversion Rate' or 'Ecommerce Conversion Rate'). This will reorder the report so that the keywords with the highest conversion rate are listed at the top of the report.

Then you can work down the list to identify suitable keywords for your paid campaigns. If you have a small budget for your paid campaigns look for keywords that have a good conversion rate and a small number of sessions. These will be the keywords that give you the biggest opportunity because it is likely that your website isn't very prominent in the organic search results. When you add these as paid keywords you will have more control over your calls to action, as well as where they are displayed based on your budget and keyword bid.

Identify 'Not Provided' Landing Pages

Although individual keywords are unavailable for people using secure search, the organic keyword report can be used to get an idea of keyword themes people are searching for on

Google. To do this click on '(not provided)' in the keyword report, then 'Other' and select 'Landing Page'.

You will now have a list of all the pages people found when they searched and this can give you some clues about the keywords people used. To start with, you will probably see your homepage as one of the landing pages – this is likely to be your most popular page for your brand terms, the majority of these searches are likely to be related to the name of your organization (and even your product or services).

If you have readable URLs for the pages on your website like '/accounting-service' or '/product/laptop-case' this will help give you an idea of the types of keywords people will be searching for to find the other pages on your website. If you don't have readable URLs or you would like to see page titles along with your landing page URLs you can use a custom report to see these details. Looking at the page title can also give you an idea about the keywords people are using to find your website. Get the custom report at http://lovesdata.co/LkNFz

> **Tip:** If you are not sure about the types of keywords people use to find pages on your website you can use the 'Landing Pages' report which is available under 'Site Content' in the 'Behavior' section. Click on a particular landing page and select 'Keyword' (above the table and below the timeline). You will now have a list of available keywords for that page. You will need to ignore '(not set)' and '(not provided)'.

Once you have identified the themes of keywords that are sending organic traffic to your website, you can use this to inform your content strategy. This can include creating new content for keywords that are not generating much traffic and refining content that is already being found by people. Another important way to understand how people are finding your website is to use the SEO reports which is covered in the "Search Engine Optimization" section in Chapter 17. These reports integrate Google Search Console data into your Google Analytics reports to provide additional insights about what people are searching for to find your website on Google search results.

Cost Analysis

The Cost Analysis report allows you to compare the performance of your Google AdWords campaigns to other third-party advertising. By uploading information, including cost, click and impression about the additional advertising you are running, you can compare the success of your different channels from inside Google Analytics. The steps to upload cost data are covered in the "Data Import" section in Chapter 22, but once you have uploaded the data you will be able to see additional metrics for your non-Google AdWords campaigns, including CTR (Click-through Rate) and advertising cost.

	Source / Medium	Sessions	Impressions	Clicks	Cost
		44,101 % of Total: 100.00% (44,101)	13,161,664 % of Total: 100.00% (3,161,664)	6,354 % of Total: 100.00% (6,354)	$404,007.34 % of Total: 100.00% ($404,007.34)
☐	1. google / cpc	15,979 (40.27%)	1,106,209 (15.07%)	98,003 (11.39%)	$109,467.07 (11.38%)
☐	2. twitter.com / social	11,004 (38.05%)	2,618,736 (36.14%)	53,439 (9.27%)	$78,319.50 (8.38%)
☐	3. linkedin.com / social	9,204 (12.50%)	3,161,664 (42.39%)	6,354 (2.42%)	$24,007.34 (3.49%)

You can also access the data you have uploaded when you create custom reports, and if you have goals configured with a dollar value or ecommerce tracking you can see ROAS (return on advertising spend) as a metric in the report.

Once you have established the objectives for your different campaigns you can use the report to establish performance. For example, by comparing the CTR (click-through rate) of your different initiatives you can identify campaigns that could be optimized to increase the number of people engaging with your messages. You can even use insights from your top performing campaigns and test those messages in under-performing initiatives.

The CPC (cost per click) column can be used to establish the relative cost for each of your campaigns in getting people to your website. If similar marketing channels, like paid search, have very different CPC amounts you could use this data along with your goal conversion data to establish your best performing paid search networks.

Tip: Remember that the Cost Analysis report includes RPC (revenue-per-click) and ROAS (return on advertising spend) data based on the last method somebody used to find your website. Use the report as a way to identify potential areas for testing and support these decisions with the Multi-Channel Funnels reports for a more complete in-depth understanding of the interactions between your marketing channels.

19

Behavior

The Behavior reports show how people interact with your website. This is typically the pages people view as they navigate through your website. You can extend the reports to get additional details about what people are doing, including your internal website search function and events to measure custom interactions.

The Overview report gives you a quick snapshot view of how people are interacting. It shows the number of pages that people are viewing, along with engagement metrics which provide a way to gauge the overall health of your website.

Terminology

A number of the terms have already been covered, including pageviews, average time on page and bounce rate, but there are some new terms in the Behavior reports.

Unique Pageviews

Unique pageviews will count multiple views of an individual page as one, if they occur in the same session. For example, someone navigates to your website, loads the homepage, then navigates to the about page and then back to the homepage. In this scenario you would have two pageviews for the homepage and one unique pageview because the person loaded the page twice in the same session.

Percentage of Exits

Exit percentages show how often people leave from a particular page (or pages) on your website. This allows you to identify particular pain points and bottlenecks in your website. For example, if a high percentage of people exit from your payment page during checkout you can investigate potential usability and messaging issues with the page.

Let's look at a simple scenario to get a better handle on exit percentage. Two people navigate to your website. The first person views your homepage and then navigates to your contact page before closing their browser. The second person views your homepage and then leaves your website.

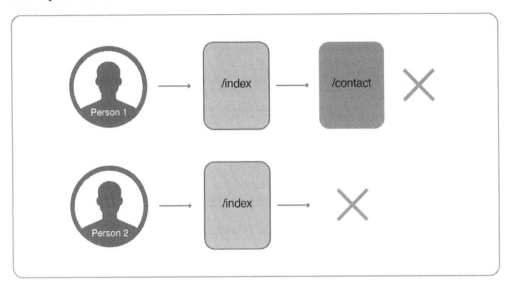

The homepage has been viewed twice and has a total of two pageviews and one exit. This means that the Percentage Exit is 50% because one exit divided by two pageviews equals 50%.

Behavior Flow

The Behavior Flow report allows you to understand the navigation paths people take through your website. When you first load the report it shows you navigation paths starting on the left-hand side with the first pages people view as they land on your website.

You can click on a particular landing page you would like to focus on and select 'Highlight Traffic Through Here'. This will highlight the navigation paths people take from that page as they navigate deeper into your website. The Behavior Flow report shows you the connections between the pages people view and these connections are presented in relative sizes, so the larger the connection, the more people are taking that particular path.

Tip: The report shows you 'Landing Page' by default as the first column of nodes (pages) on the left-hand side of the report. This is the first page people view as they load your website. The next column to the right will show you the 'Starting Page', this is really the same as Landing Page, so you might notice that the connections between the first and second column present 100% of people progressing from the Landing Page to the Starting Page.

By default the report will automatically group pages based on the structure of your URLs. If you hover over a particular node within the report and it is made up of multiple pages, you will see this presented in the overlay.

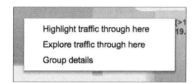

Select 'Group Details' If you want to know about the pages that are contained in the automatic grouping.

You can customize the Behavior Flow report by clicking 'Landing Page' and selecting an alternate starting point for the report. For example, if you wanted to understand the marketing campaigns that are leading to particular navigation paths you could select 'Source/Medium' or an alternate acquisition or advertising dimension.

You can apply custom segments to the Behavior Flow report to focus on particular sections of your audience.

You can customize the report to present alternate navigation paths:

- **Content Groupings** allow you to display navigation paths through particular groups of content that you have already configured in Google Analytics. For example, if you have Content Grouping set up to group different categories of product pages, such as 'clothes', 'accessories' and 'shoes', then you can use the report to understand movement between these aggregated groupings of content.

- **Automatically Grouped Pages** is the default for the report. This will present individual pages and automatically grouped sets of pages depending on your URL structure and the number of people viewing the pages.

- **Events** allow you to see the navigation paths between the different events you have implemented on your website. For example, if you have Event Tracking for video interactions and people downloading PDF files, then you will be able to see if people are triggering individual events or multiple events when they navigate through your website.

- **Pages and Events** shows you a combination of both event and pageview interactions in the report. In most cases the number of events that are measured will be much lower than the number of pageviews, so you might want to consider applying a custom segment that includes sessions where events were measured in order to use the report effectively.

> **Tip:** There are additional reports for understanding navigation paths, including Site Content, In-Page Analytics, Users Flow, Funnel Visualization and Goal Flow. You can use the report that is most appropriate for the analysis you are performing.

You can use the Behavior Flow report to make decisions about the content that you cross-promote on particular pages of your website. Start by applying a segment to the report that includes people who have completed at least one of your objectives. It is best to begin with something broad, for example a segment that includes anybody who has converted. This will mean that you include people who have completed macro and micro conversions.

> **Tip:** Remember that every website, even non-ecommerce websites, should have goals set up to measure interactions and engagement. If you haven't set up any goals then read Chapter 23 – "Goals."

> **Tip:** If you start by applying a segment that only includes one conversion action you might end up basing your decisions on a very small number of users. It is best to start with a larger group and then you can always narrow down your segment in the future.

At the top of the report, check that 'Automatically Grouped Pages' is selected. The report will now show your most popular landing pages on the left and where people navigate to on the right. Click your top landing page on the top left of the report and click 'View Only This Segment'. This allows you to just focus on where people navigate from the individual page and it removes all the other landing pages from the report. Since this is your most popular page, this is a good starting point for improving your website. In the following example you can see the most popular pages people navigate to from the website homepage.

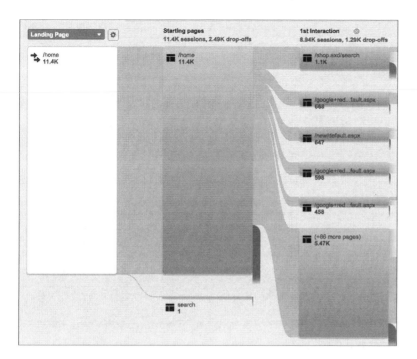

Now that you are focused on the homepage, you should ignore the group on the very left of the report and focus on the groups that are highlighted in green. This is because Landing Page and Starting Pages are really the same thing (people are not actually viewing the page twice).

Next, load the homepage and compare what is displayed with where people are navigating to. Look for pages in the report that are not clearly visible on the homepage – these can then potentially be highlighted to make them easier for people to find.

The report does not show every single page, so you will also see a 'More Pages' group at the bottom of the report. To look at the other pages people navigate to click on this group and select 'Group Details'.

> **Tip:** You can also use the Behavior Flow report to see where people leave your website. Look for pages where you expect people to continue to another page, for example landing pages, pages with forms or pages in your ecommerce checkout process. You can then start to ask questions about why people are leaving from that particular page.

Site Content

The Site Content reports show you what pages people are engaging with on your website. You can choose from the various reports available depending on your website and the type of analysis you are performing.

The All Pages report shows you all the different pages on your website. When you load the report it will show your most popular pages first, based on the number of pageviews for each page. The report is generated based on the URLs of the pages on your website. For example, if someone navigates to 'http://www.example.com/about-us', the report will show one pageview for '/about-us', and you will see everything that comes after your domain name in the report. If you have readable URLs this is a good report to use to understand your most important content.

You will notice that the All Pages report breaks down metrics for each individual page in the report. That way you can understand how much time people spend on individual pages, their bounce rate and other details.

> **Tip:** Remember when looking at Average Time on Page the time people spend on a particular page can only be calculated when they view a subsequent page. If they don't navigate to another page on your website Google Analytics can't determine time on page. This is why a page with a bounce rate of 100% will also have an Average Time on Page of zero seconds.

The starting point for using the All Pages report is to understand your most popular content. By knowing the most popular pages on your website you can consider cross promoting important content on popular pages to encourage further engagement. The report also shows you the bounce rate for each page and this can provide insights into pages that need improvement. Look for pages that have a high number of pageviews along with a high bounce rate. These pages could be improved to encourage people to navigate onto another page of your website.

To quickly find pages that have a higher than average bounce rate click on the comparison icon above the table on the right-hand side.

This will show you how the bounce rate for each page performs compared to the overall average bounce rate for all the pages on your website. Now you can quickly scan the report for the red bars which indicate a higher than average bounce rate.

If you have defined a dollar value for your goal conversions (or you have ecommerce tracking set up) you'll see different values assigned to each of your pages in the report. Page Value is an excellent way to understand the importance of your pages in contributing value to your organization. Once you have identified pages with a high Page Value you can come up with ideas to get more people to those particular pages, this will help drive even more value from your website.

Did you know? Page Value is (Goal Value + Transaction Revenue) ÷ Unique Pageviews. This means that you can use Page Value even if you are not selling online. All you need to do is define a dollar value for your goals. It also means that if people view a page more than once in a session before they convert, the page will receive the same value as the other pages seen before converting.

Let's look at how Page Value is assigned to each page in your reports. For example, you have set up a single goal and set the dollar value as $10.00 for each conversion received. You have defined a single step of '/contact.html' that results in a goal conversion if people then view '/thanks.html'. After you set up the goal you have two conversions. The first person views the following pages:

1. /index.html
2. /services.html
3. /about.html
4. /contact.html
5. /thanks.html

In this case the total value of the conversion ($10.00) is divided by five and each page receives a value of $2.00. Now the second person views the following pages:

6. /services.html
7. /about.html
8. /services.html
9. /contact.html
10. /thanks.html

Here you can see that the person viewed the '/services.html' page twice, but value is only given to the page once even if someone views the page multiple times. The total conversion value of $10.00 is divided by the four pages viewed ('/services.html' is counted once), with each page receiving a value of $2.50.

Now your report would show the following based on these two people:

Page	Pageviews	Unique pageviews	Page Value
/services.html	3	2	$4.50
/about.html	2	2	$4.50
/contact.html	2	2	$4.50
/thanks.html	2	2	$4.50
/index.html	1	1	$2.00

One thing to consider is that value is assigned to both the '/contact.html' and the '/thanks.html' pages. When you use the reports to identify important pages based on their value you should exclude these from your analysis because they are necessary for people to complete your desired action. Instead, you should focus on pages that contribute value that are not steps in your goal or ecommerce funnel. In this simple scenario you can see that the '/services.html' and '/about.html pages' are contributing value without being a direct part of the goal funnel steps.

Complex URLs

Using the All Pages report can be simple if you have easy to read URLs, but if you have complex URLs (for example, you see something like '/index.php?id=3827' in the report) you might want to consider reporting on the pages of your website based on page title instead of URL. You can do this by selecting 'Page Title' above the table in the report.

> **Tip:** You can change URLs that you see in this report by using a view-based filter, however for SEO and to meet best practice you should really consider working with your web developer to migrate your website to readable URLs.

Page Titles and SEO

The Page Title option available in the All Pages report is also useful for identifying SEO opportunities. Once you have selected 'Page Title' you can click on a particular title to see the URLs that use that particular title on your website. If there is more than one page using that title you will see the URLs listed.

For SEO you typically want to have a unique page title for each unique page on your website. If pages share the same title, this presents an opportunity to write a new more targeted title for each URL.

Content Drilldown

The Content Drilldown report gives you an alternate method for understanding the performance of your content. If your website has a folder file structure you can use the report to understand performance based on the folder structure.

For example, if someone views '/products/cameras/' and '/products/accessories/' the report will combine the two pageviews in the '/products/' folder. This allows you to quickly compare the top-level performance of your content.

Below you can see that the product pages are the most popular content sections of the website. This may not have been clear if you only used the All Pages report.

Page path level 1	Pageviews	Unique Pageviews
	296,826 % of Total: 100.00% (296,826)	220,919 % of Total: 100.00% (220,919)
1. 📁 /products/	215,729 (72.68%)	164,007 (74.24%)
2. 📁 /news/	58,783 (19.80%)	39,001 (17.65%)
3. 📁 /about/	11,476 (3.87%)	9,471 (4.29%)
4. 📁 /new/	4,969 (1.87%)	3,832 (1.73%)
5. 📁 /specials/	2,001 (0.67%)	1,546 (0.70%)

You will notice that the Content Drilldown report shows you folders and pages using small icons in the table. If you see the folder icon this means you can click on the name of the folder to see any additional sub-folders and pages in that folder. This allows you to drill down and follow the structure of your website.

Landing Pages

The Landing Pages report shows you the first pages people see as they navigate to your website. This allows you to understand the important starting points and ensure that you have considered the navigation and usability aspects of your most important landing pages.

Look for pages that have a higher than expected bounce rate and then review the content, images, graphics and style of those pages. Look for potential reasons why people would leave those pages without traveling through to another page on your website. However, it's also important to consider the particular context of the page – there will be some pages where you expect to have a higher bounce rate. If you expect people to get everything they are looking for on an individual page, then it is okay if that page has a higher bounce rate. For example, your contact page and blog pages are likely to have a higher bounce rate than other pages on your website.

> **Tip:** You can use the Landing Pages report to identify opportunities for cross-promoting your other content. This could be a banner image or short piece of text, along with a link that promotes a special offer or an important announcement that you want people to navigate to on your website.

Exit Pages

The Exit Pages report shows you the last pages people see before they leave your website. It is important to understand that everybody is going to leave your website at some point, so you are always going to have exit pages, even if you have perfect website usability design. The best way to use the report is to look for pages that have a high number of exits where you actually expect people to travel through to a subsequent page. If you see that an important page contains a form (like a landing page with a lead generation form) or a stepped action (like a page in your shopping cart checkout process) and the page has a high number of exits, this can be a sign of potential issues with that particular page.

Once you have identified a page, where you expect people to travel to another page on your website, click on the page to perform some more detailed analysis. Once you have drilled down on an individual page you can select 'Secondary Dimension' above the table to layer additional insights about people visiting the page. When you apply one of the options look at the '% Exit' column and look for rows that have a higher rate of exits.

Here are some suggestions:

- **Medium, Source and Campaign** can be used to see if particular ways people are using to find your website are leading to higher exit rates.

- **Browser and Operating System** can help identify if more people are exiting when using particular technology to view your website.

- **Network Domain** can help reveal if particular internet service providers are impacting your exits. You might find particular providers that are skewing your data.

- **Country** and other geographic dimensions can be used to see if people in particular geographic locations are more likely to exit.

- **Previous Page Path** to see if people viewing other pages impact exits or if the primary problem is people entering and leaving from the same page.

If you are unable to identify particular elements that are leading to higher than expected exits, then the next step is to review the page in your browser. It can be difficult to pinpoint the exact issues, but look at your headings, content, images, graphics and overall page design. Comparing your page to other websites can also be helpful in identifying elements that might be causing people to exit the page.

Understanding Navigation Paths

There are various ways to understand how people are navigating through your website. One of the simplest ways is to the use the 'All Pages' report. This is a great option if you are just getting started because it is easy to understand. Start by heading back to the All Pages report and click on an individual page in the 'Page' column. Now click on the 'Navigation Summary' tab towards the top of the report.

You will now see an icon of a page in the centre of the report which represents the page you have selected. You will also see the URL of the page you have selected just above this icon.

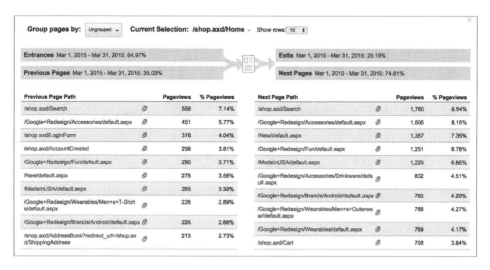

On the left you will see the percentage of pageviews for people viewing this as the first page they view on your website. Then below that you will see pages people viewed if they came from another page on your website though to the page you selected. In this example you can see that a large portion of people viewed a previous page before coming to the '/shop.axd/Home' page, and of those previous pages the most popular page was '/shop.axd/Search/'.

Then on the right of the report you can see where people go next. There will be a percent of people who exit and do not view another page, but then you will also be able to see the other pages people choose to view.

> **Tip:** Once you are in the 'Navigation Summary' tab you can click on other pages you see under 'Previous Page Path' and 'Next Page Path' and the report will update for the new page you have selected. You can also click on the 'Current Selection' page to select one of the most popular pages or search for another page on your website.

Site Speed

The Site Speed reports allow you to understand how long your website takes to load. The loading time of your website is critical to performance. This includes the technical aspects of server resources, but more importantly, loading time is critical to usability and conversion rates. Research shows that there is a direct correlation between loading time and conversion rates and that an additional one second of loading time can decrease conversions by 7%.[1] This means that if you can speed up the loading of your website you'll see measurable results.

The Page Timings report shows you the loading times of particular pages. Start by identifying your most important pages with at least a moderate number of pageviews that are also showing a long loading time. You are probably asking 'what should the loading time of my pages be?' Well, ideally your pages should load instantly, so the closer to zero seconds you can get, the better. In most cases you should try to aim for pages to load within five seconds – the longer the loading time, the more likely people are to leave your website.

> **Tip:** There are cases where a slightly longer loading time can be considered acceptable. For example, a blog post with lots of images is going to take longer to load than standard website pages. Try loading the page yourself to see what the experience is like. Visit http://lovesdata.co/QndFr for steps to simulate how your website appears on slower internet connections. If you do this and the text-based content loads quickly and then the images load after the content, this is probably an acceptable experience. If the text-based content is really slow to load, so people just see a blank page for a long time, you'll need to look at improving the loading time.

Before you start to look at how to improve the loading time, there are a couple of things you will want to check. First, ensure that the loading time calculation is based on enough data

---

1   http://www.tagman.com/mdp-blog/2012/03/just-one-second-delay-in-page-load-can-cause-7-loss-in-customer-conversions/

to ensure that it accurately reflects what people are experiencing on your website. To do this, click on the 'Technical' tab at the top of the report. Then click on the 'Data' icon (small grid icon above the table on the right) to see your data presented in a table. This will now allow you to see the 'Average Page Load Time' along with the 'Page Load Sample'.

The sample column is important because this allows you to understand how many pageviews were used to calculate the loading time. If it is calculated on the page being loaded hundreds or thousands of times this is great, but if it is calculated based on a small number of pageviews, then the data is not going to be very accurate. In the example below you can see that one page shows an average loading time of 25 seconds, but this is only based on the page being loaded 48 times.

Page ?		Pageviews ? ↓	Avg. Page Load Time (sec) ?	Page Load Sample ?
		375,718 % of Total: 100.00% (375,718)	3.32 Avg for View: 3.32 (0.00%)	3,131 % of Total: 100.00% (3,131)
1. /index.html		31,991 (8.51%)	10.47	268 (8.56%)
2. /about.html		26,920 (7.16%)	3.93	197 (6.29%)
3. /contact.html		11,713 (3.12%)	25.06	48 (1.53%)

Next, identify if the data is being skewed. For example, someone located in a particular country, using an older browser might make the average loading time appear to be high, even if the loading time for other locations is actually within an acceptable range. Start by clicking on the particular page you want to analyze in more detail. This now allows you to segment the data for this individual page by selecting different dimensions to understand the loading time in more detail.

Now click on 'Other' above the table, then search for and select 'Country'. This will show if a particular location is skewing the average loading time metric you see in the report. If the loading time for your target audience is close to the overall average it is unlikely that country is having a major impact on the data. You can change the segments you are viewing by clicking on 'Country' above the table and selecting another dimension. Try applying the following dimensions to see if there are any other factors that might be skewing your data:

- **Operating System** can be used to see if a particular operating system is slow to load your website. You might find that mobile operating systems have a slower loading time because some people will be loading your website using the cellular data if they are not connected to WiFi.

- **Browser** can show if particular browsers are taking longer to load your website.

- **Network Domain** can demonstrate if a particular internet service provider (ISP) is taking longer to load your website.

- **Medium or Source** can be used to see if a particular marketing channel results in a poor loading time. This is unlikely, but is worth quickly checking.

- **Region, Metro or City** can show a more detailed view of the geographic location and impact on loading time.

Tip: If you identify particular factors that are skewing your loading times in the report, you can create a segment that removes that particular factor. This will allow you to analyze performance without the data being skewed.

Once you've ruled out major impacts on loading time and identified that a particular page is contributing to slower overall performance, look at how you can optimize the page. The best place to start is to open the page and look at what the page includes. Generally, images and graphics are the first area you'll want to optimize to improve performance. If you open your page and you can see a lot of images throughout the page, you might want to first consider reducing the overall number of images. From here you can work with your web designer to ensure that all the images are correctly compressed. Even a single uncompressed image can significantly add to the overall loading time of your page.

The Speed Suggestions report automatically gives you suggestions to improve the performance of the loading time of your website and pages. The recommendations can range from compressing images, through to technical server configuration options. Remember that the ideal is as close to instant as possible, but you are going to have to prioritize what you can do and also understand that you might need to make some compromises along the way. Even large organizations can struggle to improve the loading times of their websites, but any improvement is a step in the right direction.

Optimization can include:

- Compressing images and graphics

- Removing redirects

- Removing whitespace from HTML, CSS and JavaScript

- Combining files like CSS and JavaScript

- Improving your server response time

Tip: For more technical resources to ensure you have a fast loading website visit http://lovesdata.co/AZtgM

The User Timings report allows you to measure the loading time of custom interactions. For example, if you wanted to measure how long it takes people to complete your enquiry or application form, then you'll require custom implementation within the code of your website to measure these times. Details can be found at http://lovesdata.co/NgbDG

Site Search

The Site Search reports allow you to understand what people are searching for once they have landed on your website and used your onsite search solution. This is a fantastic place to start understanding what people are looking for, providing great insights to inform your navigation structure, content strategy and even the products and services you are offering.

Take a moment to think about what this report is showing you – people are actually taking the time to tell you exactly what they are looking for. They have plugged a search term into your search solution looking for information. The keywords people are using to search are valuable for analysis and you can use these reports to find insights for your organization.

> **Tip:** If you have a website with more than a handful of pages you should consider adding a search solution. It will help people find information on your website and you will get the added benefit of actionable insights. The CMS you are using might have an inbuilt search option, or you can use Google Custom Search to add a search solution to your site. Google Custom Search is a free ad-supported option. Google Site Search is a paid option starting at $100 USD per year. For details visit http://lovesdata.co/mwkDw

Overview

The Overview report gives you a snapshot of your internal search solution. This includes the number of sessions that included a search, the average number of search result pages people viewed, the percentage of people who exited from a search results page and post-search engagement metrics.

Usage

The Usage report shows you the number of people using your search solution, along with engagement and conversion metrics. If you're looking after a website with thousands of pages or a large number of products your search solution will be a critical component of getting people to the most appropriate content on your site. If you see a small number of people using your search options you should review the placement of your search box. It may mean that people are having difficulty seeing a search option on your website.

If you are running an ecommerce site or focused on another type of goal, you'll want to ensure that people are converting after they have performed a search. Select the appropriate goal or ecommerce option to the right of 'Conversions' in the report table to compare the conversion rate of people using, and not using, your search solution. If people are less likely to convert after searching, check that your search is providing relevant results and that it is easy for people to use.

Search Terms

This is the best report to use if you are getting started – it will give you fast insights into what people are looking for and help you improve your site. The report shows you the actual terms that people have searched and these terms are presented by the overall number of people searching for them.

Take some time to review the terms people are using. You might just have a handful of terms, or you might have thousands of terms. Start by identifying terms that could be used to help you produce new content. For example, if people are searching for something that you don't currently have on your website, this is identifying a content gap that you can fill. You might also identify terms that could help inform the product or services you offer. People are looking for this information, so why not give it to them?

> **Tip:** Some people love clicking buttons and this includes your 'search' button. If you see the keyword 'search' or '(not set)', these are people who have searched without entering a term.

If you click on a particular term in the report you'll see the Destination Page for the term. The idea is that you can analyze particular pages people navigate to after performing a search, but unfortunately this report is one of the few reports inside Google Analytics that has been broken for a long time. Instead of seeing where people go, you will see the URLs of your search results pages which is not very useful at all.

Understanding Post-Search Navigation

Although the inbuilt report is broken for Destination Page, there is a way to understand how people navigate from a particular search results page. Start by navigating to the 'All Pages' report under 'Site Content' in the 'Behavior' section. At the top of the report, click on 'Navigation Summary', you will find this just to the right of the 'Explorer' tab.

This report shows you basic navigation paths through particular pages on your site. Next to 'Current Selection' you'll see one of your pages displayed in blue. Click the page and perform a search for the URL of your search function.

You'll need two things to do this. First, you will need to know the query parameter for your search function. If you don't know this quickly jump to "Site Search" in Chapter 24 – "Configuration Options" – which covers configuration and then come back. Second, you will need to be using a reporting view where you have not selected to strip out the query parameter from your reports. If you have stripped out the query parameter switch to an unfiltered view. Alternatively, this is also a good time to create an unfiltered view, so you have a raw set of data moving forward.

You can now search for your search query parameter in the Navigation Summary report. For example, if your search results page for the term 'contact' has a URL like '/search.php?q=contact', then you can search for **?q=** to find all your search result pages.

Page	Pageviews
/Google+Redesign/Brands/YouTube/default.aspx	31,991
/shop.axd/Home	26,920
/shop.axd/Search	11,713
/shop.axd/Cart	7,617
/Google+Redesign/Wearabies/Men+s+T-Shirts/default.aspx	7,243
/Google+Redesign/Fun/default.aspx	7,153
/Google+Redesign/Wearabies/Men+s+Outerwear/default.aspx	6,194
/Google+Redesign/Accessories/default.aspx	6,043
/Google+Redesign/Accessories/Bags/default.aspx	5,721
/Google+Redesign/Brands/YouTube/default.aspx?page_no=2	4,544

Search: ?q=

Now just click on the particular search result page that you want to analyze. The report will update and you will see two columns below the page icon. The column on the left shows you the pages where people started their search. The icon in the middle represents the search results page you are analyzing, and the column on the right shows you the pages that people went to from the search results page. You can now view the navigation for different search terms by clicking the 'Current Selection' and choosing a different search results page.

Using this technique, you can understand post-search navigation paths and also compare the pages people navigate to against your search results. If people are regularly navigating to a page that is lower down on your results page, then that page could potentially be promoted at the top of the results page to improve user navigation.

Identifying Post-Search Issues

You can also review the search terms report for terms that have a low level of engagement after the search has occurred. By identifying terms that have a lower Time After Search or lower Search Depth you can find pages that are not meeting the expectations of people searching. It could also be that your search solution isn't returning the most appropriate results for the particular term. If you do identify terms with a lower level of engagement, then try searching for those terms yourself and see what the experience is like. This can help you tune your search solution to provide better results for your users.

Look for pages that have a higher '% Search Exits', which shows you the percentage of people who are leaving your website from your search results page. A higher percentage of exits can indicate that your search solution is not providing the results people were looking for. Check the results pages for those terms and potentially tweak your search for better quality results or even add promoted suggestions for important terms.

Search Categories

If your internal search solution allows people to refine their search by selecting a category refinement, you can configure Google Analytics to report on these categories in the Site Search reports. You can find these reported in the Search Terms report. Just above the report table there is an option called 'Site Search Category' – click this to view the categories people are selecting when they search. Any searches that are performed without a category selection will be reported as '(not set)'. You can drill down into particular categories to see the individual terms that people have used in each search category.

Pages

The Pages report shows you the particular pages where people start to search. You can drill down into a particular page to see the terms that people use when they begin searching from the page. This can help identify potential navigation issues, or even content that could be included on the page. If lots of people are searching for similar terms from a page you could consider including relevant links alongside your primary content (for example in the right-hand column), in the menu or even in the footer of the page.

Site Search Best Practices

It's important to not review these reports in isolation. Make sure you open up your website and use your search solution as you are analyzing the reports. This way, you'll also be able to understand if your results are relevant to what people are searching for and better understand the experience. Testing out your search solution is also important because you might find that particular terms you see inside Google Analytics reports end up returning no results at all.

> **Tip:** You can use the Search Terms report to help you identify potential keywords for your paid search campaigns and organic SEO.

Don't forget to come back to the reports on a regular basis to review what people are searching for and ensure that your onsite search experience remains a good one.

Events

Events allow you to measure custom interactions into Google Analytics. They are highly flexible and can be used in many different ways. Overall, they allow you to get additional details about what people are doing on the pages of your website. For example, if you had a page with PDF files that you wanted people to download, then without Event Tracking you would only be able to report on the number of people navigating to the page that contained the files. You wouldn't be able to report the number of times people clicked on the page to then download the files. This means that you would be missing important insights into the popularity of the files – if a large number of people are downloading the files, you might want to consider creating additional PDFs. However, if nobody is downloading the files, you might reconsider your strategy.

To use the Events reports you need to first implement Event Tracking to collect the data. This can be done within the code of your website, or by using Google Tag Manager. Events can be a little confusing if you are getting started, because they are totally flexible and can be implemented to measure just about any interaction that occurs on a page. This can become more complicated to understand because you are also able to name these interactions in any way that you choose. If someone has already set up events and you see odd names in the reports, the best option is to identify the person who set up the events so you can find out the naming convention they have used to measure interactions. For in-depth details on how to implement events, you can read the "Event Tracking" section in Chapter 28.

This section isn't too technical, but before looking at the reports it's useful to know how events are named. When you have events implemented, you'll need to define a name for the category of the event, and the action that has been performed by a user. Looking at the PDF example again, you would want to define the *category* as 'downloads' or 'PDFs'. This way, you'll have a quick way to find all of the PDFs that people have clicked to download. You can think of the event category as a folder that contains all the data for a group of items being measured. In this example, the group (or folder) will include all PDF files on the website.

Now that you've defined a category, you need to define the *action*. In this case, you'll want to use 'click' or 'download'. Think of the action as the type of interaction that has occurred. For this example, people need to click a link on the website to download a PDF file.

There are also two optional elements that can be defined: *label* and *value*. Label is a way to get extra details or information into your reports. In this case you'll probably want to report separately on the individual PDF files that are being downloaded. Use the optional label to provide the name of the PDF (for example 'form.pdf') – this will allow you to compare the performance of the different file downloads. Finally, you can provide a numerical value – this is also optional. For example, if you wanted to report on the relative value of the different downloads that you have on your website. For this example, there is no need to assign a value for the event because all of the PDFs are similar.

Category	Action	Label	Value
download	click	form.pdf	

If there were additional PDFs to measure, then you would keep the category and action the same, but change the label to reflect the name of the file.

Tip: For more details about defining a value, read about "Goals" in Chapter 23. Some examples of values that you can use are dollar value, time, or even points if you are using events to measure an interactive website game or app.

Now we'll look at the reports that are available once you have implemented Event Tracking. To start, you have the Overview report, which gives you a top-level understanding of the custom interactions you are measuring using events. You can use this report to quickly see if you are measuring any events, along with top-level metrics and the most popular events that are being reported. You'll want more detail if you are looking to report on and analyze the performance of interactions. Let's jump into more detailed reports to understand what is available.

The Top Events report shows the events that have been measured. By default, the report shows you the most popular event categories on your site. Here you can see that the events category has been defined for different types of interactions, including downloads, outbound links and interactions on website forms:

Event Category	Total Events	Unique Events
	34,866 % of Total: 100.00% (34,866)	**26,592** % of Total: 100.00% (26,592)
1. downloads	**24,148** (69.26%)	22,690 (85.33%)
2. outbound links	**7,669** (22.00%)	1,504 (5.66%)
3. form interactions	**1,525** (4.37%)	1,086 (4.08%)

If you want to see more detail for a particular category click the category name to see the associated actions. You can then click on the action to see the optional labels if they have been defined with the event. Alternatively, when you navigate to the Top Events report you can switch from the default (which shows you category) to quickly see all of the actions or all of the labels in the report. To do this, simply select 'Action' or 'Label' above the reporting table.

The Pages report shows you the particular pages where your events are being triggered. For example, if you wanted to see the PDF files that were being downloaded from the '/about.html' page you can click on the page to see the particular events that have been triggered on that page. Then you can look for the events that show when someone has clicked to download a PDF file.

> **Tip:** Remember that if you use the Pages report, there could be additional events triggered on the other pages that you are not currently analyzing. To see all the events, you can use the Top Events report instead.

In summary, the Top Events reports allows you to understand interactions based on the way you have named your events, including category, action and label. The Pages report allows you to drill down to see which events have occurred on individual pages.

Finally, the Events Flow report visualizes the different event interactions that users perform. This allows you to see the flow of interactions. For example, if someone downloads a file and then watches a video that you are measuring using events, you will see this behavior visualized in the report.

AdSense

Google AdSense allows content websites to allocate space to display ads. Google then allows people to place ads through Google AdWords using the Google Display Network which can then be displayed in these allocated advertising spaces. When someone clicks on the ad, Google charges the advertiser and part of this revenue is shared back to the owner of the content website through Google AdSense.

The AdSense reports allow you to link Google Analytics with your Google AdSense account for insights about how those ads are performing on your website. This can help you make decisions about where ads are placed within your content and how to improve the revenue you are generating.

You can link your Google AdSense account by clicking on 'Admin' and then selecting 'AdSense Linking' under the 'Property'. Once linked, you will have access to details about the ads being displayed on your website. The most important report is the AdSense Pages report which shows you the revenue, clicks, CTR and other metrics for each of the pages where ads are being displayed. This allows you to understand your most valuable content. You can also use the AdSense Referrers report to understand which sources and mediums are driving people to your website and then resulting in clicks and revenue.

> **Tip:** Visit http://lovesdata.co/SPdWW for more details on Google AdSense. You can also find additional details about the AdSense reports at http://lovesdata.co/GTKgV

Conversion Testing

Conversion testing is where you present different website content to your users and then measure the impact on conversions in order to improve your conversion rate. Testing enables you to get greater value out of your existing traffic and can be applied to any type of website. For example, if you have an ecommerce website and you tested a new checkout process that increased conversions by 25%, you would have achieved a significant improvement to your sales. If you had a services-based website, then testing a new contact form that increased leads by 60% would give you more opportunities to sell your services.

Conversion testing can also be used to improve the overall usability of your website, so even if you aren't selling online or generating leads, you should still think about ways to improve your online experience. Maybe you have an online quiz that could be improved or perhaps you could get people to engage deeper into your website content by developing a test to reduce the number of people bouncing from your landing pages.

Running conversion tests on your website puts you in control of driving continual improvement and helps remove or reduce the arguments about who has the best idea for improving your website or online experience.

The Value of Conversion Testing

Conversion testing enables you to increase the value received from your website. This could be monetary value if you are looking after ecommerce or lead generation. It could also be symbolic value or an improved user experience if you are looking after a content website.

Let's say that you have 20,000 website users for a given time frame and of those users 2% convert to achieve a total value of $100,000. You then set a target to increase value to $150,000.

Current:	Target:
20,000 users	
2% conversion rate	
$100,000 value	**$150,000** value

If you don't make any changes to your website it is likely to continue converting about 2% of users, so what option do you have to hit the target? Well, you would have to increase traffic by 50% to meet your objective:

Current:	Target:
20,000 users	**30,000** users
2% conversion rate	2% conversion rate
$100,000 value	**$150,000** value

This makes sense, but it would take a mammoth effort to increase users by that much. It would likely mean that you'd have to increase your online advertising budget dramatically which would also eat up the additional value you set out to achieve. You could also do a whole lot of SEO work, but this would take a significant amount of time and it's no guarantee that this would result in achieving the new traffic target.

Instead of trying to increase traffic you can use conversion testing to try and increase the conversion rate. If you were to increase the conversion rate by 50% then you would achieve the goal without having to increase traffic.

Current:	Target:
20,000 users	20,000 users
2% conversion rate	**3%** conversion rate
$100,000 value	**$150,000** value

If you are able to improve the conversion rate further you will achieve even greater value. Then look at ways to increase the amount of traffic received to further capitalize on the improvement.

Content Experiments

Content Experiments allow you to run tests to improve your website. Typically, you run tests to improve the conversion rate of a particular goal, but you can also run conversion tests to improve usability. Content Experiments allows you to run A/B tests using Google Analytics.

Tip: They are called A/B tests because a portion of people will see the original page (version A) and another portion of people will see the variation you are testing (version B).

Using Content Experiments requires some steps and if you are just getting started, it is likely you'll need some assistance from your web developer and designer. This can make it a little daunting if it is your first time running a test, but it can help you achieve measurable improvements, so it is worth investing the time to do so.

There are a number of steps to follow when conversion testing. It's important to cover these steps and understand what you need to do to ensure the best chance of launching a successful experiment.

Steps:
1. Identify page(s) to test
2. Develop hypothesis
3. Create variations
4. Develop page
5. Place code
6. Preview
7. Launch
8. Analyze

It's really important to understand that not every experiment will result in a positive improvement to your conversion rate. Sometimes you might run a test that isn't statistically significant. This basically means that the difference between the original and test variation isn't significant enough to see a measurable result. If this happens you should review the test variations you created and see if there is any opportunity to create a new variation to run another test.

> **Tip:** If you run a test without much traffic, then you might not see a winning test variation for your experiment. Check how many variations you have created. A low traffic website should only ever put one variation against the original page, because more variations will take longer to test. You can also use a testing calculator to estimate the duration of a test based on your traffic and expected improvement. You can find a testing calculator at http://lovesdata.co/Wlfx9

Content Experiments Setup Steps

The first step is to identify the page you want to improve. You'll need to plan your experiment and work with your designer and developer to create a new variation (or variations) of the page you want to test. They will need to create a physical page on your website in order to set up and use Content Experiments. For example, if you decided to test your contact page and the original page on your website is '/contact-us.html', you would need to create a page like '/contact-us-2.html' to use as your test page.

> **Tip:** You can name your test page anything you like, so if you don't want '/contact-us-2.html', you could use '/contact-us-now.html' or something else that is more user-friendly and less likely to make people think you are running a conversion test.

Once you have created the variation page (or pages) log into Google Analytics and select 'Experiments' under the 'Behavior' section and click 'Create Experiment'. From here you will be guided through the following steps:

1. Name your experiment.
2. Choose a metric as the objective, for example a particular goal conversion.
3. Choose the amount of traffic to include in the experiment. Unless you have a lot of traffic, you should keep this at 100%.
4. There are additional options before proceeding to 'Configure Your Experiment' where you will need to enter the details of your original page and test variation page (or pages).
5. You will then be given the special Content Experiment code that needs to be placed on your original page. This code is just for that individual page.
6. Finally you can review and launch your test.

Once your test has been launched, people will begin to be included in the experiment and you'll be able to check back to see data in the report. You will see one of the following messages:

- **'Running'** will be displayed if the test has just been set up and you will need to wait until more data is available.

- **'Winner Found'** means that one of your variations has outperformed the other options and is now the winner.

- **'No Winner'** means that there is no clear difference between the variations.

- **'Time Limit Reached'** means that your test has run for the maximum of three months and there is no clear winner.

Tip: You should try to run experiments for a minimum of three weeks. This will help balance out things like weekend changes and other trends that occur each week.

Not every test will result in a winner. You might even find that particular test variations are worse than your original variation. This might seem negative, but it means you will then know what does not work, so you can rethink your optimization strategy. You should always consider testing a learning experience.

Alternative Tools

Content Experiments has both advantages and disadvantages. The advantages are that it is free and since it is built on Google's infrastructure it can handle large volumes of traffic. The disadvantage is that it requires work to create your alternate page (or pages) to test and you need to modify the code on the original page you are testing against.

Optimizely (visit http://lovesdata.co/YKqtO for details) and Visual Website Optimizer (visit http://lovesdata.co/eWQpT for details) are two good alternatives to Content Experiments because they allow you to use a visual editor to make changes to the page (or pages) you want to test. This can help save time and money if you are not familiar with coding.

20

Conversions

Under Conversions you'll find a collection of reports that allow you to understand the high value tasks you are trying to get people to complete. To begin using the reports, you'll need to configure goals. If you are selling online, you can also implement ecommerce tracking to understand what people are purchasing. Every website or mobile app should have a defined purpose and you need to configure goals to reflect your objectives. Goals can be configured to measure a wide variety of conversion actions, from people completing contact forms to watching videos, registering for events, making purchases, downloading files or even engaging with your content.

Tip: This section of the book focuses on understanding the Conversions reports, if you don't have any data within the reports you might want to read Chapter 23 – "Goals" – and the "Ecommerce" section (below) in this chapter for details on setup and implementation.

Terminology

Goal Completions

Goal Completions are the total number of conversions, however Google Analytics will only count one conversion per goal within a session. If someone comes to your website and completes your contact form, then navigates through a couple of pages on your website and goes back and completes the contact form again, this will mean they have completed the goal twice but Google Analytics will only count one conversion for the session.

> **Tip:** This is not the case with ecommerce transactions, every time someone purchases something a new transaction will be reported, even if they perform back to back transactions without leaving your website.

Goal Value

When you configure goals, you're able to define an optional dollar value for the conversion action. The goal value will show you the total value based on the dollar value you have defined along with the total number of goals. If you have defined a dollar value of $10.00 for a goal conversion and there are five conversions, the goal value will show $50.00. This allows you to compare values and you will see goal value available in other reports. Assigning an appropriate value is covered in the "Goal Value" section in Chapter 23.

Goal Conversion Rate

The Goal Conversion Rate shows you how good your website is at converting. It is calculated by dividing the total number of conversions by the total number of sessions. If you had 10,000 sessions and 200 goal conversions your goal conversion rate would be 2% which is (200 ÷ 10,000) x 100.

Total Abandonment Rate

The Total Abandonment Rate shows you the percentage of people who start one of your goals, but fail to complete your desired action. If you have a goal where you want people to complete your contact form on '/contact-us.html' which then directs successful completions to '/thank-you.html', then an abandonment will occur when someone views '/contact-us.html' but fails to view the thank you page.

If 2,000 people start your goal and 1,800 people abandon before they complete the goal, then your Total Abandonment Rate would be 90% as (1,800 ÷ 2,000) × 100 = 90%.

Goal Completion Location

The Goal Completion Location (or Goal URLs) show you where a conversion has occurred. In most cases this will be the page you have defined as the conversion URL. If you set the conversion page as '/thank-you.html' you would see this URL as your Goal Completion Location because this is the page where the conversion occurred.

If you have defined a goal based on events, then the goal URL will be the page where the event occurred. For example, if you are using events to measure PDF downloads and you created an event-based goal based on those downloads, then the goal URL will be the page where the PDF was downloaded because this is where the event triggered and met your goal conversion criteria.

For engagement-based goals, the goal URL will be the page where the engagement criteria was met. For example, if you created an engagement-based goal for people who spend over two minutes on your website, then the goal conversion will occur when they have been on your website longer than two minutes. So at two minutes and one second the page someone is on will be reported as the goal URL.

Goal Reports

The Goals Overview report gives you a summary of all the conversion data for the date range selected. You'll be able to see the total number of conversions, goal conversion rate and other metrics, along with the number of conversions for each individual goal that has been configured in your reporting view.

Goal Option:	
All Goals ▼	
All Goals	3,858
Goal 1: Registration	1,676
Goal 4: Contact	154
Goal 5: PDF Download	156
Goal 6: Social Media	202
Goal 7: Video	1,504
Goal 8: Quiz	25
Goal 9: Sponsorship	2
Goal 10: Newsletter	119
Goal 11: Help	20
Goal 2: Newletter [off]	0
Goal 3: Contact [off]	0

When you load the report you will see data for all goals combined. If you want to focus on an individual goal click the 'All Goals' button below 'Goal Options' and select the desired goal. The report will now refresh and just show data for your selected goal.

The Goal URLs report shows you the locations of where your goal completions have occurred. In most cases your goals will be based around people viewing particular thank you pages on your website, so this report allows you to see the actual pages that are meeting your goal conversion criteria. You can use the report to ensure that the thank you pages are as you expected based on your goal configuration. If you identify a page that you don't expect as a conversion page, then you can investigate the reason. It might be that your configuration is matching additional pages that you didn't expect, or it could be that you have an event or engagement-based goal.

The Reverse Goal Path report shows you the pages people view before they make it to your defined conversion page. On the left you will see the final thank you page and then stepping to the right you will see what they saw before converting. You can see up to three steps before the conversion page in the report.

In the detail below you'll see that people who converted on the 'thank you' page viewed the 'contact us' page before converting. You can also see that there was no step before the 'contact us' page which is indicated by '(entrance)'. This indicates there is only one step leading to the conversion page, and this was the most popular path for people who converted.

Goal Completion Location ⑦	Goal Previous Step - 1 ⑦	Goal Previous Step - 2 ⑦	Goal Previous Step - 3 ⑦	Goal Completions ↓
1. /thank-you	/contact-us	(entrance)	(not set)	2,052 (53.19%)

If you have a goal where you have defined a number of steps leading to the conversion you will see the different ways people follow those steps. If you notice steps out of order you will want to check the usability of the process. You might find that there are ways for people to skip steps or even begin the funnel process on steps that you did not expect.

Use the Reverse Goal Path report to identify the most popular paths people use to reach your conversion page, and then look for ways to increase the number of people taking that particular path. This might include highlighting a page that people see before converting within your navigation or the content of your website. Remember that you can also use the report to identify usability issues when people take unexpected paths to conversions.

Tip: The Reverse Goal Path is just one report available for understanding how people travel through the funnel steps defined for your goals. Additional reports can be used to understand funnel paths, including Funnel Visualization and Goal Flow.

The Funnel Visualization report provides a simple way to visualize how people travel through your goal funnel steps. Start by picking the goal you would like to analyze by selecting the name of the goal under 'Goal Option'. Now you will see the steps that have been defined in the goal settings starting at the top of the report and stepping down to the final conversion page. At each step in the funnel you will see where people enter a particular step (this is the number on the left) and people abandoning from a particular step (the number on the right).

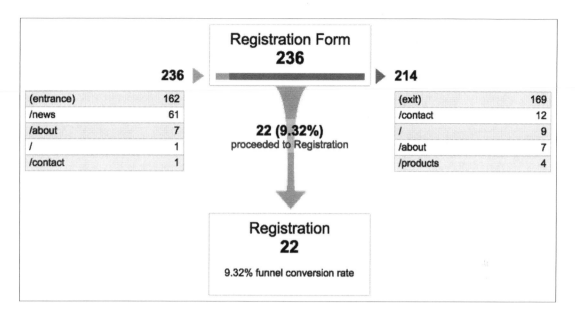

The report gives you a summary of the pages that people view before entering a step on the left and the pages that people navigate away to on the right. If you see '(entrance)' this tells you that they are coming directly into that particular funnel step without viewing a previous page on your website. Where you see '(exit)' this tells you there are people who leave your website from a particular step without ever traveling on to view another page on your site.

Tip: The Funnel Visualization report is one of the few reports that does not allow you to apply segments, so if you want to segment your funnel you will want to use the Goal Flow report instead.

Look for steps that have a large red bar, this indicates where people are not traveling on to the next step in the funnel. This can also be a good place to start with optimization (including usability, design and testing). If you can get more people through a particular step, they are more likely to continue traveling through the funnel. Think of the big red bars as the major bottlenecks in your goal funnel.

You will be able to see the percentage of people who travel from one step to another and also the overall Funnel Conversion Rate, which is the percentage of people who begin the funnel and make it to the conversion page.

Tip: The Funnel Visualization report is not detailed enough to provide you with insights into people who skip steps or repeat particular steps in your funnel. Instead the report backfills data where people skip particular steps. For example, if someone travels from your first funnel step, skips your second step and then views the conversion page, the report will show the person viewing the first and second step before conversion. Visit http://lovesdata.co/hjXhh for more details about goal backfilling. If you want to understand your funnel in more detail then you will want to use the Goal Flow report that provides much more detail about how people navigate through your funnel steps.

The Funnel Visualization report does not allow you to perform in-depth analysis, so think of it as a starting point for understanding your goals and funnel performance. Once you are ready to perform more detailed analysis you will want to start using the Goal Flow report.

The Goal Flow report is a bit like the Funnel Visualization report, but with greater flexibility and the ability to see more granular detail. It is entirely focused on the funnel that you have defined for your particular goal. You read the report from left to right and each node (green box) represents a step that has been defined for your goal.

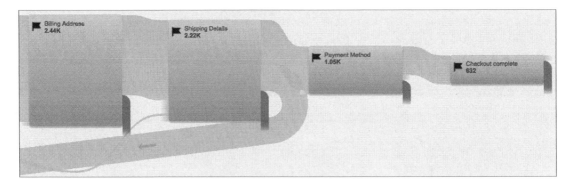

You can modify how people are grouped in the starting node of the report. By default, the report will group people based on their source, this is the last method they used to find your website before conversion. You can change the way people are grouped by clicking on 'Source' and selecting an alternate way to segment your audience. The segmentation that you choose will depend on the type of analysis you want to perform. For example, if you are focused on analyzing the performance of social media through your funnel you can select 'Social Network' or if you want to see funnel performance by people's geographic location you can select 'Country'.

Just like the User Flow report you can click on a particular step and click 'Highlight Traffic Through Here' to focus on a particular step in the funnel. When you focus on a particular step, you might also see additional connections in the report. These connections can show you where people are skipping particular steps in your funnel and also where people are looping back to repeat steps. In the example below you can see that some people have skipped a step and others are looping back after they view the conversion page.

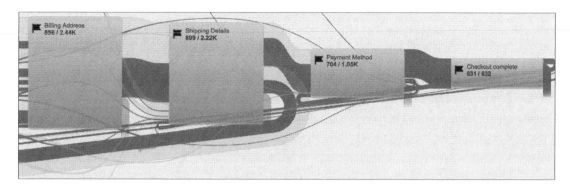

If you see people skipping steps you will want to review usability and how people navigate between steps. There might be technical problems with the process that you need to review or maybe there are links in the funnel that should be removed. If people are looping back this could help you identify opportunities to modify where people go at particular points in your funnel.

From here you will want to analyze the steps through your funnel in more detail. Click on a step in the funnel where you see a large portion of people abandoning the step. You can find this by looking for steps where there is a large red bar traveling towards the bottom of the report. Now click on the step and select 'Explore Traffic Through Here'. This will now give you more detail about how people enter the particular step and also where they travel to next.

You will be able to see the pages people view before the step and people entering at the step – this is the green bar. On the right, you'll see where people go – this might be the next step or conversion page, but can also be other pages on your website. You will also see people who exit your website completely, this is shown in red and indicates drop-offs. You can hover over each element to find additional details.

> **Tip:** You can apply segments to the Goal Flow report for greater detail and to perform in-depth analysis of particular audience segments.

Ecommerce

The Ecommerce reports provide details about transactions, your checkout process and other ecommerce transaction details. The Overview report provides a top level summary with quick top ten snapshots of your top selling products, product categories and product brands.

Important: This section covers the newer Enhanced Ecommerce reports, however you might still be using the older ecommerce reports. Visit http://lovesdata.co/Ky02M for a comparison of the old and new reports. Details about implementing Enhanced Ecommerce can be found in Chapter 28 – "Ecommerce Tracking".

You'll be able to see the total amount of revenue generated for the date range, along with the total number of transactions and the average order value for each of these transactions. The ecommerce conversion rate is the total number of transactions divided by the total number of sessions. This provides a quick gauge about the performance of your ecommerce website. Ecommerce conversion rates vary widely, but a general guide is one to three percent[1].

Under Campaigns you will see transactions, revenue and average order value for your inbound marketing campaigns that are using campaign tagged URLs and from your Google AdWords campaigns.

The reports can also include data for internal website promotions, coupon codes and affiliate details. If your ecommerce tracking code has been implemented to collect these details you will see this data presented in the overview report.

Tip: Your ecommerce reports should be accurate, but they are unlikely to match exactly to your backend sales data. They are designed to provide insights about your website and marketing performance and trends to drive overall optimization. They are not intended for things like financial reporting.

Shopping Analysis

The Shopping Behavior Analytics funnel shows you how many people are completing transactions and the steps leading to those transactions. On the left you will see the total number of sessions. On the right, the number of sessions where people viewed a product page, then added an item to the shopping cart, viewed the checkout page and finally completed the transaction.

Below the funnel you can see the number and percentage of sessions that leave at each step. The additional blue boxes for the shopping cart steps indicate that people have started at that particular step in the funnel. This will include people who begin the checkout process in one session and then finish it in another, as they will be seen to enter at the step they left off from the previous session.

---

1   http://moz.com/blog/ecommerce-kpi-benchmark-study

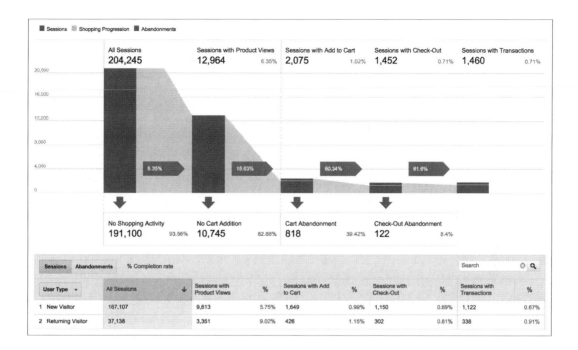

Below the funnel there is a table that you can adjust to see particular dimensions and metrics. By default it will show you the number of sessions at each stage of the funnel broken down by your new and returning users.

You can change how the table is broken down by clicking on the 'User Type' drop-down and selecting another dimension. For example, selecting 'Source' allows you to see data for each funnel step based on how people have found your website. This allows you to identify particular steps where people are more or less likely to convert based on particular audience segments. Once you identify audience segments that are more likely to travel through each checkout step you can begin to develop strategies to increase the size of this audience.

If you find segments that are not successfully making it through the checkout process, you can identify the steps that are causing abandonment and analyze their behavior in greater detail. A good way to perform further analysis is to create a custom segment and then review the more detailed reports available in Google Analytics. Start by applying your new segment to the 'Landing Pages' report under 'Site Content' in the 'Behavior' section. You might find that people included in this segment are having a different experience navigating through the website. You should also compare your under-performing segments to people who are more likely to complete the checkout process, which can help identify opportunities for improvement.

> **Tip:** You can switch the table in the Shopping Behavior Analysis report to focus on areas where people leave your checkout funnel by clicking 'Abandonments'.

You can also click on particular elements in the funnel to create custom segments based on the steps in your checkout process. Clicking on the blue bar in 'Sessions with Add to Cart' allows you to create a segment that includes everybody that has added an item to their shopping cart. After you've clicked on an element in the funnel you can name your segment, select if you want it available in any Google Analytics reporting view, or just the view you are currently using, and then click 'Create Segment'. The segment will continue to be applied as you navigate to other reports.

The Checkout Behavior Analysis report is similar to these reports, but it is purely focused on your checkout steps, not the steps leading up to your shopping cart. The steps displayed in the report will again depend on your ecommerce tracking code and the number of steps that have been implemented on your website.

> **Tip:** The name of each step in the Checkout Behavior Analysis report is defined in the administration section. Navigate to 'Admin' and select 'Ecommerce Settings' under the 'View' column on the right, you can now define the names for each funnel step. Note: If you are not able to edit these settings, then you don't have edit-level permissions for this reporting view.

You can define additional options for each step of your checkout process in the ecommerce tracking code. If these options are defined you can click on the arrow displayed between steps in the report to see the number of sessions selecting these options.

Product Performance

The Product Performance report shows the most popular products being purchased based on the product name defined in the tracking code. You can use this to identify products that are resulting in the greatest revenue and products to promote on your website and in other marketing initiatives. Depending on your ecommerce tracking code, you can also view by 'Product SKU', 'Product Category' and 'Product Brand' using the links above the table in the report.

You will see the following in the Product Performance report:

- **Product Revenue** is the total amount of revenue generated by that particular product.

- **Unique Purchases** counts a product once even if people purchase multiples in the same transaction.

- **Quantity** is the total number of units sold of a particular product.

- **Average Price** is the average price paid for the product. For example, if a product is sold twice, once for $10.00 and then for $20.00 the average price would be $15.00.

- **Average Quantity** is the average number of units sold in a transaction.

- **Product Refund Amount** is the total refunded value for a particular product.

- **Cart-to-Detail Rate** indicates how popular an item is based on people viewing the product and then adding it to their shopping cart. For example, if two people view the product page and then one person adds it to their shopping cart, then the Cart-to-Detail Rate would be 50%.

- **Buy-to-Detail Rate** indicates the percentage of people who view a product page that then go on to purchase the product. For example, if four people view the product page and then one person purchases the product, then the Buy-to-Detail Rate would be 25%.

Tip: Use the Buy-to-Detail Rate (or the Cart-to-Detail Rate) to identify products that are more engaging with your audience. You can then review the product pages for these items against product pages for less engaging items to identify areas for improvement on your product pages.

Sales Performance

The Sales Performance report provides ecommerce data when the transaction ID is sent to Google Analytics after a successful checkout. The report also shows any refunded amount associated with particular transaction IDs. Clicking on a transaction ID will show you the items purchased in the transaction.

Selecting 'Date' above the table allows you to see the total value for individual days. The date is listed in the format of year, month and day. For example, 1 January 2015 would be displayed as '20150101'. Clicking on a date will show you all the products purchased on that particular day.

Product List Performance

The Product List Performance report allows you to see where products have been seen on your website and if people engage further to view the product detail page right through to people purchasing. To use the report you need to be passing a value to the ecommerce tracking code about where the product is seen using the 'Product List' option. This allows you to completely customize what you see inside the report. Here are some examples of what you might want to consider tracking as lists:

- Category pages that contain multiple products
- Products automatically displayed on your homepage
- Related products displayed on individual product detail pages
- Products displayed in your website's search results

Let's look at a scenario to understand this in detail. If you have a new products page that automatically lists your 10 latest products you can define this page as the 'New Products' list using the ecommerce tracking code. Then when someone views the page each of the 10 products will be reported as being seen on the 'New Products' page.

If someone then clicks through to view one of these products in more detail, it will be reported as a 'Product List Click'. This continues on if they add the item to the shopping cart and for those people who purchase.

This report provides powerful insights into the most important places people are seeing products and if they engage further into your ecommerce checkout process. Use the report to identify your top performing areas for listing products using the 'Product List Views' and the 'Product List CTR' columns. Pages with a high product CTR (click-through rate) can be used to place products and increase sales.

Marketing

The Marketing section contains reports that allow you to understand the impact of your marketing on ecommerce transactions. The Internal Promotions report is similar to the Product List Performance report looked at previously, however this report is specifically designed to provide insights about products that you are featuring using internal website promotions. For example, if you have a 'Featured Items' section on your homepage you can track the impressions of these items, along with clicks, to understand the success of your internal website promotions.

The Order Coupon report allows you to see coupons that are being redeemed against an entire order and the 'Product Coupons' shows you coupons used for individual products. Use this to understand which coupons are being redeemed and which coupons are providing the greatest value.

The Affiliate Code report allows you to view any affiliate details you are sending to the ecommerce tracking code. For example, if you have affiliate marketing partners that are sending people through to your website, then you can pass the name of the affiliate into the ecommerce tracking code to report on affiliate sales. Alternatively, you can use the affiliate option to measure anything you would like associated with the transaction.

21

Multi-Channel Funnels

Multi-Channel Funnels Reports

The Multi-Channel Funnels reports allow you to gain a deeper understanding of the impacts of your different marketing channels on your conversions. Unlike the standard reports previously looked at, these reports enable a conversion to be attributed to more than one marketing channel. For example, someone finds your website after clicking your ad on Google, later they see an interesting tweet and click through to your website and then purchase from your online store. In the standard reports the conversion would be attributed to Twitter, but the Multi-Channel Funnels report shows you both touchpoints leading to the conversion. This allows you to understand the marketing channels that are closing conversions and those that are assisting conversions.

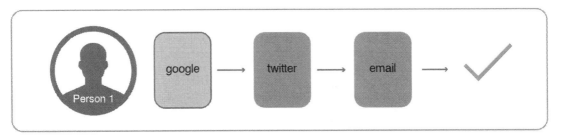

The Multi-Channel Funnels reports are all about how you attribute a conversion to a marketing channel (or multiple marketing channels). There are different types of attribution, including last click attribution, where 100% of the conversion is attributed to the last method of accessing the website. This is similar to the method used in the standard reports. Then there is first click attribution where 100% of the conversion is attributed to the first method of finding your website. Finally, there is mixed or multi attribution, where a conversion is attributed to multiple marketing channels.

The Overview report shows you the total number of conversions received, along with the number of conversions that were assisted. An assisted conversion is a conversion where someone engaged with a marketing channel, but then later converted after engaging with another channel. Continuing the example, the first method of accessing the website was through Google and then the channel that was used before the conversion was Twitter. This means that there was one conversion and one assisted conversion, because the final conversion was assisted by the first method of finding the website (in this example it was Google).

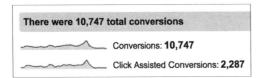

Looking at the Overview report you can see that there were 10,747 conversions and 2,287 assisted conversions. In other words, out of a total of 10,747 conversions 2,287 were the result of people engaging with more than one marketing channel. If you subtract the 2,287 assisted conversions from the total of 10,747 conversions, this tells us there were 8,460 conversions which occurred after people engaged with a single marketing channel. For example, people who found the website on Pinterest and immediately converted without engaging with any other marketing channels. The Overview report also includes the Multi-Channel Conversion Visualizer which allows you to see the interactions of your channels. Each circle represents a channel and the overlap shows you conversions which were the result of people engaging with multiple channels. Hover over a circle to see the effect of the individual channel on conversions and then hover over the intersections to see the effect of people engaging with multiple channels.

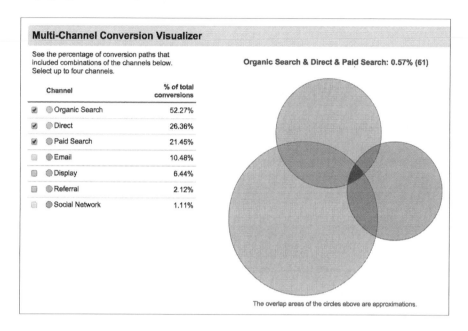

Multi-Channel Conversion Visualizer

See the percentage of conversion paths that included combinations of the channels below. Select up to four channels.

Organic Search & Direct & Paid Search: 0.57% (61)

Channel	% of total conversions
☑ ◉ Organic Search	52.27%
☑ ◉ Direct	26.36%
☑ ◉ Paid Search	21.45%
☐ ◉ Email	10.48%
☐ ◉ Display	6.44%
☐ ◉ Referral	2.12%
☐ ◉ Social Network	1.11%

The overlap areas of the circles above are approximations.

Tip: The Multi-Channel Conversion Visualizer allows you to look at the interactions of different channels by using the checkboxes next to the channel names.

By default, the Multi-Channel Funnels reports will provide data for all of your goal conversions and ecommerce transactions. If you would like to focus on one or more conversion actions you can select them by using the 'Conversion' selector at the top of the report. You can also switch from all channels to only focus on Google AdWords campaigns and select the number of days for the lookback window.

The lookback window determines how much historical data Google Analytics should use to create the reports. The default lookback window is 30 days, but you can adjust this to include anywhere from 1 day to 90 days worth of historical data. For example, if a conversion occurred on 31 January and the lookback window was set to 30 days, then the report would include any marketing touchpoints from 1 January to 31 January that contributed to the conversion. In the following example, you can see the touchpoints that would be included within the reports based on a 30-day lookback window.

To include touchpoints before 1 January you can extend the lookback window to include additional days. It's also important to understand that if you extend the lookback window to the maximum 90-day window, any conversions that occurred before the 90 day window will still not be included in the report. For example, if someone first found your website six months ago, then this would fall outside of the lookback window. So, there is a limit to how far back you can go with the Multi-Channel Funnels, but for the majority of organizations a 90-day lookback window should be more than enough.

> **Tip:** If you are offering a product or service that has a long buying cycle, then you should factor this into how you use the Multi-Channel Funnels report, along with the lookback window. For example, if you are selling a high-cost item, then the consideration could span many months that would fall outside the lookback window. If this applies to you identify goals that have shorter decision lead times. Registering for your email newsletter or downloading product brochures are likely to be the sort of tasks that people perform with minimal time between touchpoints. You can also use customizations to collect extra information, such as a custom dimension to capture details about a user's first visit.

The Assisted Conversions report shows you how your marketing channels are contributing to conversions. You will see the number of assists for each channel along with the assisted value. Remember that an assist is anything that helps lead to a conversion without closing the deal.

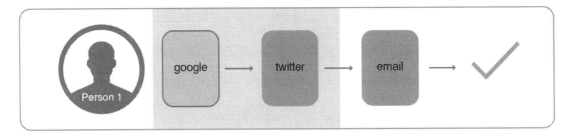

You can quickly compare each channel's ability to assist conversions by comparing 'Assisted Conversions and Value' to 'Last Click Conversions and Value'. The last column in the report, called 'Assisted/Last Click or Direct Conversions', presents this as a ratio. It is a calculation that compares the assisted to last click conversions. For example, if a channel accounted for 100 assisted conversions and 50 last click conversions the ratio value would be two. If another channel accounted for 50 assisted conversions and 100 last click conversions the ratio value would be 0.5. As you can see by this example, the ratio tells you if a channel is better at assisting or closing a conversion. The higher the number, then the better the channel is at assisting. The lower the number (or closer it is to zero), then the channel is better at closing conversions as the final touchpoint.

MCF Channel Grouping ⑦	Assisted Conversions ↓	Assisted Conversion Value	Last Click or Direct Conversions	Last Click or Direct Conversion Value	Assisted / Last Click or Direct Conversions
1. Direct	28,060 (54.16%)	$553.75 (51.33%)	87,601 (47.55%)	$1,647.00 (44.59%)	0.32
2. Organic Search	16,322 (31.50%)	$311.75 (28.90%)	73,257 (39.76%)	$1,431.00 (38.75%)	0.22
3. Referral	5,951 (11.49%)	$184.75 (17.13%)	9,867 (5.36%)	$362.00 (9.80%)	0.60
4. Social Network	645 (1.24%)	$14.50 (1.34%)	6,232 (3.38%)	$144.00 (3.90%)	0.10
5. Paid Search	326 (0.63%)	$6.00 (0.56%)	2,724 (1.48%)	$43.00 (1.16%)	0.12
6. Email	227 (0.44%)	$3.00 (0.28%)	821 (0.45%)	$15.25 (0.41%)	0.28
7. Display	190 (0.37%)	$3.50 (0.32%)	3,717 (2.02%)	$50.50 (1.37%)	0.05
8. (Other)	92 (0.18%)	$1.50 (0.14%)	16 (0.01%)	$0.50 (0.01%)	5.75

The reports give you greater understanding into the performance of your marketing initiatives. You can immediately see that not every channel is going to close conversions and this is important to understand, especially when you're making decisions around allocating your marketing budget. If you were to solely base your marketing decisions on last click attribution, then it is highly likely to result in an overall decrease in conversions.

For example, when using last click attribution you might find that the majority of your conversions came from organic search and referrals. So you decide to cut the budget that you allocated to paid search, display and email, however these channels drive huge numbers of assisted conversions. By cutting their budgets the flow-on effect could be that your organic search and referral traffic drops significantly, which could also lead to a significant drop in conversions. By using the Multi-Channel Funnels report, you can prevent this scenario from occurring because you can immediately see the relationship between your different channels.

You can then inform your marketing strategy for different channels based on their effectiveness at assisting or closing conversions. If a channel is better at assisting a conversion consider ways to help improve the number of assisted conversions. This can include ensuring that the best cross-promotions are being presented on landing pages and analysing the performance of the channel in driving specific conversion actions. For example, if you establish that your organic search channel is good at assisting conversions, then you can identify opportunities to highlight particular micro conversions that lead people towards your primary conversion action.

Tip: You can further modify the Assisted Conversions report to show 'Days before Conversion'. This will show the number of assists that occurred each day within the lookback window. Selecting 'Path Position' groups the number of interactions required before a conversion occurs. So you will see the total number of conversions that occurred after a single interaction, than those after two interactions and so forth.

Apart from channel groupings (which will be covered in detail shortly) you can also present more granular details by selecting 'Source/Medium', 'Source' only or 'Medium' only. Selecting 'Other' allows you to choose from even more options to view your attribution data. For example, selecting 'Campaigns' will show you attribution for your Google AdWords campaigns and any campaign tagged URLs you have created.

Once you have selected 'Campaigns' you'll see a portion of your traffic that is '(not set)'. Remember that this is everybody that has been to your website, but doesn't have a campaign name associated with their interaction. This will include things like organic search, referrals, direct traffic and any sessions that are not associated with a campaign name.

Important: If you compare the last click conversions in the Multi-Channel Funnels reports to the conversions in the standard reports you might notice a difference between the number of conversions reported as direct. This is because the standard reports give credit to the last non-direct method of somebody accessing your website. For example, if somebody came to your website from Twitter and then came back directly, the standard reports would show a last click conversion attributed to *Twitter*, while the Multi-Channel Funnels reports would show a *direct* last click conversion.

Channel Groupings

Channel Groupings allow you to customize how your marketing touchpoints are presented within the Multi-Channel Funnels reports. The default channel groupings will automatically assign your traffic into the following categories:

- Organic Search
- Paid Search
- Display
- Social Network
- Referral
- Email
- Other Advertising
- Direct

You can also create your own custom channel groupings to meet your individual needs. Use custom channels to compare affiliate partners to referrals, compare your email news-letter to email promotions, add an offline channel for TV, radio or print ads, or even aggregate some of the default channel together to provide a top-level view to begin your analysis.

To create a custom channel grouping click 'Channel Groupings' above the table and select 'Create a custom Channel Grouping'. You can also select 'Copy MCF Channel Grouping template' which will copy the configuration of the default groupings which you can then modify and edit as you choose.

Select 'Create a custom channel grouping' to start from scratch and make a custom channel grouping that focuses on important social networks. Start by naming the custom grouping 'Important Social Networks'. Click 'Define a New Channel' and name the new channel 'Other Social Networks'. Now you need to define your rules, so click 'Ad Content' and search for 'Social Referral Source' and select it. Next click 'Contains' and select 'Exactly Matches' and type 'Yes' into the input field. This first channel will be used to capture anybody that has engaged with one of your lower priority social networks. It allows you to still see that they came from social, but that it wasn't from one of the channels being actively managed.

Channel Grouping Settings

Name

Important Social Networks

CHANNEL DEFINITIONS

1.   Other Social Networks

     Define rules

     Social Source Referral ▾   exactly matches ▾   Yes   — OR AND

     Done   Cancel

Tip: You can customize the colors used to display your custom groupings. This can make it easier to see your most important channels.

Now you need to create custom channels for the individual social networks. Do this by creating filters where you set the 'Social Referral Source' to 'Yes', but also add the 'Source' of the particular social network. For example, for a Facebook grouping you would create the following channel:

This can be repeated for other important social networks you want to see as separate channels within the reports.

If you are using campaign tags to measure inbound links from your social media campaigns you will have to modify the configuration of your groupings to take this into account. Let's say you post on Facebook, but you also run paid ads that direct people through to your website. If you are using Google Analytics campaign tags on the inbound links for your ads this will mean that your Facebook traffic is potentially seen as two different types of traffic within Google Analytics.

If you have used the method outlined in this book for campaign tagging your paid campaigns on social media, then you will probably have campaign tags that use the following naming:

Campaign	Source	Medium	Term	Content
facebook ads	facebook.com	social		my post

This will mean that a portion of your Facebook traffic will have the source 'facebook.com' with the medium of 'social' for your paid ads and your free posts will have the medium of 'referral'. This means you will need to adjust your channel configuration accordingly. In this case use the following configuration to match all your Facebook traffic:

Tip: If you have used another way to name your campaign tags you will need to adjust your confirmation accordingly. For example, if you defined the medium as 'cpc' (for cost per click) adjust the regular expression in the previous example to become **(referral|cpc)** to match the free and paid traffic.

Repeat the process for each social network until you have created a separate channel for each network that is important. Now take a quick look at the custom channel configuration. It's important to highlight that the order you created for your custom groupings is critical to what you will see in the report. You need to imagine that each custom channel you have created is a filter, and all of your data is poured in at the top and slowly filters down through the different steps. If you were to put the first channel created (the one for 'Other Social Networks') at the top of the list, this would mean that all your social traffic would be captured by that filter and the traffic won't trickle through to the subsequent filters. So make sure individual social networks come first and that the 'Other Social Networks' channel comes last. This will ensure that all the specific social networks are in the report and then any from other social networks are clearly labelled as you would expect.

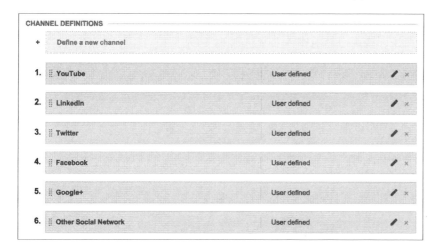

Tip: You can create additional custom channel groupings to focus on your other important marketing channels and further customize how data is presented in the report.

Configuring Branded Paid Search and Generic Paid Search Channels

You can configure Google Analytics to separate your paid search traffic into the more granular categories of branded paid search and generic paid search. This allows you to understand how these different categories of keywords are performing.

Tip: Remember that 'branded' should be used for keywords that include your company name and product names, including your trademarks and copyrights. For example, Apple would include terms like 'iPhone', 'iPad', 'MacBook' and 'Apple' as their brand terms. This leaves 'generic', which refer to descriptive words of your products and services. For Apple this would include terms like 'laptop' and 'table'.

To configure the channel groupings for your brand terms, navigate to the 'Admin' area and ensure you have the appropriate view selected from the drop-down list on the right-hand side. Then click 'Channel Settings' and select 'Manage Brand Terms'.

Here you are likely to see some automated suggestions for your branded terms based on historical data. Take a moment to review each suggestion and click the 'Add' button next to each suggestion you would like to include as a branded term. As you add terms they will move to the right and appear under 'Active Brand Terms'.

When you configure your brand terms, you don't need to enter different variations of the same keyword. This is because Google Analytics will automatically look at the brand terms you provide and match them to plurals, different capitalization and even other terms that contain your brand term. For example, adding 'android' would match 'androids', 'android phone' and 'tablet with android'. However, it is important to add misspellings since 'android' will not match 'anroid' automatically.

You should aim for a final list along the following lines:

Active Brand Terms
loves data
love data
lovesdata
lovedata

You don't need to include extra terms as they are already matched by the list:

Unnecessary Terms	Why?
loves data training	contains 'loves data' so already matched
lovedata sydney	contains 'lovedata' so already matched
ceo at loves data	contains 'loves data' so already matched

It's up to you to decide which brand terms you want to include in the channel grouping. In the example above you could have used the term 'love' as the brand term and this would match all the different variations looked at. However, this would also match terms like 'data love' and 'love analytics', which you might not want to classify as brand terms.

Now that you understand how the brand term matching works, it is a good idea to review your paid keywords report to check to see if there are any other brand terms that you should be adding to the list. I recommend opening up a new browser window or tab, so that you can quickly add any additional terms without having to try and remember the terms you have already added. A quick way to do this is to hold down your 'Command' (Mac) or 'Alt' (PC) key and click 'Reporting' in the main navigation. In the new tab that opens, navigate to the 'Acquisition' reports, select 'AdWords' and then 'Keywords'.

Start by extending the date range so that you are looking at three to six months worth of data. This is really important if you are running a small campaign, since a shorter date range will include less data and you might miss seeing other branded terms. Spend some time scanning through the terms to see if there are any that are branded but you haven't added to the channel configuration.

> **Tip:** Remember that you will be looking at the top 10 keywords, so use the arrows at the bottom of the report or the 'Show Rows' option to ensure you scan through all the keywords.

This report shows you the actual keywords that you are bidding on and since there can be a difference between what you are bidding on and what people actually search for, you will want to repeat this process one more time. Click 'Matched Search Query' above the table to see the actual keywords people are entering when they search. Now spend some time scanning through these terms, again adding any suitable brand terms to the channel configuration.

Now that you have your brand terms you can head back to your browser tab with the 'Manage Brand Terms' configuration option and enter the brand terms you have identified. Remember that you don't need to add every single variation that includes your brand, just your core list along with any misspellings you have identified. Now click 'Save'.

> **Tip:** If it is the first time you have configured your brand terms, you'll be prompted to step up the channel groupings. Simply click 'Yes' to set up the branded and generic grouping and then make sure you click 'Save' at the bottom of the page.

Now that you have created your list of brand terms you can use the keywords report anytime you want to check which keywords you are matching as branded terms.

Once you're happy with your list of brand terms you can use the Paid Keywords report to check that you aren't missing any other terms. Start by copying the brand terms from the 'Manage Brand Terms' configuration and navigate to 'Reporting', then select the 'Keywords' report under 'Acquisition'. Once the report has loaded, click 'Advanced' next to the search box above the table.

Click 'Containing' and select 'Matching RegExp' (which stands for matching regular expression). Now you need to take your list of branded terms and change them into a regular expression. If your list is something like the following:

Active Brand Terms

loves data
love data
lovesdata
lovedata

Then your regular expression will read **(loves data|love data|lovesdata|lovedata)**. This creates a list of items to search for, so when you perform your search within the report it will look for 'loves data' or 'love data' or 'lovesdata' or 'lovedata'. The pipes (vertical lines) in the regular expression create the 'OR' statements.

> **Tip:** If you have fewer branded terms, then simply modify your regular expression. For example, you might have **(term one|term two)** if you just have two branded terms. If you have lots of branded terms you can extend the regular expression to become **(term one|term two|term three|term four|term five)** to match all five terms. You can learn more about this in the "Regular Expressions" section in Chapter 27.

Now that you have converted your list into a regular expression, you can enter it into the advanced search field and click on 'Apply'.

The report will update and you'll see all the keywords that match your brand term configuration. If you notice any keywords that you don't want to include as brand terms in your channel grouping review the configuration and modify the terms that you selected as branded.

> **Tip:** You can repeat these steps to perform the same search for your Matched Search Queries (the actual keywords people are searching for when they click on your paid search ads). Just click 'Matched Search Queries' above the table and perform the regular expression search again.

Next, perform another search to identify potential brand terms that are missing from your configuration. Start by selecting 'Matched Search Queries' above the table and click on 'Edit' if you still have the advanced search applied (or click on 'Advanced' if your advanced search has been removed from the report). This time, click on 'Include' and select 'Exclude' and change 'Containing' to 'Matching RegExp'. Enter the same regular expression you used previously. Click 'Add a Dimension or Metric', search for 'Keyword' and then select it as your search criteria. Ensure that this new criteria is set to 'Include'. You can now use either the default 'Containing' option or the 'Matching RegExp' option depending on how detailed you want to search, select 'Containing', then enter a critical part of your primary brand term. For 'loves data' you might search for 'lov' as this is an important part of the term. By leaving the rest of the term off, you are able to catch misspellings of the brand name.

When you apply the search, you'll be presented with a list of terms that include 'lov' somewhere in the search queries, but are not being matched by the existing list of brand terms. You can now use this list to decide if there are any other terms you want to add to the configuration. Using this technique every few months will help ensure you maintain an up-to-date and accurate list of brand terms. It can be a good idea to schedule this report as a regular email by clicking 'Email' at the top of the report. You could even click on 'Shortcut' so you can get back to the report quickly whenever you need. Adding it as a shortcut will also save the advanced search, so you won't need to re-enter it each time you want to use the report.

Impression Reporting

If you are running Google AdWords campaigns targeting the Google Display Network you can configure Google Analytics to include impressions for video and other rich media ads within the Multi-Channel Funnels reports. This allows you to understand the impact of your video campaigns even if people don't immediately click through to your website.

To include these impressions within the reports you need to have linked your Google AdWords account to Google Analytics and have updated your tracking code to support the Google Display Advertising features.

In order to configure impression reporting, you'll need to have edit permission for the Google Analytics account. Navigate to 'Admin' and click 'AdWords Linking' under the property. Here you will see your linked Google AdWords account. Click on your account and then click 'Edit' next to 'Link Configuration'. If the account has impression data available you can click the checkbox to enable impression reporting and then click 'Save'.

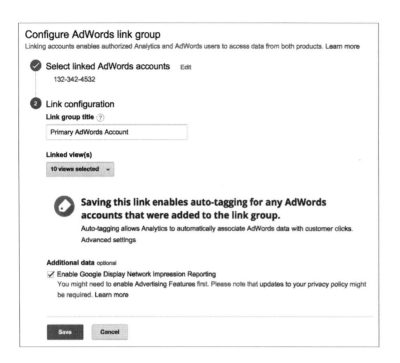

Tip: If you don't see the option for enabling impression reporting, then either your tracking code has not been updated, or you are not currently running any display campaigns.

Once you have configured impression reporting, moving forward you will see impression data within your Multi-Channel Funnels reports. Impressions are highlighted by icons which indicate if people saw your video or rich media ad, but did not click through to your website.

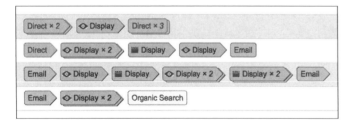

Impression reporting allows you to evaluate the success of your campaigns even if people don't click through to your website. This is especially the case if you are running video ads on YouTube, since most people view the ad without clicking through to your website. Apart from impressions being displayed within the report you can choose to include or exclude impressions and rich media from the reports by using the 'Interaction Type' option at the top of the reports.

You can focus on impressions based on particular ad types when creating custom channel groupings. For example, you can create a grouping that includes an 'Ad Format' of 'Video' to analyze the performance of your YouTube video ads.

You also have access to new dimensions to assess performance. Navigate to the 'Assisted Conversions' report within Multi-Channel Funnels and click on 'Other' to the right of 'Medium' above the table. The list of dimensions includes 'Above the Fold', 'Video Played Percent' and 'True View'.

'Above the Fold' allows you to understand if your ads were seen without people needing to scroll, 'Video Played Percent' tells you how much of your video was watched, and 'True View' tells you if people watched more than 30 seconds of your video ad.

> **Tip:** You can also make use of the impression dimensions when creating custom Conversion Segments within the Multi-Channel Funnels reports.

Top Conversion Paths

The Top Conversion Paths report is a visualization of the touchpoints that lead to a conversion. Here you can see that 125 conversions occurred after people found the website via a paid search ad and then later returned to the website via an organic search. If you were looking at last click attribution, this shows paid search was helping to assist those conversions.

People can engage with the same touch-point multiple times before they convert. This is shown in the report with a multiplier, so if you see '× 2' this means the touchpoint was used twice. You will see there is a huge range of different ways people interact with your touchpoints before they convert.

Just like the Assisted Conversions report, you can adjust the lookback window, select particular conversions, and focus on paths where people engaged with your Google AdWords campaigns. By default, the report will show you paths where there were at least two touchpoints. To see all conversion paths (including those with a single touchpoint), click on '2 or More' under 'Path Length' and select 'All'.

You can use this report to understand the complexity of your marketing channel interactions and identify paths that lead to more conversions. Look for opportunities where cross-promoting your different marketing channels makes sense. If you see that your paid search campaigns are assisting conversions that are being closed by your email marketing, then you have the opportunity to ensure the landing pages you use for your Google AdWords campaigns include your email newsletter sign-up form. It's important to maintain the primary objective of your landing pages, so consider ways to include your sign-up form without being pushy.

Other cross-promotion opportunities can include creating remarketing campaigns to re-engage people who haven't converted yet, aligning marketing messages across channels and creating ads on social media. You should also review your landing pages to see if there are opportunities to cross-promote other products and services you offer and even highlight any current promotions you are running.

You can focus your analysis on particular channels by creating Conversion Segments, which allow you to specify the particular channels that you would like to see within the report. Start by clicking 'Conversion Segments'. You will see the default segments on the left and on the right you can create your own custom segments. Create a custom segment that includes any path with a paid touchpoint. Click 'Create New Conversion Segment' and name your segment 'Any Paid Interaction'. Now select 'Include' and 'Any Interaction'. Search for 'Medium', then select it and click 'Containing' and select 'Matching RegExp'. Enter **(cpc|ppc)** as the value and click 'Save Segment'.

The report will now update and only include paths where people engaged with at least one of your paid touchpoints. You can apply multiple Conversion Segments and you always have the ability to remove the segments to go back to the default report.

Time Lag

The Time Lag report shows you the number of days between the first touchpoint and the conversion occurring. The report will include a number of conversions that had a '0 [zero] Day Time Lag', meaning that those conversions had their first touchpoint within the same day of the conversion occurring. The report then steps through the number of days since the first touchpoint, and shows you for each number of days the total number of conversions and the conversion value.

You can use the report to identify trends for particular conversion actions and particular marketing channels. Use the conversion selector to switch between your different conversions and use the conversion segments to narrow the focus of the report. You'll want to create custom segments for the particular marketing channels you want to analyze in detail.

Look for channels where there are clear trends in the Time Lag report. If you notice there are particular time lags where more conversions are occurring, this can be used to decide when you launch your campaigns.

You can also focus on strategies to try and reduce the time it takes for people to convert. The idea here is that, by making changes to your website and user experience, you can take people from consideration to decision in a shorter time frame. For example, providing additional information, adding live customer support, and simplifying the conversion process could help to reduce the time it takes people to decide on purchasing your product or service. Once you have tested or made these changes, you can use the Time Lag report and the Assisted Conversions report to see the impact of the change on the time it takes people to make a decision.

To compare the change, select a date range after the changes were implemented and then compare this to the prior date range. Looking at the Time Lag report you should see a shift with more conversions occurring towards the top of the report. It can be easier to visualize this in the Assisted Conversions report by selecting 'Days Before Conversion' above the timeline.

Path Length

The Path Length report is similar to the Time Lag report, but it presents the number of touchpoints needed for conversions to occur. Here you can see that 143,156 conversions occurred after people engaged with a single touchpoint, while people engaging with two touchpoints resulted in 21,082 conversions.

Path Length in Interactions	Conversions	Conversion Value	Percentage of total ■ Conversions ■ Conversion Value
1	143,156	$2,848.00	77.70% 77.11%
2	21,082	$426.75	11.44% 11.55%
3	7,275	$162.00	3.95% 4.39%
4	4,363	$84.50	2.37% 2.29%
5	2,407	$42.25	1.31% 1.14%

By applying Conversion Segments to the report you can analyze the performance of your marketing channels and look for quick insights about individual channels. In this example, three Conversion Segments have been applied: 'All Conversions', 'Any AdWords Search Interaction' and 'Any Display Interaction'.

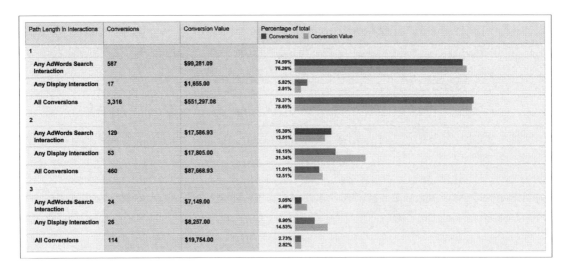

Path Length in Interactions	Conversions	Conversion Value	Percentage of total ■ Conversions ■ Conversion Value
1			
Any AdWords Search Interaction	587	$99,281.09	74.59% 76.28%
Any Display Interaction	17	$1,655.00	5.82% 2.91%
All Conversions	3,316	$551,297.08	79.37% 78.65%
2			
Any AdWords Search Interaction	129	$17,586.93	16.39% 13.51%
Any Display Interaction	53	$17,805.00	18.15% 31.34%
All Conversions	460	$87,668.93	11.01% 12.51%
3			
Any AdWords Search Interaction	24	$7,149.00	3.05% 5.48%
Any Display Interaction	26	$8,257.00	8.90% 14.53%
All Conversions	114	$19,754.00	2.73% 2.82%

You can also see that display advertising performs well in comparison to the other channels where there are two or three marketing touchpoints. Use these insights to review your display campaigns. You could allocate additional budget to display advertising to see if this will further increase conversions. If you're running remarketing campaigns and conversions drop from the second interaction your messaging and calls to action might need to be reviewed. If you're not running remarketing campaigns, then you could test out remarketing to see if it has a positive impact on conversions where there are multiple touchpoints.

Tip: You can also use the same segments on the Time Lag report to identify trends based on time. For example, if you notice that your remarketing ads have a higher level of performance at 14 days, then you could adjust your timings based on the report.

Attribution

The Model Comparison tool is available within the Attribution reports. The tool allows you to compare ways to assign credit to your marketing touchpoints. So far we've discussed last click attribution and the lack of clarity provided by giving all the credit for a conversion to the last touchpoint. Remember that first click attribution is where all the credit is given to the first touchpoint. The Model Comparison tool allows you to apply and compare these different ways of crediting marketing touchpoints, also known as 'attribution modelling'. Let's look at the different models that are available.

MCF Channel Grouping (?)		Last Interaction		Time Decay	
		Conversions ↓	Conversion Value	Conversions	Conversion Value
1.	Direct	434,522.00 (61.06%)	$6,051.25 (61.03%)	429,506.99 (60.36%)	$5,999.48 (60.51%)
2.	Organic Search	143,642.00 (20.19%)	$2,341.75 (23.62%)	146,128.62 (20.54%)	$2,363.68 (23.84%)
3.	Social Network	67,346.00 (9.46%)	$817.50 (8.25%)	68,491.35 (9.63%)	$831.79 (8.39%)
4.	Referral	45,336.00 (6.37%)	$561.00 (5.66%)	46,837.23 (6.58%)	$578.94 (5.84%)
5.	Display	16,274.00 (2.29%)	$88.25 (0.89%)	16,441.32 (2.31%)	$88.96 (0.90%)
6.	Paid Search	4,418.00 (0.62%)	$54.25 (0.55%)	4,130.66 (0.58%)	$51.16 (0.52%)
7.	Email	33.00 (0.00%)	$0.25 (0.00%)	36.65 (0.01%)	$0.33 (0.00%)
8.	(Other)	9.00 (0.00%)	$0.25 (0.00%)	6.15 (0.00%)	$0.11 (0.00%)

Last Interaction

By default, this tool will show the total number of conversions and conversion value based on the last method people used to find the website. This is where 100% of the conversion value is assigned to the last method of accessing your website.

The problem with the Last Interaction model is that any marketing initiatives that helped in assisting a conversion are not considered. For example, if you are running paid ads on social networks, they might appear to perform poorly when you apply the Last Interaction model. However, they might be extremely important in raising initial awareness that then leads to a conversion from another marketing channel.

Last Non-Direct Click

The Last Non-Direct Click model is very similar to the Last Interaction model, but if the last method of accessing your website was direct, then it uses the last non-direct channel instead. The Last Non-Direct Click model is used in the standard Google Analytics reports (including the Real-Time, Audience, Acquisition, Behavior and Custom reports). Historically, it has been the most common method used to evaluate the performance of marketing channels. Here are three examples to understand how this model works.

Someone finds your website on a social network, returns later by performing an organic search and a few days later remembers your URL and types it into their browser. In this case you'll have three sessions. Since the last session was direct, the model will look at the previous method of accessing the website. In this case it was an organic search, so the search will receive 100% of the credit for the conversion.

Somebody else finds your website using a link on another website, remembers your website's URL and then comes back the next day by typing the URL into their browser. They then return again a few days later, again typing the URL into their browser. In this case there are three sessions, the first a referral and the second and third sessions would be direct. This means that the referral would receive 100% of the credit for the conversion.

Another person finds your website by clicking on one of your paid search ads, then the following week returns by typing in your URL into their browser. The following day they click on a banner ad you are running. In this case, the banner ad will receive all the credit for the conversion, since it was the last method used to find your website before the conversion that was not direct.

The Last Non-Direct Click model has the same drawback as the Last Interaction model, since assisting channels don't receive any credit when a conversion occurs.

Last AdWords Click

The Last AdWords Click is similar to the Last Non-Direct Click model, but instead of skipping the last direct interactions, it skips any last interactions that are not from your Google AdWords campaigns. For example, someone finds your website using a link on another website, then later clicks on one of your Google AdWords ads, then the next day clicks one of your social media ads and converts. In this scenario, Google AdWords will get 100% of the credit for the conversion.

If you are looking to focus on how your Google AdWords campaigns are driving conversions, then this model can be useful for understanding overarching impact. However, you shouldn't use it exclusively as all of your conversions will be solely attributed to your Google AdWords campaigns.

First Interaction

The First Interaction model gives all of the credit for a conversion to the first method somebody used to find your website. There are two major problems with this model: firstly, giving all the credit to the first touchpoint leading to a conversion means that you neglect the channels that are assisting or closing conversions. Acting on the First Interaction model and ignoring the channels that actually drive conversions could lead to a dramatic drop in conversions.

For example, if you used the First Interaction model and it revealed that social networks were driving the majority of conversions, you might decide to cut your budgets for all your other channels. However, if social simply drives awareness at the first touchpoint and doesn't lead to conversions, then reducing the budgets for other channels would also lead to a reduction in conversions.

The second major problem with the First Interaction model relates to the lookback window, which is the amount of historical data Google Analytics looks at before the final conversion occurred. The lookback window can be adjusted to a maximum of 90 days. In some cases this could be missing important touchpoints, especially if you have a long sales cycle.

Remember that the biggest problem with the First Interaction model is that the longer you look back in time, the more unlikely it is that the first touchpoint actually had an impact on the final conversion.

Linear

The Linear model looks at all the touchpoints that lead to a conversion and spreads the value evenly across all of these touchpoints. For example, someone found your website by performing an organic search, then later used a link on another website, clicked on a paid search ad and then completed a goal action worth $90.00. In this case, there were three touchpoints and the $90.00 value would be evenly divided, so that each touchpoint would get $30.00 credit for the conversion.

The Linear model provides a better distribution of credit than the previous models covered because it goes beyond a single touchpoint. However, allocating more credit to channels that are closing conversions is important.

Time Decay

The Time Decay model gives more credit to the most recent touchpoint leading to a conversion and credit is reduced as you step back through the touchpoints prior to the conversion occurring.

The Time Decay model is complicated when it comes to assigning credit to each touchpoint. This is because the amount of credit reduces based on the number of days before the conversion occurred. For example, if the final touchpoint was assigned a value of $10.00 based on the model, then a touchpoint that occurred seven days before would receive $5.00 (or half the value of the final touchpoint). If there was another touchpoint 14 days before the final conversion then this touchpoint would receive $2.50 (or a quarter of the value of the final touchpoint). This is because by default the model reduces the credit assigned every seven days going back in time.

Did you **know?** The way the Time Decay model reduces value based on time is known as 'exponential decay'. Google says the "Time Decay model has a default half-life of 7 days, meaning that a touchpoint occurring 7 days prior to a conversion will receive half the credit of a touchpoint that occurs on the day of conversion."[1]

This model is recommended if you are going to use one of the default models available within the Model Comparison tool, as more credit is assigned to the marketing channel that closes the conversion. It also takes into account touchpoints that lead to the conversion without over-assigning credit to the initial touchpoints.

Position Based

The Position Based model splits the value of a conversion between all the touchpoints, with 40% going to the first touchpoint, 40% to the last touchpoint and the remaining 20% divided equally between the middle touchpoints. In the diagram below there are four touch-points. If the conversion is worth $100.00, then the first and last touchpoint would receive $40.00 each and the two middle touchpoints would receive $10.00 each.

The Position Based model allocates a large portion of credit to the first touchpoint, which does not reflect the importance of touchpoints that are closer to the final conversion action.

Tip: The Time Decay model is a better starting point than the Position Based or other attribution models. Once you have applied the Time Decay model to your analysis, you can always look at developing a custom model that emphasises particular touchpoints and channels to reflect your needs. For details on creating a custom attribution model visit http://lovesdata.co/gDcaY

Using the Model Comparison Tool

Once you're familiar with the default attribution models available within the tool, you can select models to understand the performance of your channels. You can compare multiple models and see the difference in conversions between the models, simply click 'Select Model' and choose the model that you would like to compare.

This example compares Last Non-Direct Click to the Time Decay model. You can see how the Time Decay model has impacted the final conversion numbers compared to the Last Non-Direct Click model.

---

1   https://support.google.com/analytics/answer/1665189?hl=en

Tip: Just like the Multi-Channel Funnels reports, you can also adjust the Model Comparison Tool by selecting particular conversions, focus solely on Google AdWords, adjust the lookback window and apply 'Conversion Segments'. All of these options are available at the top of the report. You can also switch from the default channel grouping, for example by selecting 'Source/Medium' or even your own custom channel grouping.

Next, let's walk through how you can make the data actionable by applying Avinash Kaushik's methodology.[2] Before getting started, you need to determine the lookback window for your analysis. This is the amount of historical data (based on days) you want to include before the conversion occurred. Determining your lookback window can be tricky and will require a little bit of intuition and your knowledge of the conversion (or sales) cycle to the number of days you include.

Navigate to the Time Lag report found within 'Conversions' and then 'Multi-Channel Funnels'. Select a date range that is a minimum of three months – ideally use six months or even longer to have a better picture of your conversion cycle.

Tip: If there were any major spikes in traffic from particular marketing campaigns or seasonal events, then try and avoid these in your date range. This might mean reducing the date range so that you don't include the spike.

Now, select a particular conversion action from the drop-down list. You'll want to perform this analysis on individual conversion actions, otherwise the data will be skewed. For example, if you were to mix macro conversions and micro conversions, then the micro conversions are likely to make your conversion cycle look shorter than it really is because micro conversions are usually quick and easy for people to perform.

Next, select a lookback window that makes sense for the particular conversion action you have selected. If you are analysing a conversion with a longer conversion cycle, like purchasing a product or service worth thousands of dollars, then you will want to extend the lookback window to 90 days. However, if you are analysing a conversion for a low cost item or a micro conversion where you expect people to act quickly, then you will want to stick with the default 30-day lookback window or even reduce it slightly.

Tip: Selecting the lookback window will require you to apply your best professional opinion. At worst you can always repeat the process again with a different lookback window and compare the results.

---

2   http://www.kaushik.net/avinash/multi-channel-attribution-modeling-good-bad-ugly-models/

Looking at the report, you might see longer time lags grouped together into buckets of days. In the example below you can see that there are three buckets; 12 to 30 days, 31 to 60 days, and 61 to 90 days.

Time Lag in Days	Conversions	Conversion Value	Percentage of total Conversions / Conversion Value
0	4,302	$223,762.71	76.44% / 68.25%
1	153	$17,515.08	2.72% / 5.34%
2	90	$1,142.10	1.60% / 0.35%
3	55	$129.95	0.98% / 0.04%
4	48	$271.95	0.85% / 0.08%
5	44	$512.30	0.78% / 0.16%
6	67	$2,869.45	1.19% / 0.88%
7	49	$935.55	0.87% / 0.29%
8	32	$1,266.30	0.57% / 0.39%
9	34	$633.15	0.60% / 0.19%
10	17	$1,131.57	0.30% / 0.35%
11	25	$140.90	0.44% / 0.04%
12-30	364	$21,279.06	6.47% / 6.49%
31-60	254	$52,988.44	4.51% / 16.16%
61-90	94	$3,261.69	1.67% / 0.99%

Click on the plus sign next to each bucket to expand the report and see all of the days listed out. Now look at the total number of conversions at the top of the report and calculate 80% of these conversions. For example, if you had 355 conversions, then 80% of 355 would be 284. Now add up the number of conversions row by row in the report until you are at that 80% mark or slightly over.

You might need to adjust the percentage up from 80% based on your knowledge of the conversion cycle. For example, if you use 80% and the number of days in the conversion cycle seems too low, then repeat the process with 90% of the total conversions.

Next, add the custom attribution model to your reporting view. To do this visit http://lovesdata.co/zEwcW and click the 'Import' button. Select the appropriate reporting view and click 'Create'. Now, enter your conversion cycle as the lookback window (if your conversion cycle is 0 to 25 days, then enter '25') and click 'Save'.

Navigate back to the Model Comparison Tool within 'Attribution' and then 'Conversions'. Now when you click 'Select a Model' and scroll to the bottom of the list, you'll see your custom model.

Avinash recommends comparing the Time Decay model to your custom model to begin analysis. Select the particular conversion action you are analyzing from the drop-down and set the lookback window to the same number of days as you set for your custom model (which is the same as your conversion cycle).

Tip: If you're starting out, you might want to compare the Time Decay, Last Non-Click Interaction and your custom model. This allows you to see the differences between the standard reports (Last Non-Click Interaction) to your custom model and can help you familiarize yourself with the differences in conversion data between the models.

Now look at the percentage change in the conversions column and look for the major shifts between the models (highlighted by green and red arrows). From here you want to develop tests for the way you allocate your marketing budget. The idea is to allocate additional budget to the upward shifts when you are comparing models (highlighted by green arrows) and potentially even decrease your budget where there is a downward shift (highlighted by red arrows). The best way to start is to allocate additional marketing budget to the better channels. This way there is no risk of cannibalizing your other channels, even if the test fails.

Here is an example of how you could apply this technique. Say you have a monthly marketing budget of $5,000. You might test assigning an additional $1,000 to the marketing channel that shows the greatest opportunity.

You will then need to monitor the results of your additional budget allocation and look for a lift in conversions for the channel. To do this, you'll want to compare a date range before your test to the date range of your test and look for an increase in conversions. You will need to ensure that you are accounting for any major influences, like seasonal trends, website changes and marketing campaigns (one option is to use the Benchmark reports). You'll also want to monitor the CPA (cost per acquisition) to see if it increases significantly during your test. The additional budget might not be performing as well as it should, which might mean you need to review the creative and the placements of the display ads to ensure that major changes weren't made during your test. Ideally, just increase the budget for the test without changing placements, the ads or any other targeting.

Tip: Avinash makes some additional recommendations for the methodology to work, including the need to campaign tag all your inbound marketing and uploading cost data for all your advertising. You can read his blog post at http://lovesdata.co/gDcaY

Once you have confirmed the success of your test, you can look to reallocating your regular monthly marketing budget to the channel and then repeat the process. Remember that testing with additional budget is one way to test. Once you're confident in your testing you can look at reallocating existing budget instead.

22

Advanced Interface Features

Segments

Segments allow you to focus on particular sections of people visiting your website, to perform in-depth analysis. You can think of segments like a temporary lens you can apply to your reports to better understand their behavior. These temporary lenses can be applied and removed at any time and you can even compare different segments against one another. As you normally browse your reports inside Google Analytics you are looking at all your website sessions, meaning that absolutely everybody accessing your website is included in reports.

There are some good default segments that can be found in every Google Analytics account. To find these pre-defined segments, navigate to the 'Standard Reporting' tab and select the 'Overview' report under the 'Audience' menu item. Now click 'Add Segment' (you will find it below the name of the report and above the graph). On the left you will see a category called 'System' that includes all the pre-defined segments. Click on the box next to the segment you want to apply to your report – let's select 'Search Traffic' and now click on 'Apply'. You'll now see that the Audience Overview report has been refreshed and you are now only seeing data for people that have found your website using a search engine.

You'll also notice that for each segment applied to your report there is a chart showing the percentage of traffic included in the segment.

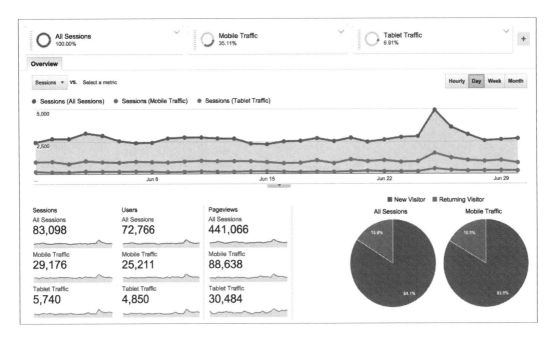

You can now navigate to different Google Analytics reports and the segment will stay selected. For example, if you navigate to 'Acquisition', then 'All Traffic' and then 'Source/ Medium', you will only see the search engines people have used to find your website. This is because the segment is still applied to your reports. If you navigate to 'Referrals' (also under 'All Traffic') you will see a lot of zeros and a message saying "There is no data for this view". This is because the Advanced Segment only includes search engine traffic and since a referral is not a search engine, there isn't any data available. Another way to think of it is that you are looking at a referral report and asking for search engines – they simply cancel each other out and nobody matches the criteria defined by the segment.

Tip: If you navigate to a report and see zeros or data that you were not expecting, check to see if you have a segment applied. Removing or changing the segment might give you the information you were looking for.

You can also apply multiple segments at the same time, allowing you to quickly compare performance and trends between segments. For example, navigate to 'Overview' under the 'Audience' menu item and then click 'Add Segment'. In the 'System' category, select 'All Sessions', then 'Search Traffic' and also 'Referral Traffic', then click 'Apply'. You can now see all three segments plotted on the timeline and below the timeline you can also quickly compare data. For example, you can compare the number of sessions and further down, you can even compare top-level engagement metrics, like pages per session and bounce rate to quickly gauge performance.

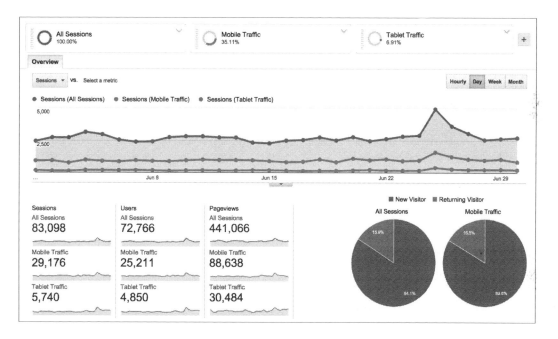

To remove a segment click on the grey downward arrow on the right-hand side of the segment (at the top of the report) and click 'Remove', or you can click on the 'Add' button and deselect the segments you no longer want to apply.

> **Tip:** If you log out and then log back into Google Analytics, the segments you previously applied to your reports will no longer be applied. If you want to use the segments you were using previously, simply re-apply the segments to your reports.

Session and User Segments

Google Analytics allows you to choose between session-based or user-based segments. This allows you to decide if you want to include people based on a single session, or if you want to include people based on all the information that is available about them from multiple interactions (sessions). Choosing one type of segment over the other will produce different results, so your decision will come down to what you want to see in the reports, and how you want to analyze your data. Let's look at some different scenarios to understand the difference between session and user segments.

Generally, user-based segments are best suited when you want to analyze the behavior of individuals where the particular behavior (or interaction) you are focusing on could occur during any number of sessions on your website.

Session-based segments allow you to compare interactions that include the same criteria and where you want to focus your analysis. For example, if you want to analyze the navigation paths people take through your website after they click a link in your email newsletter, then you probably want to start with a session-based segment. If you're using campaign tags on the links in the email newsletter, you could create a segment to include all sessions where the medium is defined as 'email'. Then use the Content reports and even the Users Flow report to better understand the paths people take and the content they engage with after they come to the website from the email newsletter.

Let's look at the alternate option to better understand the difference between the types of segments. If you were to create a user-based segment for the email newsletter, you would be saying that you want to see everybody who at some point came to the website via the email newsletter. For example, if someone found the website by searching on Bing, they then signed up for the email newsletter and a few weeks later receive a newsletter and click on the link to return to the website. That person (user) is now associated with Bing and the email newsletter, so creating a user-based segment is like saying "I want to include anybody who at some point engaged with my newsletter". Since the user is also associated with Bing, you'll see both Bing and the email newsletter when you apply this user-based segment.

So when you want to focus on particular criteria, in this case the email campaign, it is best to use a session-based segment as it will only include sessions that match that specific criteria.

System Segments

The System Segments provide a great starting point to perform more in-depth analysis of your data and are the same across all Google Analytics accounts. You can choose from the following session-based segments:

- **All Sessions** includes all website sessions.
- **Bounced Sessions** includes interactions where people only viewed a single page during a particular session.
- **Direct Traffic** includes sessions where people have come directly to your website.
- **Mobile and Tablet Traffic** includes people visiting your website on their mobile or tablet.

- **Mobile Traffic** includes people visiting your website on their mobile.

- **Non-bounce Sessions** only includes sessions where people viewed two or more pages.

- **Non-paid Search Traffic** includes sessions where people have come from an organic (free) search. This will include all the major search engines, including Google, Bing and Yahoo.

- **Paid Search Traffic** includes sessions where people have come via a paid search campaign. This will include your Google AdWords traffic if you have correctly linked Google AdWords and Google Analytics. This segment will also include any custom campaign tracking where the medium is set to one of the standard paid traffic values. This includes 'cpc' for cost-per-click, 'ppc' for pay-per-click, 'cpa' for cost-per-acquisition, 'cpm' for cost-per-thousand impressions, 'cpv' for cost-per-view and 'cpp' for cost-per-phone call.

- **Referral Traffic** includes sessions where people have come to your website using a link on another website.

- **Search Traffic** includes sessions where people have come from a search engine. This segment will include both organic and paid search traffic.

- **Tablet and Desktop Traffic** includes people visiting your website on their tablet, desktop or laptop.

- **Tablet Traffic** only includes people visiting your website on their tablet.

- **Sessions with Conversions** includes any single session that included a goal conversion.

- **Sessions with Transactions** includes any single session where a purchase was made.

The system segments also include the following user-based segments:

- **Converters** includes people who have completed a goal conversion or transaction at least once during one or more sessions.

- **Made a Purchase** includes people who have completed at least one transaction during one or more sessions.

- **Multi-session Users** includes people who have been to your website multiple times during the selected date range.

- **New Users** includes people who had not previously been to your website including anytime before the selected date range.

- **Non-Converters** includes people who have never completed a goal conversion or transaction.

- **Performed Site Search** includes people who have performed at least one site search.

- **Returning Users** includes people who have previously been to your website, including before the selected date range.

- **Single Session Users** includes everybody who has only been to your website once during the selected date range.

> **Tip:** Your users will include people who visit your website multiple times. If somebody clears their cookies or is not identified as the same user, then this will show up two separate users inside Google Analytics (unless you have implemented the user ID feature).

If you are measuring a mobile app the default segments will be slightly different. The mobile app default segments include:

- All Sessions
- Android Traffic
- Direct Traffic
- iOS Traffic
- Mobile and Tablet Traffic
- Mobile Traffic
- New Users
- Other Traffic (Neither iOS or Android)
- Paid Search Traffic
- Referral Traffic
- Returning Users
- Sessions with Conversions
- Sessions with Transactions
- Tablet and Desktop Traffic
- Tablet Traffic

Custom Segments

Custom Segments allow you to build segments based on your own specific requirements. Start by thinking about your most valuable audience members and create segments to help analyze these groups of people in more detail. By identifying these groups you can better understand how they become your most valuable users and use these insights to improve the experience for them further and even apply the knowledge to your less valuable audience segments. Let's look at some examples of custom segments.

Geographic Segmentation

Creating custom segments based on the geographic location of your audience is a great starting point for segmentation. This is because most organizations know where their target audience is located or can easily establish the locations of their most valuable clients and customers.

For example, you might only offer your products and services to people located in the United States, but you find visitors from all around the globe in your Google Analytics reports, including people from the United Kingdom, Australia, Canada and many more. However, your target market is only those people located in the United States. In this case you could create a Custom Segment to just focus on people located in the United States and temporarily remove those people located in other countries. This allows you to specifically focus on your target audience and understand how that particular section of your audience is finding and engaging with your website.

Start by selecting 'Add Segment' (which will be a greyed out option above the timeline graph). Now click on 'New Segment', name the segment 'US Traffic' and from within the 'Demographics' section click on 'Continent' to the right of 'Location' and select 'Country'. Next type 'United States' and click 'Save'.

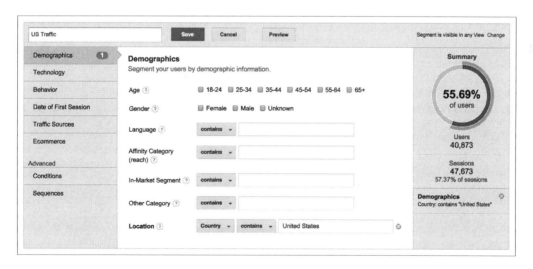

Your custom segment will now be applied to your report. You can now navigate between your reports and the segment will continue to be applied.

> **Tip:** A good way to check your custom segment is correctly set up is by navigating to the report (or reports) that relate to your segment. For example, navigate to the 'Location' report under 'Geo' in the 'Audience' section to test the segment including people located in the United States. You should expect to see only the elements you have chosen to include in your custom segment.

Don't worry about making a mistake when you create a segment, because you can always edit it later. Clicking the downward arrow on a segment you have applied to your reports allows you to:

- **Edit** the segment to make changes.

- **Copy** the segment to make a new segment.

- **Share** the segment's configuration with other people. This only shares the configuration and not your data.

- **Build Audience** to create a remarketing list for your Google AdWords campaigns using the segment.

- **Remove** the segment from being applied to the report (selecting 'Remove' will not delete the segment).

Conditions and Sequences

You can further control how people are included within your custom segment by using 'Conditions' and 'Sequences'. A condition allows you to build up one or more statements that must be met for people to be included within your segment. For example, you might create the following condition-based segment:

This would mean that the segment includes sessions where people are using an Apple device and they are located in Canada.

A sequence based segment can be used to include people based on particular criteria being met in a particular order. For example, you might create the following user-based sequence:

This segment will include people who came to your website from your email newsletter, before later converting for your lead generation goal. You can further control the sequence-based segment by choosing between 'Any User Interaction' and 'First User Interaction'. Selecting 'First User Interaction' means that the person needs to have completed step one first without anything else occurring previously. Continuing the sequenced-based filter example, if you changed the 'Sequence Start' to 'First User Interaction' this would only include people who came to your website from your email newsletter on their first session before converting. While selecting 'Any User Interaction' would include people who came from your email newsletter and converted even if the session from the email newsletter wasn't the first session.

Another option is to change how people move from one step to the next within the segment. The default option of 'Is Followed By' means that other interactions can occur between each step, while selecting 'Is Immediately Followed By' means that nothing else can occur between the steps.

Examples of Custom Segments

The best starting point is to create custom segments to reflect your highest value prospects and customers. This does not necessarily need to be dollar value, it can simply be your most important audience members. Consider creating custom segments based on:

- **How people find your website**
  - For example, social media traffic or people clicking on campaign tagged links from your email marketing.

- **Audience demographics**
  - For example, age, gender and other demographics.

- **High value customers**
  - For example, people who have converted with a value of more than $500 or people who have converted multiple times.

- **Landing pages**
  - For example, people who have visited one of your marketing campaign landing pages.

- **Branded and generic keywords**
  - People finding your website using branded and generic keywords (remember that this will primarily be for paid keywords as most organic keywords are not provided).

- **Viewing important pages**
  - People who have viewed an important page (or pages) on your website, like the shopping cart or a contact form.

- **Custom dimensions**
  - If you are measuring custom information about audience members into Google Analytics you can create segments using your custom dimensions.

Tip: You can add pre-configured custom segments to your account by visiting http://lovesdata.co/166ca

Data Import

Data Import allows you to combine external data with your data inside Google Analytics. This can be used to extend what is available within your reports and provide additional insights into your audience and their behavior. Data Import works by joining additional data to existing data. For example, let's say you have multiple authors for your blog, you can use the URL of each blog post as the key to join data and then extend this by uploading the name of the author for each key.

Default page data inside Google Analytics:

Page	Pageviews
/blog/summer-is-here	2,837
/blog/new-features	1,038
/blog/summer-specials	991

External data linking authors to blog posts:

Author	Page
Melissa	/blog/summer-is-here
James	/blog/new-features
Sarah	/blog/summer-specials

Default data and external data combined in Google Analytics:

Page	Author	Pageviews
/blog/summer-is-here	Melissa	2,837
/blog/new-features	James	1,038
/blog/summer-specials	Sarah	991

This now allows you to understand the relative performance of the blog authors and tie this to people's behavior on the website.

Data Import allows you to import:

- **Cost Data** to understand relative advertising costs and additional data about your custom marketing campaigns, including impressions, clicks and cost.

- **User Data** that allows you to upload data against individual users if you have implemented user ID. For example, you can upload your own demographics or custom data for particular individuals.

- **Product Data** to extend ecommerce product data if you choose to only send a product ID when an ecommerce transaction occurs. Based on this ID you can upload additional data including product name, brand and category.

- **Campaign Data** allowing you to use a single parameter for campaign tagging URLs (utm_id) and then upload additional campaign data, including source, medium and campaign name for each campaign ID.

- **Refund Data** which enables you to refund ecommerce transactions and upload partial refund data for particular products in a transaction.

- **Content Data** to add additional details to pages on your website, including page author and other custom data.

- **Custom Data** to upload custom data to Google Analytics.

Regardless of the data you are looking to import, the main thing to consider is that you need a key to connect your upload data to and this key needs to be available in your reports. Some of the Data Import options will have a key available by default. For example, Content Data uses the page URLs that are already in your reports. However, if you don't have the key available, you will need to make this available before you begin uploading data. This might mean using campaign tagged URLs to use Cost Data or setting up ecommerce tracking to use product or refund data. If you want to use Custom Data you will need to implement a custom dimension or user ID before you can upload your data.

Cost Data Import

The Cost Analysis reports allow you to view the ROI (Return On Investment) of your paid campaigns by including advertising cost and comparing it to the value your website is generating based on your goal values and ecommerce transactions. In order to do this you need to upload your advertising cost data into Google Analytics, otherwise the report will only report on the ROI of your Google AdWords campaigns (since cost data for these campaigns are automatically available). You can also include impressions and clicks when you upload data for the report. This allows you to compare how people are engaging with your ads along with the conversion data.

Uploading Cost Data into Google Analytics

Before you start, it's important to understand that custom data is uploaded to a property inside Google Analytics and is then applied to one or more views. If you have a large-scale implementation you'll have to repeat the process if you want data available within views that are contained in different properties. In most cases you won't need to worry about this, but it is good to remember that uploading cost data is at the property level and not the account level.

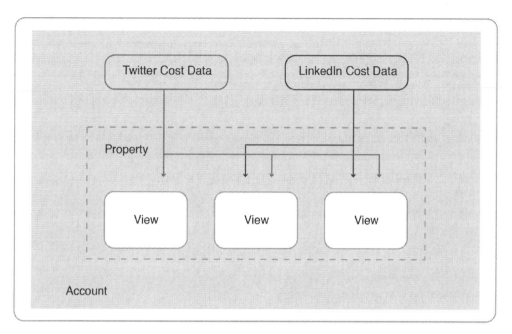

There are a number of steps you need to follow to upload cost data into Google Analytics. Here is a quick summary of what's required:

1. Ensure you're using campaign tags

2. Download cost data from non-AdWords sources

3. Set up custom data source

4. Format data for upload

5. Upload data into Google Analytics

Step 1: Check Campaign Tags

The first thing you need to check is that you're using campaign tags on your inbound links. This ensures that you can match your cost data to data that is available in your Google Analytics reports. The campaign tags you create will become the key that you use to combine the data together inside your reports.

As a minimum, you need to be defining the source and medium for your inbound links using campaign tags. However, if you are also defining the campaign name, keyword and ad content, then you have the option of uploading more detailed data for those additional campaign tags you have used.

Tip: You can only upload cost data if you are using campaign tags. To learn more read Chapter 18 – "Campaign Tracking."

Step 2: Download Data

Now, you'll need to download your cost data for each of your advertising channels. This will typically involve going to each advertising platform and finding the reporting section to access your campaign data. When you download data, always look for reports that give you a daily breakdown for your advertising. This is important because when you upload data to Google Analytics you need to upload data for each day your ads have been running.

The types of data you can upload for your campaigns will be covered in a moment, but for now, try to download a complete set of data for each day your campaign has been running. You might not use every column from your advertising platform report.

LinkedIn

You can download your LinkedIn ad data from LinkedIn Campaign Manager. You can find this under the 'Reporting' tab. Make sure to download your data using the 'Day' option.

Twitter

You can download your Twitter ad data from the 'Campaigns' tab by selecting 'Export'. Select 'Daily' and 'CSV' before clicking 'Download'.

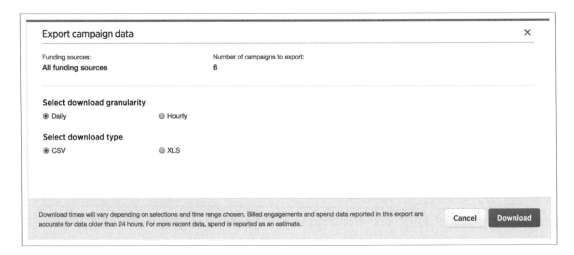

Facebook

Download your Facebook ad data from the 'Reports' section. On the top right-hand side look for the 'Dates' option, click on 'All Days' and select '1 Day Per Row'. Then click 'Export' and select 'CSV'.

If you are downloading data from another advertising network look for an option to download the data as a CSV file or Excel spreadsheet. If this is not available you can go with another format, but it might mean more work formatting the data.

Step 3: Set Up Custom Data Source

Now you need to set up your custom data source. Navigate to the 'Admin' section and select the appropriate property. In the property select 'Data Import' and click the 'Add New Data Set' button. Now select 'Cost Data', click 'Next Step' and name the dataset and select the view (or views) where you want the data to be available in your reports.

You can create a new data source for each of your advertising channels. For example, one for your LinkedIn ads, one for your Facebook ads and another for your Twitter ads. Alternatively, you can create a single data source and use it to upload all of your data. This can make it quicker to upload data, since you do not need as many files, but it also makes it a challenge if there is a mistake and you need to re-upload data as everything is combined in one data source.

There is no right or wrong, so if you are running ads on a manageable number of channels you will probably want to have these as separate data sources so that everything is logical and easy to manage within your property.

Now you need to select the data that you will be uploading. Generally you will want to upload clicks, cost and impression data, unless you are unable to provide data for one of these from your advertising. Start by clicking 'Select One' under 'At Least One of these Columns Must be Provided' and then click 'Clicks' and repeat for 'Cost' and 'Impressions'.

You also have the option of providing additional information for your advertising campaigns. You can include the following optional dimensions:

- Referral Path
- Ad Content
- Ad Group
- Ad Slot
- Ad Slot Position
- AdWords Campaign ID
- AdWords Criteria ID
- Campaign
- Destination URL

- Display URL
- Keyword
- Matched Search Query

Adding these additional dimensions allows you to produce more granular reporting with your cost data. Let's say you are running ads on Twitter that direct people to your website and you have two very different campaigns. One campaign directs people to purchase and another is for a free promotion. Since both campaigns are on Twitter, use the source 'twitter.com' and the medium 'social'. This means that if you upload cost data against the source and medium you won't be able to understand the performance of the individual campaigns.

When uploading cost data, you can select 'Campaign' as an extra column and include the two different campaign names. This will allow you to see your advertising cost for each individual campaign.

In order for your cost data to be correctly attributed to each campaign, you'll need to ensure you're uploading cost data for the correct campaign name, source and medium. How this works will be covered in more detail shortly, but in brief, use the following campaign tags for your inbound links on Twitter:

http://www.company.com/landing-page?utm_source=**twitter.com**&utm_medium=**social**&utm_campaign=**twitter**%20**purchase**%20**ads**

http://www.company.com/landing-page?utm_source=**twitter.com**&utm_medium=**social**&utm_campaign= **twitter**%20**promotion**%20**ads**

Then split your Twitter advertising costs when uploading the data, along the following lines:

Source	Medium	Campaign	Advertising Cost
twitter.com	social	twitter purchase ads	$1,239.00
twitter.com	social	twitter promotion ads	$560.00

If you have additional details about your campaigns you can extend this method and upload additional data for elements like keyword and individual ad content. However, you'll need to be able to tie the extra data to that element for the reports to make sense. For example, if you wanted to upload the cost for individual keywords the keyword will need to directly correspond to the campaign tag parameters that are already available in your reports.

Tip: You can check the level of granular data you can upload by comparing your existing Google Analytics campaign data with the advertising report data you downloaded in step two. If you can easily combine the two sets of data together based on a particular campaign tag element you are likely to be able to upload this into your reports. To see what data is already in your Google Analytics reports navigate to 'Campaigns' in the 'Acquisition' section. Then click on the name of the campaign you are reviewing. Now click on 'Other' above the table and search for and select 'Ad Content'. If you see something other than (not set) you can upload data for individual ads. Repeat the process by clicking 'Ad Content', then search for and select 'Keyword' (under 'Acquisition'). If you see something other than (not set) you can upload data for individual keywords.

In most cases you'll want to at least select 'Campaign' from these additional options, since you typically set the campaign name when creating tagged URLs. However, this means adding an extra row to your data before uploading.

Once you're happy with the cost data you will be uploading (by selecting the columns you will provide) you can then choose the 'Import Behavior'. The default is 'Summation' and this option will sum data if there are multiple rows that contain the same 'Source' and 'Medium' keys. For example, if you had previously uploaded data for the 'linkedin.com' and 'social' combination for a particular day and the cost was $100, and then you later uploaded cost data for the same day and the same 'linkedin.com' and 'social' combination of $200, the reports would show a total cost of $300.

If you change this to 'Overwrite', then the most recent data you upload would replace the previous value. Continuing the example, this would mean that the particular day would now show $200 for the 'linkedin.com' and 'social' combination.

Once you are happy with your cost data upload settings you can click 'Save'. Now you'll see the options available for uploading your data. Click on 'Get Schema', this will show you the columns that you will need to include in your file when you upload your data.

Click on the 'Download Schema Template' to download a template file. This will be a CSV file that you can open in Excel which includes the headings for each column.

Now that you have the template file, you can click on 'Done' and then 'Done' again. You will now see your cost data upload source.

Step 4: Format Data

Now that you have downloaded the schema template, you need to get all of your data into that format. For example, if your schema header looks like:

```
ga:date,ga:medium,ga:source,ga:adClicks,ga:adCost,ga:impressions,ga:campaign
```

This means the first column will contain the date, the second the medium and so on.

Open the template you downloaded in Google Sheets or Excel so you can compile your data. You will have something along the following lines:

ga:date	ga:medium	ga:source	ga:adClicks	ga:adCost	ga:impressions	ga:campaign

Next, you will need to convert the data you have downloaded into the correct format. For example:

ga:date	ga:medium	ga:source	ga:adClicks	ga:adCost	ga:impressions	ga:campaign
20140810	cpc	twitter.com	135	1239.00	10732	twitter purchase ads
20140810	cpc	twitter.com	93	560.00	3090	twitter promotion ads

Tip: The first column is the date and takes the format of year, month and then day. So, 10 September 2014 would be '20140910'.

If you have been working in Excel or Google Drive export this as a CSV ready for upload. This will give you a file that contains something like:

```
ga:date,ga:medium,ga:source,ga:adClicks,ga:adCost,ga:impressions,ga:campaign
20140810,cpc,linkedin.com,135,1239.00,10732,twitter purchase ads
20140810,cpc,twitter.com,93,560.00,3090,twitter promotion ads
```

You're now ready to upload the data into Google Analytics.

Step 5: Upload Data

The easiest way to upload the data is through the Google Analytics interface. Navigate back to the data source you created (navigate to 'Admin' then select 'Data Import' for the appropriate property).

Click on 'Manage Uploads' for the particular data source where you want to upload the data. Then click on 'Upload File' and select your file. Once your file has been uploaded it will be processed and your data will appear in the 'Cost Analysis' report. Depending on the amount of data you have uploaded, it takes a minimum of one hour before the cost data will appear in your report.

Analysis

From here you can begin analyzing campaign performance from within Google Analytics. The Cost Analysis report is available in the Acquisition section. The report will automatically calculate CTR (click-through rate) and average CPC (cost-per-click) using the click and impression data.

Click on the 'Cost' column to order the report based on the cost data that is available. This will quickly show your most important campaigns based on advertising spend. You can also use this to quickly identify other advertising channels where you haven't uploaded cost data for the selected date range. These will show zeros in the cost column.

The report can give you a quick initial gauge as to the performance of your campaigns by looking at the 'Click-through Rate' column. Look for source and medium combinations that have a high click-through rate – this can indicate that your ads are more engaging for your target audience. Also look for source and medium combinations with a lower click-through rate – these are potentially advertising channels where you can begin your optimization efforts to improve engagement.

When comparing the combinations, remember that the 'Google/CPC' row can include display advertising, which will reduce your overall click-through rate. Remember to factor this in before jumping to a conclusion.

> **Tip:** If your uploaded data also includes campaign name information you can compare campaign performance by clicking 'Campaign' above the table.

The Cost Analysis report is quite simple, but the benefit of uploading cost data goes beyond this standard report. You can also create custom reports using the uploaded data for more detailed analysis. Before you perform more detailed campaign analysis, it's important to ensure you have goals configured and if appropriate, ecommerce tracking, as this will provide deeper insights.

You can create a custom report that includes 'Impressions', 'Clicks' and 'Cost' data along with 'Cost Per Goal Conversion' and 'Goal Conversion Rate'. This allows you to begin comparing performance based on how much conversion actions cost on average, along with advertising cost and how well the channel converts. Go to http://lovesdata.co/709lR to add this custom report to your account.

The report is read from left to right, allowing you to see source and medium combinations with the greatest reach based on impressions. You can then focus on the click-through rate and bounce rate columns to understand which campaigns are driving the highest levels of engagement. If a combination has a low click-through rate you should review the relevance of your ads to your target audience. If you see a high bounce rate this can indicate a disconnect between your ad and your landing page. You can then review your campaigns in more detail to understand where you are sending people to on your website. Modifying the landing page or sending people to a different landing page could help improve results. If you notice a combination with a low bounce rate you can review the landing pages of those ads to see if they are suitable for less successful campaigns.

Looking at the 'Goal Conversion Rate' and 'Cost Per Goal Conversion' columns are a good way to see if your campaigns are achieving results. Look for campaigns that have a lower than expected conversion rate or a higher than expected cost per conversion and begin by focusing on improving those campaigns. If a particular campaign has a high conversion rate you can consider reallocating budget to that campaign in order to improve your overall conversions while maintaining the same advertising budget.

You can also customize this report further by including particular macro and micro conversions in the custom report. You can do this by editing or copying the report and selecting individual goals instead of using the combined conversion rate and cost per conversion metrics. In the custom report you also have the option of adding 'ROI' (Return On Investment), 'RPC' (Return-Per-Click) and 'Margin' as a metrics. These can provide additional context to the performance of campaigns, but rely on you defining a dollar value for your goals or ecommerce tracking. You should aim to assign a dollar value for all your conversions and then add 'RPC' to the custom report. This will show you how much you make on average each time someone clicks on your ad. You can also add 'ROI' and 'Margin', but remember these are really looking at the value achieved against your advertising cost and don't take into account any of your other supply or production costs.

Tip: You might want to factor in elements like human resource (the amount of time to create and manage your campaigns), profit margin (if you are focused on ecommerce transactions) and even CLV (Customer Lifetime Value) when performing analysis. To do this you can export your data from Google Analytics and use Google Sheets or Excel. Alternatively, you can also upload these elements as additional custom data – read "Custom Dimensions and Custom Metrics" section in Chapter 28 for details.

It is also important to remember that these reports are based on last click attribution, so if someone clicks through from your ad and does not immediately convert, then they will not be included as a conversion in the calculations. Before you make a final decision about reallocating advertising budget or stopping a campaign completely you will want to use the Multi-Channel Funnels reports and Model Comparison Tool.

You'll also see your uploaded cost data in the Model Comparison Tool. In the tool you will see values for the 'Cost-Per-Acquisition' (CPA) column. Use the tool to get a more complete and accurate understanding of how your channels are driving conversions even if they were not the last touchpoint someone used before converting on your website. For details on how to use these reports read the "Multi-Channel Funnels" and "Attribution" sections in Chapter 21.

Additional Data Import

The steps to upload the other data types (user, product, campaign, refund, content and custom data) is similar to uploading cost data, however a different key will be used to join the data. For additional details on these other data types visit http://lovesdata.co/6WxlJ

Measuring Internal Website Campaigns

Now that campaign tagging inbound marketing has been covered, you might be wondering how to measure the internal promotions and offers that you run within your own website. This might include the banners featured on your homepage and other elements that are designed to promote your products and services.

The three options for measuring these internal campaigns are:

- **Event Tracking**
- **Enhanced Ecommerce**
- **Custom parameters**

Using one, or a combination, of these options to measure internal campaigns will allow you to better understand your promotions. Once you have a way to measure people clicking through, you'll be able to collect data that can be used to understand performance and importantly, insights into what is working and what isn't when it comes to the valuable real estate on your website. Depending on your objectives, this might relate to conversions or even engagement.

The campaign tags used to measure your inbound marketing efforts should not be used within your own website.

Let's look at a scenario to understand why:

1. Someone clicks through to your website. This could be from a free (organic) or paid click.

2. Google Analytics records the traffic source, medium and other details about how that person found your website. At this point a user's session also begins to be recorded.

3. Now they click on a banner within your website that uses UTM campaign tags.

4. Since the campaign tags contain traffic source, medium and other details this is again recorded by Google Analytics. Also a new session begins since Google Analytics sees that this person has used a new method (source, medium, etc.) to find a page on your website.

This means that although you will see details about your onsite promotion, you will also have two sessions recorded, even though it is really only one session. By using UTM campaign tags within your website you will be inflating your overall number of sessions and you are also highly likely to be impacting other metrics, such as bounce rate and average session duration.

Important: Do not use campaign tags within your own website. They should only be used for inbound marketing from external sources.

Option 1: Using Events

Event Tracking can be used to measure any interactions on a page, so Event Tracking suits measuring internal campaigns. They're really flexible too: when you use Event Tracking, you can define a category, action and you also have the option of adding label and value. For example, you might use the following naming convention to measure a free product trial banner running on your homepage:

- **Category:** Internal Promotion
- **Action:** Banner Image
- **Label:** Free Product Trial Offer
- **Value:** 5

If you are promoting a white paper on another page of your website, you could use:

- **Category:** Internal Promotion
- **Action:** Featured Content
- **Label:** Free White Paper
- **Value:** 2

By keeping the category on both promotions as 'Internal Promotion', it makes it easier to quickly identify all of the promotions in your reports. The action can then be used to group different promotions – for example 'Banner Image' can be used for all banners on your website. The label is then used to distinguish the individual offers being promoted and the optional value is used to prioritize the importance of the promotion. In the examples above the value is used to rank the importance of each offer out of a maximum of five.

Event Tracking does require custom code to be implemented on each link you want to measure. If you're using Google Tag Manager you can also measure particular elements based on their element ID.

Here is an example of Event Tracking that could be applied to your link:

```
<a href="/free-trial" onClick="ga('send', 'event', 'Internal
Promotion', 'Banner Image', 'Free Product Trial Offer',
5);"><img src="/images/banners/free-trial.png" alt="Free
Product Trial Offer" /><img … /></a>
```

You will then have data available within the Events reports under Behavior.

Option 2: Using Enhanced Ecommerce

If you are selling a product online migrating from the legacy ecommerce tracking to Enhanced Ecommerce will allow you to measure the products that you are promoting throughout your website.

Enhanced Ecommerce allows you to measure promotions, clicks on promotions, right through to when people add the item to their cart and checkout. For example, if you promote three featured products on your homepage, you can measure three promotions for the products. Then, if someone clicks through on a particular featured product, you can see the number of people clicking through to view that product.

Measuring promotions is a bit like Event Tracking, but this time you are defining an ID, name and optional creative and position details. Here is an example:

- **ID:** Internal Promotion 2351

- **Name:** Spring Features

- **Creative:** Green Shirts

- **Position:** 3

This will allow you to understand which promotion people see, the name of the offer, the particular creative used and where it is positioned on the page. To implement this, your code would look like:

```
ga('require', 'ecommerce');
ga('ec:addPromo', {
  'id': 'Internal Promotion 2351',
  'name': 'Spring Features',
  'creative': 'Green Shirts',
  'position': '3'
});
```

You can then also measure the number of people clicking the promotion:

```
ga('require', 'ecommerce');
ga('ec:addPromo', {
  'id': 'Internal Promotion 2351',
  'name': 'Spring Features',
  'creative': 'Green Shirts',
  'position': '3'
});
ga('ec:setAction', 'promo_click');
ga('send', 'event', 'Internal Promotion', 'click', 'Spring
Features');
```

Visit http://lovesdata.co/B4yXP for additional implementation details. Once you have implemented Enhanced Ecommerce promotion tracking you will be able to see the effectiveness of your offers in your reports.

> **Tip:** You can also use this technique to measure promotions on non-ecommerce websites using Enhanced Ecommerce.

Option 3: Using Custom Parameters

A simple way to measure internal campaigns is to use custom query parameters that you add to your links. This requires very minor changes to your links and can be a quick way to understand the effectiveness of your promotions. The main thing is not to use any parameters that are already being used (such as the parameters used by your CMS). You can use this technique to measure any details that you like, for example:

- **Type:** Banner Image
- **Creative:** Free Trial

You can then translate these to your custom parameters and apply these to the link for your promotion:

```
<a href="/free-trial?in_type=banner-image&in_name=free-
trial"><img src="/images/banners/free-trial.png" alt="Free
Product Trial Offer" /></a>
```

In this example 'in_type' is used for the type of internal promotion and 'in_name' to define the creative. After you have applied your own parameters you'll begin to see these displayed in the Site Content reports in Google Analytics.

You might want to exclude the following two parameters from some of your reporting views, because they will make your pages reports a little messier than usual. This is because the page will now appear as two rows in your reports (instead of one). You will see:

```
/free-trial
/free-trial?in_type=banner-image&in_name=free-trial
```

An extra optional step is to use the internal site search reports to see your internal promotions in your reports. However, this should not be used if you have an internal search function as people clicking on your promotions will be mixed with people actually searching on your website.

23

Goals

Goals allow you to measure high-value interactions that occur on your website. You should create goals that reflect your objectives, for example generating leads, sales or deep engagement with your website. You should set up goals for your different objectives, even if you are not trying to drive monetary value (like leads). Even without these monetary conversions you should still be able to define your objectives and translate these into appropriate goals.

Start by identifying your macro conversion actions – these are the most important actions you are trying to drive on your website. Examples of macro conversions include:

- Submitting a contact form
- Registering for a special offer
- Requesting additional product or service information
- Signing up and creating an account

Then you should identify your micro conversion actions – these are your secondary objectives. They might not translate directly into value, but they should lead people towards those actions. For example, people commenting on your blog could be tracked as a micro conversion. They aren't necessarily ready to become a customer, but they are engaging to a much deeper level than someone who only reads your blog post. Micro conversions are important because they allow you to have a more complete picture of your website performance. This is especially important for understanding the effectiveness of your marketing initiatives since only a small number of people will be ready to complete one of your macro conversion actions, but they might complete a micro conversion. Examples of micro conversions include:

- Subscribing to email newsletter

- Downloading a PDF

- Watching a video

- Writing a comment or review

- Sharing on social media

- Adding to wish list or a rating

> **Tip:** Depending on your objectives, you might have different macro and micro conversions. For example, if you are a content, community or news website, then your macro conversions might include some of the micro conversions that have been covered, along with objectives around monetizing your content.

Once you have identified your macro and micro conversions it's time to set them up as goals in Google Analytics. You will need to have administrator-level access to configure goals and once you have them set up you will begin to see data in your reports.

Page-based Goals

The most common type of goals are based on people viewing a particular page on your website. In most cases, you want to set up page-based goals to track the 'thank you' page someone views after completing your desired action. This type of goal is ideal for tracking people completing forms, stepping through an ecommerce checkout and any other stepped process you are trying to get people to complete.

Setting Up Destination Goals

To set up a page-based goal start by identifying the steps you want people to complete in order to get to your desired 'thank you' page. Unless you already know the URLs of each step, the best way to find the correct page URLs is to complete the process yourself. For example, if you want to track contact form conversions start by loading your website and navigating to the contact form you want to track as a goal. Next you will need to write down the URL of the page as it appears in the URL bar of your web browser. Following the same example, write down 'http://www.company.com/contact.html'. Next, complete and submit the form so that you are taken to the 'thank you' page. Now write down the URL of the 'thank you' page. In this example, it's 'http://www.company.com/thanks.html'.

You now know the steps people must complete for the contact form goal. Now it's time to configure Google Analytics in order to begin tracking the goal into the Conversion reports. Click on 'Admin' and then in the 'Profiles' tab click the name of the profile where you would like to set up the goal. Now click on the 'Goals' tab in the profile.

If there are already goals set up in the view you will see them in the 'Goals' tab. There are four sets of goals available in the tab and each set can contain five goals each. The sets are designed to group related goals together. For example, if you have several forms you would like to track you could set these up under 'Goals (set 1)', then if you want to track people downloading files, these could be set up under 'Goals (set 2)'. Using the different sets is not critical, but it does help streamline where you see your different conversions in your reports.

Click on 'New Goal', name the goal and select the 'Goal Slot ID' for where you would like to add the goal. In this example, you're setting up a goal for your contact form, so let's name the goal 'Lead'. Select 'Destination' as the 'Type'. Next, enter the 'Destination' or final 'thank you' page URL for the goal. Looking back at your notes you can see that the 'thank you' page URL was 'http://www.company.com/thanks.html'. You only need to enter the page path, not the complete URL, so enter **/thanks.html** as the 'Destination'.

For the 'Match Type' keep the default setting on 'Equal To'. This does exactly as the name suggests and will only report a conversion if someone views the '/thanks.html' page. Match types, and how they can impact your conversion numbers, are explored in a moment.

Leave 'Value' blank for now (this will be covered further in this section). Because there was an additional step to complete (opening the contact form for this example), enable the 'Funnel' option. This allows you to define the steps that lead to the 'thank you' page.

Next, enter the page path of the contact form. Looking at your notes you can see the contact form is located at 'http://www.company.com/contact.html'. Again, you only need to enter the page path, so just enter **/contact.html** as the URL. Then name that step 'Contact Form'.

> **Tip:** If you are setting up a goal that has multiple steps leading to the 'thank you' page, for example a shopping cart checkout process, you can add additional steps by clicking 'Add Another Step'. You can add up to 20 steps leading to your goal conversion page.

Leave the 'Required' option for your first funnel step deselected. This option will be covered shortly, but in the majority of cases you don't need to use it, so leave it unchecked if in doubt.

Click 'Create Goal' and the goal is now configured.

Match Types

Match Type is how Google Analytics is going to decide if pages match your goal configuration and if a conversion will be reported. There are three match types that you can select from: 'Equal To', 'Begins With' and 'Regular Expression'.

Equal To does just as the name suggests – it will only match the URLs you enter in the goal configuration exactly. For example, if you select 'Equal To' and enter **/thanks.html** as the destination, the goal will only report a conversion if someone makes it to the '/thanks.html' page on your website. If they go to '/thanks.html?id=contact' or '/contact/thanks.html' or any page other than '/thanks.html' a goal conversion will not be reported.

Begins With is a more relaxed way to match the URLs in your goal configuration. Selecting 'Begins With' will still match page URLs even if there is extra information after the destination page URLs you have defined for your goal. For example, if you enter **/thanks.html** as the destination, a goal conversion will be reported if someone makes it to the '/thanks.html' or '/thanks.html?id=contact' pages on your website.

Regular expression is an advanced way to match URLs for your goal configuration. It gives you the greatest amount of flexibility in how goal conversions are reported, but is also the most complicated match type. For example, if you select 'Regular Expression' as the match type and enter **/thanks\.html$** it would require that '/thanks.html' has to be at the very end of the page URL for a goal conversion to be reported. This would mean that '/thanks\.html$' would match both '/thanks.html' and '/contact/thanks.html' and someone viewing either of these pages on your website would result in a conversion. For more on how you can match URLs using regular expressions read the "Regular Expressions" section in Chapter 27. You can also download a regular expression cheat sheet at http://lovesdata.co/THYyF

> **Tip:** The match type you select applies to the goal URL and the URLs in your funnel settings. For example, selecting 'Regular Expression Match' means that you will also need to use regular expressions in the goal funnel steps.

Goal Value

Assigning a value to your goal conversions is an essential way to focus on the impact of conversions and also to understand the relative importance of different goals that you have set up. There are a number of ways to define a goal value which depend on the type of website you're looking after and the information available. We'll walk through three different techniques for assigning a dollar value to your goals: calculated values, estimated values and symbolic values.

> **Tip:** If you are looking after a website that does not have a focus on generating sales or leads you might feel that you want to skip over assigning a goal value. However, everybody that has goals should be assigning a goal value. Assigning values (even symbolic values) will allow you to prioritize the importance of your goals and allow you to use metrics that are only available once you have assigned a goal value.

Important: If you are selling items online do not use goals to measure sales. Instead use ecommerce tracking, which is specifically designed to report on the different values of items that are being sold, and your checkout steps.

Calculated Value

The first place to start when assigning a goal value is to see if you can calculate the value of a goal. This is suited to any website or organization where the final conversion occurs offline, for example, if your website is generating leads which are then followed up by your sales team, or if you are promoting a product that people purchase in-store.

If you have information about the value of the final conversion that occurs use your historical data to calculate the average value of a conversion. Let's say you are looking after a website that promotes business consulting services for individuals and you know that each client is worth an average of $3,000 to your business. Next, you can work out the total number of new clients and the total number of online leads you received over a given period of time.

Let's say you find that over a two-month period there were 10 new clients and that they came from 40 online leads from your website's contact form. This means that the contact form provided a total value of $30,000. You can now divide this by the 40 initial leads received. This shows that, although not everybody who completes the contact form becomes a client, on average each form submission is worth $750. This means you have a value that can be used for your goal.

What if you haven't previously set up a goal for key actions on your website, like in the leads example? Then you should check the All Pages report to see if you can identify the number of historical conversions that have occurred. Alternatively, if you can check previous emails for people who have submitted your form you could also use this to help calculate your dollar value. Otherwise, you can always set up your goal with an estimated dollar value and once you have enough data you can adjust the value in your goal settings.

> **Tip:** You might have different conversion actions on your website that you can apply different dollar values to using this method. For example, you might have a form on your 'services for business' page and another form on your 'services for individuals' page. You should try to calculate the value of each goal, rather than combining them to use a single dollar value.

Estimated Value

Assigning an estimated value is where you use your best judgement to estimate the value of a particular conversion. This can be useful if you have a general idea of what a goal conversion is worth, but you currently don't have enough data to calculate a value.

Let's say you are setting up goals for a plumber and they don't want to provide exact sales figures. You can try to gauge the average value of a lead based on the information they tell you. For example, if they say their average job is worth $500 to $1,000 dollars and they receive one lead from their website every day and convert 50% of those leads. In this case you can estimate that they receive 30 leads per month with 15 becoming jobs for a value of approximately $700 to $800. This means the estimated total value is $10,500 based on 15 jobs multiplied by $700. Then divide the total estimated value by the 30 leads that were received, resulting in an average lead value of $350. This could be adjusted up or down if you feel the figure is too high or too low.

> **Tip:** This can be a really good technique to begin discussing what a goal conversion is really worth and to highlight the importance of moving towards a calculated dollar value.

Symbolic Value

The final option is to use a symbolic dollar value, where you assign value based on the importance of the goal. This is especially useful for organizations not generating leads or sales, and websites primarily focused on content. The best way to assign symbolic values is to start by listing out all the different website goals. Then you can assign values based on the importance of each goal against the objectives of your website.

Let's say you are looking after a tourism website that is designed to provide information about traveling to New Zealand. The website is designed to promote New Zealand as a great place to visit, but does not allow people to book flights, accommodation or other tourist activities directly on the website.

Goals for the website might include:

- Creating a travel plan
- Sharing content on social networks
- Visiting external tour provider websites
- Contacting travel agents

You can then assign symbolic values based on the importance of the goals. If getting people to book travel to New Zealand is the primary purpose of the website you can assign a value of $100 for people who contact a travel agent. Then assign $25.00 for people who visit the website of an external tour provider, since they might look at multiple tour websites before booking. $10.00 could be assigned to people who create a travel plan and $2.00 for people who share content on a social network.

This immediately allows you to focus on the most important goals, while understanding that lower-priority goals still drive some symbolic value for the website. If you're unable to calculate or estimate a goal value you should definitely be able to assign a symbolic value to begin making better use of your goals and goal value metrics in the reports.

> **Tip:** Remember that symbolic and estimated goal values can be used as a starting point to begin focusing on the real value and purpose of your website. You can always adjust the values you have assigned by editing your goal settings at a later point.

Required Step

Required step is one of the most confusing configuration options available within Google Analytics. It is an optional setting that only modifies the Funnel Visualization report for the particular goal. It does not change any of the other reports that present the data for the goal. We'll look at a simple scenario to understand the impact of this setting.

Let's say you want people to register as a member of your website, and registration requires people to complete two steps before they are a member. First they need to review the membership details page located at '/member-overview.html' and then they need to enter their personal details on the '/member-address.html' page before they are taken to the '/member-welcome.html' page. Based on these pages, the goal would include the following steps:

Step 1: /member-overview.html

Step 2: /member-address.html

Destination: /member-welcome.html

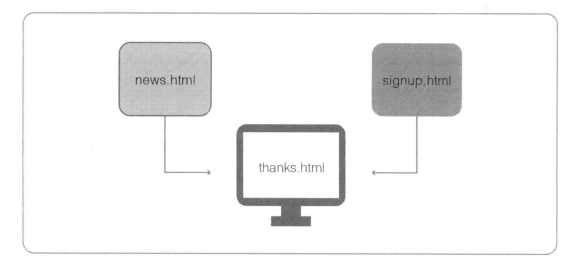

Let's say you have selected 'Required' for the first step for the goal configuration:

Destination

| Equals to ▼ | /contact-thank-you | ☐ Case sensitive |

For example, use *My Screen* for an app and */thankyou.html* instead of *www.example.com/thankyou.html* for a web page

Value OPTIONAL

Off   Assign a monetary value to the conversion.

Funnel OPTIONAL

On

Use an app screen name string or a web page URL for each step. For example, use *My Screen* for an app and */thankyou.html* instead of *www.example.com/thankyou.html* for a web page.

Step	Name	Screen/Page	Required?
1	Contact Form	/contact-us	Yes

+ Add another Step

Verify this Goal   See how often this Goal would have converted based on your data from the past 7 days.

Create Goal   Cancel

Two people complete the goal, the first person views step one, step two and then converts, while the second person skips step one and only views step two before converting. In this scenario the goal would report a total of two conversions in the Overview report and the Goal Flow report, but would only show one conversion in the Funnel Visualization report.

The idea behind the setting is that it allows you to focus on a particular starting point for your goal while still giving you the complete number of conversions. In the majority of cases you do not need to use the 'Required' option, but now you know what it does!

Tip: Remember that selecting 'Required' for the first step of your goal only modifies the Funnel Visualization report.

Event-Based Goals

You can trigger goals based on interactions you are already tracking with Events inside Google Analytics. Event-based goals do not allow you to define steps leading to the interaction, so they are suited to single step actions. Examples of event-based goals include tracking downloads, clicks on outbound links and people watching videos or engaging with interactive content on your website.

The first thing you will need to do is ensure that events are being tracked into Google Analytics. To do this, navigate to 'Events' in the 'Behavior' reports and then select 'Top Events'.

If you want to measure people clicking on PDF downloads as a goal you can now use events to trigger a conversion. To create the goal select 'Event' as the goal type after entering a suitable name and then click 'Next Step'. You can now define any of the event elements you would like to match in order for a conversion to be triggered. In the example above, you can see that the event category is 'Download'. If the event label is set to 'PDF' then you can define these in the goal configuration. This will mean that when an event is logged where the category is 'Download' and the label is 'PDF' you will see a conversion in your reports. Here is what your configuration will look like:

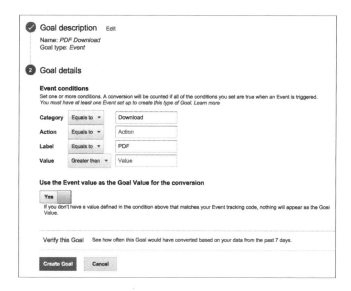

Tip: You can use any combination of category, action, label and value. You can even choose to use the event value as the value of the conversion in the goal configuration.

Engagement-based Goals

Goals based on engagement allow you to trigger a conversion based on someone spending a certain amount of time, or viewing a certain number of pages, on your website.

Engagement-based goals are best suited to content or branding websites without any page or event-based goals.

Mixing Engagement-Based Goals with Other Goal Types

Best practice is to avoid setting up engagement-based goals in Google Analytics views that already have page or event-based goals. This is because the engagement-based goals will inflate your total conversion numbers. This makes it difficult to use the 'total conversion' numbers in reports as this number will now include multiple types of conversions.

If you already have page or event-based goals set up in a view, create a new duplicate view and set up the engagement-based goals in that duplicate view. This will ensure that your existing view remains consistent and you can then make use of the engagement-based goal numbers in the new view.

Alternatively, if you do not want to go to the trouble of creating a new duplicate view, you can create a Custom Segment in your existing view to replicate the engagement-based goals.

Create a Custom Segment for Sessions Over Five Minutes

1. Click 'Add Segment'

2. Click the 'New Segment' button

3. Name the segment 'Sessions Over 5 Minutes'

4. Select 'Conditions', click 'Ad Content' and change it to 'Session Duration'

5. Select 'Contains' and change it to 'Greater Than' and enter '300' as the value (300 is 5 minutes x 60 seconds)

6. Click 'Save'

Create a Custom Segment for Sessions with Over Five Pageviews

1. Click 'Add Segment'

2. Click the 'New Segment' button

3. Name the segment 'Sessions Over 5 Pageviews'

4. Select 'Conditions', click 'Ad Content' and change it to 'Pageviews'

5. Select 'Contains' and change it to 'Greater Than' and enter '5' as the value

6. Click 'Save'

24

Configuration Options

There are configuration options that can be set for each of your reporting views. They allow you to define important aspects of your account, like the time zone used for your reports, through to setting up reports for your internal search function and even tweaking your content reports.

View Settings

These settings allow you to modify information and data that you see within reporting views. Since they are applied to each individual view, you will need to repeat any changes you make across all the views that you want the settings applied to.

To find the view settings, navigate to the admin area and click 'View Settings' after you have selected the desired view from the drop-down list.

View Name

Under 'Basic Settings' you can rename the view allowing you to easily distinguish the different reporting views created. Typically, the first view created in your account will be named something like 'www.company.com', so you can change this to something more descriptive such as 'Company [RAW] 01/01/12'. '[RAW]' has been included to indicate that this is a view without any filters applied. The date has also been included to indicate when the view was originally created. This allows you to quickly understand what will be contained in the reports.

If you had another reporting view that excluded your own company's internal sessions, you might name this 'Company [Filtered] 01/06/12'. This way, you know at a glance that the data is filtered to remove your company's sessions, and that it was set up after the original raw view was created. You can use your own naming convention for your custom views, but make sure it is easily understood by everybody who has access to the account.

Website URL

Next you'll see 'Website URL'. This is not a critical setting and does not determine what is (or is not tracked) into your reports. If your URL is not correct there is no reason to panic. The main thing this setting does is allow you to quickly jump to pages of your website from within the reports. For example, if you are looking at the 'Landing Pages' report in 'Site Content' you will see a small outbound link icon.

If your website URL is set to 'www.company.com' and you see '/index.html' in the report, this small icon will automatically link to 'www.company.com/index.html'. If your website URL is actually 'www.newcompany.com' this will mean the link goes to the wrong website. You can change the setting to use your correct URL. This is also the case with the In-Page Analytics report, if you navigate to this report and see the wrong website loading it means you will need to change the URL in the view settings.

Time Zone

The time zone setting is important as this is the time zone used to create your reports. The time zone is originally set when you first set up your Google Analytics account. Generally, the best approach is to use the time zone where the majority of people who will be performing analysis and reporting using the reporting view are located. Alternatively, you could set the time zone based on the location of your primary audience.

If you change the time zone for a view that already contains data, then changing this setting can result in a data gap in your reports or an overlap of data. Hopefully you don't need to change this setting and even if the wrong time zone is set, then you might want to consider leaving it and creating an entirely new view with the alternative time zone. This will mean that the data within the view remains consistent for reporting and analysis.

If the view is linked to a Google AdWords account, then the view will inherit the time zone setting from the Google AdWords account. If this is the case, the best option is to change the time zone from within Google AdWords. Alternatively, you can also unlink Google AdWords, but when you relink it again the time zone will revert back to the Google AdWords account time zone.

> **Tip:** To change the time zone of your Google AdWords account you will need to contact Google AdWords support since you can't make this change yourself.

Default Page

Setting the default page is a simple way to clean up your content reports. Setting the default page allows you to specify the index or homepage for your website. By default, Google Analytics doesn't know your exact index page, so you might see the following in the All Pages report:

Page	Pageviews
/	2,392
/products/	1,991
/services/	1,794
/index.php	1,138

If your index page hasn't been configured as the default page, you are likely to see a number of pageviews for '/' and further down in the report you are likely to see a number of pageviews that are also for your index page. In the example above you will notice that there is a row for '/' as well as '/index.php', which are really both the homepage. Depending on how your website has been developed, you may see one of the following common index pages in the report:

- index.php
- index.html
- default.aspx
- home.jsp

To check to see if you have multiple index pages, navigate to 'Behavior', 'Site Content' and 'All Pages'.

Then click on 'Advanced' to the right of the search box under the timeline.

Click on 'Containing' and select 'Matching RegExp' (regular expressions). For more details read the "Regular Expressions" section in Chapter 27

Now enter the following in the field to the right of 'Matching RegExp' and click the 'Apply' button:

```
^(/(index|default|home)?\.?(html|htm|php|asp|aspx|jsp)?)$
```

This will automatically check for the most common index pages. If you have more than one row reported after clicking apply, it is likely that you need to set your default page.

If you only have one row after following these steps, then you only have one index page being tracked and you shouldn't have to take any further action.

If you have three or more rows after clicking apply, then you have multiple index pages and you will need to use an advanced filter to clean up your reports instead. For more details visit http://lovesdata.co/Fo9lZ

If you see multiple rows for your homepage within the report page, then this can be used to define the default page in your view settings. In the example above, this is '/index. php'.

Navigate to 'Admin' and under 'View' click on the name of the profile that you are going to set the default page for.

Click on the 'View Settings' tab and now you can define your default page.

In the example above, the page was '/index.php', however you shouldn't enter **/index. php**. Instead remove the forward slash and just enter **index.php** as the default page.

This is because the default page setting will look for all pages that are reported with a forward slash on the end and add the defined default page to the end of the page URLs. For example, if the original pages report looked like the following:

Page	Pageviews
/	2,392
/products/	1,991
/services/	1,794
/index.php	1,138

Then if you entered **/index.php** as the default page, you would see the following in your reports:

Page	Pageviews
//index.php	3,530
/products//index.php	1,991
/services//index.php	1,794

So by entering **index.php** without the forward slash your report would be much cleaner:

Page	Pageviews
/index.php	3,530
/products/index.php	1,991
/services/index.php	1,794

As shown, setting the default page is a quick way to clean up your content reports and prevent duplication. Setting the default page only works from set up onwards, so remember that if you set the default page today it will not clean up your historical data.

Exclude URL Query Parameters

This setting allows you to clean up pages that are duplicated in your content reports to streamline your reporting and analysis. For example, if you notice '/index.php' and '/index.php?linkedin=012' you can use this setting to prevent the page from being duplicated in your reports. In this example 'linkedin' is a query parameter that is used to distinguish different ads that are being displayed on LinkedIn. When someone clicks the ad they are taken to the '/index.php' page, but the query parameter results in a duplicate page in reports. By adding **linkedin** to the exclude URL query parameters setting this duplication will be prevented and the page will simply be reported as '/index.php' instead of '/index.php?linkedin=012' moving forward.

If you identify multiple query parameters that you want to remove from your reports you can add multiple query parameters by separating each one with a comma.

Tip: You can also exclude and manipulate query parameters using filters. However, one difference is that the 'Exclude URL Query Parameters' setting takes effect before filters are applied (during the processing of data for your reports).

Currency Display

Changing the currency display setting is a purely cosmetic option that modifies the currency code displayed in reports. For example, if you see €1.00 in your reports and then change the currency from Euros to US Dollars, you will then see $1.00 in your reports. Changing the currency display setting will not perform any type of currency exchange.

> **Tip:** If you sell items in multiple currencies you can modify the Google Analytics ecommerce tracking code to define the particular currency used during checkout. Google Analytics will automatically convert those currencies into the local currency you have set as the 'Currency Display' in the view settings. For more details visit http://lovesdata.co/Z2Pnq

The exception to this, is for your Google AdWords campaign data. If you have linked Google AdWords and Google Analytics, then cost data from your Google AdWords account will automatically be converted into the currency you have selected for the Google Analytics view. Visit http://lovesdata.co/gbPOj for details.

Ecommerce Tracking

The Ecommerce Tracking setting makes the Ecommerce reports visible in the particular view. It does not mean that ecommerce values will be automatically tracked into your reports – you still need to modify your tracking code to include the ecommerce transaction and item details.

Site Search

You can configure Google Analytics to track your website's internal search solution into the Site Search reports. Analysing the terms people are searching for within your website can provide valuable insights into potential navigation issues, ideas for new website content and potentially even highlight opportunities for new products and services.

> **Tip:** If you don't have an internal search function on your website, you can leave the 'Site Search' setting off.

Site Search reports are valuable because people visiting your website are actually taking the time to tell you exactly what they want. Listen to what they are asking for!

Start by navigating to your website and performing a search. Search for something that you know will return search results. For example, searching for 'contact', 'about' or your company name should return results from your internal website search solution.

After you've performed a search, look in the URL bar of your browser window and look for the keyword you originally searched for. For example, after searching for 'contact' you see: 'http://www.company.com/search.php?q=contact'

Once you see your keyword in the URL bar look to the left and you should see an equals sign. Now look to the left of the equals sign. Look for a letter or a word that sits after either a question mark (?) or an ampersand (&), but before the equals sign. In this example there is a 'q' between the question mark and the equals sign. This is called a query parameter and this is what makes the search results change based on what people are searching for. Look at your website and identify the query parameter that drives your search solution. It might not be a 'q', other common query parameters for search solutions include 'query', 'term', 'searchquery' and 'searchterm' to name a few. Here are some examples of how those might look in your URL bar:

`http://www.company.com/sitesearch.aspx?query=contact&catego-ry=general` – in this example the query parameter is 'query'

`http://www.company.com/index.php?id=search&searchterm=contact` – in this example the query parameter is 'searchterm'

`http://www.company.com/search?term=contact` – in this example the query parameter is 'term'

You might have slightly different URLs for your search function depending on the solution you are using and how it has been set up for your website.

If you see the keyword that you originally searched for, but you don't see any equals signs, question marks or ampersands, then it will take some extra work to get the reports set up – this will be covered shortly. For now, let's look at the examples above, which are the most common types of URLs for search functions. Each of these examples has a query parameter and once identified can be used to configure Google Analytics to report on what people are searching for within the website.

Let's say that the query parameter is 'q' from the search results page of 'http://www.company.com/search.php?q=contact'. Now, you need to navigate to 'Admin' and select 'View Settings'. Towards the bottom of the settings page you will see 'Site Search Settings', click the button to turn it on.

Now you can enter the query parameter for your search function into the settings. For this example, simply enter **q** and then click 'Save'.

You'll notice there are some additional options for the Site Search reports. First, there is an option to 'Strip Query Parameters out of URL'. This option does not change the Site Search reports, but instead modifies how your search result pages will be displayed in the All Pages and other Site Content reports.

By default, the different things people search for will be displayed in the All Pages report. In the following example, the search results pages start with '/search.php'. After searching for this URL in the report you can see all the different search related URLs:

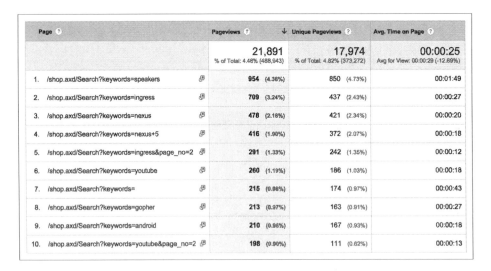

Page		Pageviews	↓ Unique Pageviews	Avg. Time on Page
		21,891 % of Total: 4.48% (488,943)	17,974 % of Total: 4.82% (373,272)	00:00:25 Avg for View: 00:00:29 (-12.69%)
1.	/shop.axd/Search?keywords=speakers	954 (4.36%)	850 (4.73%)	00:01:49
2.	/shop.axd/Search?keywords=ingress	709 (3.24%)	437 (2.43%)	00:00:27
3.	/shop.axd/Search?keywords=nexus	478 (2.18%)	421 (2.34%)	00:00:20
4.	/shop.axd/Search?keywords=nexus+5	416 (1.90%)	372 (2.07%)	00:00:18
5.	/shop.axd/Search?keywords=ingress&page_no=2	291 (1.33%)	242 (1.35%)	00:00:12
6.	/shop.axd/Search?keywords=youtube	260 (1.19%)	186 (1.03%)	00:00:18
7.	/shop.axd/Search?keywords=	215 (0.98%)	174 (0.97%)	00:00:43
8.	/shop.axd/Search?keywords=gopher	213 (0.97%)	163 (0.91%)	00:00:27
9.	/shop.axd/Search?keywords=android	210 (0.96%)	167 (0.93%)	00:00:18
10.	/shop.axd/Search?keywords=youtube&page_no=2	198 (0.90%)	111 (0.62%)	00:00:13

This is what you would see if you choose not to strip out the parameters. Alternatively, if you would like to only use the Site Search reports and not see all the different pages show up in the All Pages report you can choose to strip out the parameters. This will mean that moving forward the All Pages report will display a single search results page:

Page		Pageviews	↓ Unique Pageviews	Avg. Time on Page
		21,364 % of Total: 4.46% (479,484)	**13,109** % of Total: 3.62% (361,949)	**00:00:25** Avg for View: 00:00:29 (-11.03%)
1.	/shop.axd/Search	**17,336** (81.15%)	10,215 (77.92%)	00:00:27

It is up to you if you want to keep all the different search results pages separate or combine them into one. If in doubt do not strip out the parameter, as having additional pages in your report does not have any major drawbacks.

If your website search function allows people to search particular areas of your website you can also enable 'Site Search Categories' to see the category selections people are making when they search. The process for identifying your search categories is just like finding your search query parameter. Start by selecting a category, entering a search term and then searching.

Then look at your URL bar and look for the query parameter of your category selection. Here, after selecting 'Lowest Price' as the category the URL for the search results page changes to:

- http://www.company.com/search.php?q=shirts&refine=lowest
  – in this example the query parameter for the search category is 'refine'

Once you have identified the query parameter for your search category you can enter this into the settings page.

Alternate Setup Options

If you did not see the keyword in the URL bar after your search, or it did not appear using a query parameter, you have some alternate options to set up and use Site Search reports. Start by performing a search and looking at the URL. This time, try searching for 'contact'.

- http://www.example.com/search.php
- http://www.example.com/index.php?id=search
- http://www.example.com/search-results.asp

In the examples above you cannot see the search term anywhere in the URLs, which means you can't configure the reports. If this is what you see return to the original page where you entered the search term and view the page source. Look for the form that is used for your search function. You may see that the form is using a 'post' method, for example:

```
<form action="search.php" method="post">
```

Changing your form to a 'get' method is likely to begin showing 'get' in your search term in the URL, along with a query parameter. Here is an example of the new form:

```
<form action="demo_form.asp" method="get">
```

Alternatively, if you do see your search term in the URL, but it doesn't include a query parameter, then you have some more advanced work to get the Site Search report working. The options include adding a view filter, modifying your tracking code or using Google Tag Manager to modify your URLs. Here are some examples where the search results page includes the keyword, but not a query parameter:

- http://www.example.com/index/search/contact
- http://www.example.com/search.php/keyword/contact/id946
- http://www.example.com/searchterm/contact

The best option in this case is to use a filter to modify the URLs so you can use the Site Search reports. Visit http://lovesdata.co/wE4hW for details.

> **Tip:** Google Tag Manager can also be used to configure Site Search reports even if you do not have a query parameter available within the URL. It is a technical solution, so you might need help from your web developer or the person looking after your Google Tag Manager implementation. View details at http://lovesdata.co/BcdP2

Copy View and Move to Trash Can

If you have 'Edit' level permission inside Google Analytics you will see the options 'Copy View' and 'Delete View' on the top right corner of the view settings page. When you copy a view it will copy all the view settings, filters and other configurations you have made and create an entirely new reporting view with those options. However, it is important to remember that this process will not copy data within your reports, just the configurations, so data will only be logged into this new view from set up moving forward.

You can also delete views by moving them to the trash can. Once you have confirmed that you want to delete a view it is moved to the 'Trash Can'. The view will continue to collect data even though it is located in the trash can, but after 35 days the view (and data) will be permanently deleted.

Filters

Filters allow you to permanently modify the data coming into a reporting view. This allows you to create dedicated views that only include certain data. For example, you can apply a filter to a view to exclude your own sessions from being reported.

In most cases you will want to create a new view before you apply a filter. This is because once you apply the filter you won't be able to compare data *before* the filter was applied to data *after* the filter was applied, since you will be choosing to exclude at least a portion of the sessions. If you are just starting out it's best practice to have the following views set up:

- **Raw view** that doesn't have any filters applied
- **Primary view** where you are excluding your own sessions (along with any other appropriate filters)
- **Test view** that you use to try out filters before applying them to your primary view

In a lot of cases you can use segments to narrow the focus of your reports without having to permanently modify the data that is collected into the view. Read the "Segments" section in Chapter 22 for details. Here is a summary of the differences between filters and segments:

Filter	Segment
Permanently modifies data	Temporarily modifies data
Only applies after configuration	Can be applied to historical data
Allows you to filter based on IP address (which is not available in the interface)	Allows you to filter based on dimensions and metrics available in the interface
Filters are applied to create one set of data	Multiple segments can be applied at the same time to compare trends
Modifies data for everybody who has access to the reporting view	Custom segments can be created by each user who has access to Google Analytics

Excluding your IP Address

The best way to exclude your own sessions from showing up within a view is by creating a filter using your IP address. This means that sessions from your IP address are discarded before they become available within the reporting view. This provides cleaner and more actionable data, as it will report on the data about your customers (and potential customers) and not your own interactions with your website.

The first step is to determine your IP address. If you are on a small business or home connection you might want to consider upgrading to a static (or fixed) IP address, as in most cases a dynamic (or changing) IP address is standard. A static IP address is the best way to ensure that you are actually excluding your own interactions.

Once you have your IP address you can head to 'Filters' in 'Admin' and select 'New Filter'. Name your filter and select 'Exclude' as the 'Filter Type' and then select 'Traffic from the IP Addresses' (as the 'Source or Destination') and then 'That Contain' (as the 'Expression'). You can now enter your IP address and click 'Save'.

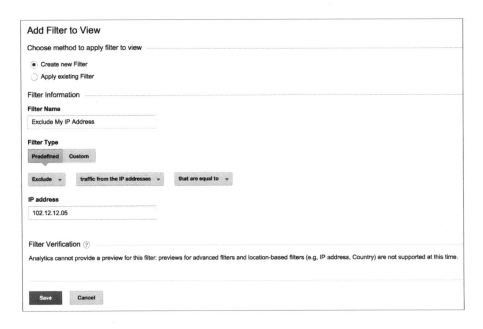

Only Including a Folder

Another common filter is to only include a particular folder of your website within the reporting view. This is primarily used for medium and larger scale websites where you only want to give access to the sub-set of data to particular people in your organization. Here is an example of the filter configuration if we only wanted to include data from the '/news/' folder:

If you don't need to restrict access you won't need to use this filter.

Tip: As you become more advanced you can use filters to do even more data modification in Google Analytics. You can use advanced filters to exclude multiple IP addresses at once and even clean up URLs you see in your reports. For more tips on using filters visit http://lovesdata.co/n3dF6

25

Using Reports

Improving Google AdWords

Using Bounce Rate

The Campaigns report in Google Analytics (under 'Acquisition' and 'AdWords') reflects the campaigns that you have set up inside your Google AdWords account. You can see the number of people that came from clicks on your ads along with website engagement, all broken down by campaign. You'll also be able to see the number of goal conversions, and if you have set up ecommerce tracking you can see the dollar value generated by your campaigns.

Campaigns with a low bounce rate (lower than 30%) are likely to be performing well, with traffic being directed to engaging landing pages and landing pages that relate well to the targeted keywords.

> **Tip:** Remember that bounce rate is the percentage of people who only view a single page on your website. If people get everything they need on the landing page (for example contact details or product information), then a high bounce rate might not necessarily be a bad thing.

Campaigns with high bounce rates (for example over 60%) are likely to be using less targeted landing pages, which are not closely related to the keywords. Click the name of a campaign with a high bounce rate to view the Ad Groups in that particular campaign. You might find that there are one or two Ad Groups that are skewing the overall campaign bounce rate higher.

Clicking the name of an Ad Group will allow you to see the particular keywords you are using in Google AdWords. You can then see which landing pages are being used by clicking 'Secondary Dimension' and selecting 'Destination URL'. You'll now see the keyword you are bidding on, along with the particular landing page or pages used in your ad variations. It's likely that you'll find keywords with higher bounce rates don't relate well to the landing page being used inside Google AdWords.

> **Tip:** If a keyword has a low bounce rate but isn't driving any conversions try adjusting your ad variations to include calls to action like 'buy now' and 'inquire today'. You can also modify your keywords to focus more on driving conversions. For example, you could change the keyword 'gift basket' to 'buy gift basket'.

Using Goal Conversions

You can evaluate the success of campaigns, ad groups and even keywords by comparing them against your goal conversions. Navigate to the 'Campaigns' report (under 'Acquisition' and 'AdWords').

Now select 'Comparison' as the report view (small icon with bars either side of a vertical line above the table) and compare against the conversion rate for the goal you want to focus on. This will now show you the overall effectiveness of your Google AdWords campaigns in driving conversions against the overall performance of your website.

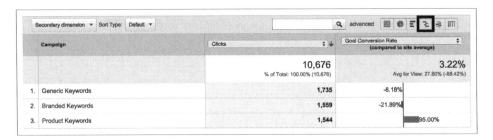

The custom report includes an Ecommerce Transactions tab if you're running an ecommerce website. If this is you, select 'Ecommerce Transactions' and compare your campaigns against the 'Ecommerce Conversion Rate'.

Tip: If you want to compare performance against an individual goal, you can use the standard Campaigns report in Google Analytics (under 'Acquisition' and 'AdWords'), then select the particular goal tab before selecting 'Comparison' view and choosing the individual goal to view performance.

Consider reallocating your advertising budget to campaigns that are performing well – this will mean you receive more for your advertising dollars.

You can also click on the names of poorly performing campaigns to view the Ad Groups and then click on the Ad Groups to view the keywords. Once you have identified individual keywords that are not performing well in terms of conversions, you can review your landing page content and also the appropriateness of keeping those keywords in your Ad Groups.

Identify Poorly Converting Keywords

The first step to identifying poorly converting keywords is to ensure that your goals are configured correctly inside Google Analytics. You should also configure goals for your macro and micro conversions, as some keywords might be better at driving initial engagement, while others are better at driving higher value conversions.

Navigate to the 'Keywords' report under 'AdWords' in the 'Acquisition' section. This will show you all the keywords you are bidding on within your Google AdWords account. Select the goal or ecommerce conversion you would like to use to the right of 'Conversions' on the top right of the table. Now click on the 'Conversion Rate' column heading to order the keywords with the highest conversion rate at the top of the table. Then click the 'Conversion Rate' column a second time so that your keywords with the lowest conversion rate are first.

Next, click 'Default' to the right of 'Sort Type' and select 'Weighted'. This will now show you your poorly performing keywords. Selecting 'Weighted' as the sort type takes into account the number of sessions along with the low conversion rate.

Now, review these keywords and prioritize any that need adjustment or further optimization. It's a good idea to review each keyword over the previous 12 months to see if there are any seasonal trends you need to account for. You can also use the 'Top Conversion Paths' report within 'Multi-Channel Funnels' to see if the keyword is assisting conversions. To do this, navigate to the report, select 'AdWords' as the 'Type' above the timeline graph, then select 'AdWords Keyword Path' below the graph and finally search for the keyword you are analyzing.

You will now be able to see the total number of conversions that included people searching for the particular keyword.

Keywords and Matched Search Queries

There is a difference between the keywords that you bid on in your Google AdWords campaigns and the keywords that people use to find your ads on Google. This is because you can choose different keyword matching options when you add keywords in Google AdWords.

In Google Analytics you can easily compare the two, by navigating to the 'Search Queries' report (under 'Acquisition' and 'AdWords'). In this report you'll see the actual search terms that result in people clicking your ads and visiting your website.

Now, click 'Secondary Dimension' and select 'Keyword'. You'll be able to see the Matched Search Query (the term entered on Google), along with the actual keyword you're bidding on. This allows you to quickly identify how well your keyword matching options are working. You're also likely to find keywords that should be removed from your Google AdWords campaigns (using negative keywords) and new keywords to add to your Ad Groups.

When using this report, remember that you can also use the bounce rate, goal completions and revenue (if you have an ecommerce website) to evaluate the performance of the particular keyword.

> **Tip:** Before removing a poorly performing keyword, consider creating a more targeted landing page with appropriate content and a strong call to action. Removing a keyword might reduce your advertising spend, but you might also be missing out on a potential client.

Evaluating Marketing Campaigns

Google Analytics can be used to report on, compare and even improve your marketing campaigns and budget allocation. In order to receive accurate and reliable data to drive action, ensure that you're using campaign tracking to track your marketing initiatives (read Chapter 18 – "Campaign Tracking) and that you have also set up goals (read Chapter 23 – "Goals").

> **Tip:** If you are selling online you can use ecommerce value and transactions to report on marketing campaign success.

Start by creating a custom report that lists source and medium by sessions, conversions and conversion rate. This will allow you to identify campaigns (using source and medium) by overall popularity and compare this against conversion rate to ensure your different initiatives are driving action on your website.

Source/Medium	Sessions	Conversions	Conversion Rate

Then for each of the source/medium combinations, add in some offline data to better evaluate success. If you're generating leads from your website, you could adjust your table to become:

Source/ Medium	Sessions	Online Leads	Online Lead Rate	Offline Conversions	Conversion Rate

Ideally you would then calculate the ROI of each of the marketing channels. Try to include your total advertising cost and human resources into the 'Cost' column.

Cost	Profit	ROI (Profit/Cost)

You can now use this to see the relative costs and ROI of the different marketing channels. This helps you understand the top performing initiatives, and those that cost more on average to generate a conversion. Use this information to help inform your marketing strategy and how to allocate your budget between the different channels. Before you make final decisions on particular campaigns, also consider the attribution of your campaigns and how they might be assisting conversions in your overall marketing mix. Review "Multi-Channel Funnels" in Chapter 21 for more details on attribution.

Improving SEO

SEO (Search Engine Optimization) is the process of optimising your online presence to improve your performance for organic (free) search results. For most people, this means improving your visibility within Google's results to drive more traffic to your website. The way people perform SEO continues to change, but the starting point is always the content of your website. This is because search engines need content in order to understand what your website is about and to include it within search results.

However, SEO continues to become more and more difficult because search engines continue to evolve. For example, Google's search results begin to understand individual user preference and behavior and present results that are more likely to appeal to that particular individual. This means that two people could both search for the same keyword on Google, but see very different results. As the experience becomes more personalized, it becomes harder to optimize content.

As SEO becomes more complicated, there are still ways to improve your website for organic search results. Focus on your audience and content when thinking about this type of optimization because you could end up with content that appeals to search engines, but not your desired target audience. As you use Google Analytics to identify optimization opportunities, always ensure that you have a defined objective for your content and website.

Let's look at a number of ways you can use Google Analytics to optimize your website for organic search results.

Not Provided Organic Keywords

When someone searches on Google and clicks on an organic listing Google no longer passes the individual keyword data through to your website. This means that Google Analytics and other analytics tools are unable to report on individual organic keyword data coming from Google search results. There are a two options for getting insights into the organic keywords people are using to find your website.

The first option is to link Google Analytics to your Google Search Console (Webmaster Tools) account to access the 'Search Engine Optimization' reports within 'Acquisition'. These reports show you the different search queries that people are using to find your website. Read more about "Google Search Console (Webmaster Tools)" in Chapter 11.

The second option is to use the keywords report to understand which landing pages people are finding from organic search. Navigate to 'Organic' under 'Keywords' within the 'Acquisition' section. Now click on '(not provided)', and 'other' above the table, then search for and select 'Landing Page'. This now shows you the pages people first land on after they have performed a search where the keyword is not provided. This won't give you the specific keywords, but you can use the landing pages to build up an understanding of the types of keywords and keyword themes people are searching for. Typically, your homepage will be found for your branded keywords and individual pages will have content that relates to the keywords people are using.

Optimizing Organic CTR

Click-through rate (CTR) is an important way to measure and improve your paid search campaigns, but Google Analytics also allows you to see the CTR of your organic keywords in Google search results. This enables you to test different headings and descriptions for your SEO and measure the results.

The difference between optimizing organic and paid search results using CTR is that for organic optimization, you need to spend a little more time monitoring the changes in order to determine what has worked.

Start by selecting the previous two full calendar months in Google Analytics and then navigate to the 'Queries' report under 'Acquisition' and 'Search Engine Optimization'. Find the keyword that you're looking to optimize your website for and record the current CTR and Average Position along with the date range you are using. For example:

Keyword	CTR	Average Position	Date Range
chocolate baskets	1.15%	7	1 April to 31 May

Now that you have a benchmark for the performance of the keyword you'll need to find which page (or pages) from your website is being displayed in search results.

Search for the keyword and identify the page on your website. Now use the Landing Pages Report (also under 'Search Engine Optimization') to record the performance of that page in Google search results. For example:

Page	CTR	Average Position	Date Range
http://www.site.com/chocolate-baskets.html	0.75%	11	1 April to 31 May

Next, develop a new headline and description for the page to improve the relationship to the keyword you are optimizing. Go back to the Google search results page and note down the headline and description that is being displayed. For example:

Gift Baskets by Online Gift Baskets & Co
www.site.com/chocolate-baskets.html
Gift baskets from $39.95 with fast shipping. ... Wine Gifts, Coffee Gifts, Wedding Gifts, Chocolate Gifts, Tea Gifts, Congratulations ...

Elements of the keywords that people search for are highlighted in bold in search results. In this example you can see that the keyword isn't actually in the headline or description. Develop a new headline and description that includes the actual keyword you are trying to optimize and also try to include a call to action in the description.

If you're advertising on the same or similar keywords with Google AdWords you can also look at the ad variations in your account that have a high CTR. These ads, their ad copy and calls to action can be used to help develop better headlines and descriptions for your organic optimization.

If you're currently investing in SEO, but not Google AdWords, this is a great reason to consider allocating a small budget to a Google AdWords campaign to help improve your SEO.

Here is an example of a headline and description that includes the keyword:

Chocolate Baskets - Milk, Dark & White Chocolate
www.site.com/chocolate-baskets.html
Huge selection of Chocolate Baskets from $39.50 with fast shipping.
Order a Milk Chocolate, Dark Chocolate or White Chocolate Basket today!

The headline and description now have a strong relationship to the keyword and therefore people are more likely to visit the website as a result. Now, develop a new headline and description for your website based on the keyword you are optimizing.

Tip: You might need to also change the URL of the page that relates to the keyword you are trying to optimize. For example, for the keyword 'chocolate baskets' it is better to have a page URL of '/chocolate-baskets.html' than it is to have '/chocolate-gifts.html'.

You'll now need to edit the heading and description meta tags of the page in order for Google and other search engines to update your website details in their search results pages. This can take anywhere from a few hours to a month, depending on the size of your website and how often you've updated your website in the past. Once you can see your new title and description in Google search results note down the date and wait for the same number of days as your benchmark date range. In the example this was 61 days (1 April to 31 May).

For example, if you updated your website on 1 June and then saw the new heading and description in Google search results on 30 June, you would need to wait until you had data in Google Analytics for 1 July to 30 August.

Once you have enough data you can compare the new date range against your benchmark to see if you have improved in Google search results. For example:

Keyword	CTR	Average Position	Date Range
chocolate baskets	1.15%	7	1 April to 31 May
chocolate baskets	3.00%	3	1 July to 30 August

And for the page:

Page	CTR	Average Position	Date Range
http://www.site.com/chocolate-baskets.html	0.75%	11	1 April to 31 May
http://www.site.com/chocolate-baskets.html	1.50%	6	1 July to 30 August

From this example, you can see the improved CTR and the average position of the website in search results.

> **Tip:** Try also improving the content on the particular page you are optimizing to further improve results.

This is a great technique for improving your organic rankings. Ideally, you would use this method for optimizing every keyword and every page on your website, but this is not always practical. Start with your most important keywords, measure the results and continue the process. Like all SEO techniques, you need to perform this technique on an ongoing basis to stay ahead of your competitors.

Identifying Inbound Link Opportunities

Search engines also look at inbound links and where these links are coming from as a component of how they rank websites in search results. Google Analytics allows you to see websites that are already linking to you and you can use these insights in your optimization process.

Start by reviewing websites that are already referring traffic. Navigate to the 'Channels' report under 'Acquisition' and then click on the 'Referrals' channel. This will allow you to see the websites that are sending you traffic. You'll want to spend some time looking through this report, and use it to understand who is linking to you, and also how they are linking to your website.

Click on an individual website in the referrals report to see the page or pages in that site that include a link to your website. The little outbound link icon to the right of the page URL allows you to quickly open the page in a new window.

> **Tip:** If you don't see the link to your website try right clicking and selecting 'View Source'. You can then search for part of your domain or URL to find the link. If you still can't find the link it might be because the link has been removed from the page. It could also be that the link is in a forum or on a news website and the link has moved off that particular page. In this case look for a way to view the additional pages that might contain the link to your site.

When you have identified the link to your website you can decide if there are any opportunities for you to engage with the particular site or encourage them to link to more of your content. For example, if someone has included a link to your content in their blog post you could contact them to see if they are interested in sharing more of your content, or you could even develop exclusive content for them to release.

If you find people talking about your brand on a social network, in comments or in a forum, use this to better understand the types of content they are interested in – this can inform your overall content strategy. If they are saying negative things about your brand or content, be careful about how you engage with them online and if their comments are justified, then you could use this to fix your existing content or help inform future content and strategies.

The way people link to your website can also be optimized for SEO. This isn't always possible, but if you know the person linking to your website, you might be able to get them to change the link. For example, if you are trying to optimize for the keyword 'fresh cut flowers', a link that says 'click here' or 'http://www.site.com/product' is not as good as a link that specifically includes 'fresh cut flowers'.

If you're running display ads through Google AdWords you can also use insights from the Placements report to identify additional linking opportunities to complement your paid advertising. Navigate to 'Acquisition', the select 'AdWords', 'Display Targeting' and 'Placements' (under the graph). You can then drill down into the different types of placements you are running on the Google Display Network to see the individual sites where your ads have displayed.

Identify placements that relate closely to your content and brand and look for opportunities to engage on these sites. For example, news-related sites could be a potential place to engage using topical comments on articles that relate to your business. Blogs and content sites could be contacted for potential guest posts or to provide exclusive content or promotions. Community and forum sites could be places to engage and build your reputation for sharing with the community.

When you identify link and engagement opportunities always remember that you need to focus on building and delivering value to the audience and owners of the site. Posting links to your content should not be the starting point. You need to build a dialogue, create value and engage with people so they want to learn more about your brand and content.

Measuring SEO

You can measure the results of your SEO using segments in Google Analytics. Selecting the 'Organic Traffic' system segment will just show you visitors who found your website via organic searches on Google, Bing, Yahoo and other major search engines.

Use the 'Compare To Past' option in the date range to establish if your SEO initiatives have increased the number of visitors coming to your website in the current reporting period. You can quickly compare your SEO traffic to your overall website traffic by selecting the 'All Sessions' system segment.

Improving Website Design

Google Analytics provides a range of reports about the devices people use to access your website. These can be put to use to inform user experience and design components of your website.

Desktops, Laptop, Tablet and Mobile Users

Your reports will include all the different devices people use to view your website by default. However, the experience of a mobile user compared to somebody using a desktop can be dramatically different. It is important to take this into consideration when analyzing how people engage with your website.

A good way to distinguish between how people experience your website is by applying segments to your reports. There are default segments you can apply by selecting 'Add Segment' above the graph – choose from: 'Mobile Traffic', 'Tablet Traffic', 'Mobile and Tablet Traffic' and 'Tablet and Desktop Traffic'. You can also create a custom segment to only include people using desktops and laptops. To add this segment to your account visit http://lovesdata.co/ZbUkx

> **Tip:** In most cases, tablet users behave in a similar way to desktop users so applying the 'Mobile Traffic' and 'Tablet and Desktop Traffic' default segments should provide enough detail. Alternatively, you can apply the 'Mobile Traffic', 'Tablet Traffic' and 'Desktop Traffic' segments for a complete view in your reports.

Screen Size

You can see the different size screens your visitors use to access your website by selecting 'Screen Resolution' in the 'Browser & OS' report (under 'Audience' and then 'Technology'). This report gives you an indication of the total available screen space your website could be displayed in, but keep in mind that not everybody will have their browser set to the full size of their screen. Remember that by default this will show all devices, including mobile devices with smaller screen sizes.

Browsers

People can access your website on lots of different browsers, such as Internet Explorer, Safari, Firefox and Google Chrome. Depending on how your website is developed and what browsers people are using, your website might look perfect or it might not. Cross-browser testing allows you to see how your website appears (renders) in different versions of different browsers.

The Browser & OS reports in Google Analytics (under 'Audience' and 'Technology') allow you to see the different browsers people use to view your website. Selecting a particular browser will show you the different versions of that browser people are using.

You can then use a cross-browser testing tool to preview how your website looks in the different browsers without having to install them.

As an example, let's say you looked at your Google Analytics reports and found that 2,310 sessions were from Internet Explorer 11.0, and this made up 32.75% of your Internet Explorer traffic. If your cross-browser test showed that your website appeared a little odd on that browser, then you would probably want to invest in correcting the issues. However, if your website appeared incorrectly on Internet Explorer 4.0.1 and this browser only had 19 sessions, making up 0.73% of your Internet Explorer traffic, then it probably isn't worth the investment in correcting the problems.

Browser Size

Understanding if the width of your website design works for the majority of your website visitors is always important. After all, you don't want information or navigation being obscured due to people using particular browser sizes when viewing your website.

The In-Page Analytics report (under 'Behavior') allows you to understand exactly how people experience your website and if any elements are being cut-off or obscured.

Select 'Browser Size' and you'll see a translucent orange overlay appear over the areas the particular visitors are not seeing when they access your website. Remember to click the configuration icon and select the layout of your website (justified left, centred or justified right).

Select 'Visitors To This Page' to include the screen size of people who visit your website, but may not have seen the page you are looking at in the report. Moving the slider left and right allows you to understand how people experience your website. In this example, you can see that 97% of people accessing the website have a good experience because all of the main content is visible.

> **Tip:** Applying the custom advanced segment to only include people using desktops and laptops will ensure you are not including people using mobile devices with smaller screens. This will prevent the report from being skewed by those devices.

Depending on your website objectives and the particular page on your website, it can be important to have primary information, links and calls to action visible 'above the fold' (or in other words, visible without people needing to scroll). The Browser Size report in In-Page Analytics also allows you to understand what is visible to people without requiring them to scroll.

If you have links or navigation 'below the fold' select 'Show Bubbles' and de-select 'Browser Size'. If people are scrolling (and clicking links lower down on the page) you will see an orange bar at the bottom of the page with the percentage of clicks that occur lower down on the page. If these links are important you might want to consider placing them higher up on the page to ensure people can see them.

Website Loading Speed

The time it takes to load pages on your website impacts on the user experience of your website. A fast-loading website provides a positive experience for people because they can quickly get to the information they are looking for. A slow-loading website is not only frustrating, but can also reduce conversions, increase abandonment and have a negative impact on your SEO and Google AdWords campaigns.

It has been shown that a one second reduction in loading time can lead to a 7% increase in conversion rate.[1] Even if you're not trying to drive conversions on your website, reducing the loading time of your website will lead to higher levels of visitor engagement and reduce website abandonment.

Google Analytics allows you to see the loading time of your website in the Site Speed reports (under Behavior). The Page Timings reports shows you the average loading time of individual website pages, allowing you to quickly identify slow-loading pages that can be optimized.

The great thing about the Site Speed reports is that they show you the loading time of your website as it is experienced by real people – it's not a theoretical report but based on real people accessing your website.

Tip: The Site Speed reports are based on a sample of pages being loaded and aren't calculated every time a page is loaded on your website. This means you should check the sample size before you start to worry too much. If a page has an average loading time of 20 seconds, but it is based on a sample of 2 pageviews, there might not be anything wrong with the page. You can see the sample size by choosing the 'Technical' report set.

Tip: Look for slow-loading pages with a minimum sample size of 100. If you don't have a lot of website visitors try extending the date range to increase the sample size.

Once you've identified a page or pages on your website that are slow to load you will need to work with your web developer and designer to speed things up. This usually means making changes to code, images, graphics and other files to optimize their loading time.

Try Google's PageSpeed Insights tool at http://lovesdata.co/XdXIz for suggestions that can speed up your website.

---

1   http://blog.tagman.com/2012/03/just-one-second-delay-in-page-load-can-cause-7-loss-in-customer-conversions/ and http://blog.kissmetrics.com/loading-time/

Improving Navigation

In-Page Analytics

There are a number of reports available in Google Analytics to help you understand how visitors navigate your website. The In-Page Analytics report (under 'Behavior') provides you with a visual indication of the links that people use to travel from one page to another.

It's important to understand that this report is not a heatmap report (that shows you exactly where people are clicking). It simply shows you elements that then link to another page on your website, so if you have two links to the same page they will both be overlaid with the same information. This is why sometimes when you add all the percentages together they add to more than 100%.

Looking at the homepage of your website, you can see which menu items and links people use to navigate deeper into your website. Consider reordering and prioritising these elements to make the most popular links easier to find on the page. You could consider reordering your menu so that the most important content is closer to the top left corner of the page.

You can also identify links that are rarely used – these elements could be de-emphasised in the page and in your menu. Start by selecting a date range of at least three months and look for links that either haven't been clicked (i.e. don't have overlay information) or have a very low percentage of clicks (e.g. under 1%).

> **Tip:** In-Page Analytics uses your current website to present the report. If you have recently changed your website, the data overlaid on the report may include data that was collected before you changed your website. It's best to use the report before you make changes to your website and then wait until enough data is collected based on your latest changes before making more decisions.

Landing Pages

The Landing Pages report (under Behavior and Site Content) shows you the most popular entry points to your website. This is the first page people view when they access your website. Your top landing pages are great places to consider cross-promoting other areas of your website.

If you can't think of appropriate pages to cross-promote on your top landing pages, then click on a particular landing page in the report and then select the 'Entrance Paths' tab (above the timeline).

You will now see the top ten pages people view after the particular landing page. Also think about pages that you want to promote and pages that are important for driving conversions on your website, these could also be promoted on your top landing pages.

Site Search

The Site Search reports allow you to see what people are searching for on your website. You will potentially find keywords that relate to website content that can be used to improve navigation.

Start by using the 'Search Terms' report (under 'Behavior' and then 'Site Search') for search terms that could indicate potential bottlenecks in navigation. For example, if you see a number of visitors searching for "contact details", then your 'contact us' page might be hidden or not be presented in your primary navigation.

Tip: Different people can use different variations and even misspellings of particular terms when they use your website's search solution. Spend some time looking through the list and identifying common themes or related terms as the report shows you the exact terms people are entering into your search solution.

The Pages report in the Site Search reports allow you to see the particular pages that people start to search from. Click 'Secondary Dimension' (below the timeline and above the table) and then select 'Search Term'. This allows you to see both the pages that people start to search from and also the particular terms they use.

Look for terms that indicate that they are not finding the content they are looking for on the page they are already viewing. For example, if people are searching for "graduate" and "graduate opportunities" from your careers page you could highlight the link to the graduate pages on the particular page people start searching from.

26

Model for Successful Analysis

Integrating Google Analytics into your business will provide lasting benefits and a clear structure for the way you apply the tool, beyond simply reporting on historical trends. The value of Google Analytics is unlocked when you use the tool to drive improvement.

There are three key stages to this model. The first is measuring your website and creating reports; the second stage is performing analysis; and the third stage is making a change to stimulate improvement. The stages are then repeated to continue the cycle.

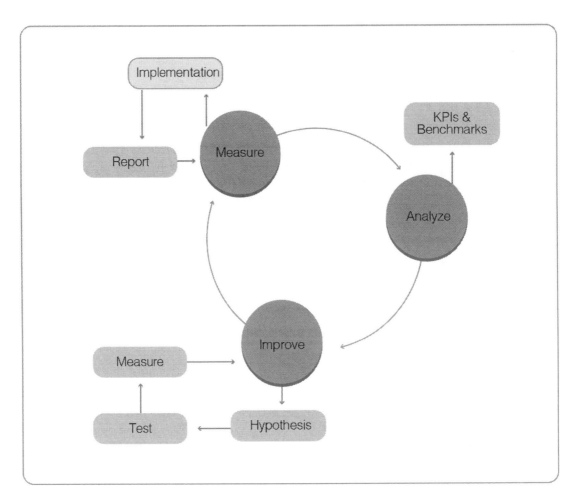

1. Measure

Before applying the model you need to ensure that you have tracking code in place and that you're measuring the key interactions occurring on your website. This forms your 'Implementation' – you need to have at least a basic implementation in order to have data available in your reports.

It is quite common to get stuck in the implementation phase when beginning to use Google Analytics. However, the focus needs to be on analysis, which can result in a measurable improvement. An initial review of your implementation and performing an initial check of the data available in your reports should be enough to at least identify what is, and is not, being tracked. You can then begin to build a wishlist for your implementation. If you wait until your implementation is exactly the way you want, you will find the time you spend on the implementation means you are behind in other areas. Balance your implementation wishlist against analysis and optimization.

> **Tip:** Read "Analytics Implementation Model" in Chapter 28 for a model that specifically covers the ongoing management of your implementation.

The implementation component of the model can be included within particular cycles. For example, you might aim to initially apply the cycle every two months, but you might only include reviewing your implementation every four to six months.

The main element to focus on within the 'Measure' stage is that you have enough data available in your reports to progress to the 'Analyze' stage. In some cases you might find there are small tweaks that you need to make in order to get the data you need. This could be as simple as setting up a custom segment, configuring a new goal or even rolling out custom tracking in Google Tag Manager. Once you have the data available in Google Analytics you can move to the next stage.

2. Analyze

This stage is where you spend time digging into the data and drawing out insights. A good starting point is to look for things that seem strange in your data. This could be a mix of good and bad. For example, you might find a landing page with a really low bounce rate, or another page with an extremely high bounce rate. You can then begin to ask questions about why these pages have dramatically different bounce rates and try to list out ideas about why they might be different.

It is important to layer different questions on top of the data you see in your reports. Continuing the example of two landing pages, you should layer questions about your audience and how they are finding the particular page. Try to ask yourself what might be impacting on bounce rate. Are there particular devices that are skewing the average bounce rate? Are there particular traffic sources and mediums that have different bounce rates for each of the landing pages?

Try to focus your analysis on one particular element of your website. If you need some ideas on where to start read Chapter 15 – "Reports" – for starting points.

> **Tip:** If you're stuck and are not sure where to begin your analysis, look at the Intelligence Events reports. These reports automatically identify significant changes in your data.

It can be helpful to develop benchmarks and KPIs (Key Performance Indicators) for your analysis. This allows you to focus on changes that are occurring within your data as a way to identify areas that are performing well and flagging areas that are falling below your intended thresholds.

Your analysis should aim to identify an area of improvement that you can then begin to test in the next stage.

3. Improve

Once you have identified a potential area of improvement in your analysis, you then need to action that change. Depending on your analysis the change you make could be directly applied to the website or it could form the basis of an experiment where you test the change before rolling it out.

The best way to decide about how to apply the improvement to your website is to gauge what impact the change is likely to have. For example, if you've identified that your homepage is slower to load than other pages on your website, then making a change to speed up the loading time will have a positive impact across your entire audience. Alternatively, if you identify that an important landing page has had a moderate drop in conversion rate then you might want to run a conversion test on this page instead of rolling out a blanket change for all of your traffic.

If you determine that a conversion test is the best way to implement the improvement, you will need to develop a hypothesis for your test, create and deploy the test and finally measure the results of the test.

> **Tip:** For more details on running a conversion test read "Content Experiments" in Chapter 19.

After you make an improvement to your website or you finalize a conversion test, it is important to report on the impact of the change. This could be a simple summary where you compare a critical metric before the change was made to after the change was made.

Applying the Model

Making continual improvements to your website doesn't necessarily need to be a complicated process. The main thing is to ensure you are using Google Analytics to drive improvement and not just for creating reports.

When you begin to apply the model choose on a time frame to run your optimization cycle. This might be every two months at the start, and then you can always run the process more regularly once you are comfortable with the interface. Google Analytics provides a fantastic platform that you can encourage others in your organization to use, creating your own processes, documenting what has worked and what hasn't worked. Giving people access to the reports will mean more people can be involved in the optimization process and share the workload.

27

Advanced Options

Custom Reports

You can create your own custom reports when the standard reports don't quite meet your specific requirements. Before you begin creating your custom report you need to be familiar with the difference between dimensions and metrics. Remember that dimensions are the rows of information and metrics are the columns of data. These elements will form the building blocks of your custom report.

Let's start by creating a custom report that focuses on engagement from social media. Navigate to 'Customization', then click 'New Custom Report' and name the report 'Social Media Engagement'. Now skip down and select 'Add Dimension' – this is where you add the rows of information to the custom report. For this report search and select 'Social Network' as this will return the names of the different social networks as rows in the custom report.

Next, you need to add some metrics. Just above the dimension select 'Add Metric' and search for and select 'Users'. Repeat this to add 'Sessions', 'Bounce Rate', 'Pages Per Session' and 'Average Session Duration'.

You'll also need to add a filter to the report to only include social media traffic. To do this click 'Add Filter', then search for and select 'Social Network'. Change 'Include' to 'Exclude' and then enter **(not set)** in the filter field.

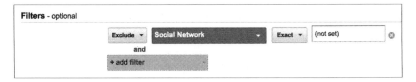

Finally, click 'Save' to view the custom report. You'll now have a custom report that specifically focuses on engagement from social networks. You have the option to edit the report if you would like to further adjust what you see in the report.

Click on 'Edit' at the top of the report. Now under the dimension of 'Social Network' click 'Add Dimension', then search for and select 'Landing Page' and click 'Save'.

The report will look the same, except the name of each social network will be blue. This means you have added a drill down level in the custom report. Clicking on the name of a social network will show the particular pages that people landed on when they came to your website from that particular social network.

Let's create another custom report. This time you're going to create a custom report that only includes the '/2013/', '/2014/' and '/2015/' folders from your website. Navigate to 'Overview' in the left column and then click 'New Custom Report', name the custom report '2013 to 2015 Folders' and add the following metrics:

- Pageviews
- Unique Pageviews
- Average Time On Page
- Bounce Rate

Then add 'Page' as the dimension. Now click 'Add Filter', then search for and select 'Page'. Check that the filter is set to 'Include' and change 'Exact' to 'Regex'. Now enter the following regular expression in the filter field:

^/201[3-5]/

This regular expression will match pages starting with '/2013/', '/2014/' and '/2015/'. If you aren't comfortable with regular expressions yet you could use the following which is easier to understand:

^/(2013|2014|2015)/

Now click 'Save' and your report will only contain the content in the folders you have defined.

> **Tip:** You can modify this custom report to focus on the folders or pages that are appropriate for your website. For example, you could use **^/(index|about|contact)\.php** to only match the '/index.php', '/about.php' and '/contact.php' pages on your website.

Getting Started with Custom Reports

There are two quick ways to get started with custom reports. Firstly, you can copy the majority of the standard reports available in the 'Reporting' tab to meet your needs. Try navigating to the 'Channels' report under 'All Traffic' in the 'Acquisition' section and click 'Customize' at the top of the report. This will automatically send you through to the custom report template where you can tweak what is included and not included in your version of the report.

The second option is by adding pre-created custom reports to your account that you can use or customize further. You can find these at http://lovesdata.co/0cEJ4

Advanced Custom Reports

There are additional options you can use when creating a custom report.

You can add multiple tabs to your reports which allows you to include different pieces of information in the same custom report. You can also name each of the tabs in your custom report.

There are different types of custom reports you can create. In these examples the 'Explorer' report type has been used which is similar to the majority of the standard reports you find in Google Analytics.

The 'Flat Table' option allows you to combine multiple dimensions together within a single report. In the social media report created previously a drill down dimension was added to see the landing pages. If you used the 'Flat Table' custom report you could combine these into a single view. The custom report would look something like:

Social Network	Landing Page	Users
Google+	/blog	637
Google+	/about-us	472
Twitter	/contact	403
LinkedIn	/blog	294
Twitter	/blog	289
Etc.		

The 'Map Overlay' type allows you to create a custom report that includes a geographic map. The 'Metric Groups' allow you to add additional metrics in a particular reporting tab. For example, if you wanted to quickly switch between conversion and engagement metrics you could add these metrics within separate metric groups.

Regular Expressions

Regular expressions allow you to search for and match (or not match) particular elements within text. They are advanced, so you might not need them straight away, but as you use Google Analytics more they will speed up the way you use and customize the interface and will also give you more flexibility in configuring views.

The following example is not a regular expression but it will help you understand the concept of regular expressions if you're just getting started. What would you get if you searched on Google for 'google analytics case study filetype:pdf site:google.com'?

Well, the search results would only include PDF files, hosted on google.com that contain the keyword 'google analytics case study'.

This is not really a regular expression, but it does show you how they work, in that you are defining your search term to only include particular search results that match your criteria.

Different characters and symbols are used in regular expressions to do different things, just as 'filetype' and 'site' in the example defined what should be included in search results.

> **Tip:** If you haven't used regular expressions before they can be a little daunting, but when you become more comfortable using Google Analytics they will help speed up the way you refine what you include in particular reports and segments.

Now we'll look at how regular expressions work and cover examples of how they can be used in Google Analytics.

Wildcards

As a regular expression a full stop matches any single character where the full stop is placed. For example, **goo.gle** matches 'gooogle', 'goodgle' and 'goo8gle' because there is a single character where the full stop is placed.

An asterisk matches zero or more of the item that came before the asterisk. For example, **goo*gle** would require zero or more additional 'o's where the asterisk is placed. This means that it would match 'google', as there are no additional extra 'o's. It would match 'gogle' because the 'o' before the asterisk is removed (or in other words zero 'o's) and would also match 'gooooogle' because there are additional 'o's.

A plus sign is similar to the asterisk, but requires one or more of the previous item (instead of zero or more). For example, **goo+gle** would match 'google' and 'gooogle' because they both contain at least one extra 'o'. However, it would not match 'gogle' because we need at least *one or more* 'o's.

A question mark matches zero or one of the item that came before the question mark. For example, **labou?r** would only match with and without the U, meaning it would match 'labour' and 'labor'. You can see how this could be applied to match the United States and United Kingdom spelling of the word.

A pipe creates an 'OR' statement, allowing you to match any one item within a list. For example, **apple|banana|orange** would match 'apple', 'banana' or 'orange'.

Syntax	Meaning	Example	Matches
.	Any single character	go.gle	google, goggle
|	Or	demo|example	demo, demos, example
?	Zero or one times	demos?123	demo123, demos123
*	Zero or more times	goo*gle	gogle, google, goooogle
+	One or more times	goo+gle	google, goooogle

Anchors

A caret sign can be used to ensure that what you are trying to match is at the beginning. For example, **^/folder** would match '/folder/page.html' because '/folder' is at the beginning. However it would not match '/other/folder' because '/other' is at the beginning (and not '/folder').

A dollar sign is the opposite to caret sign. It's used to ensure what you are looking for is at the end. For example, **page$** would match 'specialpage' because page is at the end, but it would not match 'pagedetails' because page is not at the end.

Syntax	Meaning	Example	Matches
^	Starts with	^demo	demos, demonstration
$	Ends with	demo$	my demo

Grouping

Parentheses along with pipes allow you to create a list of items to match. For example, **(thanks|confirmation)** would match 'thanks' or 'confirmation'. You can also create lists using square brackets and extend these lists using a hyphen. For example, **[a-d]** would match 'a', 'b', 'c' or 'd'.

Syntax	Meaning	Example	Matches
[]	List	analy[zs]e	analyze, analyse
-	Range	demo[2-4]	demo2, demo3
()	Items	my(demo|example)	mydemo, myexample

Escaping

Now you might come across a scenario where you want to match something like 'thanks.html'. You'll notice that it contains a full stop. And a full stop, as you have seen, is a regular expression. In this case you want to match the full stop literally as a full stop and not as a regular expression. To do this, add a backslash before the character you want to match literally. In this example, **thanks.html** would become **thanks\.html**. If you didn't add the backslash **thanks.html** might match 'thanksbhtml' or 'thanks8html'

Syntax	Meaning	Example	Matches
\	Escape	USD\$10	USD$10

Examples of Regular Expressions

Let's say you want to match two particular pages in your Google Analytics report. You can use regular expressions to create an 'OR' statement. This is where you want to match one or the other. If you wanted to match '/thanks.html' or '/confirmation.html' you could use the following regular expression:

```
^/(thanks|confirmation)\.html
```

In this example, the brackets create a list and the pipe creates the 'OR' statement. If you then decided you also wanted to match '/registration.html' you could modify the regular expression to become:

```
^/(thanks|confirmation|registration)\.html
```

You can use a similar regular expression to match folders (directories) on your website. For example, if you wanted to only see your '/services/' and '/news/' folders you could use the following regular expression:

```
^/(services|news)/
```

Regular expressions can be used in various ways in Google Analytics. You can use regular expressions in the search box that is found above the table in reports.

The following regular expression can be used to find all pages ending with '.html':

```
\.html$
```

The following regular expression will match 'company.com', 'company.co.nz' and 'company.co.uk':

```
company\.(com|co\.nz|co\.uk)$
```

The following regular expression will match 'Canada', 'Australia' or 'New Zealand':

```
(canada|australia|new zealand)
```

Regular expressions can be used when configuring custom segments, custom reports, dashboards and when setting up goals. Simply look for the regular expression matching option, often listed as 'RegEx'.

Tip: Download a useful regular expression cheat sheet at http://lovesdata.co/THYyF

Universal Analytics

Universal Analytics is the evolution of Google Analytics and opens up new measurement opportunities. It provides a new method of tracking which can be used for greater insights into the behavior of your audience. It includes the ability to measure people interacting with websites and mobile applications (using JavaScript tracking code and SDKs for mobile apps), but adds additional measurement functionality.

Unlike the traditional methods for measuring interactions on websites and apps, Universal Analytics allows you to measure individuals across multiple devices. For example, if someone registers for the members area on a website using their laptop and then later logs into an app on their phone, these interactions can be tied together by setting a user ID in the tracking code. This then gives you the ability to report on the number of people moving between different devices and gain deeper insights into the behavior of your audience.

You could also use the user ID to merge Google Analytics data with other data already available for particular users. For example, you could merge data from a CRM (Customer Relationship Management) tool with Google Analytics to understand how particular customer segments interact on your website and mobile apps.

Apart from the JavaScript tracking code and SDKs to measure mobile apps, Universal Analytics also allows you to measure custom interactions using the Measurement Protocol. The Measurement Protocol is a way to feed different types of data directly into your Google Analytics reports and is useful when the JavaScript tracking code or SDKs are difficult to implement. For example, you could measure offline interactions to report on how many people are swiping their membership cards at brick-and-mortar stores by using the Measurement Protocol to send the custom interaction into Google Analytics. The possibilities with the Measurement Protocol are almost endless, from in-store interactions to measuring gaming consoles, almost any device that can detect or measure an interaction can be customized to log this information into Google Analytics.

> **Tip:** For more details on the Measurement Protocol visit http://lovesdata.co/xCh2U

Google Analytics Premium

Google Analytics Premium provides additional enterprise-level features based on an annual subscription fee. The Premium version is designed specifically for large-scale implementations that are collecting large volumes of data. Features of Google Analytics Premium include:

- Written contract that guarantees minimum service levels from Google
- Larger data collection limits
- Faster data processing into reports
- Unsampled data export
- Dedicated account management and support
- Data-driven attribution modelling tool
- Additional integrations, including Google BigQuery and DoubleClick

Types of organizations using Google Analytics Premium include:

- Travel
- Finance
- Ecommerce
- Consumer Goods
- Government

For more details on Google Analytics Premium visit http://lovesdata.co/WfHUh

28

Tracking

There are two ways to set up tracking for your website. You can install the Google Analytics tracking code on all the pages of your website, or you can install Google Tag Manager. Installing the Google Analytics tracking code in your website is usually the quickest option as you can generally use a plugin or modify your website template to install the code. However, if you want to extend the tracking code to include things like event tracking, ecommerce tracking or other customizations then this means you will need to modify tracking code on individual pages on your website. This is where Google Tag Manager can be more efficient as it allows you to manage your tracking code and measure some custom interactions without needing to further modify the code on your website.

> **Tip:** In most cases, you should consider using Google Tag Manager as it can help streamline your Google Analytics implementation. This is covered in Chapter 29 – "Google Tag Manager".

Tracking Websites

When you sign up for a new Google Analytics account, you'll be prompted to enter your website's details. This will provide you with the Google Analytics tracking code. If you're embedding the code directly within the code of your website you'll need to ensure that this tracking code is placed immediately before the closing **</head>** tag on all the pages of your website.

If you are using Wordpress, Joomla or another CMS (Content Management System) for your website using a plugin can be a quick way to implement the Google Analytics tracking code. In most cases you will only need to copy and paste the tracking ID for these plugins to work.

Tracking ID   Status: Receiving Data
UA-123456-1

Website tracking
This is the Universal Analytics tracking code for this property. **To get all the benefits of Universal Analytics for this property, copy and paste this code into every webpage you want to track.**

Tip: If you need to find your tracking code for an existing Google Analytics property navigate to 'Admin' and select 'Tracking Code' in 'Tracking Info' under the Property column.

You can place the same tracking code on the primary domain as well as sub-domains to track people as they move between the different sections of your website. For example, placing the same tracking code on 'http://www.company.com', 'http://blog.company.com' and 'http://promo.company.com' will automatically track people as they move between the different sub-domains.

Tracking Multiple Websites

The Google Analytics tracking code can be placed on multiple websites. However, there are some considerations depending on what you would like to see in your reports. Adding the default tracking code to multiple websites will mean that when people travel from one website to the other you will see two users and two sessions in your reports.

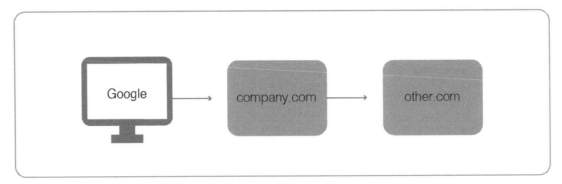

Using the default tracking code will also mean that you will see two source and medium combinations in your reports. Looking at the scenario above you will see Google as the source and medium, as the person entered 'http://www.company.com' and you will also see a referral of company.com when the person then travelled to 'http://www.other.com'. Setting up cross domain tracking will mean that only the original method for finding 'http://www.company.com' is displayed in your reports and you will see more accurate data with only one user and one session reported.

To set up cross domain tracking, you need to modify the tracking code on your primary domain. In this example this is 'http://www.company.com':

```
<script type="text/javascript">

  (function(i,s,o,g,r,a,m)
{i['GoogleAnalyticsObject']=r;i[r]=i[r]||function(){
    (i[r].q=i[r].q||[]).push(arguments)},i[r].l=1*new Date();a=s.
createElement(o),
    m=s.getElementsByTagName(o)[0];a.async=1;a.src=g;m.parentNode.
insertBefore(a,m)
    })(window,document,'script','//www.google-analytics.com/
analytics.js','ga');

  ga('create', 'UA-123456-1', 'auto', {'allowLinker': true});
  ga('require', 'linker');
  ga('linker:autoLink', ['other.com'], false, true);
  ga('send', 'pageview');

</script>
```

You will notice that the code has been modified to automatically track people as they travel across to the other website. The tracking code will now automatically track people traveling to pages on 'other.com'.

You will then need to modify the tracking code used on 'http://www.other.com':

```
<script type="text/javascript">

  (function(i,s,o,g,r,a,m)
{i['GoogleAnalyticsObject']=r;i[r]=i[r]||function(){
    (i[r].q=i[r].q||[]).push(arguments)},i[r].l=1*new Date();a=s.
createElement(o),
    m=s.getElementsByTagName(o)[0];a.async=1;a.src=g;m.parentNode.
insertBefore(a,m)
    })(window,document,'script','//www.google-analytics.com/
analytics.js','ga');
```

```
ga('create', 'UA-123456-1', 'auto', {'allowLinker': true});
ga('require', 'linker');
ga('linker:autoLink', ['company.com'], false, true);
ga('send', 'pageview');

</script>
```

Tip: Cross domain tracking can also be set up in Google Tag Manager.

Finally, you need to make sure that Google Analytics will not treat movement between your domains as referrals (which would create a new session). Go to 'Admin' click on 'Tracking Info' and 'Referral Exclusion List', then add 'company.com' and 'other.com' to the list.

Tracking Mobile Websites

The Google Analytics tracking code automatically tracks smart phones, including Android phones and iPhones. This is because modern mobile devices load the JavaScript tracking code and log cookies, the two requirements for Google Analytics to track people accessing your website.

You will find the dedicated Mobile reports in the Audience section and you can also apply segments to your reports to perform more detailed analysis of your mobile traffic.

In most cases you will already have your mobile traffic included in your reports, however if you have your mobile website on a dedicated sub-domain or another area of your website you should check that you have implemented the same tracking code on those pages you have used on your website.

Event Tracking

Event Tracking allows you to track custom interactions that people are performing on your website, so that you can understand the specific actions occurring on particular pages.

The most common use for Event Tracking is to measure the number of files being downloaded from your website. For example, you might have a PDF that contains additional information about your products or services that people click to download. Without Event Tracking, you would only be able to report on the number of people visiting the page that contains the link to the PDF, but not if people are actually clicking to download the file. Event Tracking will give you a clearer picture as to the number of people downloading the file. Additionally, if you have multiple files available to download, you can track all of them using Event Tracking to compare their popularity.

Another common use for Event Tracking is to measure people clicking on email links on a website. For example, the info@company.com email address on a contact page. Measuring the number of people clicking links to navigate away from your website is also a common use for Event Tracking. These links are called *outbound links* as they direct people off your website. For example, if your website was 'www.company.com', and you provided a link on one of your pages to 'www.partnerwebsite.com', then you would be creating an outbound link to the partner website. If you have links that will send people to different websites, then setting up Event Tracking will allow you to understand where people are leaving your website, and also track and compare the links on your website that they are selecting.

> **Tip:** Event Tracking only tracks defined interactions that people are performing on your website, so when we're talking about tracking downloads, email links and outbound links, we're really talking about tracking the clicks on those elements. For example, with download tracking we're not actually tracking if people successfully download a particular file and open it on their computer, we're simply tracking the number of people who click to download the file.

Event Tracking is totally flexible and can really be used to track any type of interaction into Google Analytics. In addition to tracking downloads and links, Event Tracking can be used to track engagement with video and Flash content, interactive menus, scrolling banners and anything interactive on your website.

> **Tip:** If you're just starting to use Google Analytics or are not familiar with coding the best way to think of Event Tracking is like campaign tracking, but it is set up in the source code of your website. The main reason it is similar to campaign tracking is that it is flexible and it is up to you to decide how to name events. How you decide to name your events (just like campaigns) will be seen inside your Google Analytics event reports (it's important not to use campaign tracking on your own website because it will result in inflated session data).

Event Tracking allows you to define a 'category' and 'action' for the event and also an optional 'label' and 'value'. Whatever names or values you give these elements will be what you see inside your reports. Let's look at how these elements are used to help you decide how to define them.

Event Category

The event category allows you to define a top-level grouping for your event reports.

For example, if you're setting up events to track multiple files you could define the category as **download**. You would then see the total number of clicks to download all your files. You could then drill down into your 'download' category to see the individual files that people are choosing to download.

Another example is if you want to track multiple videos you have on your website, you could define the category as 'video' to see the total number of interactions with your videos and then drill down to see the particular videos that people are choosing to watch.

If you defined both of these categories (download and video) you would see the following in your event category report:

Event Category	Total Events
video	1,780
download	943

You can see that because two different top-level categories are defined, these are reported inside Google Analytics. The Total Events column shows the total number of category interactions. In this example, you can see the total number of people interacting with videos and the total number of clicks to download files.

Event Action

The event action enables you to describe the user's interaction in order to see more detail inside your reports. Just like event category, you can define your own name as the event action, so it is totally flexible and can be customized to your own particular needs.

Continuing the video tracking example where the event category was defined as 'video', you'll now need to define an event action. If you're setting up events to track the play button in your video keep the category as 'video' and then define the event action as 'play'. This will now allow you to understand the total number of times people start to play the videos.

You might also want to track the number of people who watch the entire video. Again you would keep the category as 'video', but you would now define the event action as 'completed' and set up the event to only record data after people had completed watching the entire video. You could now compare people choosing to play videos against the number of people watching to the very end of your videos. Once you implement Event Tracking in your videos you can drill down into the event category of 'video' to see the following:

Event Action	Total Events
play	1,271
completed	501

You can now see the number of people who start watching and finish watching a video.

Remember that you can define event actions as anything you choose. For download tracking you could name the event action as 'click' for all of the files you want to track. But they would all have the same event action which doesn't really provide any useful insights.

Instead, you can choose to name the event action as the type of file people are choosing to download. In this example PDF files are being tracked, so you would define the event action as 'pdf'. If there were additional PDF files, you would continue to define the action as 'pdf', but then if you added some Word documents for people to download, you would define the action for those files as 'doc'. Now you will be able to drill down into the event category of 'download' and see the following:

Event Action	Total Events
pdf	829
doc	114

You'll be able to see the number of people that are clicking to download the PDF and Word documents. You might even use this report to decide the best file formats to use in future.

Event Label

Defining a label for Event Tracking is optional, but as we'll see it is very useful to take the time to use the event label parameter. Think of the label as a way to get more detailed information into your Google Analytics event reports.

Continuing with the download tracking example, you can now report on the total number of clicks to download files and even report on the types of files that are being downloaded. However, something really important is missing – the ability to report on the individual files that people are downloading. This is where event labels can provide more detail in reports.

For the PDF file, you've now defined the event category as 'download' and the event action as 'pdf'. All you need to do is define the event label as the name of the individual file, so for this example the label will be 'information.pdf'. You'll now be able to use the event label report to see the total number of times people have selected to download the particular PDF file:

Event Category	Total Events
information.pdf	603

Once you set up Event Tracking with appropriate labels for the different downloads, you'll also be able to compare the popularity of all the files being tracked:

Event Label	Total Events
information.pdf	603
brochure.pdf	183
application.doc	43

Event Value

Defining a value for your event is optional and not used as often as event label. Event value allows you to define a numerical value for the interaction you are tracking. For example, you could use value to track the time someone spends watching a video. That way, when you are tracking the number of people who finish watching your video, you also know the duration of the video they watched.

Event value could also be used to define a dollar value for the interaction, for example if you have determined that downloading a particular file has a value of $2.00, you could then pass **2** as the event value for that particular download.

If you are using Event Tracking to track a Flash-based game you could use the event value to track the score or level someone has reached within the game.

Implementing Event Tracking

Once you have decided on suitable values for your event categories, actions, labels and values, you'll need to implement Event Tracking. In most cases you will want to implement Event Tracking using Google Tag Manager as this streamlines the configuration of your tags and also allows many elements, like downloads and outbound links to be automatically tracked without needing any additional tracking code. We'll cover this in Chapter 29 – "Google Tag Manager." Let's look at how Event Tracking works if the Google Analytics tracking code is embedded directly on your website (and you're not using Google Tag Manager).

Continuing with the download tracking example, the naming convention will be:

Event Category	Event Action	Event Label (optional)	Event Value (optional)
download	file type (e.g. pdf, word, etc.)	file name (e.g. information.pdf)	

All of the files use the event category of 'download' for top-level reporting, the event action will record the file type (for example 'pdf' for PDF downloads) and the event label represents the name of the individual file (for example 'information.pdf'). Finally, the optional event value will not be used in this example.

Now the code for files being tracked with events needs to be modified. In the code of the website, the first file to be tracked using events looks like:

```
<a href="/files/information.pdf">Download Information PDF</a>
```

This is for the 'information.pdf' file, so now you need to apply Event Tracking code to the link using the naming convention chosen. The link in the code will now look like:

```
<a href="/files/information.pdf" onclick="ga('send', 'event',
'download', 'pdf', 'information.pdf');">Download Application
Document</a>
```

The extra elements highlighted above are the special Google Analytics Event Tracking code. Now, when someone clicks on the link to download the file; 'download' is the category, 'pdf' is the action and 'information.pdf' is the label.

If another file uses the following code:

```
<a href="/files/application.doc">Download Application Document</a>
```

You would adjust the appropriate elements in the Event Tracking code, so the link would now become:

```
<a href="/files/application.doc" onclick="ga('send', 'event',
'download', 'doc', 'application.doc');">Download Application
Document</a>
```

You can then continue this process to track all the files on your website. But what if you have hundreds or even thousands of downloads available on your website that you want to track? Well, you can go through this process and manually edit the code for every file or you can use Google Tag Manager to automatically track all the downloads. Even if you are going to use Google Tag Manager, it is still important to understand how Event Tracking works and how the Event Tracking elements appear inside your reports. Read Chapter 29 – "Google Tag Manager" – for details.

As discussed, the Event Tracking code allows you to define the category, action, label and value for the website elements you want to track as events. Here you can see how the Event Tracking elements are placed in the Event Tracking code (where '1' is the optional event value):

```
ga('send', 'event', 'event category', 'event action', 'event
label', 1);
```

Remember that Event Tracking is totally flexible and can be used to track specific interactions occurring on the pages of your website.

Best Practices for Event Tracking

As you have seen, Event Tracking is perfect for tracking downloads and videos, but it can also be used to track other interactions occurring on your website. Here are some additional ideas for using Event Tracking along with best practice suggestions for naming and defining Event Tracking parameters.

Tracking Email Links

Some people don't like completing website forms, so having email addresses as links on your website can help people get in contact with you, but they are not tracked by default. Here is a naming convention for tracking email (mailto) links:

Event Category	Event Action	Event Label (optional)	Event Value (optional)
email	click	info@company.com	

If you have different email links used throughout your website consider using the event action to define the type of email address or the department the email will go to. For example, event action could be 'customer support' for help@company.com and support@company.com. Then the event action could be 'staff member' for individual staff email addresses such as james@company.com and rebecca@company.com.

In this example the event value has been left blank, but you could use this if you have calculated a dollar value for people clicking on your email links.

Tip: Some people prefer to define the event category as 'mailto' as this is the technical name for an email link.

Tracking Outbound Links

Tracking outbound links using events is similar to tracking email links, but you change the event category to 'outbound' and use the event label to report the particular website people are navigating to.

Event Category	Event Action	Event Label (optional)	Event Value (optional)
outbound	click	google.com	

Just like email links, you could also use the event action to classify the theme or category of the website you are linking to on your pages.

Tracking Videos

The best option for tracking videos is to track the number of people selecting to play the video and the number of people who complete watching the entire video. The optional event label should be used to report the individual videos that people are watching. You can also consider using the optional event value to report on the duration of the video. In the following example, the video duration (in seconds) is being recorded.

Event Category	Event Action	Event Label (optional)	Event Value (optional)
video	play	about us	
video	completed	about us	65

Implementing Event Tracking to report on your videos will depend on the video service you are using and how you are embedding the video on your website. If you are embedding YouTube videos on your website visit http://lovesdata.co/QkQFx for a solution.

Tip: You could also track people engaging with other video controls, like 'pause' and 'volume', but the most actionable data will be seeing if people actually complete watching your video content.

Tracking Other Interactions

Remember, Event Tracking is completely flexible and you can track almost any interaction that occurs on a page of your website. Additional options for Event Tracking include:

- People interacting with form fields
- Internal website banners and promotions
- Interactive elements, including AJAX
- Tracking interactions in mobile apps

Event Tracking and Bounce Rate

Event Tracking will prevent a bounce from being reported if someone engages with an element that has Event Tracking implemented.

For example, let's say you have a video that you have on your 'about us' page and you have set up events to track every time someone clicks on the play button to watch your video. If someone comes to the 'about us' page, watches the video and then leaves your website you will have one pageview reported for the page and one event reported for the video. By default Event Tracking will mean that this visit is no longer considered a bounce, even though a bounce is usually understood to be someone viewing a single page on your website.

In most cases you probably want this scenario to be reported as an engaged visit – they have after all selected to watch your video. However, if you would prefer that this scenario is still considered a bounce, you have the option of adjusting the Event Tracking code to report the bounce. This is called a non-interaction event, where you only want to report on events and do not want it to adjust bounces or bounce rate.

Inside Google Tag Manager you can set 'Non-Interaction Hit' to 'True' so that someone triggering the event will still be considered a bounce if they don't go on to view another page. Example code:

```
ga('send', 'event', 'videos', 'play', 'about us',
{'nonInteraction': 1});
```

Ecommerce Tracking

Ecommerce tracking enables you to measure transactions and other sales-related information into Google Analytics. Once you've implemented ecommerce tracking, one of the biggest benefits is the ability to understand the value generated from your different marketing campaigns. You can also use ecommerce data with a whole range of other dimensions too. This allows you to ask a whole range of questions about people purchasing online, including:

- Where are they located?
- What devices do they use?
- What are my most popular items?
- Where do people abandon the shopping funnel?
- How do high value customers find the website?
- What website pages are most valuable?

You'll need to work with your web developer to implement ecommerce tracking because transactions (and the steps leading up to transactions) need to be sent to Google Analytics using special code. This needs to all happen dynamically, or in other words, all the ecommerce details sent to Google Analytics need to be specific to each person purchasing the product. For example, if someone visits your website and purchases a blue t-shirt for $25.00, then those details need to be sent to Google Analytics. If someone else purchases red socks, then those details need to be sent for that particular transaction.

Important: If your ecommerce tracking has already been set up, then you might be using the standard ecommerce tracking code. Standard ecommerce tracking only collects details on the final receipt page after each purchase is made. There is a newer way to measure ecommerce called Enhanced Ecommerce that allows you to collect information for all stages leading up to and including the purchase. We're going to focus on Enhanced Ecommerce, if you are using the older standard code you might want to consider upgrading to take advantage of the new features and reports.

Not sure if you are using standard ecommerce or Enhanced Ecommerce? Navigate to 'Ecommerce' in the 'Conversions' reports. If you see the following menu options (along with data in the reports) then you are using Enhanced Ecommerce:

If you don't see these options, then you are using standard ecommerce (Enhanced Ecommerce requires the reports to be enabled, along with special Enhanced Ecommerce tracking code).

Enhanced Ecommerce tracking allows you to measure your shopping cart process. It's also flexible, so if you have a checkout process that takes three steps, or just a single step, you can define these in the tracking code.

You can also implement Enhanced Ecommerce to understand how people engage with products before they start the checkout process. This includes tracking clicks on product promotions and people viewing product detail pages.

Enhanced Ecommerce requires the analytics.js tracking code and the Enhanced Ecommerce plug-in enabled, in order to measure ecommerce data for your reports. The most efficient way to implement Enhanced Ecommerce is by using Google Tag Manager and a data layer. The amount of work required to implement ecommerce tracking in this manner is similar to implementing the tracking code directly on each page of your website, but there is the additional benefit of greater flexibility and a streamlined implementation.

Using a data layer with Google Tag Manager is covered later, but first let's explore how you would modify the Google Analytics tracking code to measure ecommerce transactions.

Here is the default Google Analytics tracking code:

```
<script>
  (function(i,s,o,g,r,a,m)
{i['GoogleAnalyticsObject']=r;i[r]=i[r]||function(){
  (i[r].q=i[r].q||[]).push(arguments)},i[r].l=1*new Date();a=s.
createElement(o),
  m=s.getElementsByTagName(o)[0];a.async=1;a.src=g;m.parentNode.
insertBefore(a,m)
  })(window,document,'script','//www.google-analytics.com/
analytics.js','ga');

  ga('create', 'UA-123456-1', 'auto');
  ga('send', 'pageview');

</script>
```

And here is an example of the modified tracking code used to track ecommerce transactions on the final receipt page:

```
<script>
  (function(i,s,o,g,r,a,m)
{i['GoogleAnalyticsObject']=r;i[r]=i[r]||function(){
  (i[r].q=i[r].q||[]).push(arguments)},i[r].l=1*new Date();a=s.
createElement(o),
  m=s.getElementsByTagName(o)[0];a.async=1;a.src=g;m.parentNode.
insertBefore(a,m)
  })(window,document,'script','//www.google-analytics.com/
analytics.js','ga');

  ga('create', 'UA-123456-1', 'auto');

  ga('require', 'ec');

ga('ec:addProduct' {
  'id': 'TID654321',
  'name': 'Branded Tshirt',
  'category': 'Apparel',
  'variant': 'red',
  'price': '19.95',
  'quantity'': 1
});
```

```
ga('ec:addProduct', {
  'id': 'TID654321',
  'name': 'Mens Socks',
  'category': 'Apparel',
  'variant': 'blue',
  'price': '5.95',
  'quantity': 2
});

ga('ec:setAction', 'purchase', {
  'id': 'TID654321',
  'revenue': '39.99',
  'tax': '3.19',
  'shipping': '4.95',
});

  ga('send', 'pageview');

</script>
```

Important: All of the data assigned to the ecommerce parameters need to be dynamic. In other words, they need to change based on the particular transaction that has occurred.

Ecommerce tracking can be used to measure a number of different values, from product name to category, right through to coupon codes and other data. For more details go to http://lovesdata.co/kY59S

Tip: Hosted ecommerce platforms like Shopify and Bigcommerce include Google Analytics integrations to measure transactions into your reports. Visit the support section of your platform for details on setting up tracking for your store.

The approach for tracking ecommerce transactions with Google Tag Manager is similar to modifying the tracking code. You will implement a data layer that dynamically generates the transaction-related data, which is then used by Google Tag Manager.

Here is an example of Google Tag Manager code along with a data layer:

```
<script>
window.dataLayer = window.dataLayer || [];
dataLayer.push({
  'ecommerce': {
    'purchase': {
      'actionField': {
        'id': 'TID654321',
        'revenue': '39.99',
        'tax': '3.19',
        'shipping': '4.95'
      },
      'products': [{
        'id': 'PID765123',
        'name': 'Branded Tshirt',
        'category': 'Apparel',
        'variant': 'red',
        'price': '19.95',
        'quantity': 1
      },
      {
        'id': 'PID123445',
        'name': 'Mens Socks',
        'category': 'Apparel',
        'variant': 'blue',
        'price': '5.95',
        'quantity': 2
      }]
    }
  }
});
</script>

<!-- Google Tag Manager -->
<noscript><iframe src="//www.googletagmanager.com/ns.html?id=GTM-
AB1EF2"
height="0" width="0" style="display:none;visibility:hidden"></
iframe></noscript>
<script>(function(w,d,s,l,i){w[l]=w[l]||[];w[l].push({'gtm.start':
new Date().getTime(),event:'gtm.js'});var f=d.
getElementsByTagName(s)[0],
j=d.createElement(s),dl=l!='dataLayer'?'&l='+l:'';j.async=true;j.src=
```

```
'//www.googletagmanager.com/gtm.js?id='+i+dl;f.parentNode.
insertBefore(j,f);
})(window,document,'script','dataLayer','GTM-AB1EF2');</script>
<!-- End Google Tag Manager -->
```

You then need to configure the tag for the final receipt page in Google Tag Manager.

> **Tip:** Instead of passing complete transaction and product details, you also have the option of passing the product and transaction ID and then uploading the additional data to Google Analytics. This reduces the amount of data that needs to be included in the data layer, however it does mean additional work to upload the extra information into Google Analytics.

The data layer can be used to send additional information about how people are engaging with your products, right through to the checkout steps. For details visit http://lovesdata.co/AFuiO

Ecommerce Accuracy

Google Analytics, like any web analytics tool, is unlikely to be 100% accurate and it should go without saying that for tax auditing and any other business-critical financial reporting, you should use your ecommerce system and not Google Analytics. Revenue figures in Google Analytics should be used to optimize website and marketing activities and increase sales, not for generating tax or auditing reports.

That being said, when you compare the dollar figures from your Google Analytics reports to your ecommerce system you'll want to see 95% accuracy. In other words if Google Analytics is plus or minus 5% in comparison to your actual ecommerce revenue then you should not be concerned about your setup. On the other hand, if Google Analytics is only reporting 70% of transactions occurring, you need to investigate why there is a large percentage of missing data in your reports.

The best way to troubleshoot your ecommerce tracking code is to go through the process yourself. Using a test login and a test credit card and actually stepping through your checkout process will allow you to view the source code for each step and ensure the ecommerce tracking is correct.

Tracking Mobile Apps

You can use Google Analytics to measure people using your Android and iOS mobile apps by including the SDK (Software Development Kit) in your app. Alternatively, you can use the Google Tag Manager SDK to help streamline your data collection and also push changes to your app. While tracking mobile apps is similar to tracking interactions on your website, you'll need to spend time planning the elements and interactions that you want to measure.

The SDKs allow you to measure:

- **The number of screens** people use in the app.
- **Events for tracking** additional interactions.
- **Ecommerce transactions for in-app purchases** or virtual currency.
- **Custom dimensions for custom information** about your audience or what they are doing in the app.
- **Custom metrics for other data** you want to report on, like number of in-app search results or number of points collected.
- **Custom timings** to measure how long particular actions take, like moving between levels or completing a stepped process.
- **Exceptions and crashes** to understand app errors and crashes.
- **Campaigns** to see the initiatives that are driving app installations.
- **When people share and like content** in your app with **social interactions**.
- **User ID** for tying in-app interactions to website and offline interactions.

The SDKs allow you to define when to send data to Google Analytics. You can use a 'Periodic Dispatch' or a 'Manual Dispatch'. This means that data does not need to be sent as each interaction occurs in the app (which helps to conserve battery and reduce data loss due to network issues). You can also make use of remarketing and demographic reports by implementing 'Display Features' in your app.

Tip: Start planning as early as possible to map out the data you want to collect from your app and involve your app developer as early as possible to ensure tracking is implemented before you deploy your app.

For details on implementing Google Analytics for your mobile app visit http://loves data.co/HWaWJ

Custom Dimensions and Custom Metrics

Google Analytics allows you to add your own dimensions and metrics to extend the default information and data already being collected on your website. This allows you to measure things specific to your organization, for example:

- Logged in and logged out users
- Comments on blog posts
- Author of individual blog posts
- Newsletter subscriber
- Existing members and customers
- Membership levels and types
- Anonymous customer ID

- Customer lifetime value
- Customer demographics
- Information from your CRM

Start by considering how you would like the custom dimension or metric to be tied to the person's interaction. Should it be at the user level, so that every time the person visits the website it is measured? Should it just be for the session or for the individual hit (for example pageview)? The way you define this will depend on what you are measuring, and how you would like the data to be available in your reports. This is called the 'Scope' and it can be tricky to decide the first time you set up a custom dimension or metric, but you can always try it on a test area of your website to begin with.

The scopes you can choose from are:

- **Hit-level** means the value will be tied to an individual interaction, like a pageview or event.
- **Session-level** where the value is tied to all the hits (including pageviews) in a single session.
- **User-level** where the value is applied to the current and future sessions.

Tip: You can also use a **product-level** scope to provide additional information for products you are measuring with ecommerce tracking.

Here are some examples of when you might use a different scope, depending on what you are measuring:

Example	Scope	Why?
Author of individual blog posts	Hit (pageview)	To attribute author details to each page within reports.
Comments on blog posts	Hit (pageview)	To attribute the comment to the particular page of the blog post. This also ensures multiple comments on different pages are tracked correctly.
Weight of items being sold online	Product	For insights into shipping costs of products being purchased.
Logged in and logged out users	Session	People can be logged in or logged out for any given session.
Existing members and customers	User	To know if people are already members or customers (regardless of whether they are logged in or not).

Once you have decided on an appropriate scope, the next step is to set up the custom dimension or metric in Google Analytics. Navigate to 'Admin' and select 'Custom Definitions' in the 'Property' column. Now select 'Custom Dimensions' and click 'New Custom Dimension'. You will now be able to enter a name for your custom dimension and select the appropriate scope. Now click 'Create' and you will be presented with examples of how to implement the custom dimension in the Google Analytics tracking code and mobile SDKs.

Now you need to modify your tracking code, so that your custom dimension is included before the pageview (or other type of hit) is sent to Google Analytics. You also need to ensure that the value of the dimension is dynamically set in your tracking code so that the correct information is tracked. For example, if you are measuring logged in users the tracking code should look something like:

```
...
ga('create', 'UA-123456-1');
ga('set', 'dimension1', 'logged in');
ga('send', 'pageview');
</script>
```

While for logged out users it should look like:

```
...
ga('create', 'UA-123456-1');
ga('set', 'dimension1', 'logged out');
ga('send', 'pageview');
</script>
```

> **Tip:** You can use Google Tag Manager to send custom dimensions and metrics to Google Analytics. This can be done using tags and triggers or even using a custom data layer.

You'll notice that the custom dimension is given an index. This simply identifies the number for a particular custom dimension. The first dimension you set up will have an index of '1', the second an index of '2' and so on.

> **Tip:** Custom metrics are set up using similar steps, but you will need to select between 'Integer', 'Currency' and 'Time' as the value of your custom metric. Custom metrics can be set with a 'Hit' or 'Product' scope.

Troubleshooting Tracking Code

When you are using customized Google Analytics tracking code (or are working with external developers who are installing tracking code), there are a number of things that can go wrong, causing inaccurate data inside your Google Analytics reports.

In most cases the best way to troubleshoot your tracking code is by using your web browser to check the source code of your website. It sounds obvious, but one of the most common issues with tracking is the incorrect implementation of the tracking code.

No Tracking Code

If somebody forgot to put the tracking code on the website or they removed the tracking code, you won't have any data available in your reports. Navigate to 'Admin' and you will find the tracking code you should use in the 'Tracking Info' section of the 'Property' column.

Incorrect Tracking Code

Start by logging into Google Analytics and finding the property ID (for example UA-123456-1) for the particular website you want to check.

The Google Analytics tracking code installed on the website needs to have this exact property ID. If the property ID is different to the one that you found in the account list, then the website is sending data into a different Google Analytics property.

This can occur if someone made a mistake and implemented the wrong code, or if someone else previously set up a Google Analytics account. If someone else has already set up a Google Analytics account, then the best option is to request access to that existing account. This is much better than removing the tracking code and placing a new one because this would mean that the historical data won't be available in the new Google Analytics view.

Formatted Tracking Code

Extra formatting in the tracking code, like an extra space or paragraph return can break the Google Analytics tracking code, preventing data from being logged into your reports. This tends to happen when someone copies the tracking code into an email and then sends it to the developer for implementation. Emails can be automatically formatted, for example adding a line break to ensure that a line doesn't exceed a certain number of characters. When this happens to the tracking code it usually isn't noticed, but it will prevent the tracking code from working when implemented.

Tip: If you need to send the tracking code to your web developer, send it as a plain text file.

Modified Tracking Code

The Google Analytics tracking code can be modified to meet custom tracking requirements. Ideally, all tracking code modifications should be tested before being applied to your website. If modifications are not applied in the correct order, or if the existing order of the tracking code function is changed, this can cause incorrect tracking into your reports.

Example of **incorrectly** modified tracking code:

```
...
ga('send', 'pageview', '/my-own-page');
ga('create', 'UA-123456-1', 'auto');
</script>
```

In the example above, you'll notice that the pageview is sent before the property ID has been defined. This means that nothing will be tracked into Google Analytics.

Example of **correctly** modified tracking code:

```
...
ga('create', 'UA-123456-1', 'auto');
ga('send', 'pageview', '/my-own-page');
</script>
```

Tracking into Multiple Profiles or Accounts

You can simultaneously track into multiple Google Analytics properties by modifying the tracking code or adding multiple tags in Google Tag Manager.

Let's look at an example where the code has been **incorrectly** modified:

```
...
ga('create', 'UA-123456-1', 'auto');
ga('create', 'UA-654321-1', 'auto', {'name': 'secondTracker'});
ga('send', 'pageview');
</script>
```

In this example the pageview will not be tracked into the second property because there is no function to send the pageview data.

Here is another example of **incorrectly** modified tracking code:

```
...
ga('create', 'UA-123456-1', 'auto');
ga('create', 'UA-654321-1', 'auto');
ga('send', 'pageview');
ga('send', 'pageview');
</script>
```

In this case the first property will receive two pageviews, while the second property won't receive any data.

Now let's look at an example of **correctly** modifying the tracking code. Below you can see that the code has been modified to track into two accounts:

```
...
ga('create', 'UA-123456-1', 'auto');
```

```
    ga('create', 'UA-654321-1', 'auto', {'name': 'secondTracker'});
    ga('send', 'pageview');
    ga('secondTracker.send', 'pageview');
</script>
```

Placement of Tracking Code

The Google Analytics tracking code should be placed just before the closing </head> tag found at the top of all pages of your website. You can also place the code anywhere between the opening <body> and closing </body> tags on your pages, but placing it at the top will give you more accurate data inside Google Analytics.

> **Tip:** The Google Tag Manager code should be placed immediately after the opening <body> tag on all the pages of your website.

If the tracking code is placed before the <title> tags within the <head> tags you might not get correct information for your Page Title report inside Google Analytics. This is because the Google Analytics tracking code might load before the <title> tag, meaning that the Google Analytics tracking code is unable to correctly read the page titles on your website. If you see '(not set)' appearing in your page title report, then this is the likely cause. To correct the problem and get accurate information, move the tracking code below the <title> tag.

Browser Extensions

Browser extensions can help you check and troubleshoot your Google Analytics implementation. Chrome extensions are covered, but some of the extensions are also available for other browsers.

Tag Assistant

Google's Tag Assistant extension provides a quick way to check which Google Analytics tags are firing on a particular page, and it also provides top-level recommendations about the tracking code. For example, you can quickly check if you're using the latest version of the tracking code and if there are any errors or recommendations to streamline your implementation.

To add the extension to Chrome visit http://lovesdata.co/1n0v3

Developer Tools

The 'Inspect Element' option available in Chrome allows you to see the hits that have been sent to Google Analytics. To view the hits, right click on a page and select 'Inspect Element', select the 'Resources' tab, click 'Frames', click the name of the website, then 'Images' and look for the '__utm.gif' image or images. These are the hits sending data to Google Analytics. You can also review the query parameters of the URL to understand what data is being sent with the hit.

Web Developer

The Web Developer extension allows you to quickly view the cookies stored in your browser for the particular website you are viewing. This provides a quick, visual way to check the value of the Google Analytics cookie to make sure they are correct or if they are being overridden as you travel between different sections of your website. You can also see if there are multiple sets of Google Analytics cookies that are being stored for the particular website.

Visit http://lovesdata.co/DyrEl to add the extension to Chrome. Once you have installed the extension, select 'Cookies' and then 'View Cookie Information'.

Analytics Implementation Model

Aligning your implementation with your measurement needs and using an implementation plan can help you stay focused on collecting valuable data to assist with decision making. It's easy to become sidetracked with the latest features and wanting to implement highly custom-ized measurement solutions, but unless you are going to apply the data and reports to drive improvement, you can find yourself heavily invested in a technical implementation that might never be used. Applying the implementation model will help to reduce this by continuing to tie your implementation to your business objectives.

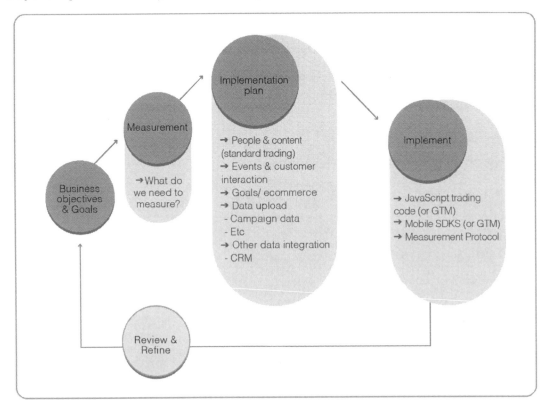

1. Business Objectives and Goals

The first stage is to outline your business objectives. You can use the same approach that was covered in Chapter 5 – "Model for Successful Online Advertising" – where you list business objectives based on the marketing funnel steps of awareness, engagement, conversion and retention. Focus on the business objectives that directly relate to your website and list them out under these headings.

Awareness	Engagement	Conversion	Retention

Once you've defined your objectives you shouldn't need to revisit this stage unless your objectives changed based on a shift in business strategy.

Tip: For additional details on identifying your business objectives read Chapter 5 – "Model for Successful Online Advertising."

Once you have listed your objectives, the next step is to identify the website goals needed to measure people's interactions that will result in these objectives being met. For example, if you listed 'generate sales leads' you will need to review your website to identify how people can complete this particular task on your website. You might then identify the following:

- Submit contact form
- Click on an email link
- View location details

Take the time to brainstorm different options for each of your objectives. You might also identify additional micro conversions and other interactions indicating which people are more likely to help meet your business objectives. List all of these potential goals for each of your business objectives and the more goals you list, the better.

If you end up with a large number of potential goals, consider prioritizing these. For example, you might have first, second and third priority goals.

2. Measurement

Now you need to spend time considering each goal and asking yourself 'what do I need to measure?'. In some cases this will be clear, for example, if you identified 'submit contact form' as a goal, then you would need to make sure the contact form is being measured.

In other cases, you might need to spend more time considering the different options and researching possible solutions. For example, if you identify 'view location details' consider the different options available to measuring this interaction. You might simply use the number of times the location page is viewed, or you might want to think about measuring people clicking on the map or entering their address to find their nearest location.

When you are working on identifying what needs to be measured, it can be helpful to load your website and in some cases use a whiteboard or piece of paper to sketch the page and highlight the different ways people can interact to achieve the goal.

3. Implementation Plan

Once you've identified the elements that can be measured, you can begin to develop an implementation plan. This is where you translate what you want to measure into how it can be measured. Continuing the contact form example, you can identify that this needs to be set up as a goal in Google Analytics. This also might highlight the need for website changes or other technical assistance to achieve your measurement needs. If the contact form doesn't have a 'thank you' page, then this will need to be addressed before you can configure the goal.

In other cases you might need to review the Google Analytics features and options available that can be used to measure the interaction. A good starting point for this is to review Chapter 11 – "Google AdWords Reporting." The following popular tracking and configuration options are also useful starting points.

Tracking options include:

- Events
- Cross-domain tracking
- Ecommerce
- Social interactions
- Advertising features (used for demographics and interests)
- Custom dimensions
- Custom metrics
- User ID

Configuration options include:

- Goals
- Site search
- Data import

Once you have identified what you want to measure and how to measure it, it is a good idea to review these against your original goals and business objectives. It is important that the time and resources invested in measuring these elements matches up against what you need for reporting and analysis. If you have identified something to measure that is not closely aligned to an objective, then don't make this a priority and consider leaving it until the next time you review your implementation.

4. Implement

The next stage is to implement the tracking and configuration changes to begin collecting data. This will generally need the involvement of your web developer to make changes to your tracking code or Google Tag Manager implementation.

Before you make changes to your live website, it is a good idea to test the implementation to ensure it correctly sends the data to Google Analytics. If you're making use of an entirely new feature that you haven't used before it can be good to set up a testing area where you can use a completely separate Google Analytics property to see if the data appears correctly in your reports.

If you are using Google Tag Manager you can make changes to your tags and triggers and use the preview mode to test the tracking before publishing the tags to your live website. Google Tag Manager keeps a version history of changes so you can always roll-back to a previous version if something goes wrong. However, it is a good idea to keep your own documentation to outline changes that you are making to your implementation.

> **Tip:** If you're correcting tracking code problems or implementing new features, it can be helpful to add a short description of the change as an annotation in Google Analytics. This allows you to quickly refer to these changes as you are using the reports.

5. Review and Refine

Following implementation, you should create a schedule to continue the process of reviewing and refining your implementation. Reviewing your measurement needs every three to six months, even briefly, can help identify new opportunities, but remember to always tie your review to your business objectives.

> **Tip:** Your Google Analytics implementation should be seen as an evolving component of your overall website strategy. As new measurement and analysis needs arise, your implementation will need to change to meet these requirements.

29

Introduction to Google Tag Manager

Google Tag Manager (GTM) allows you to centrally manage (and consolidate) your different analytics tags in one place. It enables you to place a single tag across your website and then remotely update your tracking without having to change any code on your website. You can also use Google Tag Manager in your mobile apps to manage your tracking without having to resubmit your app for approval each time you make a change. It is well suited to medium and large scale organizations where updating and adding new tags can take considerable time and place additional burden on your IT resources. By remotely managing your tags you can be quicker at rolling out updates and test tracking code changes before making them live. You can use Google Tag Manager to manage your Google Analytics tracking code, but also tags from Google AdWords, DoubleClick and other third-party tools.

Tip: If you're looking after a smaller website, don't have multiple tags or have a simple Google Analytics implementation, you might not need Google Tag Manager. However, there are some benefits, like being able to track custom interactions using Event Tracking without having to modify your code (it will also allow you to centrally manage tags if you add more tags in the future).

Overview

To get started using Google Tag Manager, you need to understand the core elements. When you sign up for Google Tag Manager you begin by creating an account. You'll generally want a similar structure to that of your Google Analytics account setup, in that each Google Tag Manager account should only be used to manage the tags for related websites. If you're looking after unrelated websites, like a company website and a personal blog, then create separate Google Tag Manager accounts, just like you would for your Google Analytics accounts.

Once you have created your account you'll need to create a container. The container sits within your account and will be used to manage the tags for a specific website. You can create multiple containers within your account if you need to manage tags for multiple websites (or even apps). Again, these sit within a single account, so they should all relate to the individual organization.

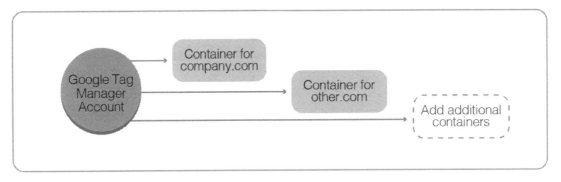

There are three important components that sit within each container. These are *tags*, *triggers* and *variables*. Tags are used to send information to Google Analytics and act as the replacement for the standard Google Analytics tracking code. Since we're just getting started let's focus on using tags to track a website into Google Analytics, but remember that you can use them to send information into other tools too.

Tip: Tags can also be used for other more advanced purposes, for example event and ecommerce tracking.

Next there are triggers – these allow you to specify when particular tags should, and should not, be applied. For example, when you first set up Google Tag Manager, there is the option to select 'All Pages' as your trigger. This means that your tracking code will fire on all pages of the website. If you then wanted to add an extra tag to an individual page you could create a trigger that only includes a desired page.

Finally, there are variables which store pieces of information when someone views your websites. Variables can be used in combination with tags and triggers. For example, the default Page Path variable stores the page that someone is viewing on the website. If they were viewing 'http://www.company.com/thank-you.html' then the Page Path variable would be '/thank-you.html'. This could then be used by the trigger to check if someone was viewing the 'thank you' page.

Basic Website Set Up

Let's start with the basics and look at how Google Tag Manager can deploy Google Analytics to measure your website.

Start by visiting http://lovesdata.co/HXxaG and signing up for a Google Tag Manager account. You'll need to name your new account and then name your first container. Typically you will want the name of your container to be the same as the name of your website.

Now that you have created a container, you are given the Google Tag Manager code that needs to be placed on the pages of your website. The code should be placed immediately after the opening <body> tag on your pages.

If you already have Google Analytics installed on your website, then it is still okay to place the code on all your pages. This is because you can set up Google Tag Manager without publishing your tags, allowing you to preview and test your tags before they are live on your website.

If you are setting up Google Tag Manager on a new website, that doesn't have any existing Google Analytics tracking code installed, you will need to create a new Google Analytics account and note down the Web Property ID. Alternatively, if Google Analytics is already installed on your website, you can view the source code of your website to find your Web Property ID or find it in your Google Analytics account.

> **Tip:** Don't know your Web Property ID? It will look something like 'UA-12345678-1' and can be found in the 'Admin' tab of your Google Analytics account under 'Tracking Info'.

Now that you have your Web Property ID, head back to Google Tag Manager. Navigate to the new container just set up. Once you're on the overview page for the container, select 'Add a New Tag'. Name the tag 'GA Tracking', select 'Google Analytics' as the tag type and choose 'Universal Analytics'.

Enter the tracking ID that was previously found for your website – this will look something like 'UA-123456-1' – and enter this as the 'Tracking ID'. There are also additional options, but for now let's leave the default settings, including the 'Tracking Type' as 'Pageview' and click 'Continue'. Now select 'All Pages' so the tag fires on all the pages of your website and click 'Create Tag'.

Now you can preview the tracking before publishing the tags on your website. Click on the downward arrow to the right of the 'Publish' button. From the options click the 'Preview' button. You'll now see an alert that indicates you're in preview mode.

Open a new browser window and navigate to your website. A special panel will load at the bottom of your website, telling you which tags have fired on the page you are viewing. You should now see a message saying that your 'Universal Analytics' tag has fired once.

Next, navigate through to your website and you should see that the tag you have set up fires once on every single page.

Important: Read "Migrating from Tracking Code to Google Tag Manager" in this chapter (below) before you publish your container inside Google Tag Manager. There are some important things to consider and you will want to develop a plan before you launch the new tracking on your website.

Once you're happy and ready to publish your tracking tags, click the 'Create Version' button and then 'Publish'.

> **Tip:** Google Tag Manager includes version control which allows you to store all the changes you make to your tracking codes. You can even roll back to a previous version if something goes wrong.

Your website is now using Google Tag Manager and you should see data showing up in your real-time reports.

Automatic Tracking with Google Tag Manager

Google Tag Manager can automate the measurement of some custom interactions. The most common examples are to automatically track people clicking to download files and clicking on outbound links.

Measuring Outbound Links

First, navigate to 'Variables' in the left-hand side column and enable 'Click URL' under 'Clicks'. This will allow you to make use of the URLs contained in the links on your website.

Navigate back to 'Tags' and create a new 'Google Analytics' tag for 'Universal Analytics'. Name the tag 'Outbound Links'. Enter your 'Tracking ID' and select 'Event' as the 'Track Type' and enter 'Outbound Link' as the 'Category' and 'Click' as the 'Action'. For the 'Label' option, click the variable icon to the right of the input field (small building block icon) and select 'Click URL'. Then click 'Continue'.

Select 'Click' as the trigger and then select 'New' (this is only displayed the first time your create a trigger). Name the trigger 'Link Click – Outbound Links' and select 'Just Links' as the trigger type. Deselect 'Wait for Tags' and 'Check Validation' and click 'Continue'.

> **Tip:** To improve the accuracy you can leave 'Wait for Tags' and 'Check Validation' enabled, however you will want to test the tracking to ensure it doesn't conflict with any other scripts being used on your website.

Select 'Some Clicks' and configure the firing condition for 'Click URL', 'Does Not Contain' and then enter your domain name without the 'www.', for example 'company.com'. This filter prevents links to other pages of your website from being tracked.

Click 'Save Trigger' and then 'Create Tag'.

Now you can preview and check that the new tag is working correctly. Open the browser window and navigate to a page that includes outbound links. Then, open the outbound link in a new tab by 'control' clicking on a PC (or 'command' clicking on a Mac). This will preserve the main tab with the Google Tag Manager preview panel and you should see the outbound link tracked on the 'Summary' panel.

Measuring File Downloads

The steps to measure file downloads are similar to measuring outbound links, but with a few differences. Again, you need to ensure that 'Click URL' is enabled within 'Variables'.

Create a new 'Google Analytics' tag for 'Universal Analytics'. Name the tag 'File Downloads'. Enter your 'Tracking ID' and select 'Event' as the 'Track Type' and enter 'File Downloads' as the 'Category' and 'Click' as the 'Action'. For the 'Label' option, click the variable icon to the right of the input field (small building block icon) and select 'Click URL'. Then click 'Continue'.

> **Tip:** Instead of entering your tracking ID (or property ID) for every single tag, you can create a variable that includes your ID, then reuse this variable with all of your tags. Navigate to 'Variables' and click 'New' under 'User-Defined Variables' and select 'Constant'. Name your variable 'Tracking ID – company.com' and enter your tracking ID (for example UA-123456-1) and then click 'Create Variable'. Next open a tag and remove the existing tracking ID. Now click on the variable icon and select the tracking ID variable you created before saving the tag.

Select 'Click' as the trigger and select 'New'. Name the trigger 'Link Click – File Downloads' and select 'Just Links' from the 'Targets' dropdown. Deselect 'Wait for Tags' and 'Check Validation' and click 'Continue'.

Then select 'Some Clicks' and configure the firing condition for 'Click URL', 'Matches RegEx (Ignore Case)' and then enter:

```
\.(pdf|docx?|zip|xlsx?|pptx?|exe|txt)$
```

This will match the following files: pdf, doc, docx, zip, xls, xlsx, ppt, pptx, exe and txt. You can modify the regular expression to include additional file types or remove particular file extensions.

Finally, click 'Save Trigger' and then 'Create Tag'.

Measuring Banners

You can use Google Tag Manager to automatically track clicks on banners and other promotions on your website. To measure these interactions you need to check that the image (or other element) uses a link that can be identified based on the 'class' or 'ID' attribute. Here is an example of the code used to create a banner that switched between two promoted items:

```
<ul  class="featured">
<li>
  <a href="/blog/latest-updates" class="slider">
    <img src="/images/banners/latest-updates.jpg" />
  </a>
</li>


<li>
  <a href="/blog/spring-specials" class="slider">
    <img src="/images/banners/spring-specials.jpg" />
  </a>
</li>
</ul>
```

You can see that both links have a class of 'slider' which can be used to track banner clicks in Google Tag Manager. If the link you want to measure does not have a class or ID, then you will need to modify your code to add one of these elements before proceeding.

Important: Ensure that the class or ID is specific to the links you want to track. If the name of the class or ID is used for other links on your website, they will also be measured unless you define the page (or pages) where the banners are located within the trigger.

Ensure that 'Click Classes' (or 'Click ID') and 'Click URL' are enabled in 'Variables'. Create a new 'Google Analytics' tag for 'Universal Analytics', name the tag 'Banner Clicks'.

Enter your 'Tracking ID' and select 'Event' as the 'Track Type' and enter 'Banner' as the 'Category' and 'Click' as the 'Action'. For the 'Label' option, click the variable icon to the right of the input field (small building block icon) and select 'Click URL'. Then click 'Continue'.

Select 'Click' as the trigger and select 'New'. Name the trigger 'Link Click – Banner' and select 'Just Links' from the 'Targets' dropdown. Deselect 'Wait For Tags' and 'Check Validation' and click 'Continue'.

Select 'Some Clicks', then choose 'Click Classes', 'Equals' and enter 'slider' as the value (if your class is different then enter the value for your website). Click 'Save Trigger' and then 'Create Tag'.

> **Tip:** If you only want to measure clicks on the banners for a particular page (or pages) you can use a regular expression to only include clicks occurring in those pages. For example, selecting 'Page URL, 'Matches RegEx (ignore case)' and entering 'company. com/?$' will only include clicks occurring on 'company.com' and 'company.com/'. Clicks on other pages will be ignored.

Advanced Google Tag Manager Options

Google Tag Manager can be used to meet advanced measurement needs. In some cases this will mean further customization of tags, triggers and variables, as well as modifying website elements, using custom code, right through to implementing a data layer.

Advanced implementations can be used to measure:

- Interactions with form fields
- Form submits
- Cross-domain tracking
- YouTube videos
- Scroll depth

For Google Tag Manager technical resources visit http://lovesdata.co/rppMo

Data Layer

Google Tag Manager can be used with a data layer to further extend what you can track. The data layer is used to store extra information that can then be used by Google Tag Manager. For example, you could dynamically include the name of blog post authors in the data layer in order to collect this information and pass it to Google Analytics from Google Tag Manager.

> **Tip:** The data layer can be used for ecommerce tracking and extending ecommerce tracking with additional data, including promotions, product views and more.

Fore more on implementing a data layer visit http://lovesdata.co/5tkIh

Migrating from Tracking Code to Google Tag Manager

Migrating from the standard Google Analytics tracking code to Google Tag Manager can be a complicated task if you're looking after a medium or large-scale website. There are some important things to consider before you get started. Planning out your migration will help reduce the number of pain points you encounter.

Start by establishing the general scope of the migration. Are you going to be migrating a single website or multiple websites? From there you will also want to get an idea of the number of pages that are contained on each website and how the tracking code has been applied to those pages. If you are running a single template file that spans all pages the existing tracking code is likely to be implemented in the template. This means that you can leave the existing tracking code and add the Google Tag Manager code to the template.

If you're dealing with multiple websites or discover that the existing code is implemented using multiple templates or some other special customizations, you will want to develop a stepped plan where you stage the migration in clearly defined steps. For larger implementations you might want to consider moving through particular sections of the website to allow for more time to check and test the new code.

You will need to review the existing implementation and document any tracking code customizations. Any customizations that have been made are likely to stop working when you move to Google Tag Manager. Look for any customizations that have been made, including:

- Sub-domain and cross-domain tracking
- Ecommerce tracking
- Event tracking
- Custom variables
- Social interactions
- Virtual pageviews
- Tracking into multiple properties
- Any other customizations

It is best to involve your web developer as early as possible in the process. They will have the best idea of what has been implemented on the website and if any customizations have been made. Once you have established a full list of customizations you can begin planning the migration into Google Tag Manager.

Tip: When you are planning your migration it is also a good opportunity to plan any new customizations that you haven't yet implemented. You might not want to implement these immediately, as there are likely to be enough challenges with the first stage of migration. However, it doesn't hurt to plan ahead and also ensure you are making use of any existing customizations.

Steps for migrating to Google Tag Manager:

1. Identify the tracking code (or codes) used on the website (or websites).

2. Identify if any customizations have been made to the tracking code.

3. Create your Google Tag Manager account.

4. Install Google Tag Manager on your website in parallel to the Google Analytics tracking code, but do not publish any tags in Google Tag Manager.

5. Create a testing property in Google Analytics and use this to test the Google Tag Manager implementation.

6. Configure Google Tag Manager with your tracking code (or codes).

7. Configure any tracking customizations in Google Tag Manager. This might include setting up a data layer on your website for some elements like ecommerce transactions.

8. Check that all tracking has been replicated in Google Tag Manager.

9. Preview and test that Google Tag Manager is correctly firing tags on your website.

10. Update Google Tag Manager to use your primary property (instead of your testing property).

11. Simultaneously publish your tags from Google Tag Manager and remove all instances of the Google Analytics tracking code implemented directly on the website.

Index